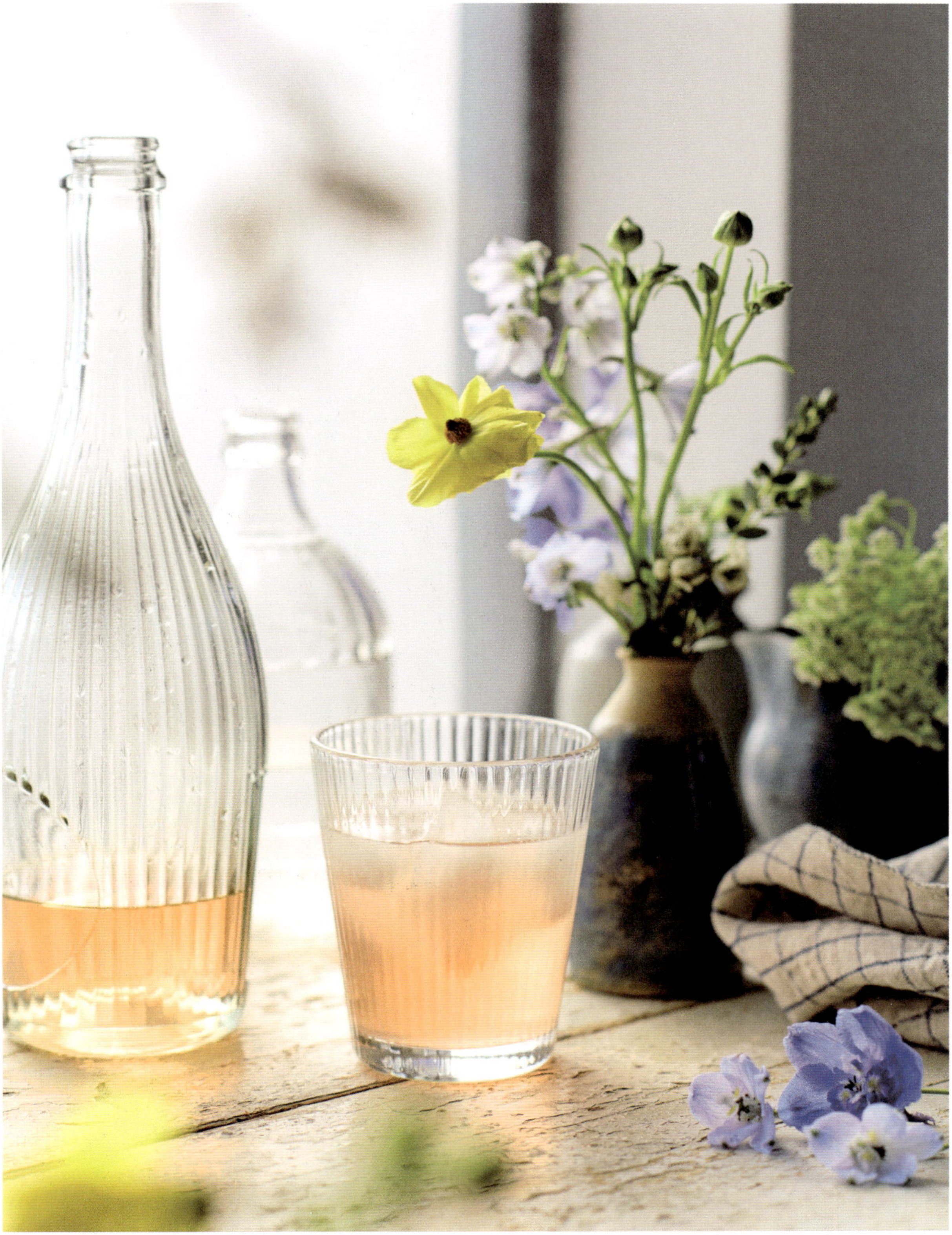

The Scandinavian Year

Food and thoughts from Sweden, Denmark and Norway

Brontë Aurell

Photography by Peter Cassidy

RYLAND PETERS & SMALL

Dedication
To my mother, Lena.

Senior Designer Megan Smith
Editor Gillian Haslam
Head of Production Patricia Harrington
Creative Director Leslie Harrington
Editorial Director Julia Charles
Food Stylist Kathy Kordalis
Prop Stylist Tony Hutchinson
Picture Researcher Jess Walton
Illustrator Maïté Franchi
Indexer Vanessa Bird

First published in 2025 by
Ryland Peters & Small
20–21 Jockey's Fields
London WC1R 4BW
and
1452 Davis Bugg Road,
Warrenton, NC 27589

www.rylandpeters.com
email: euregulations@rylandpeters.com

10 9 8 7 6 5 4 3 2 1

Text copyright © Brontë Aurell 2025
Design and commissioned photography copyright © Ryland Peters & Small 2025.
See right for full image credits.

ISBN: 978-1-78879-718-4

Printed and bound in China.

The author's moral rights have been asserted. All rights reserved. No part of this publication may be reproduced, stored in a retrieval system or transmitted in any form or by any means, electronic, mechanical, photocopying or otherwise, without the prior permission of the publisher.

A CIP record for this book is available from the British Library. US Library of Congress Cataloging-in-Publication Data has been applied for.

The authorised representative in the EEA is Authorised Rep Compliance Ltd., Ground Floor, 71 Lower Baggot Street, Dublin, D02 P593, Ireland
www.arccompliance.com

PHOTOGRAPHY CREDITS

All photographs by Peter Cassidy apart from those on the following pages:
11 above left rolf_52/AdobeStock; above right Benjamin Edwards/RPS; below Oleksandr Dibrova/AdobeStock; 18 Nassima Rothacker/RPS; 19 below right living4media/Jonathan Birch; 31 above right Wirestock/AdobeStock; below left StockFood/Kati Neudert; below right mariannerjensen/AdobeStock; 47 hans_chr/AdobeStock; 55 below left Debi Trelcar/RPS; above right Catherine Gratwicke/RPS; 67 above right House of Pictures/Tia Borgsmidt; below left Sofie K/AdobeStock; below right gadagj/AdobeStock; 74 below right Nassima Rothacker/RPS; 87 above left Nikolai Sorokin/AdobeStock; above right henjon/AdobeStock; below left Sergey Kamshylin/AdobeStock; below right Amaiquez/AdobeStock; 107 above left House of Pictures/Tia Borgsmidt; below left stefanholm/AdobeStock; 127 above left Mari Mur/AdobeStock; above right Polly Wreford/RPS; below Mirek/AdobeStock; 161 above left House of Pictures/Este Sorri; above right Alexander/AdobeStock; below left Igor Korobko/AdobeStock; below right House of Pictures/Matilda Lindeblad; 168 above left Olonkho/AdobeStock; 180 below right Debi Treloar/RPS; 181 above left Polly Wreford/RPS; 199 below right House of Pictures/Annabelle Antas; 215 above left House of Pictures/Sussie Bell; below left House of Pictures/Sussie Bell; below right living4media/Etsa.

NOTES

• Both British (Metric) and American (Imperial plus US cups) measurements are included in these recipes for your convenience; however work with only one set of measurements within a recipe.
• All spoon measurements are level unless otherwise specified.
• All eggs are medium (UK) or large (US), unless specified as large, in which case US extra-large should be used. Uncooked or partially cooked eggs should not be served to the frail, young or pregnant.
• When a recipe calls for the grated zest of citrus fruit, buy unwaxed fruit and wash well before using. If you can only find treated fruit, scrub well in warm soapy water before using.
• Always check that any flowers used for garnish are food-safe and pesticide-free.

Contents

Introduction	6
January	8
February	28
March	44
April	64
May	84
June	104
July	124
August	144
September	158
October	178
November	196
December	212
Basic recipes	234
Index	238
Acknowledgements	240

Introduction

There is something magical that happens when we enter a kitchen that isn't only about sustenance. We all recall dishes from our childhoods, and cooking is about creating memories. Perhaps it's a sandwich on a picnic in the sun, maybe a bag of chips/fries in the rain on the way home from school, a homemade birthday cake, a special meal on a first date, a fun ice-cream flavour on a holiday. The connection between food and memory is so strong that just by eating a bite of a special something can transport us back home to just *that* memory and feeling, even if only for a brief moment.

During the last decades of writing and working with food from Scandinavia, I've raised my children (who are half Swedish, half Danish) here in London where I live. I've been fascinated by how we as parents instil our culture in our children not just via language or traditions, but also through the foods we eat. A different kind of mother tongue, developed through taste and all those special moments in childhood.

I've spent decades writing down recipes on paper napkins in my café for second- and third-generation Scandinavians, helping them search for long-lost tastes and recipes and evoking remote childhood memories, revisiting feelings, places and people deep in their memory bank. Food can be a temporary remedy for homesickness, soothing a longing for a place or a person we can't be with in that moment of time. One bite, and you can be back in the arms of your parents, with your childhood sweetheart or on a night out with your best friends.

This book is part traditional, part evolved and most definitely a collection of recipes that I've built on and moved with in my life as a Scandinavian emigrant. It is not encyclopaedic (there are plenty of books for that), but it is how I cook at home with my family. As we go through the year in our own hybrid Scandinavian way, we eat, we live and we grow. This book is a love letter to my children, hoping that they take with them in life these bites of their heritage and pass it on to new, special people in their own lives. Mostly, however, this is a thank you to my mother, Lena. In writing this book, I've relived my own childhood and all the values and culture that shaped me when growing up in her kitchen back home in Denmark. The kitchen is where I feel her the most, but also where I miss her the most. It is grief, healing and rebirth, all in one year, recipe by recipe.

As life evolves and families grow up, so do the recipes we cook. We change ingredients, flavour notes and the methods we use to cook things. As we become globetrotters in our own right, like nomadic emigrants holding on to the traditions and culture of our grandparents, we substitute local ingredients and change recipes according to what is available around us, in turn, creating our own new recipes for our families and friends from which to make new memories. Food culture is about tradition, but it's also a beautiful evolution: all our shared experiences thrown together in a big pot and cooked with love.

INTRODUCTION 7

The start of the year brings darkness. It's cold. It's wet. So much snow. No more looking forward to the Yuletide celebrations. And everyone seems worried about their waistlines in a way that was all but forgotten before the turn of the year. No wonder bears prefer sleeping through it all.

On the flip side, January brings promise – to yourself or for the year ahead to be better than the last; to bring change and hope. There's comfort and consistency – and very few surprises. The monotony of this all brings calm and time for reflection. We know that, eventually, it will end and our initial desire to only eat healthy salads will eventually balance out with foods that bring us a different kind of happiness. January is the month of patience and quiet comfort in the little things. To me, it's family, friends and cosy nights in (yes, *hygge* indeed).

We enjoy the winter season's stored harvest of dark kales and cabbages, and root vegetables of all shapes and sizes. As the frozen ground sleeps outside, we have our pickles and preserves to see us through.

JANUARY

WHO ARE WE?

Somewhere along the way, I changed from being Danish to *Scandinavian*. This only happens outside Scandinavia. I've been an emigrant for longer than I've lived at *home*, so the lines blurred somewhere while moving from place to place. I don't think this is simply because I married a Swede, although it has made culture feel more fluid across the different places in which we have lived and loved. As we met people from outside Scandinavia, we realised that others see us as one, not the three countries of Denmark, Sweden and Norway. We became 'the Scandinavians', perceived as so similar in language, values and outlook. However, in Scandinavia we see ourselves as different to each other.

Scandinavia is a geographical definition (the peninsula of Norway and Sweden with the addition of Denmark). It does not include Finland or Iceland – when they *are* included, we refer to the 'Nordics'. Scandinavia is geography, Nordic is a union of the five aforementioned countries, plus Greenland, the Faroe Islands and the Åland Islands.

It's often a misconception that Scandinavia is not a big place. In fact, at almost 1.1 million square km/ 425,000 square miles, it's three-and-a-half times the size of the UK, or Texas and California combined. While our values, cultures and languages have so many similar notes, the food we can grow on the lands varies immensely from north to south and west to east.

To drive a car from the top of mainland Norway to the southern part of Denmark would take you 32 hours in one stretch. There are polar bears on the Norwegian islands and plenty of moose on the mainland, while sometimes-sunny Denmark specialises in pig farming. Scandinavia is as Arctic as it is Germanic.

As the rugged mountain landscapes of the north give way to the bicycle-friendly flats of the south, we share our Viking heritage, Norse mythology and a love of pickled herring. United by food, language roots and a passion for an annual television musical song contest, we are sometimes as similar as we'd like to be seen as unique (when it suits us). Over the centuries, we've fought, made up, fought again and eventually ended up as peace-loving, hotdog-eating people who appreciate good design and very salty liquorice.

Danes regards themselves as the descendants of the Vikings and the old rulers of the peninsula. Swedes, the inventors (from flat-pack bookcases to food packaging and dynamite). Norwegians, the keepers of the most beautiful landscapes.

To a Norwegian and Dane, Swedes are often seen as a forward-thinking and tech-savvy bunch. Always very organised and a bit like a big brother, Sweden sets a good example for approaching things level-headedly and with self-control. Norway calls Sweden its *söta bror* – 'sweet brother' – but Sweden doesn't reciprocate this term of endearment (it's far too cool). Norwegians often envy Sweden and all its cheap(er) food.

To a Swede, the Norwegians are the summer house-loving people who wear sweaters and are generally quite jolly in their beautiful country. Norway is the only country to rival Sweden at skiing. An underlying attitude of 'well, you got all your money from oil' is occasionally sensed but, more than anything, Norwegians are seen as happy-go-lucky, confident, outdoorsy people who are easy to get on with (even if they maybe eat a little too much fish and have an odd fondness for caramelised goat's cheese). Even when a Norwegian person is angry they can sound jolly, on account of the natural inflection that ends every sentence.

Danes are the often-dressed-in-black cool people, with many men sporting Viking-style beards. They're seen as laid back and free, on account of there being no state-run alcohol shops in Denmark, so Danes can buy alcohol at *any time* we want (in other Nordic countries, alcohol sales are strictly regulated). Both Sweden and Norway have issues understanding Danes when they speak Danish because they sound as though they have hot potatoes in their mouths when they speak and the Danish system of naming numbers is extremely complicated. Denmark's little brother syndrome is strong: it's by far the smallest of the three countries, with only one hill of 147 m/482 feet to call a 'mountain'.

As similar as we are, so different.

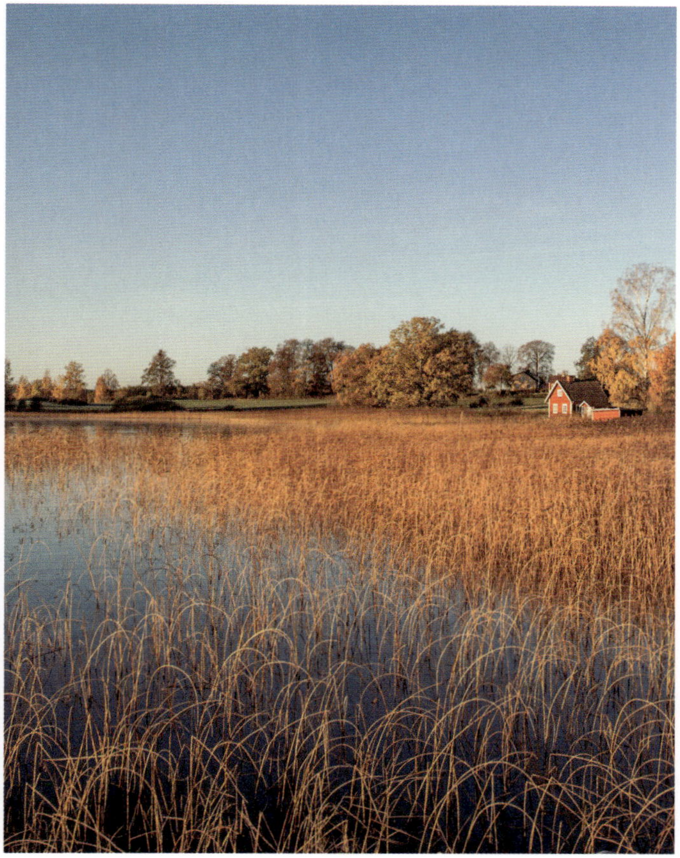
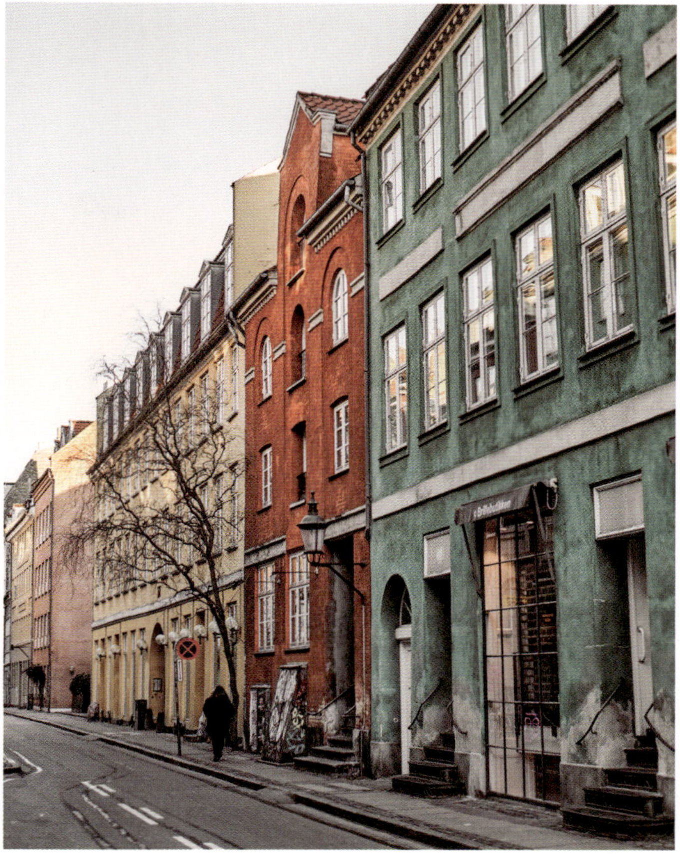
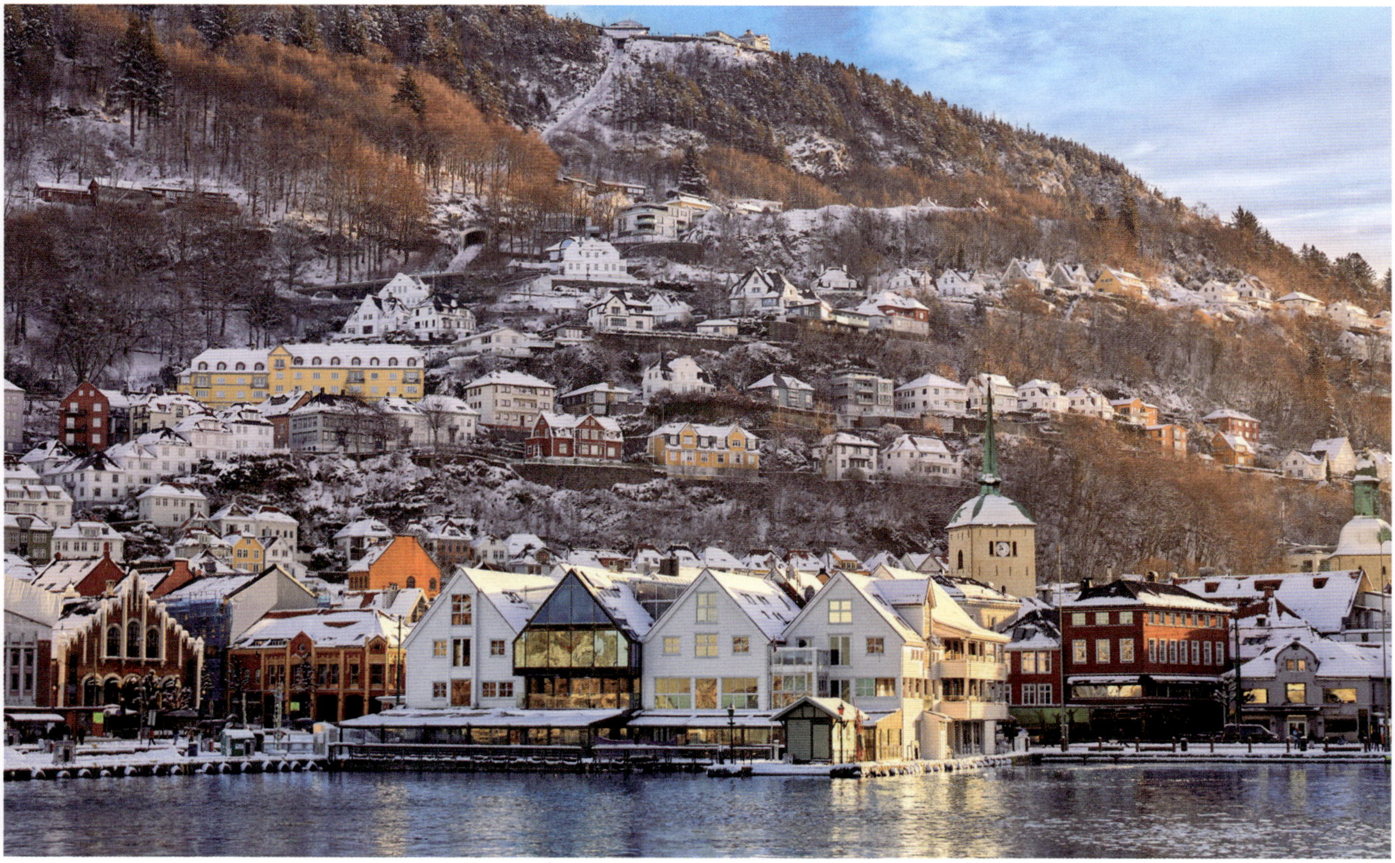

Jerusalem artichoke soup — *Jordskokkesuppe*

As winter takes hold across the northern countries, we huddle up and hibernate, desperately longing for daylight. There is something comforting about making a hearty soup and watching the snow fall outside, listening to the crackle of the fire in the background. Many wonder how we get through those dark and cold months – the answer is we surround ourselves with all kinds of comfort: warmth, candles, family and a good bowl of soup.

Jerusalem artichoke can be a little hard to digest for some people. If you have time, soak them in water with added lemon juice for 15 minutes before cooking, as this helps to break down the inulin (or dietary fibre).

butter, for frying
1 onion, peeled and chopped
450 g/1 lb. Jerusalem artichokes (peeled weight)
800 ml/3¼ cups vegetable stock
½ teaspoon grated nutmeg
oil, for frying
100 ml/⅓ cup plus 1 tablespoon cream
400 g/14 oz. haddock loin (optional)
25 g/1 oz. toasted hazelnuts, roughly chopped, to serve
fresh thyme leaves, to garnish (optional)
salt and freshly ground black pepper

SERVES 4

Melt a knob/pat of butter in a saucepan. Add the onion and fry, without colouring, for around 15 minutes over a low heat.

Wash and peel the Jerusalem artichokes. Set aside two of the longer artichokes and cut the remainder into 1-cm/½-inch cubes.

Add the cubed artichokes to the pan with the onions and fry over a low heat for a few minutes, then add the stock and leave to simmer, uncovered, for 20 minutes. Season with salt, pepper and the nutmeg.

Meanwhile, in a frying plan/skillet, add a glug of oil. Thinly slice the two reserved artichokes, then add to the pan and fry until super crisp. Remove from the pan and drain on paper towels.

If you are adding haddock to the soup, melt a little butter and oil in the pan used to fry the artichokes. Add the haddock and gently fry, flipping only once, until done – the cooking time depends on the thickness of the fish, but a total frying time of around 5 minutes is approximate.

When the cubed artichoke is super soft, blend the soup with a stick blender until smooth, then add the cream and check the seasoning.

Serve hot in bowls with the fish added at the last minute (if using), and the hazelnuts and artichoke crisps on top. If you wish, garnish with a few fresh thyme leaves.

VARIATIONS Add small, freshly chopped pieces of apple just before serving, if you want a hint of freshness. Small crispy fried pancetta pieces also work really well with this soup.

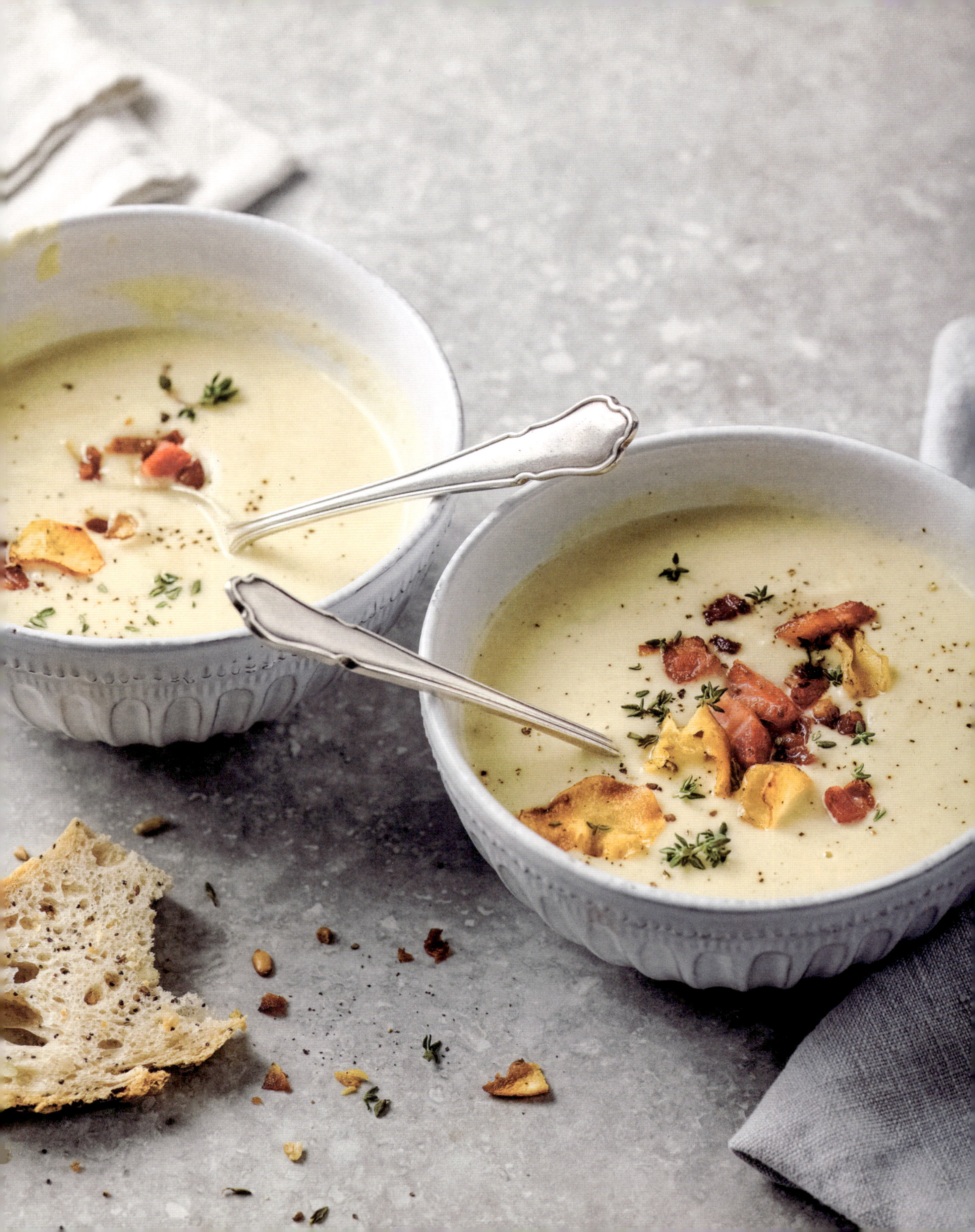

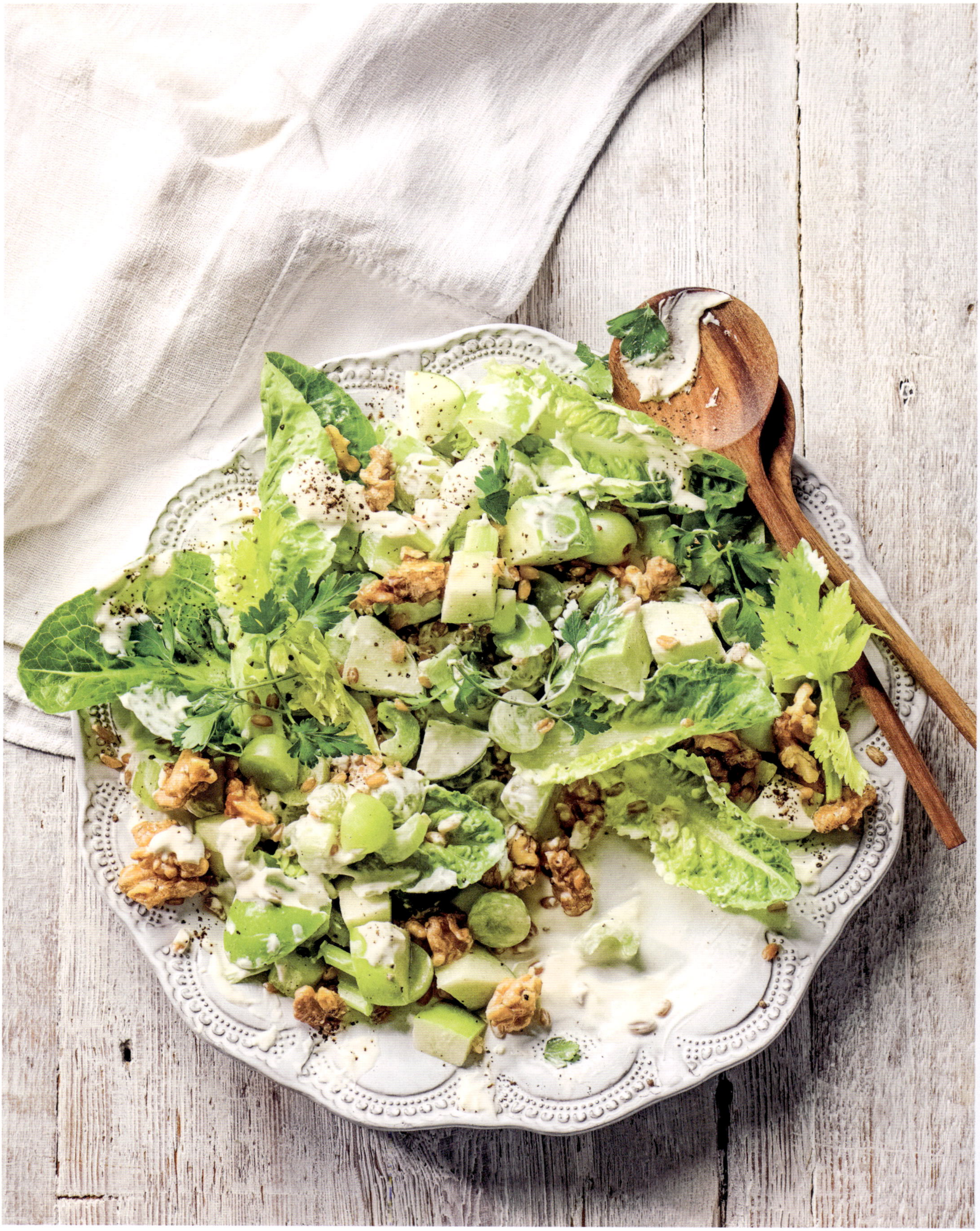

Waldorf salad with spelt grain

Waldorfsalat med spelt

As a 70s child, I am always going to have some fond memories of the exotic creamy salads that were popular back then. One of these is the Waldorf. It has always remained popular in Norway and, reading up on the reasons why, it seems that the link between Norway and the Waldorf Astoria Hotel – where this salad was invented – is a lady called Jørgine Boomer. Jørgine was born in Norway and emigrated to the US when she was 16. Her husband bought the Waldorf Astoria in 1918 and together they managed the hotel for many years. That she was an influence on this salad's popularity back in Norway is purely speculation, but is not entirely unlikely.

This is a slightly non-traditional version of the classic salad with added grain and a lighter dressing.

60 g/generous ½ cup chopped walnuts
2 tablespoons date syrup or golden/corn syrup (optional)
4 sticks celery, peeled (see note) and chopped into 1-cm/½-inch pieces
2 green apples, cored and chopped into 1-cm/½-inch pieces
a small bunch of green grapes, halved if large
100 g/3½ oz. cooked spelt grain (I use the ready-cooked grain pouches)
2 Gem lettuce, leaves separated
2 tablespoons freshly chopped flat-leaf parsley

DRESSING
3 heaped tablespoons crème fraîche
3 heaped tablespoons Greek yogurt
1 teaspoon honey
2 tablespoons cider vinegar
½ teaspoon Dijon mustard
a good squeeze of fresh lemon juice
salt and freshly ground black pepper

SERVES 4 AS A GENEROUS SIDE

Lightly toast the chopped walnuts. At the last minute, just as you turn off the heat, coat the walnut pieces with the date or golden/corn syrup (or leave uncoated if you prefer).

To make the dressing, mix all the ingredients together.

In a bowl, mix the chopped celery, apples and grapes. Mix in the dressing and season to taste. Add the spelt grain.

Scatter the crispy lettuce leaves over a serving plate, add half the salad mixture across, then add half the walnuts. Top with the remaining salad mixture, then scatter over the parsley and remaining walnuts.

NOTE I peel the celery lightly with a peeler if eating it raw – this removes the stringy bits.

Haddock with beetroot and parsnips

Stegt kuller med rødbeder

This recipe can be made with your white fish of choice, but I do love haddock. However, if making this back in Scandinavia, I would most likely use cod, as haddock isn't as popular there. The roasted beets combine well with a creamy parsnip mash and fresh tart apple bites.

If you want to cook your own beetroot rather than using pre-cooked, boil or roast until tender, then cool and peel, before proceeding with the recipe.

4 pieces of haddock loin, approx. 600–800 g/1 lb. 5 oz.–1 lb. 12 oz. total weight (cod also works well for this)
vegetable oil
salt and freshly ground black pepper

PARSNIP PURÉE
600 g/1 lb. 5 oz. parsnips
300 ml/1¼ cups whole milk
100 ml/⅓ cup plus 1 tablespoon cream
1 bay leaf
1 garlic clove
a pinch of grated nutmeg
a few drops of white wine vinegar

ROAST BEETROOT
400 g/14 oz. cooked beetroot/beets, cut into wedges
a glug of olive oil
1 tablespoon balsamic vinegar
2 sprigs of fresh thyme

TOPPING
30 g/2 tablespoons browned butter
1 tart apple, skin left on, cored and finely diced
sprigs of fresh dill

SERVES 4

To make the parsnip purée, set half a parsnip aside to make crisps, then peel and cut the remainder into even-sized chunks. Place in a saucepan with the milk, cream, bay leaf and garlic and boil until cooked through and soft, about 15 minutes. Transfer the parsnip (discard the bay leaf and garlic clove) to a blender and add as much of the liquid as is needed to blend to a smooth purée – you may not need it all. Season with nutmeg, salt, pepper and a few drops of vinegar.

To roast the beetroot/beets, preheat the oven to 195°C/175°C fan/375°F/Gas 5. Add the cooked beetroot to a small roasting dish with the oil, vinegar and thyme and roast for around 15 minutes.

To make the parsnip crisps, thinly slice the reserved half parsnip with a peeler, then fry in a hot pan with vegetable oil until browned. Leave to drain and crisp up on paper towels.

In a frying pan/skillet heated with a bit of oil, fry the haddock until just cooked through – the length of time depends on the thickness of the fish. Turn once during cooking. Season well.

To make the browned butter, melt the butter in a pan until it froths and turns brown.

To serve, if necessary gently warm the parsnip purée. Divide the purée between serving plates, then place the fish to one side. Add the beetroot wedges and chopped apple on top, then decorate with dill sprigs and parsnip crisps. Finish with a few spoonfuls of the brown butter. Enjoy immediately.

NOTE The parsnip mash is delicious on its own served as a side dish to a roast dinner – simply top with the fresh apple and browned butter.

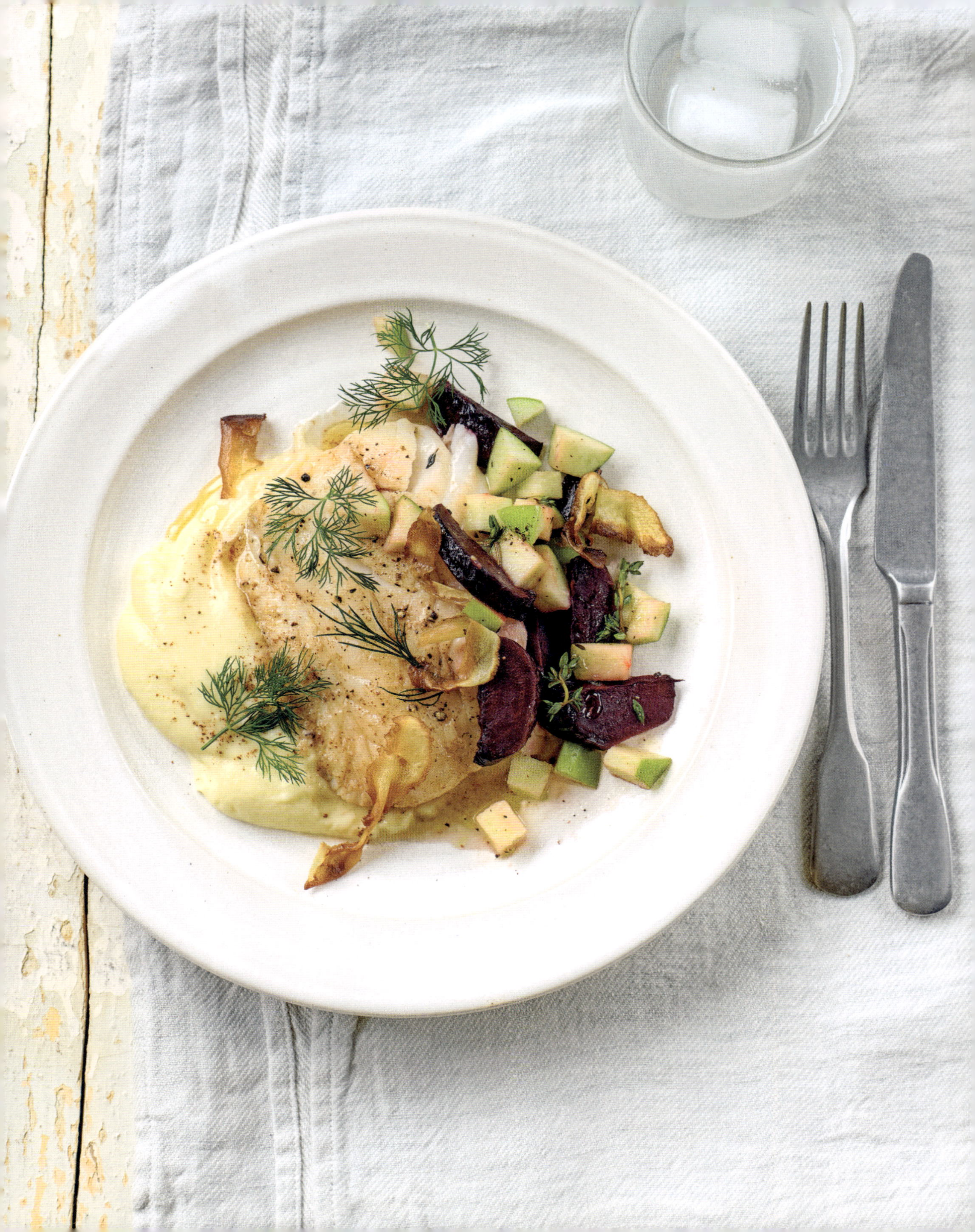

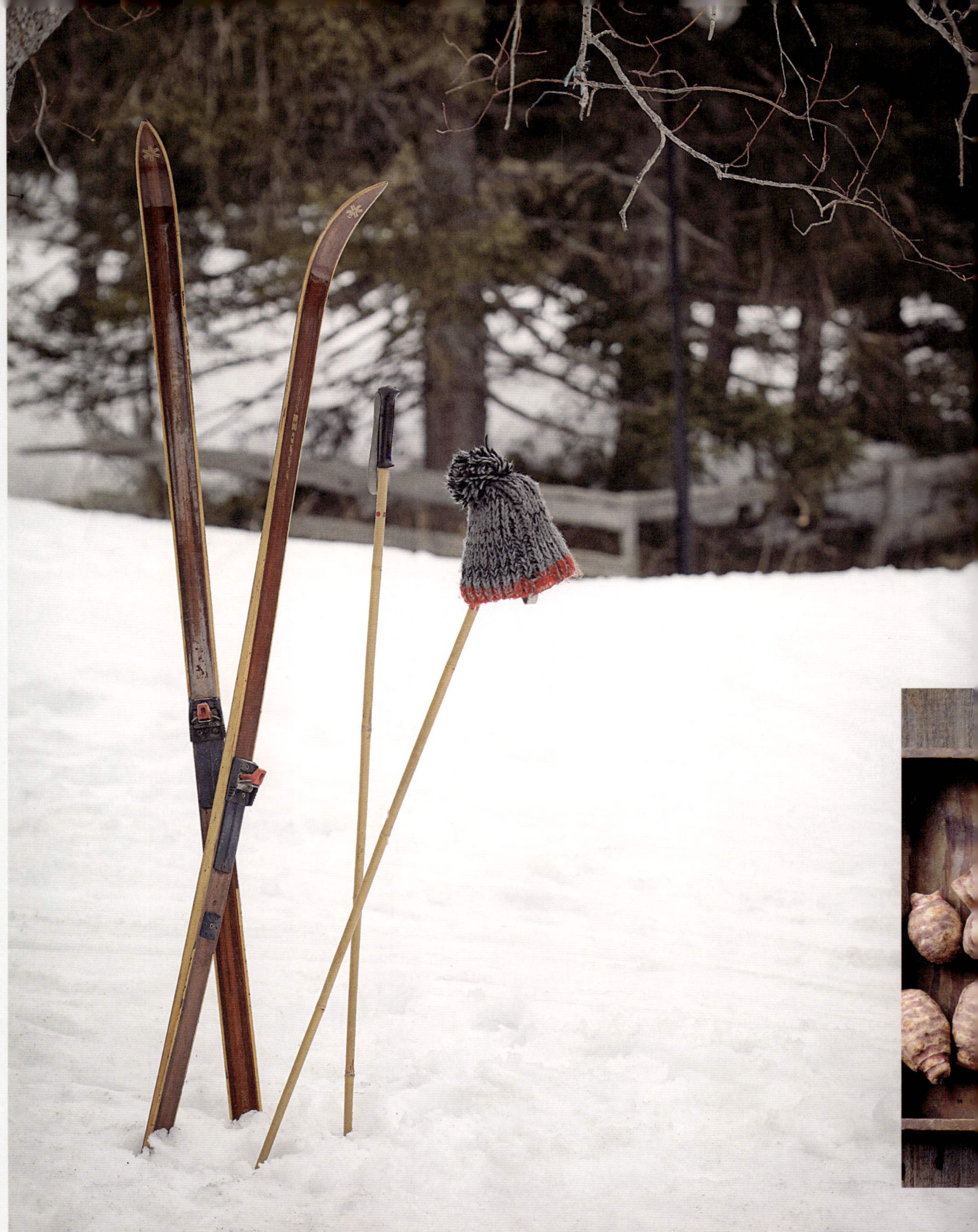

JANUARY 19

My mother's Danish meatballs

Everyone's mother makes the best meatballs. Except my kids also always preferred my mother's meatballs to mine. To be fair, Mamma Lena's meatballs were the best. When she passed away, we thought her special methods and tricks for making the meatballs in her own way were gone forever, but it turned out that my brother-in-law Benjamin – an excellent cook himself – had filmed her making these meatballs from start to finish. What was meant as a bit of a fun clip has become my most treasured thing: her voice, her laughter, her kitchen, her meatballs.

In a previous book I published a recipe of her meatballs where I added allspice. She wasn't impressed because it was my thing to add allspice, not hers. I have removed it in this recipe and made sure that this is just as she made them.

300 g/10½ oz. minced/ground veal

200 g/7 oz. minced/ground pork (minimum 15% content – don't buy low-fat pork)

1 teaspoon salt

1 onion, grated

1 whole egg

50 g/1 cup breadcrumbs or oats

3 tablespoons plain/all-purpose flour

½ teaspoon grated nutmeg

100 ml/⅓ cup warm whole milk, with ½ beef or chicken stock/bouillon cube dissolved into it

freshly ground black pepper

100 ml/⅓ cup plus 1 tablespoon sparkling water

75 g/5 tablespoons butter and a good glug of olive oil, for frying

SERVES 4

Place the minced/ground meat and salt in a stand mixer with the paddle attachment. Mix for about 1 minute on medium speed.

Squeeze the excess juice from the grated onion (to get rid of most of the liquid). Add to the meat and mix again, then add the egg, breadcrumbs, flour, nutmeg and milk with the dissolved stock/bouillon cube. Season with black pepper and mix until incorporated. Leave to rest in the fridge for at least 30 minutes.

Preheat the oven to 120°C/100°C fan/250°F/Gas ½.

Take the meat out of the fridge, then add the sparkling water and stir in. (If the mixture feels too wet, you can add more flour here until you have a mixture that holds its shape.) Using a tablespoon, scoop out a quantity of meat mixture the size of a large egg. Wet your hands, then use the flat of your hand to help shape the meatballs. Danish meatballs are not round, but slightly oval.

In a frying pan/skillet, heat up the butter and leave it to brown and bubble, then add a glug of oil. The large quantity of butter is essential for these meatballs, or they just don't get the right crust and flavour.

Test one small meatball first just to taste you have the right seasoning, then you can adjust as necessary and continue with the rest of the mixture. Fry the meatballs over a medium-high heat, in batches to allow plenty of room for turning, for 2–3 minutes on each side. Transfer to the warm oven for approx. 10 minutes to complete the cooking. Repeat until you have used all the meat.

Serve with sautéed or boiled potatoes and brown gravy made from good stock.

These meatballs freeze well but also keep for 3 days in the fridge. Also absolutely delicious served cold on an open sandwich.

NOTE If you do not wish to use veal, substitute with all pork – Mamma Lena often did so.

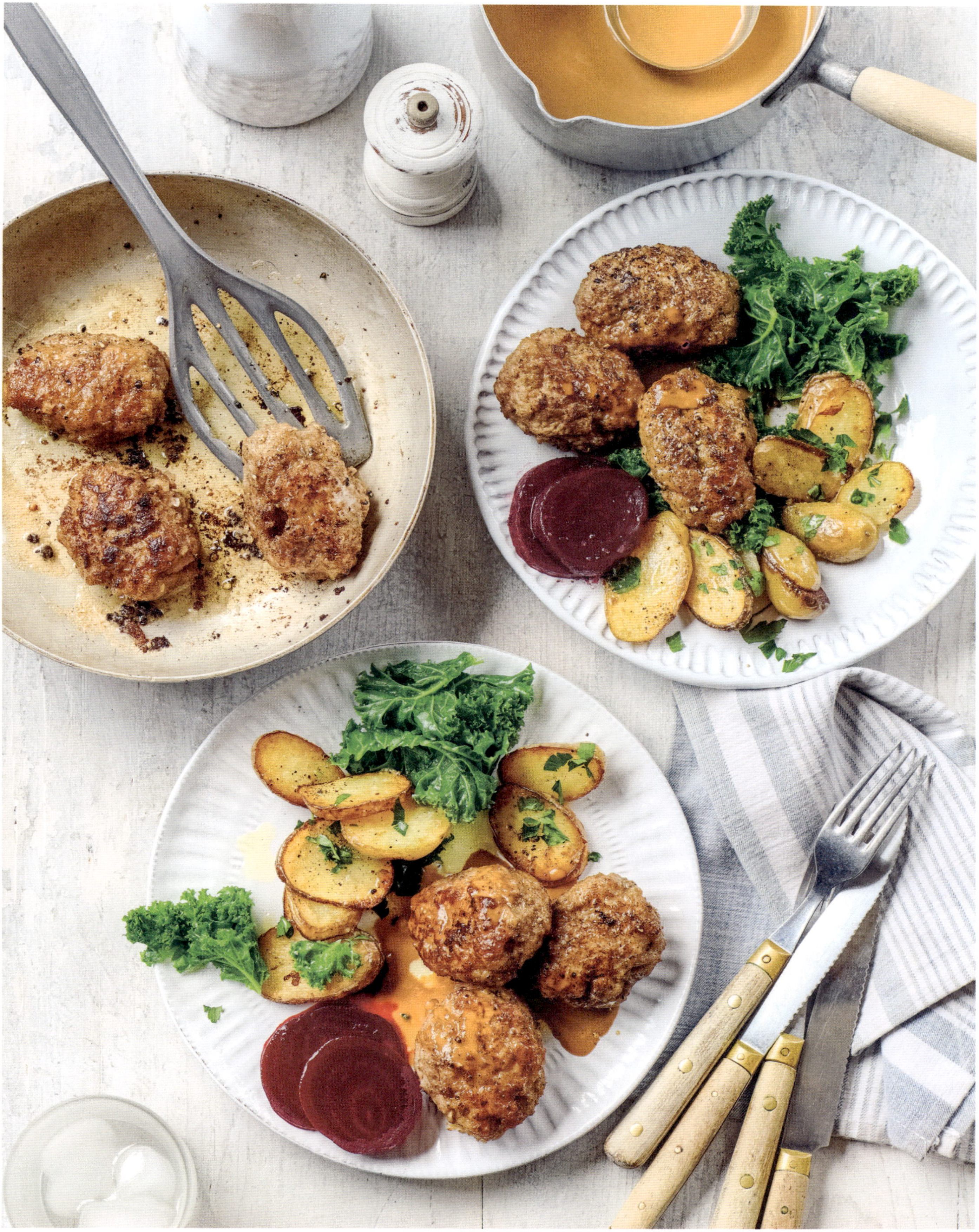

Swedish curd cake with raspberries

Ostkaka med hallon

If you are going to make this, the first thing you need to know is that it won't taste like any cheesecake you've had before. It's actually a curd cake – only called cheesecake because, well, cottage cheese is also a cheese. Originally, this was made using raw milk and rennet, but I use cottage cheese, as do many people nowadays. This version is sometimes also known as a *falsk ostkaka* ('fake curd cake'), as it does change the texture slightly compared to the rennet version – but on the flip side, it takes 3 minutes to stir together and in my opinion it tastes just as good.

There are several regional varieties, but the one from the south of Sweden is the version I make at home. Always serve this lukewarm, never cold. It does not keep, so eat up as soon as you can.

50 g/¼ cup caster/granulated sugar

3 eggs

400 g/14 oz. natural cottage cheese (not too cold or the curds won't break when mixing)

100 ml/⅓ cup plus 1 tablespoon double/heavy cream

50 g/½ cup finely chopped blanched almonds

25 g/3 tablespoons plain/all-purpose flour (or 1½ tablespoons cornflour/cornstarch, if you prefer no gluten)

1 teaspoon vanilla sugar or vanilla extract

a pinch of salt

1 teaspoon almond extract

dusting of ground cinnamon or cardamom

TOPPING

125 g/4½ oz. raspberries

2 tablespoons sugar

ovenproof serving dish, approx. 20 x 25 cm/8 x 10 inches, greased with butter

SERVES 4–6

Preheat the oven to 180°C/160°C fan/350°F/Gas 4.

In a stand mixer, whisk the sugar and eggs until light and airy. Add all the remaining ingredients apart from the cinnamon or cardamom. Give it a stir to break up the cheese curds a little and pour into your prepared dish.

Dust the top with a tiny bit of ground cinnamon or cardamom (less than ½ teaspoon – it's just for a bit of flavour).

Place in the preheated oven and bake until set and slightly golden on top. This depends on your oven but around 30 minutes is a good guideline. Keep an eye on it – it needs to be set but not overcooked.

Meanwhile, make the topping. Place 100 g/3½ oz. of the raspberries in a saucepan, add the sugar and a dash of water and boil until the raspberries have broken down and it looks like a runny jam. Leave to cool.

To serve, dollop the jam on top of the cake and decorate with the remaining berries. Always serve this lukewarm, never cold.

NOTE Instead of making a topping, you can also just use jam/preserves of your choice. I often serve this with cloudberry jam as it pairs so well with the almond and vanilla. I also sometimes serve it with cherry sauce (see page 226). I've even been known to eat this with salted caramel (see page 38), although admitting to this might get me into trouble with the Swedish food police.

Easy rye bread

Nemt rugbrød

Most authentic Danish rye bread recipes use a sourdough starter as a base, which gives depth, flavour and structure to the bread. However, if you do not have an active sourdough starter (maybe, like me, you keep killing, them), then this recipe is for you: rye bread ready in a few hours, rather than several days. Pictured on page 19.

200 g/7 oz. cracked rye kernels (see note below)

200 ml/¾ cup hot water

1 teaspoon freshly squeezed lemon juice or neutral vinegar (such as white wine vinegar)

200 ml/¾ cup room-temperature milk

15 g/½ oz. fresh yeast

150 ml/⅔ cup lukewarm water

1 tablespoon dark molasses or treacle

200 ml/¾ cup Guinness or other stout

150 g/1 cup plus 1 tablespoon wholegrain rye flour

300 g/2 cups plus 2 tablespoons white bread flour

100 g/¾ cup sunflower seeds

50 g/⅓ cup pumpkin seeds/pepitas

75 g/⅔ cup linseeds/flax seeds

1 tablespoon fine salt

approx. 50 g/⅓ cup pumpkin seeds/pepitas or sunflower seeds, to decorate

1.5-litre/3-lb. loaf pan (or use 2 smaller loaf pans), lined with baking parchment

MAKES 1 LOAF

Add the cracked rye to a bowl and top with the hot water. Leave until the rye has absorbed the water and the mixture is lukewarm (around 30 minutes).

Add the lemon juice (or vinegar) to the milk – this will curdle the milk in around 15 minutes.

Add the yeast to a stand mixer, then add the lukewarm water and allow to dissolve. Add all remaining ingredients (adding the salt last) and mix well for about 4–5 minutes. Cover the mixer bowl with a damp kitchen towel and leave to rise for about an hour. It will look gloopy and porridge like.

Using a spoon, beat the air out of the mixture. Pour into the prepared loaf pan and leave to rise again for another hour (you can also leave to rise in the fridge overnight – if so, you can reduce the amount of yeast by half). The loaf will not rise a lot, maybe only by a quarter.

Preheat the oven to 240ºC/220ºC fan/475ºF/Gas 8.

Just before baking, brush the top gently with water and prick the top of the bread all over with a fork, to a depth of 2.5 cm/1 inch below the surface – this allows the bread to stay level when baking and avoid air pockets forming. Scatter the seeds for decorating all across the top.

Pop the bread in the hot oven and immediately turn it down to 200ºC/180ºC fan/400ºF/Gas 6. Bake for approximately 1 hour, depending on your oven. When the internal temperature of the loaf reaches around 98ºC/208ºF, the bread is ready.

Rye bread is always sticky when just baked. For the best result, allow the bread to cool, then wrap in clingfilm/plastic wrap and wait 24 hours before eating, or at least until it has cooled down completely. It will slice perfectly the next day (in my opinion, the perfect slice of rye bread for an open sandwich is 7 mm/¼ inch thick). You can freeze this bread, but it does last 3–5 days after baking.

If you don't have a 1.5-litre/3-lb. loaf pan, use two smaller ones and adjust the baking time (using a thermometer to check the internal temperature).

NOTE If you cannot find cracked rye, a reasonable substitute is whole rye pulsed a few times in a food processor before using. Never use whole rye as the seed needs to be cut or the liquid will not be absorbed as well.

That 80s chocolate cake

Kärleksmums

As a child growing up in Denmark in the 1980s, this hugely popular cake was always just known as 'you know, that cake', and recipes for the best version were traded among neighbours and friends. All the while over in Sweden, this cake had a real name – *Kärleksmums* – which literally translates to 'love yummy'. It was the cake you always hoped someone would bring into school for their birthday, baked in a big rectangular pan so there was more than enough for everyone. I have no idea where it originated but for me, it is everything about our carefree childhood.

75 g/¾ cup good-quality cacao powder
150 ml/⅔ cup just-boiled water
150 ml/⅔ cup whole milk
300 g/2¾ sticks butter, softened
300 g/1½ cups caster/granulated sugar
4 large/US extra-large eggs
275 g/2 cups plain/all-purpose flour
½ teaspoon salt
1 teaspoon vanilla sugar
1 teaspoon bicarbonate of soda/baking soda

TOPPING
150 g/1 cup icing/confectioner's sugar
50 g/3½ tablespoons butter
1 tablespoon cacao powder
½ teaspoon vanilla sugar
4 tablespoons strong black coffee
50 g/⅔ cup desiccated/dried shredded coconut, plus extra to decorate
sea salt flakes (optional)

sheet pan, approx. 35 x 25 cm/ 14 x 10 inches, lined with baking parchment

SERVES 8–10

Preheat the oven to 180°C/160°C fan/350°F/Gas 4.

Mix together the cacao powder and hot water and leave to cool a little. Add the milk to the cacao mixture.

Cream the butter and sugar in a stand mixer until pale. Add the eggs one by one, taking care they are completely incorporated. Sift the flour, salt, vanilla sugar and bicarbonate of soda/baking soda into another bowl.

Add the flour mixture and the cacao mixture to the egg mixture whilst whisking continuously on a slow speed, taking care to ensure everything is just incorporated. Do not over-beat or you will end up with a heavy cake.

Pour the batter into the prepared sheet pan. Bake in the middle of the preheated oven for about 20 minutes or until a skewer inserted into the centre comes out just clean (take care not to over-bake). Cool slightly in the pan, then transfer to a wire rack to cool completely.

To make the topping, combine all the ingredients in a saucepan over a low heat and leave to melt. Spread over the cooled cake and top with extra coconut and a few sea salt flakes (optional). Leave to set before serving.

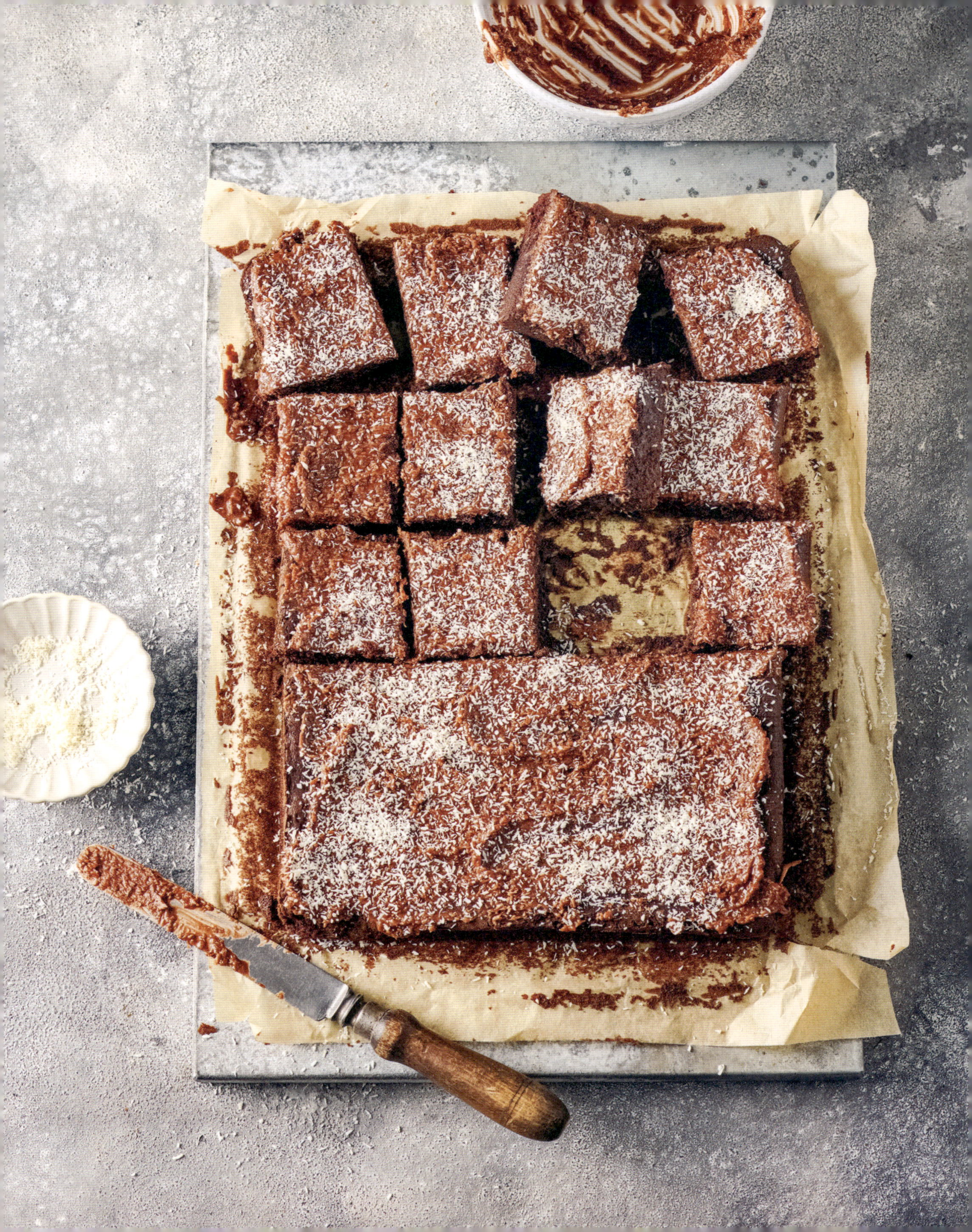

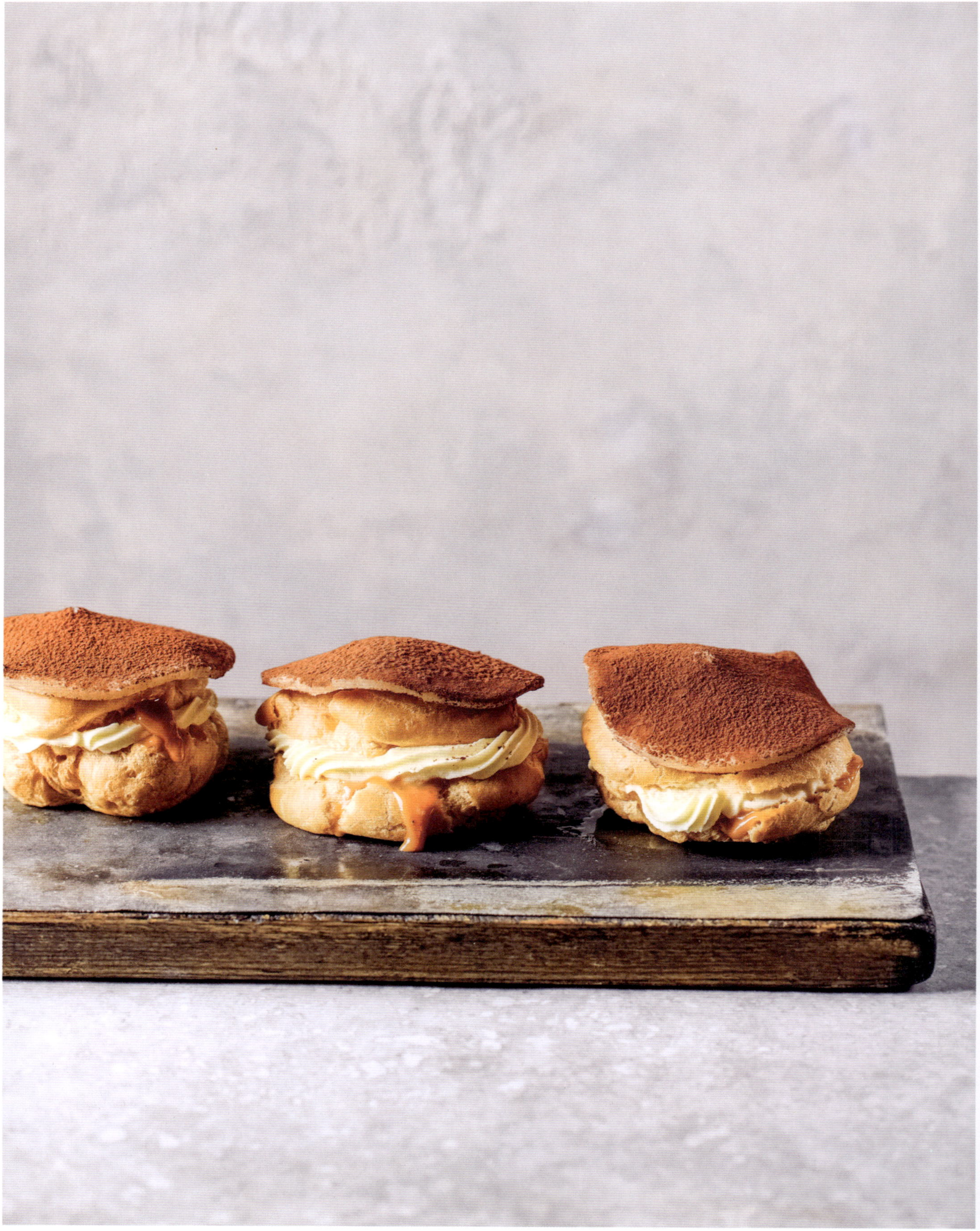

Choux buns with salted caramel

Kartoffelkager med saltkaramel

That the Danish name for these cakes is 'potato cakes' (*kartoffelkager*) is slightly misleading – they have nothing to do with potatoes, other than that they look a bit like them once the marzipan topping is added at the end (and hence this is how they got the name). Some places make these with a layered cake base, others as a choux pastry (which is what I prefer). I add a bit of salted caramel sauce to cut against the sweetness of the whipped cream and pastry cream.

1 quantity Choux Pastry Basic Batter (see page 235)
250 ml/1 cup whipping cream
¼ quantity Pastry Cream (see page 237) or 150 g/5½ oz. store-bought custard
150 g/5½ oz. Salted Caramel (see page 38 or store-bought)
200 g/7 oz. Marzipan, ideally 50% almond content (see page 237 or store-bought)
cocoa powder, for dusting

2 baking sheets, greased and lined with baking parchment
2 large piping/pastry bags fitted with large plain nozzle/tip (optional)
5–6-cm (2–2½-inch) round cookie cutter

MAKES 20

Preheat the oven to 200°C/180°C fan/400°F/Gas 6.

Prepare the choux pastry following the instructions on page 235. Spoon or pipe out around 20 buns of equal, generous size onto the prepared baking sheets. They will rise and puff up slightly, so space them apart.

Pop in the preheated oven and bake for 10 minutes, then reduce the oven to 160°C/140°C fan/320°F/Gas 3 and bake for a further 20 minutes. Do not open the door for the first 20 minutes of baking time. The buns take around 30 minutes in total.

Remove from the oven and pierce the buns immediately to allow steam to escape from the pastry. Leave to cool on a wire rack.

No more than 2 hours before serving, whip the cream to stiff peaks, then fold in the pastry cream or custard. Cut each bun open. First pipe in a dollop of salted caramel, then pipe in a generous amount of cream.

Roll out the marzipan on a surface lightly dusted with icing/confectioner's sugar. Stamp out 20 shapes to fit over the top of the choux pastry buns using the cookie cutter. Dust the marzipan shapes generously with cocoa powder and add to the top of the buns.

The coldest month of them all, no matter if you're in the south of Denmark or the northernmost islands of Norway. February brings a bitter, fierce chill that bites you right to the bone. This is deep winter with only a little light. It's also known as the month of cream buns (which probably keep us going).

In Denmark we might, by mid-February, be lucky to see the little snowdrop and winter aconite flowers peek up from the semi-frozen ground and we're reminded that, at some point, hopefully soon, the snow will melt and things will feel brighter and lighter. Mostly, though, those first green shoots come and go, quickly followed by both the first and second false springs, teasing us into submission for a bit longer.

Further north, though, there's much less chance of peeping shoots; February in the fjälls of Sweden and Norway still means heavy blankets of snow and having to dress in several layers of weather-appropriate clothing just to leave the house to pick up a carton of milk. However, February is perfect for winter sports in these mountainous regions, even if the days outside are very short and sweet, lit up by snowflakes that reflect the light as the sun hurries to set almost as soon as it rose.

FEBRUARY

THE TRADITIONS OF LENT

Many are surprised to learn how big a part the lead-up to Lent plays in the Scandinavian calendar, even if nowadays very few people ever actually give up anything. The season is called *Fastelavn* in Denmark and Norway, from the old Danish word *fastelaghen* and the old German word *fastelabend*, meaning 'the night before the fast'. It spans several days, with different ones having importance in various parts of our countries.

On the Sunday and Monday before Lent (seven weeks before Easter), Danish and Norwegian kids don fancy dress and gather at schools, nurseries and town halls. In Denmark, kids *slå katten af tønden* ('beat the cat out of the barrel') in a piñata-style game with a wooden barrel suspended from the ceiling, each child taking turns to beat it with a bat until it breaks.

In the old days, *fastelavn* was a grown-up event and the barrel-beating was done on horseback by drunken adults. It was customary to place a real black cat inside the barrel, but thankfully this horrific practice was outlawed a long time ago; today, the barrel is filled to the brim with sweets, still decorated with images of black cats as a nod to the old ways of warding off evil. After the barrel is broken, a Cat King and Queen will be crowned from among the kids – the biggest honour of them all. Usually, the royal pair are chosen based on the originality of their costumes.

When I grew up, *fastelavn* meant going from door to door begging for coins or sweets, although an American-style Halloween has now taken over as the door-knocking event of the year.

Another ancient tradition is the Danish and southern Swedish tradition of *fastelavnsris*: birch twigs decorated with colourful paper, sweets and feathers. These were traditionally used to whip young maidens of the village (in good humour). Today, no maidens are whipped, but the tradition of the decorated twigs lives on, with some kids using them to wake their parents on *fastelavn* morning. The tradition of birch twigs as a fertility symbol stems from pagan times and you'll find the same twigs in Sweden during Eastertime.

The Tuesday is known as *Hvide tirsdag* in Denmark – literally 'White Tuesday'. In Sweden, it is known as *Fettisdagen* ('Fat Day', a spin on the French *Mardi Gras*). Traditionally this was the last day to eat expensive ingredients such as white flour, eggs and sugar. Today, we eat heavy wheat buns filled with whipped cream. In Denmark and Norway, these are known as *fastelavnsboller* and in Sweden, *semlor* reign supreme. Danish *fastelavnsboller* are made either using a choux pastry dough, a laminated dough or a basic bun dough. A *semla* is a heavy wheat brioche-type bun, the top quarter of which is sliced off to form a lid. The insides are hollowed out, mixed with marzipan and a bit of milk and this is used to fill the hollow. Whipped cream is then piped on top and the lid replaced, after which the whole thing is dusted with icing/confectioner's sugar. Some Swedes enjoy this eaten in a bowl with warm milk, but most hand-deliver to the mouth.

Fettisdagen is a huge deal in Sweden. Every year, millions of *semlor* are sold and made on this day. It used to be tradition that the buns were only ever sold on the Tuesday, but nowadays you can buy them from New Year until Easter in most shops and bakeries. Until quite recently there was even a law governing when these buns could be made and sold, and if shops served them outside of those dates, they could, and would, be fined. Even today, no one sells *semlor* between Easter and Christmas.

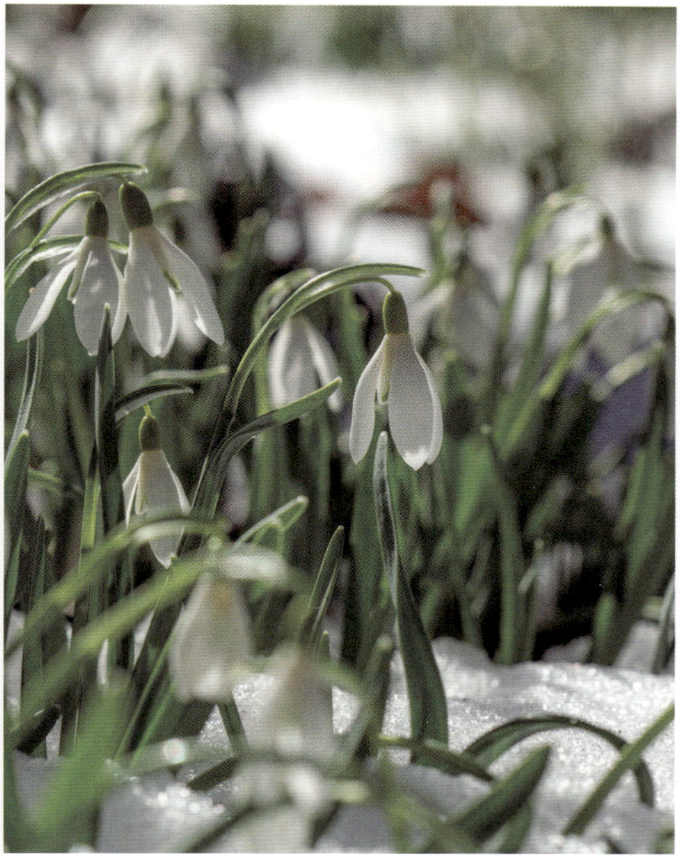

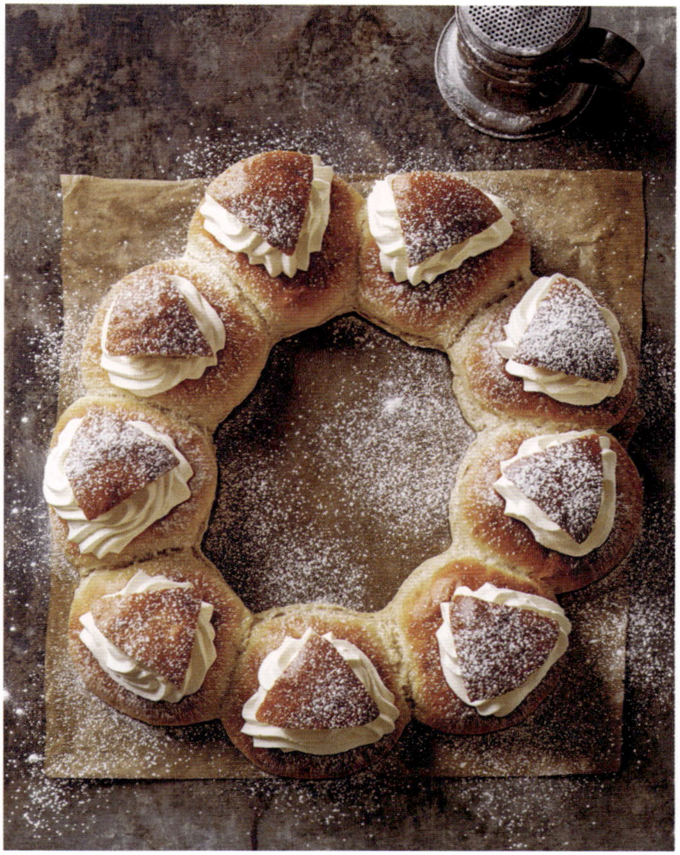

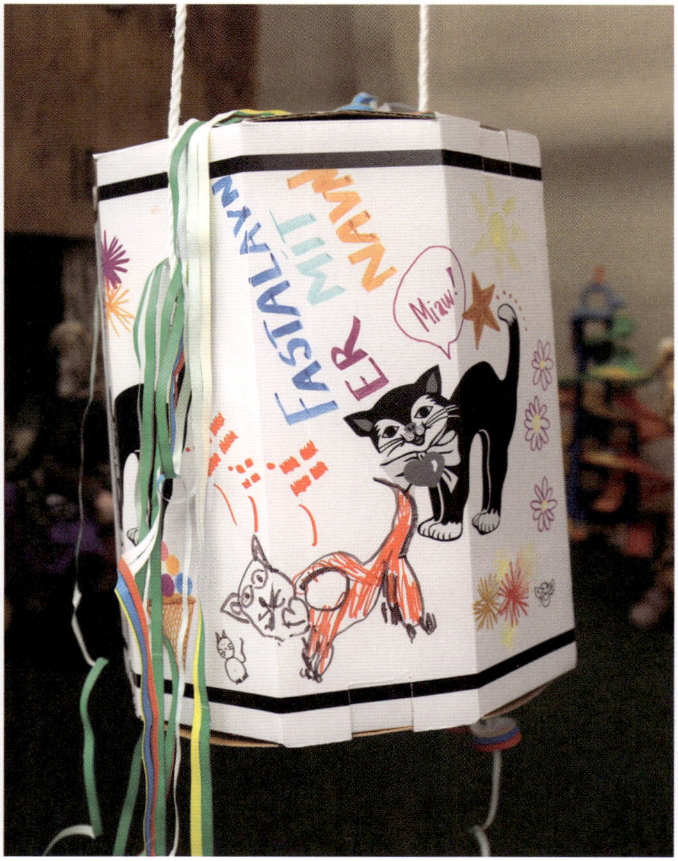
FASTALAVN
ER
MIT
NAVN
Miaw!

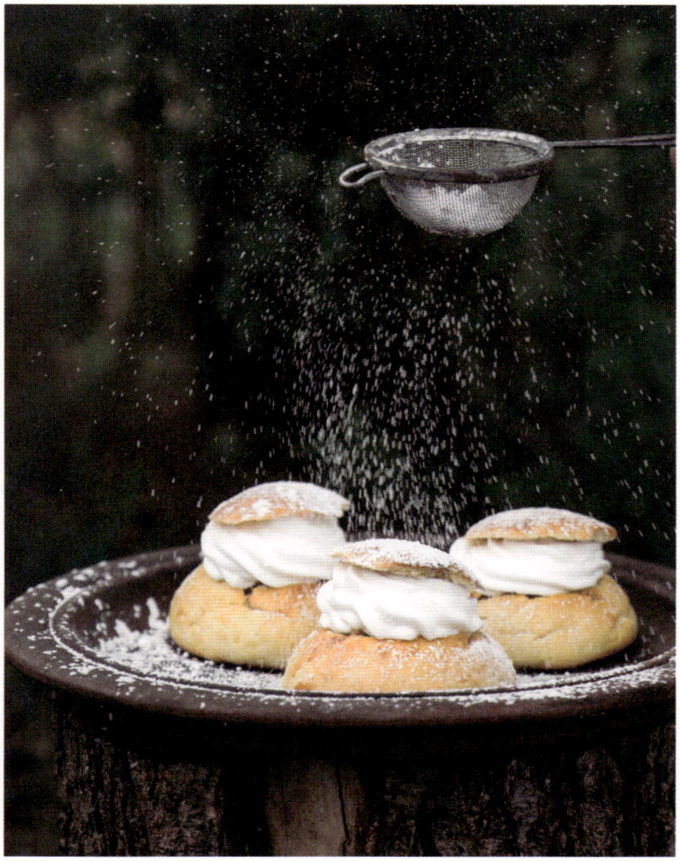

Swedish pea soup — *Ärtsoppa*

Across the Nordics there are plenty of yellow pea soup recipes. In Sweden, however, old-school tradition dictates that Thursday is pea soup day. This apparently originated from Catholic times when no meat was consumed on Fridays, so Thursday was pork-and-pea-soup day. This recipe comes from Stina Envall, who is the *husmor* (house mother) at London's Swedish Church. Stina uses whole dried yellow peas (not split ones), but this means hours of soaking before boiling. I've made her recipe with both kinds of peas and the split ones do produce a thicker result, but still a great taste (and much quicker to cook). I feel I'm teaching you to suck eggs by adding a pancake recipe, but for it's here for US readers, as this type of pancake is less common in America.

500 g/1 lb. 2 oz. yellow peas, whole or split
1 litre/4 cups vegetable stock
1 large onion, chopped
1–2 tablespoons dried thyme
1 tablespoon dried marjoram
3–4 carrots, sliced into circles
salt and freshly ground black pepper

TO SERVE
pulled ham hock or cubed ham (optional)
Dijon mustard
Pancakes (see below)

SERVES 4–6

If using whole peas, soak in water for 24 hours, then drain. If using yellow split peas, there is no need to soak but do rinse them before using.

Place the peas in a pan with the stock and bring to the boil, skimming the soup as it starts to boil. Add the onion.

If using whole peas, boil for around 1–1½ hours or until tender, topping up with water as necessary, then add the herbs and, carrots and seasoning; if using split peas, cook for about 30 minutes, then season and add herbs and carrots. Cook for a further 15–20 minutes until the carrots are tender. It is hard to specify the cooking time as it depends when the peas are soft and the soup gets a bit thicker.

Serve in bowls (traditionally we add ham hock or similar to the dish, and many spoon a bit of Dijon mustard through). Serve with pancakes.

Pancakes — *Pannkakor*

4 eggs
100 g/7 tablespoons butter, melted
180 g/1⅓ cups plain/all-purpose flour
a pinch of salt
1 tablespoon sugar
350 ml/1½ cups whole milk
100 ml/⅓ cup plus 1 tablespoon beer (optional, see note)
neutral oil, for frying

FOR SWEETER PANCAKES
additional 1–2 tablespoons sugar
1 teaspoon vanilla extract
½ teaspoon ground cardamom

MAKES 16–20 PANCAKES

Whisk the eggs with the half of the butter and the flour, salt and sugar. Add the milk and beer and whisk until it all comes together. Don't over-whisk. Add the additional ingredients, if you wish to make sweeter pancakes. Leave to rest in fridge for 30 minutes before using.

Heat a 23–35-cm/9–14-inch frying pan/skillet over a medium heat and add some oil and some of the remaining butter. When hot, add a ladleful of batter – it should just cover the entire surface of the pan, thinly. You may need to swivel the pan a bit. As soon as the top looks dry, use a spatula to turn the pancake over and fry for less than a minute on the other side.

Stack the thin pancakes on a plate and keep warm.

NOTE The beer gives the batter a lovely taste (I just add a dash of whatever is going) but you can omit it and just use extra milk instead. If you want to make these as dessert, I think a slightly sweeter version is nice – and the addition of vanilla and cardamom is one my mother always made.

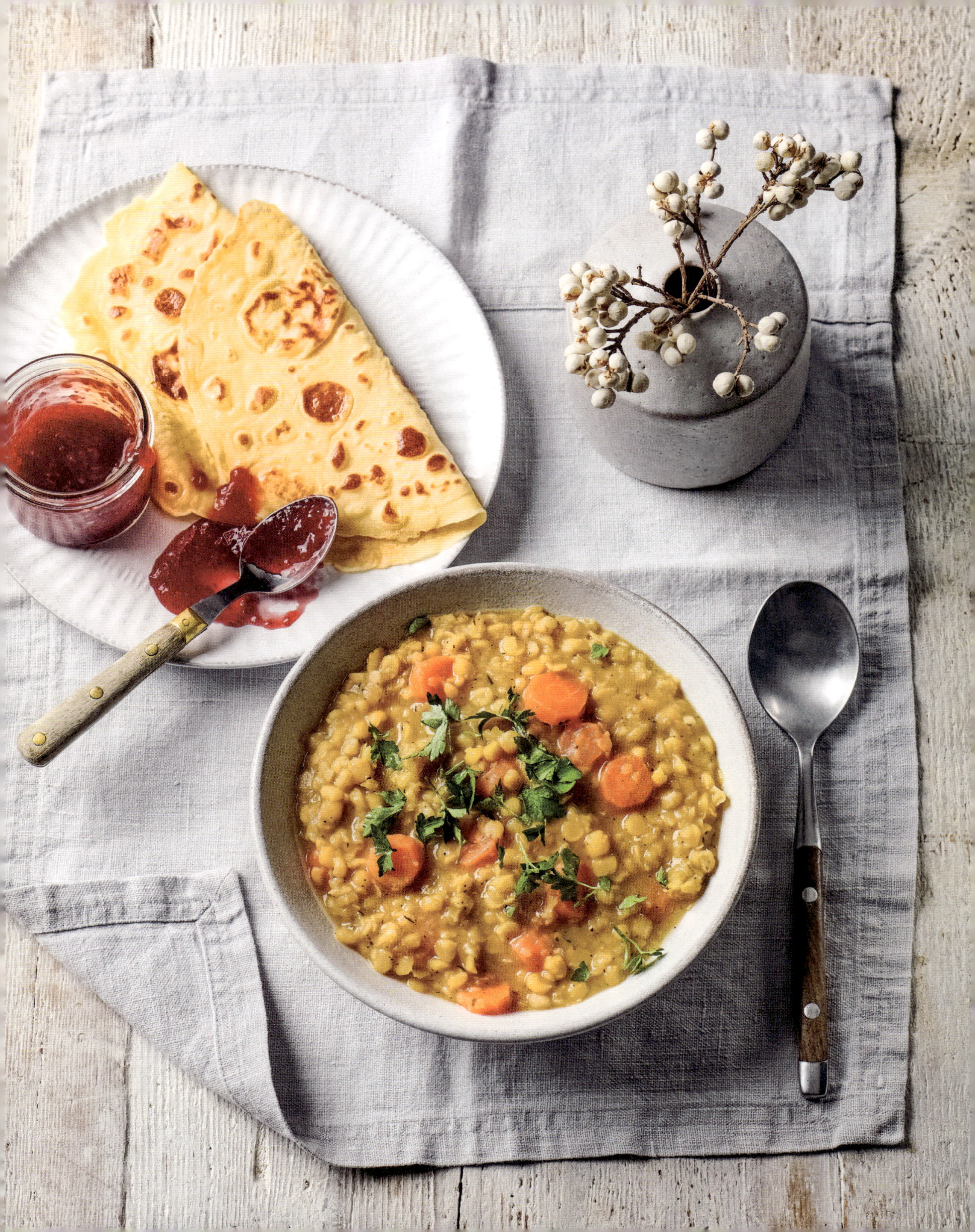

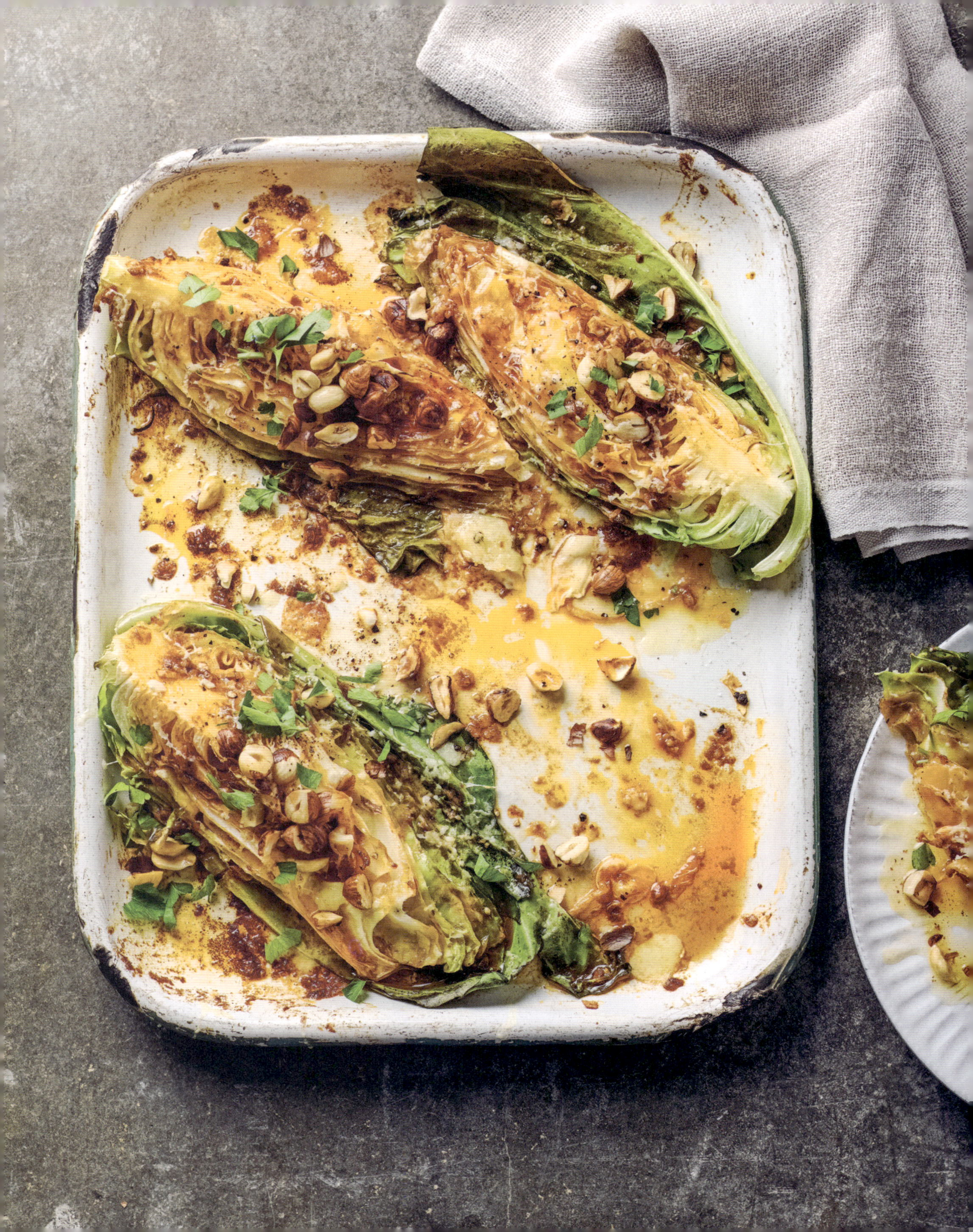

Roasted cabbage with Västerbotten cheese

Bagt spidskål med Västerbottensost

I love most kinds of cabbage, but a lot of older Nordic recipes cook it for a long time so I gravitate to recipes using raw or roasted cabbage. I serve this alongside Danish meatloaf (see page 52), meatballs (all kinds, but especially *Krebinetter*, see page 70), and also roast pork belly (see page 220) as a change from slow-cooked red cabbage.

40 g/3 tablespoons butter
a glug of oil
1 teaspoon paprika
2 garlic cloves, crushed
50 g/1¾ oz. Västerbotten cheese, grated (or Pecorino, Parmesan or other aged hard cheese)
1 head of sweetheart cabbage, cut into 4–6 wedges
25 g/¼ cup toasted hazelnuts, roughly chopped
2–3 tablespoons freshly chopped flat-leaf parsley
salt and freshly ground black pepper

SERVES 2–4 AS A SIDE

Preheat the oven to 200°C/180°C fan/400°F/Gas 6.

In a small pan, melt the butter, leave to froth up and go brown. This takes several minutes, but remove from the heat as soon as it is medium brown (dark brown will be bitter). It's done when it smells like baking biscuits.

Mix the oil, paprika, crushed garlic, half the cheese and 2 tablespoons of the browned butter in a bowl. Season well with salt and pepper.

Add the cabbage wedges to a baking tray or ovenproof dish. Brush each side with the cheese topping so all surfaces have some topping on them.

Cover with foil and bake in the preheated oven for 15–20 minutes. Remove the foil and add the rest of the cheese over the top of the cabbage, as well as drizzling the remaining browned butter over. Return to the oven, uncovered, for 10 minutes to crisp up, adding the hazelnuts for the last minute of cooking. Sprinkle the parsley over and serve immediately.

Scandinavian beetroot salad

Rödbetsallad

The iconic Scandi salad and an essential dish on any *smörgåsbord*, especially at Christmas. A super-quick side that goes well with anything from meatballs to boiled eggs. You can use plain cooked beets instead of pickled (simply adjust the seasoning).

500 g/1 lb. 2 oz. pickled beetroot/beets (approx. 2 standard jars), drained and diced into small cubes
1 tablespoon caster/granulated sugar (optional)
1 tart apple (Granny Smith or similar), peeled and cored
a squeeze of fresh lemon juice
75 g/⅓ cup mayonnaise
100 g/scant ½ cup crème fraîche or natural/plain yogurt
2–3 tablespoons balsamic vinegar
salt and freshly ground black pepper

SERVES 4–6

Taste the beetroot/beets as some brands use sweetener – if overly sweet, do not add sugar, but if too sour for your taste, add a tablespoon of sugar.

Cut the apple into cubes the same size as the beetroot. Squeeze some lemon juice over the apple, then mix with the beetroot. Mix in the mayonnaise, crème fraîche and balsamic vinegar and season. The light pink colour will go darker after a few hours. If you make ahead and prefer a lighter, creamier result, add a dollop of mayo or yogurt before serving.

VEGAN Swap the dressing for a vegan mayo.
EXTRA TART Add finely diced pickled cucumber, gherkin or capers.
NUTTY Add toasted walnuts or pumpkin/pepitas and sunflower seeds.
LIGHTER Replace the mayo and yogurt with skyr for lower calories.
HERRING SALAD Add chopped pickled herring and boiled/cooked egg.

Norwegian meatballs

Kjøttkaker

In traditional Norwegian cooking, two types of meatballs are popular. These beef meatballs called *Kjøttkaker*, literally translated it means 'meat cakes', and then there are *medisterkaker* made of pork which are usually served at Christmas along with *ribbe* (see page 220).

This beef version is served all year round, with mashed or boiled potatoes, mashed peas and a thick gravy. Of course, a good dollop of lingonberry on the side is a must. Even though they are served with similar sides to Swedish meatballs, these taste quite different and are much larger. Finishing the cooking in the gravy adds flavour to the sauce.

500 g/1 lb. 2 oz. minced/ground beef (minimum 15% fat content)
salt
½ onion, grated
½ teaspoon grated nutmeg
2 tablespoons cornflour/cornstarch
1 tablespoon plain/all-purpose flour
200 ml/¾ cup warm milk, with half a beef stock cube dissolved in it
1 egg
butter and oil, for frying.

GRAVY
25 g/1¾ tablespoons butter
25 g/3 tablespoons plain/all-purpose flour
600–800 ml/2½–3 cups stock or potato cooking water
soy or Worcestershire sauce (optional)
gravy browning
salt and freshly ground black pepper

MASHED PEAS
350 g/12 oz. frozen peas
80–100 ml/6–7 tablespoons meat stock
2 tablespoons butter

SERVES 4 (MAKES APPROX. 12 MEATBALLS)

In a stand mixer, mix together the beef and salt for a few minutes, then add the other meatball ingredients and combine. Place the mixture in the fridge to chill for 30 minutes before using.

Meanwhile, make the gravy. Melt the butter in a saucepan and add the flour. Continue to cook over a low heat until the mixture starts to colour, then start whisking in the liquid, little by little, allowing it to come to a simmer before adding more liquid. You may not need all the stock or water, but keep adding until you have a gravy of a good consistency. Season with salt and pepper and maybe a drop of soy or Worcestershire sauce. To give it colour, add a few drops of gravy browning. The gravy won't taste of much at this point, but the meatballs will be added to the sauce at next step.

Preheat the oven to 150°C/130°C fan/275°F/Gas 1.

To cook the meatballs, melt butter and oil in a frying pan/skillet and allow to brown slightly. Using a large spoon, shape the chilled mixture into approximately 12 large meatballs, each a little bigger than a large egg and slightly oblong. Fry in the fat until browned properly on all sides – you may need to do this in batches.

As you cook the meatballs, add the cooked ones to a large ovenproof dish. When done, pour the gravy over and place in the preheated oven for 15–20 minutes to finish cooking and to allow the meatballs to add a meaty flavour to the gravy.

To make the pea purée, boil the peas in the stock, then drain and blend with a stick blender – I like mine with a bit of texture. Stir through the butter and season with salt and pepper.

Serve the meatballs and gravy with the mashed peas and potatoes.

Danish beef in onion gravy

Hakkebøf

A hearty midweek meal from the traditional Danish kitchen – a favourite when I was growing up, and still a favourite in my kitchen today. This may look like a burger, but there's no bun – just lots of delicious browned onion, gravy and a beef patty. Traditionally this is served with boiled potatoes, but to be honest, we sometimes have mash or (sacrilege!) fried potatoes.

Two tips for a great result: firstly, don't mess too much with the meat (simply shape and fry) to allow the fibres of the beef to remain in the same direction as this makes a juicy patty. Secondly, it takes time to caramelise onions, so be patient.

butter and oil, for frying
3 onions, sliced
500 g/1 lb. 2 oz. minced/ground beef (minimum 15% fat content)
2–3 tablespoons plain/all-purpose flour, plus extra for dusting
500 ml/2 cups beef stock
Worcestershire sauce
salt and freshly ground black pepper

SERVES 4

In a frying pan/skillet, melt the butter and add the sliced onions. Cook over a low heat for around 15 minutes until the caramelisation process starts. You may need to add a glug of oil midway through.

Meanwhile prepare the beef patties. Split the meat into four patties and gently shape these so they have a good height of around 1.5–2 cm/¾ inch. Don't overwork the beef. Season with salt and pepper. Add a few tablespoons of flour to a plate and coat the patties lightly on both sides.

When the onions are cooked, remove from the pan and set aside. Add the beef patties to the pan and fry until browned but not cooked through. Remove the patties from the pan and set aside.

To make the gravy, heat the remaining fat in the pan (if there is not enough fat from the beef, add a bit more butter), then add 2–3 tablespoons flour to make a roux. Whisk over heat until it thickens, adding more and more stock as you go along (you may not need all the stock). Add the caramelised onion back in and season to taste with salt, pepper and Worcestershire sauce, then add the beef patties and allow to simmer for a few minutes until the patties are cooked through.

Serve with mashed or boiled potatoes, pickled cucumber and some seasonal vegetables.

Elsa's apple crumble with salted caramel

Elsas smulpaj

Smulpaj (literally 'crumb-pie') is what we call a fruit crumble in Swedish. My daughter Elsa is our household expert crumble baker and this is her recipe. If you're not a fan of salted caramel, leave it out and this is simply a very good *smulpaj* all on its own.

- 6 Granny Smith apples, peeled, cored and cut into 1–2-cm/½–¾-inch pieces
- 1 teaspoon vanilla extract or vanilla sugar
- 100 g/3½ oz. salted caramel sauce (see below or use store-bought)

TOPPING
- 150 g/1¼ sticks cold butter, cut into cubes
- 150 g/1 cup plus 2 tablespoons plain/all-purpose flour (or gluten-free flour, which is what Elsa uses)
- 50 g/½ cup ground almonds
- 50 g/½ cup porridge/rolled oats
- 125 g/⅔ cup minus 2 teaspoons caster/granulated sugar
- 1 teaspoon ground cinnamon
- 1 teaspoon mixed spice
- a pinch of salt

SERVES 6–8

Preheat the oven to 220°C/200°C fan/425°F/Gas 7.

Put the apples in a saucepan with a dash of water and the vanilla extract or sugar. Start the cooking process for a few minutes over a medium heat until starting to soften, then turn off the heat.

To make the crumble topping, rub the butter into flour in a bowl until it becomes sandy in texture, then add the other ingredients and mix again.

Add the apples to a shallow baking dish, then pipe or spoon the salted caramel all over. Cover with the crumble topping.

Bake in the preheated oven for 20–25 minutes or until the apples are cooked through and the top is nice and crisp.

Salted caramel sauce

Kolasås

- 200 g/1 cup granulated sugar
- 100 g/7 tablespoons unsalted butter, cut into pieces
- 125 ml/½ cup whipping cream
- sea salt flakes, to taste

MAKES APPROX. 400 G/14 OZ.

Heat the sugar in a medium saucepan over a medium heat, until amber in colour. Add the butter – the mixture will bubble rapidly as the butter melts. Whisk to ensure it is combined, then add the cream. Allow to boil for a minute or so, then turn off the heat and season to taste with sea salt. Cool completely before using. Store in the fridge for up to 1 week.

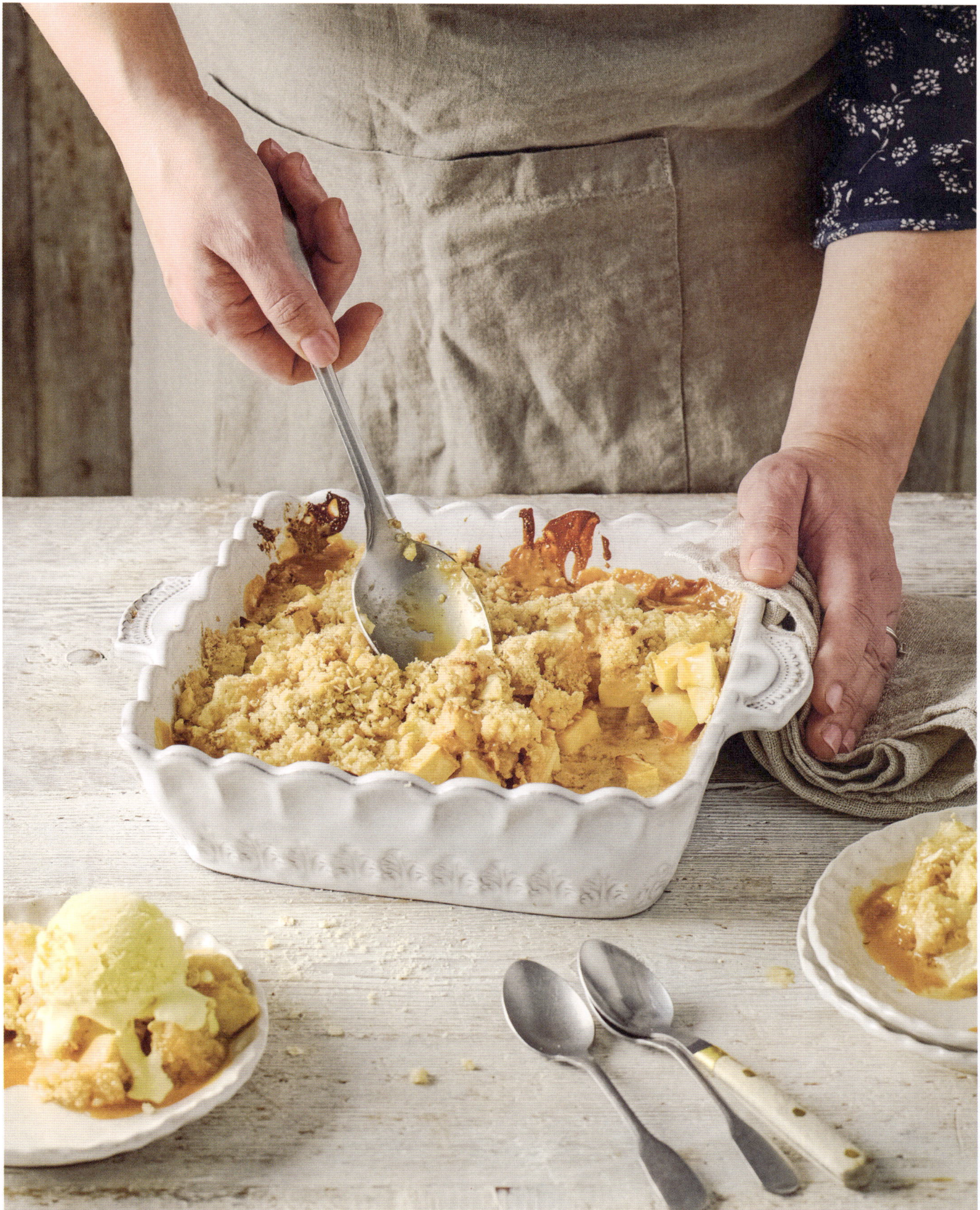

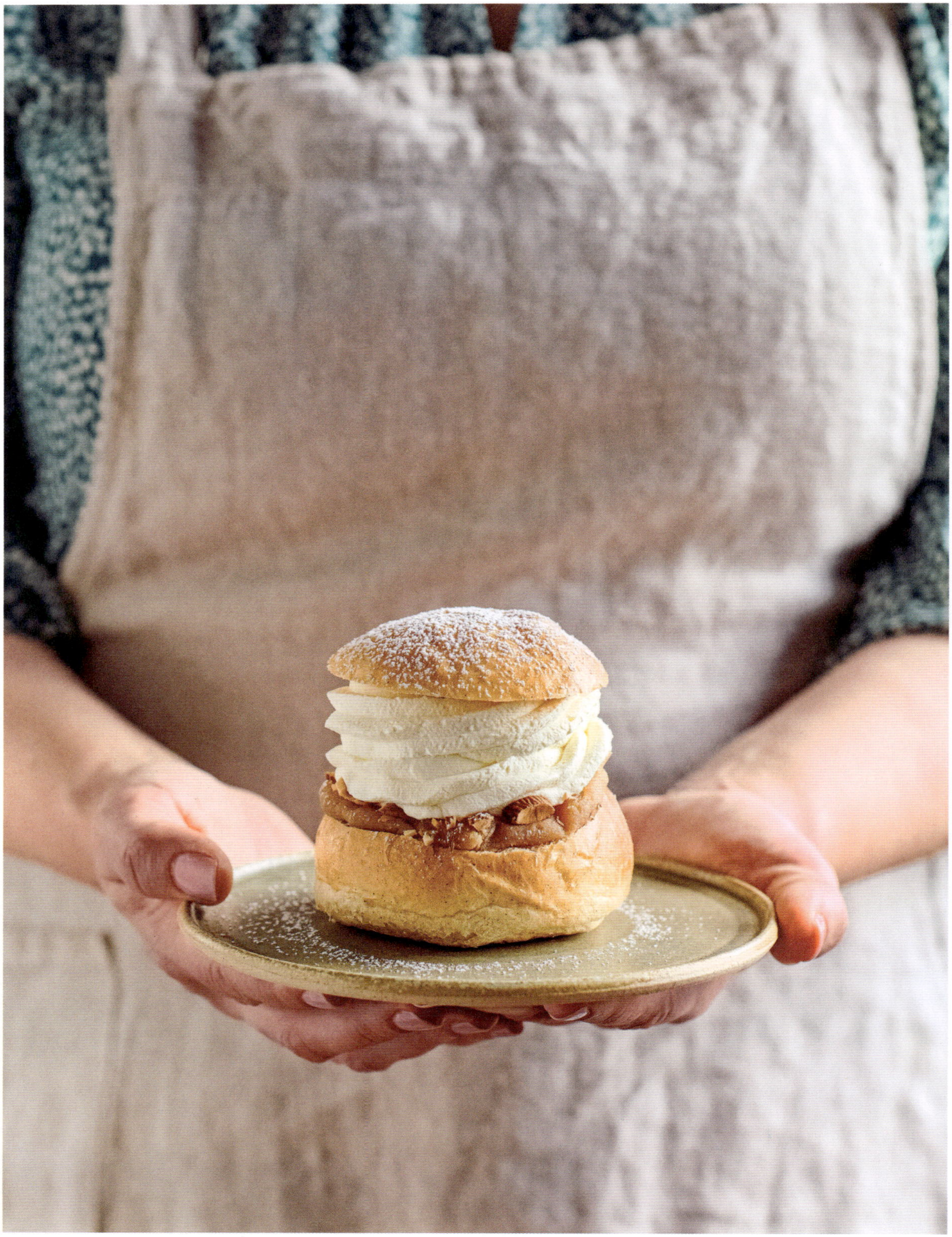

Semlor buns

Semlor

On Shrove Tuesday, Swedes buy over 8 million semlor buns (not accounting for home bakes). Across the Nordics, nobody celebrates this day quite like the Swedes. Indeed, the story goes that in 1771 poor King Adolf Fredrik feasted on 14 of these delicious cream buns with hot milk (admittedly following a full banquet of lobster and Champagne) and passed away due to severe indigestion.

There used to be a strict season for these buns – overseen by an actual law – but these days, the buns appear on sale straight after New Year and disappear just before Easter, giving us all plenty of time to enjoy them.

The traditional filling is almond paste and whipped cream, with some also enjoying these buns in a bowl of hot milk (like the king). In recent years, bakeries (including ScandiKitchen) have started experimenting with different flavours and fillings (much to the dismay of semlor purists). This has led to anything from pistachio or saffron to Prinsesstårta – and even a nacho semlor – but nothing beats the original and best. Just make sure you don't eat 14 of them.

1 quantity Basic Bun Dough (see page 234)
plain/all-purpose flour, for dusting
beaten egg, for brushing
100 g/3½ oz. Marzipan (see page 237)
a good dollop of custard or dash of milk
500 ml/2 cups whipping cream
1 teaspoon vanilla extract or vanilla sugar
1 tablespoon icing/confectioner's sugar, plus extra for dusting

piping/pastry bag fitted with a plain nozzle/tip

MAKES 12

Turn the dough out onto a floured surface. Knead again for a few minutes, then cut the dough into 12 equal-sized pieces and shape each into a ball. Place on a baking sheet, evenly spaced. Leave to rise for 25–30 minutes.

Preheat the oven to 200°C/180°C fan/400°F/Gas 6.

Brush each bun with beaten egg and bake in the preheated oven for 8–10 minutes or until baked through – keep an eye on them as they can burn quickly. Remove from the oven and cover the buns with a lightly damp kitchen towel to prevent them forming a crust as they cool.

When they have cooled completely, cut a 'lid' off the buns about 1.5 cm/½ inch from the top and set aside. Scoop out about one-third of the inside of each bun and place in a bowl. Mix the inside bits with the marzipan paste and custard until it forms a very sticky mass – add a bit more custard or milk if it's a little hard. The mixture should be almost spoonable. Spoon the filling back into the buns, dividing it equally between them.

Whip the cream with the vanilla and icing/confectioner's sugar until stiff, then use the piping/pastry bag to pipe cream on all the buns. Put the 'lids' back on and dust lightly with icing sugar, then serve immediately.

NOTE You can add some toasted chopped almonds on top of the marzipan for a bit of extra crunch and texture.

FEBRUARY

Astrid's sticky cake & my brownie

Astrids kladdkaka och min brownie

Kladdkaka means 'sticky cake' in Swedish. It's not a brownie as it contains no chocolate, is slightly underbaked (not runny but super sticky), and often served lukewarm. My eldest, Astrid, bakes a really good one. On the flip side, you do sometimes just want a brownie, so here is my recipe for the perfect super-fudgy kind.

Astrid's kladdkaka

- 225 g/1 cup plus 2 tablespoons caster/granulated sugar
- 3 eggs
- 2 teaspoons vanilla sugar or extract
- 125 g/1 cup minus 1 tablespoon plain/all-purpose flour
- 50 g/½ cup cacao powder (Astrid always uses Fazer Ögon Cacao), plus extra for dusting
- a pinch of salt
- 150 g/1¼ sticks butter, melted

23-cm/9-inch round cake pan, greased and lined with baking parchment

SERVES 6

Preheat the oven to 200°C/180°C fan/400°F/Gas 6.

Whisk the sugar and eggs until light and airy, then add the vanilla. Mix the dry ingredients together, then sift into the egg mixture and fold in along with the melted butter until incorporated.

Pour the batter into the prepared cake pan and bake in the preheated oven for 12–14 minutes. The time will depend on your oven – mine is exactly 14 minutes for the perfect level of super-stickiness, but your oven may be different. Take it out 2 minutes before you think it's ready.

Leave the cake to cool in the cake pan, unless you've given it slightly too long in the oven – in that case, remove from the pan immediately so it does not keep baking from the residual heat. Dust with cacao to serve.

My fudgy brownie

- 175 g/1½ sticks butter
- 275 g/1½ cups minus 2 tablespoons caster/granulated sugar
- 75g/3½ tablespoons golden/corn syrup
- 250 g/9 oz. good-quality dark/bittersweet chocolate (60–70% cocoa solids), broken into pieces
- 4 eggs
- 1 teaspoon vanilla extract
- 120 g/1 cup minus 1½ tablespoons plain/all-purpose flour
- 10 g/2 tablespoons cacao powder
- a pinch of salt
- 100–150 g/3½–5½ oz. nuts – pecans, macadamia, hazelnuts, pistachios or walnuts all work well (optional)

35 x 24-cm/14 x 9½-inch cake pan, lined with baking parchment

MAKES 16 PIECES

Preheat the oven to 180°C/160°C fan/350°F/Gas 4.

Melt the butter, sugar and syrup in a saucepan over a low heat until all the sugar crystals have melted, around 5–7 minutes. Turn off the heat and add the chocolate and allow to melt. Add the eggs and beat in one by one, then add the vanilla extract. Sift the flour, cacao and salt together, then fold into the chocolate mixture until uniformly combined (don't over-beat). The mixture should be nice and thick. Stir in the nuts, if using.

Pour into the prepared cake pan and bake in the middle of the preheated oven for 20–25 minutes. This brownie has no rising agent and is very fudgy – it is done when you see cracks appearing around the edges. It seems to bake a little quicker if you have added nuts, so do keep an eye on it.

Remove from the oven and leave to cool in the pan and ideally for a few hours in the fridge before eating or, even better, cut into pieces and freeze until a few hours before you need a brownie fix.

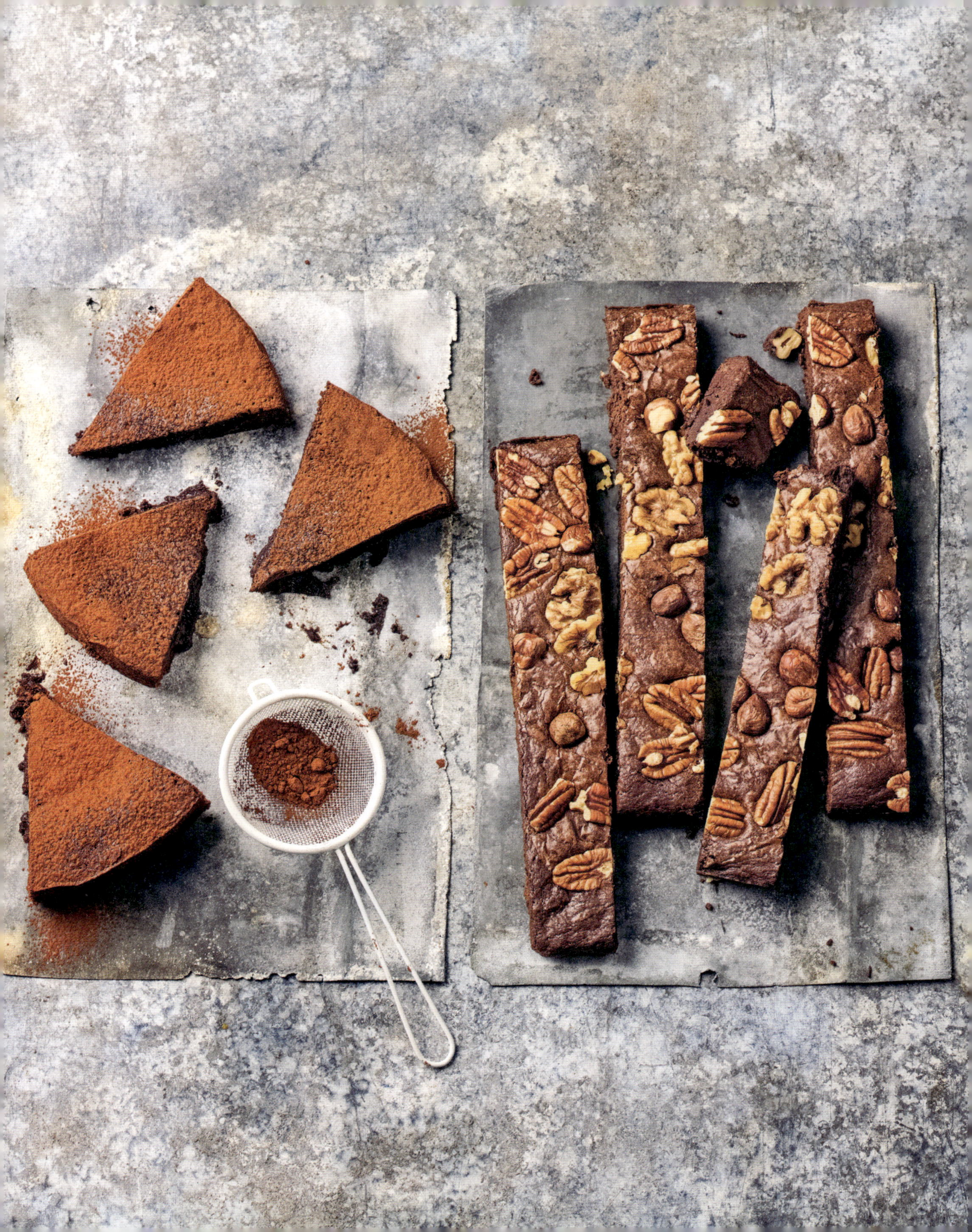

By March, the southern coastal parts of Scandinavia are starting to defrost and daylight is returning, making it much easier to spend time outdoors. However, the snow is giving out to rain – and lots of it. Even so, as the polar night ends, it feels as if we are finally coming out of hibernation. The crisp, clear nights in the north may increase the chances of catching a glimpse of the aurora borealis, while in the southern towns and cities we once again venture out to enjoy *fika* with friends in outside cafés (under thick woollen blankets, of course). Danes get back on their bicycles in droves – Copenhagen mornings are once more a determined peloton of people pedalling to work.

Early spring is a time for skiing. March sees the famous Vasaloppet ski race in Sweden, a 90-kilometre/56-mile cross-country race inspired by the 16th-century skiing followers of the future Swedish King Gustav Vasa and his attempts to overthrow the Danish King Christian II. While Danes in general are not big skiers compared to the Norwegians and Swedes (on account of the lack of enduring snow and no mountains in Denmark), Vasaloppet draws participants from near and far as people attempt to complete the gruelling race across the snowclad Dalarna region. March is also a month of other winter sports, including the indigenous Sámi community's reindeer racing.

MARCH

HAPPINESS

Year after year, the Nordic countries top the overall worldwide happiness polls.

I often wonder what happiness really means and what those poll questions ask. Is it just overall contentment with life? Is it a happy childhood or the ability to look back and think, 'I've truly lived'? How can any measure of happiness truly quantify something as qualitative as happiness? To me, happiness is in everything, from a soft cinnamon bun to *hygge* in front of the telly on a Saturday evening, as much as it is about coins in my pocket or seeing my kids flourish. Are Nordic people just extra happy because we feel comfortable being naked or that we eat a lot of those buns? If someone asks you, 'Are you content?' and your basic needs are met, how can you say no? There are many different words to describe 'happy' in Scandinavia. *Glad* is self-explanatory, whereas *lykkelig* is euphoric happiness. I think we're a calmly and collectively content people who are appreciative of this.

The Nordic countries are structured largely around the same basic principles: in a society, those who *have* must contribute more and those who *lack* must be supported. All education is free and nobody need worry about healthcare and meeting the basic needs of life (from birth to death). The status quo is a baseline which means that Maslow's Hierarchy of Needs are met in abundance for most of us. This works, because *everyone* (by and large) seems to agree that this is a good base from which to start. There are no serious political parties that want to form a different baseline than this, which makes it easier to agree on the basics.

A huge majority of Nordic people agree with high taxes in order to sustain a fairer society for all, that those who have more give back and those who do not get more. This also creates a large base of people who *feel* middle-class and rather content in that sphere. They want for none of their basic needs but, on the flip side, won't ever be able to afford a Ferrari. There is enough to go around, a sense of not too little, not too much, just the *right amount*. It's fair. In general, you are likely to trust your neighbour and leave a pram containing your sleeping child outside the café on the street as you *fika* with friends. We work short weeks, but feel more effective when at work. Women and men are equal in their basic rights and, if you lose your job, you're unlikely to end up on the street. These factors all contribute to this overall happiness.

The Swedish concept of *lagom* is exactly this: *just right*. The word is said to derive from a phrase used in Viking times – *laget om*, meaning 'around to the team' and apparently used to describe just how much mead one should drink when passing the horn around the group, ensuring enough for all. This etymology is commonly accepted to be right, although some parallels are made with the common set of rules about how much one should have of something, always relating back to the greater good for the whole group. If you take only what you need there may just be enough to go around for everyone. In essence, this is the basis of the Nordic psyche.

A band of people equal in status, income and education also allows for the less positive concept of the *Jante Law* to remain engrained in our souls. This is Scandinavia's in-depth version of 'tall poppy syndrome' and is alive and well today. It comprises ten commandments, including 'Don't think you are anything special', 'Don't think you are better than anyone else' and 'Don't think you can teach us anything'. These are harsh reminders that, to live in this *lagom* medium of semi-skimmed everything, you can't be ostentatious, flamboyant or a smartass. It's all about *balance*. Not simply because it would make you look better than others, rather because it would make others feel bad about themselves. It works by considering *everyone*.

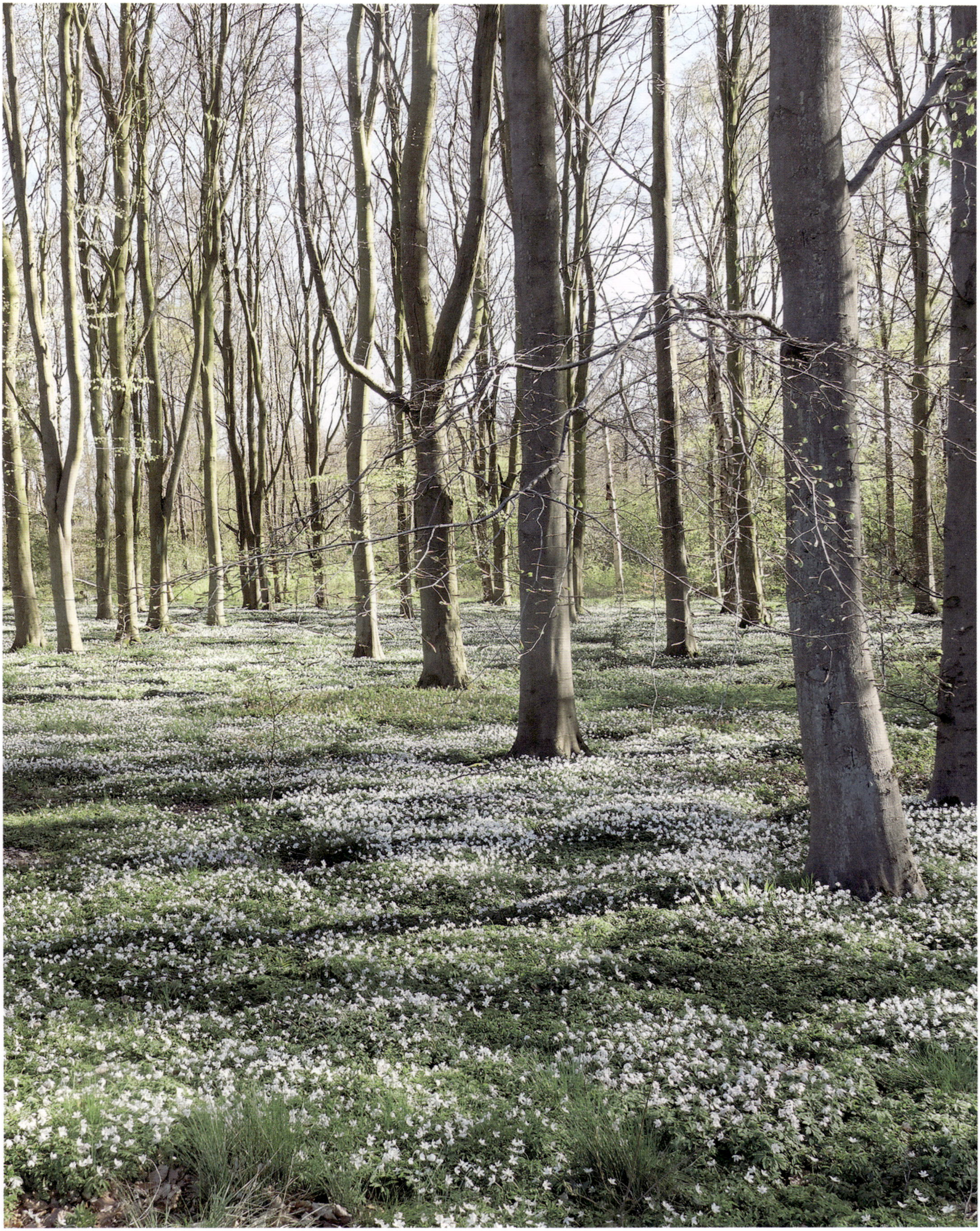

Barbro's salmon pâté

Laxpaté

For decades, my dear friend Barbro McAusland has been making her salmon pâté for the Christmas Fair at the Swedish Church in London, a highlight of the Scandinavian community's festive season. It's a bestseller at the fair and always sells out quickly, so I'm very grateful to Barbro for sharing her recipe with me for this book. This pâté is delicious on Scandi crispbread – either as a starter or as a snack – or simply part of a bigger *smörgåsbord* spread. Swedish pickled sprats (*ansjovis*) can be bought in speciality shops. You can freeze this pâté once done – seal it by melting a pat of extra butter and pour over the top of the pâté, then freeze.

- 200 g/7 oz cooked salmon, skinned, boned and all fatty bits removed
- 20 g/¾ oz shallot, chopped finely
- 10 drops of Worcestershire sauce
- 1 garlic clove, crushed
- 80 g/5½ tablespoons butter, slightly softened and cubed, plus optional 25 g/1¾ tablespoons, melted, for sealing
- 50 g/2 oz. pickled sprats (also known as Swedish *ansjovis*)
- 1 teaspoon brine from the sprats
- 2 tablespoons freshly chopped parsley
- 2 tablespoons freshly chopped dill
- ½ teaspoon cayenne pepper
- salt and freshly ground black pepper

MAKES 350 G/12 OZ.

In a food processor, blitz all the ingredients until smooth and season to taste.

Either eat immediately, or pot in ramekins, seal the top with melted butter and freeze for later use.

Simple fennel salad

Nem salat med fennikel

One of my favourite ways to eat fennel is simply raw with a good dressing, mixed with apple. This super-simple salad goes well with a piece of smoked mackerel or hot-smoked salmon on the side.

- 2 large bulbs of fennel
- 1 large tart apple, such as Granny Smith
- a small bunch of fresh dill, roughly chopped
- 50 g/2 oz. toasted walnuts, roughly chopped
- a handful of fresh pea shoots

DRESSING
- 1 tablespoon apple cider vinegar
- 1 tablespoon freshly squeezed lemon juice
- 1 teaspoon honey or sugar
- a pinch of salt and freshly ground black pepper
- 5 tablespoons extra virgin olive oil

SERVES 2–3

To make the dressing, combine everything except the oil, then add the oil while whisking until the dressing comes together.

Finely shave the fennel on a mandolin and pop it in ice cold water (this will keep it crispy). Shave the apple the same way. Combine in a bowl and add the dill. Pour the dressing over, add the walnuts and pea shoots, and serve.

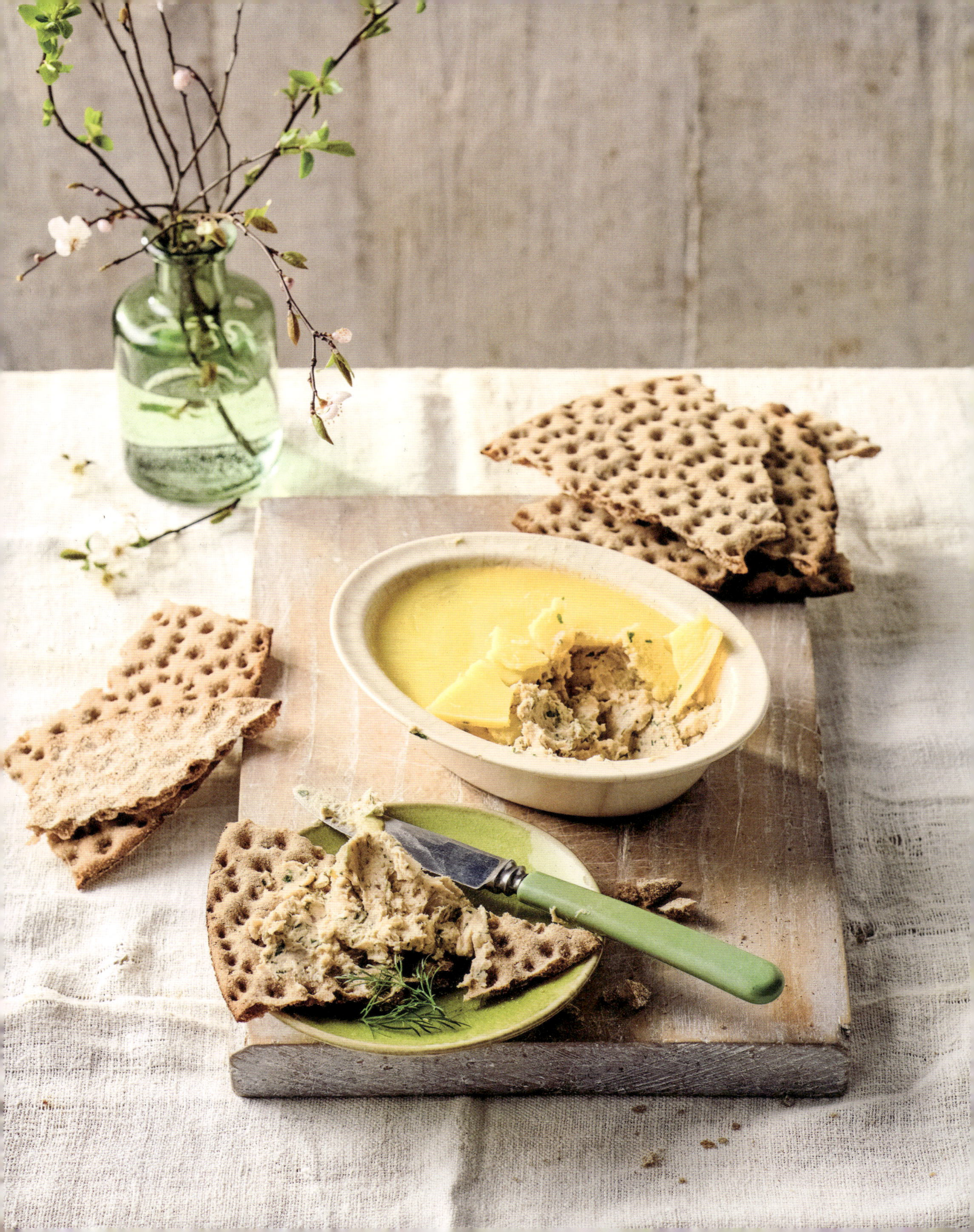

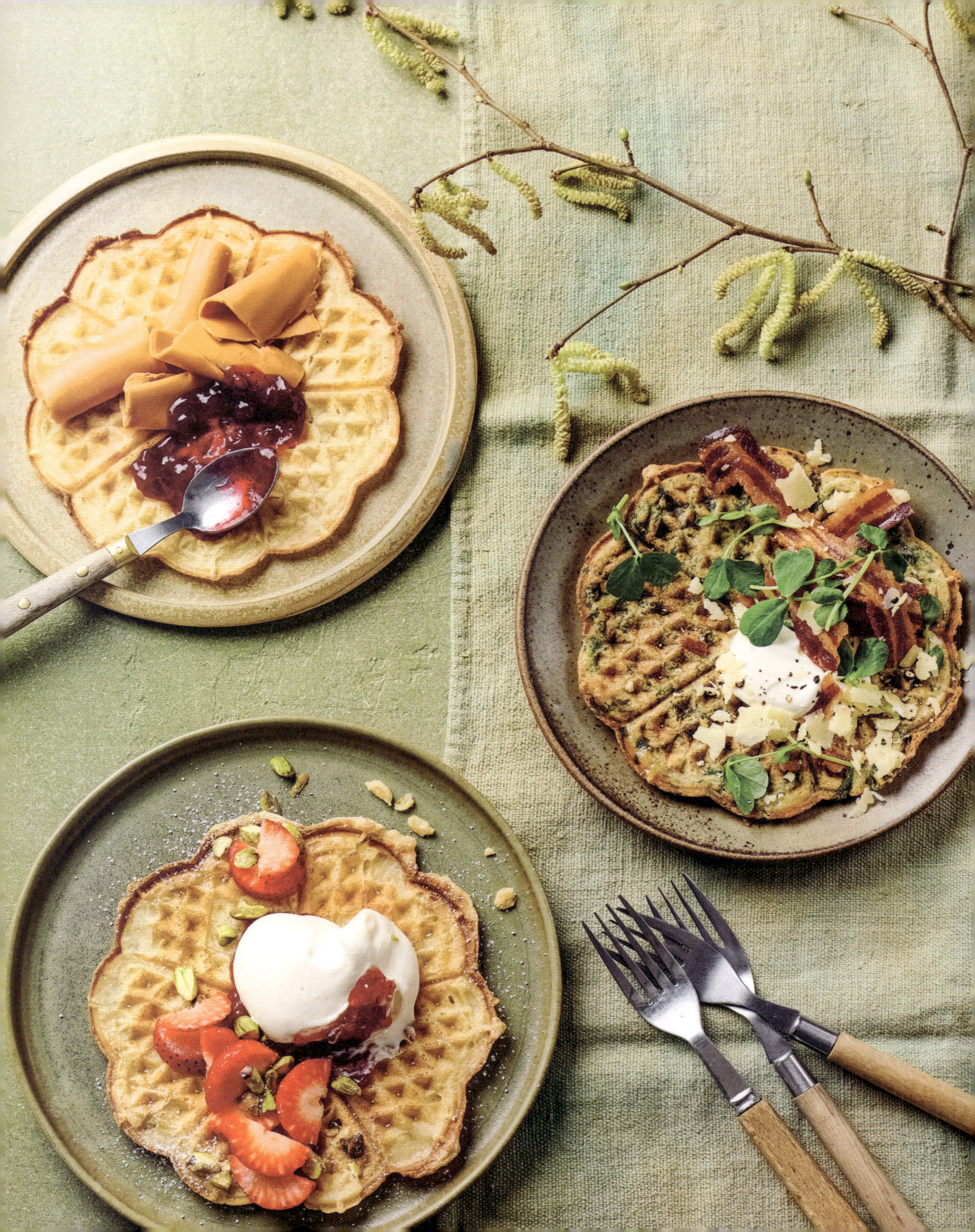

Three different waffles

Tre forskjellige vafler

Waffles are a staple snack in Norway and Sweden (we also make these in Denmark). The biggest fans are Norwegians, where every household has a recipe for the perfect *vaffel*. Often served with *brunost* (caramelised goat's whey) and a sweet jam/preserve, some people even use them to serve hotdogs. In Sweden waffles are crispier (they don't stay crispy, so you need to eat right away), served with whipped cream and jam. I also love savoury waffles and often make cheesy and veg ones.

Swedish crispy waffles

150 g/1¼ sticks butter, melted, plus a little extra for brushing
300 g/2¼ cups plain/all-purpose flour
2 teaspoons baking powder
1 teaspoon vanilla sugar or vanilla extract
250 ml/1 cup whole milk
250 ml/1 cup water
cloudberry or strawberry jam/preserve and berries, to serve
whipped cream, to serve

Mix all the ingredients together to form a smooth batter. Leave to stand for 30 minutes before using.

Heat up the waffle iron and brush with melted butter. Add a ladle of batter to the preheated waffle iron and close the lid. Leave to cook for 2–3 minutes or until golden brown and crispy. Remove and serve immediately with cloudberry or strawberry jam/preserve, whipped cream and fresh berries.

ALL RECIPES MAKE APPROX. 6–8 WAFFLES

NOTE All waffles are made in a traditional Scandi heart-shaped waffle iron. You can use other irons but cooking time will vary, as will yield. Do make sure you buy a quality one as some cheaper brands don't get hot enough.

Spinach & cheese waffles

75 g/5⅓ tablespoons butter, melted, plus a little extra for brushing
350 ml/1½ cups water
100 g/3½ oz. blanched spinach, drained and chopped
150 g/1 cup plus 2 tablespoons plain/all-purpose flour
50 g/½ cup wholegrain spelt flour (replace with white flour if you don't have spelt)
2 teaspoons baking powder
75 g/2¾ oz. Västerbotten cheese or mature Cheddar, finely grated
salt and freshly ground black pepper
sour cream, to serve (optional)

Mix the wet ingredients and spinach in one bowl. Mix the dry ingredients in another bowl. Combine into a batter and leave for 30 minutes before using.

Heat up the waffle iron and brush with melted butter. Add a ladle of batter to the preheated waffle iron and close the lid. Leave to cook for 2–3 minutes or until golden brown and crispy. Remove and serve immediately with sour cream and bacon slices.

VARIATION If you wish, add 100 g/3½ oz. cooked crispy bacon pieces to the batter (but watch the salt seasoning as the bacon is salty). Alternatively, serve with a few rashers/slices of bacon on top.

Norwegian-style waffles

3 eggs
300 ml/1¼ cups whole milk
100 ml/⅓ cup plus 1 tablespoon natural/plain yogurt
250 g/1¾ cups plus 2 tablespoons plain/all-purpose flour
75 g/⅓ cup plus 2 teaspoons caster/granulated sugar
1 teaspoon baking powder
½ teaspoon bicarbonate of soda/baking soda
1 teaspoon ground cardamom
1 teaspoon vanilla sugar or vanilla extract
100 g/7 tablespoons butter, melted, plus a little extra for brushing

In a bowl, combine the eggs, milk and yogurt. Add all the dry ingredients. Add the melted butter and whisk to form a smooth batter, taking care not to over-beat. Leave for at least 30 minutes in the fridge before using.

Heat up the waffle iron and brush with melted butter. Add a ladle of batter to the preheated waffle iron and close the lid. Leave to cook for 2–3 minutes or until golden brown and crispy. Remove and serve immediately.

Danish meatloaf

Forloren hare

Cold, dark evenings, family around the table, talking about their day – that is what this dish represents to me, past and present. This was a favourite midweek meal growing up, and now it's one of my children's favourites, too. My mother's (and my grandmother's) meatloaf dish has gradually evolved and become mine, and one day it will belong to my children. This dish is part of our family history. My mother always used only beef, but traditionally in Denmark, it's either pork and beef or pork and veal. I now add small bacon pieces to the mixture because, well, that's next-level.

100 g/3½ oz. pancetta/bacon cubes
1 onion, finely chopped
a glug of oil
100 ml/⅓ cup plus 1 tablespoon milk
1 beef stock cube
500 g/1 lb. 2 oz. minced/ground beef (minimum 15% fat content)
2 teaspoons flaked salt, such as Maldon
50 g/⅔ cup breadcrumbs
1 egg
½ teaspoon grated nutmeg
1 teaspoon Dijon mustard
a small bunch of fresh flat-leaf parsley, finely chopped (approx. 3 generous tablespoons)
1 teaspoon tomato purée/paste
200 g/7 oz. thinly sliced streaky/fatty bacon
Hasselback Potatoes (see page 225), to serve

SAUCE
100 ml/⅓ cup plus 1 tablespoon cream
200 ml/¾ cup milk
2–3 teaspoons redcurrant jelly or lingonberry jam/preserve
Worcestershire or soy sauce (optional)
1–2 tablespoons cornflour/cornstarch
gravy browning (optional)
salt and freshly ground black pepper

SERVES 4–6

Add the pancetta or bacon pieces and onion to a saucepan with a glug of oil and fry over a low heat for around 10 minutes or until the onion starts to caramelise. Take off the heat. If the bacon pieces are quite big, chop them up to avoid big lumps in your meatloaf.

Heat the milk, add the stock cube and allow to dissolve.

In a stand mixer, add the beef and salt and mix for a few minutes, then add the breadcrumbs, egg, nutmeg, parsley, mustard and purée. Add the bacon/onion mixture and the milk with stock and combine. Season. Place the mixture in the fridge to chill for at least 30 minutes before using.

Preheat the oven to 240°C/220°C fan/425°F/Gas 7.

Shape the meatloaf into a rectangle about 20 cm/8 inches long and place in an ovenproof dish. Lay the streaky bacon all across the top, taking care to tuck the ends underneath. The whole loaf should be covered.

Bake in the preheated oven for 20 minutes. Remove from oven. To make the sauce, mix the cream with 100 ml/⅓ cup plus 1 tablespoon of the milk and pour into the dish around the meatloaf, along with 2 teaspoons of redcurrant jelly or lingonberry jam (cranberry could also work here).

Turn the oven down to 200°C/180°C fan/400°F/Gas 6 and cook the meatloaf for a further 20–25 minutes. Remove from oven and drain all the creamy goodness and meat juices into a saucepan. Cover the meatloaf and allow to rest while you make the sauce.

Add the remaining milk (or use water) to the sauce (depending on how liquid much was left in the dish after cooking). Bring to the boil and taste, then add another teaspoon of jelly if necessary and season with salt, pepper and maybe a few drops of Worcestershire or soy sauce. In a small dish, dissolve the cornflour/cornstarch with a little water, add half of it to the gravy and thicken for a minute or so at boiling point. Add more cornflour if you prefer a thicker sauce. If you want a darker gravy, add a few drops of gravy browning. Strain the sauce through a sieve/strainer and keep warm. Serve the meatloaf in thick slices with Hasselback potatoes.

TIPS Replace the breadcrumbs with oats for a gluten-free option. Leftover meatloaf makes an excellent sandwich filling with crisp leaves, mustard and tomato in crusty bread.

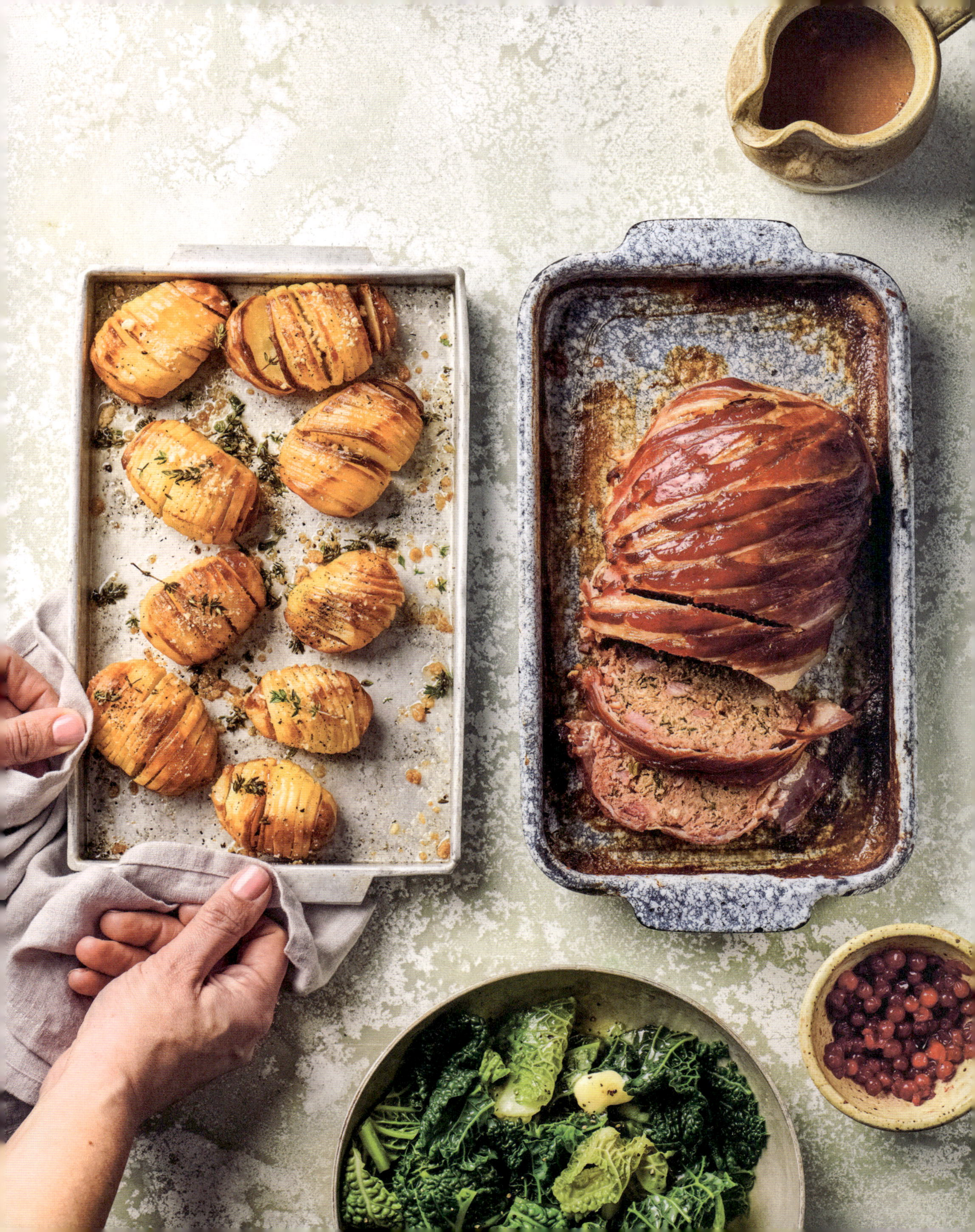

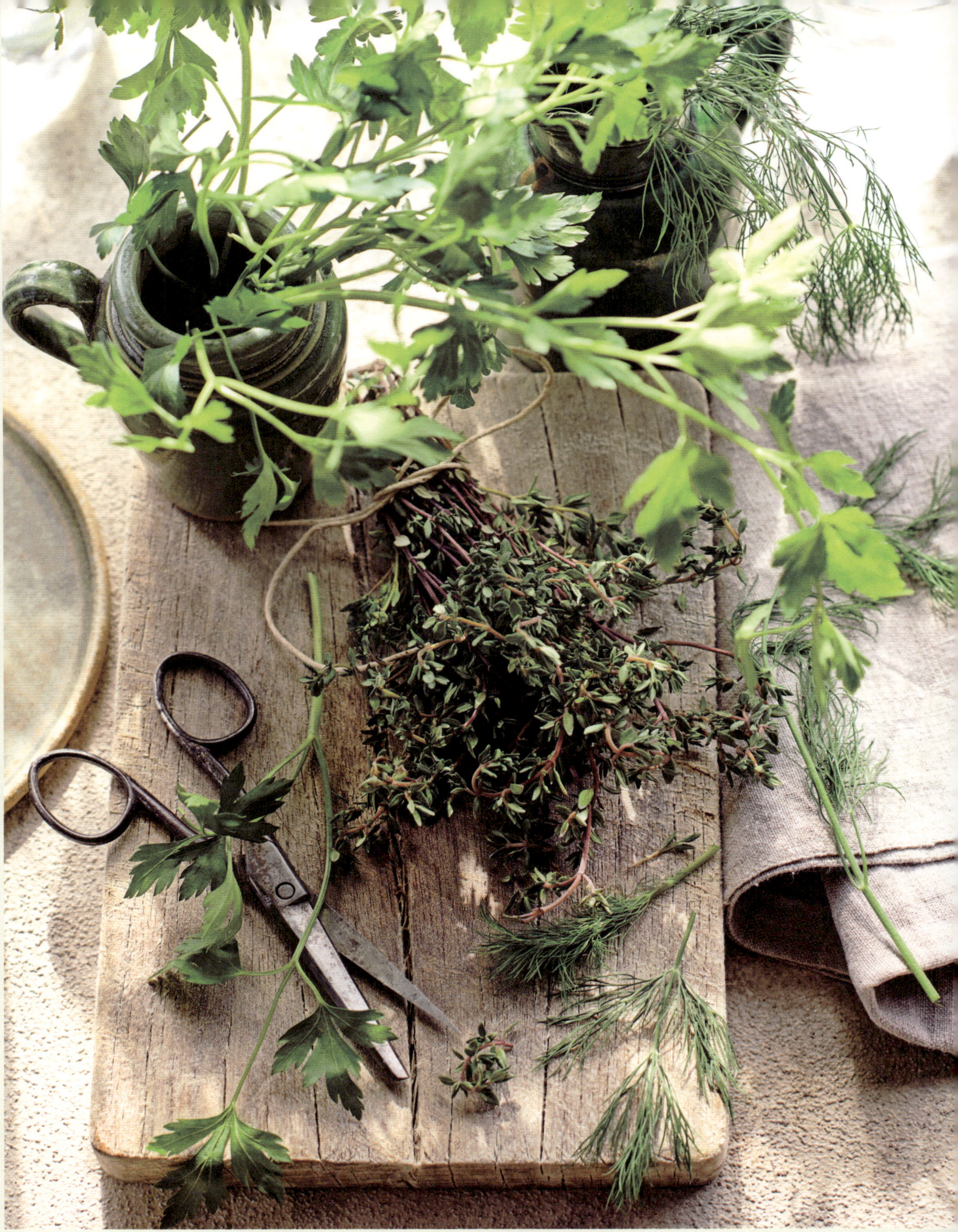

MARCH 55

One dough, seven biscuits
Sju sorters kakor

There is a tradition in Sweden that a hostess is supposed to provide seven different biscuits/cookies when someone pops by to *fika*. There is even a book called *Sju Sorters Kakor* ('Seven Kinds of Biscuit') that almost every Swede owns a copy of. First published in 1945, it's still in print, even though I've never been presented with seven types of biscuit when visiting a Swedish household!

Base dough
Grunddeg

200 g/1¾ sticks butter
300 g/2¼ cups plain/all-purpose flour
a pinch of salt
185 g/1 cup minus 1 tablespoon caster/granulated sugar
1 teaspoon vanilla sugar or vanilla extract
1 egg

Rub the butter into the flour and salt in a bowl until it resembles a sandy texture, then add the sugar and vanilla and mix again. Add the egg and mix until the dough is uniform in texture – try not to over-work it.

NOTE This makes a 700-g/1 lb. 9-oz. batch of dough. Each recipe that follows uses a full batch of dough, but you can split the dough into halves or quarters and adjust quantities for the individual recipes to fit.

Vanilla & chocolate biscuits with nuts
Kakor med nötter

MAKES APPROX. 40–45

Using a strong piping/pastry bag fitted with a large star nozzle/tip, push the dough out into logs 5–6 cm/2–2½ inches long. Arrange closely on a lined baking sheet. Chill for at least 30 minutes before baking.

Preheat the oven to 210°C/190°C fan/410°F/Gas 6. Bake for 6–8 minutes or until slightly golden. Remove from the oven and allow to cool on a wire rack.

Melt 100 g/3½ oz milk chocolate to just melted, then remove from the heat and add a further 25 g/⅞ oz. chocolate and stir to melt. Dip each cooled biscuit half in melted chocolate and place on a lined tray. Chop 30 g/1 oz. of pistachios or almonds, scatter over the chocolate and allow to set.

Chocolate biscuits
Chokladkakor

MAKES APPROX. 40

Add 120 g/¾ cup chocolate chips to the dough before chilling for at least 30 minutes.

Preheat the oven to 210°C/190°C fan/400°F/Gas 6.

Roll out the dough on a floured surface to approx. 5 mm/¼ inch thick. Using a 5-cm/2-inch cookie cutter, cut out biscuits and place on a lined baking sheet. Bake for around 7–9 minutes until slightly golden, then remove from the oven and cool on a wire rack.

Orange biscuits
Kakor med apelsin

MAKES APPROX. 40

Add the zest of 1 orange plus 1 tablespoon orange juice to the dough, then chill for 30 minutes.

Preheat the oven to 210°C/190°C fan/400°F/Gas 6.

Roll out the dough to approx. 5 mm/¼ inch thick. Using a 4–5-cm/1½–2-inch cookie cutter, cut out biscuits and place on a lined baking sheet. Bake for 7–9 minutes or until just starting to go golden at the edges, then remove and cool on a wire rack.

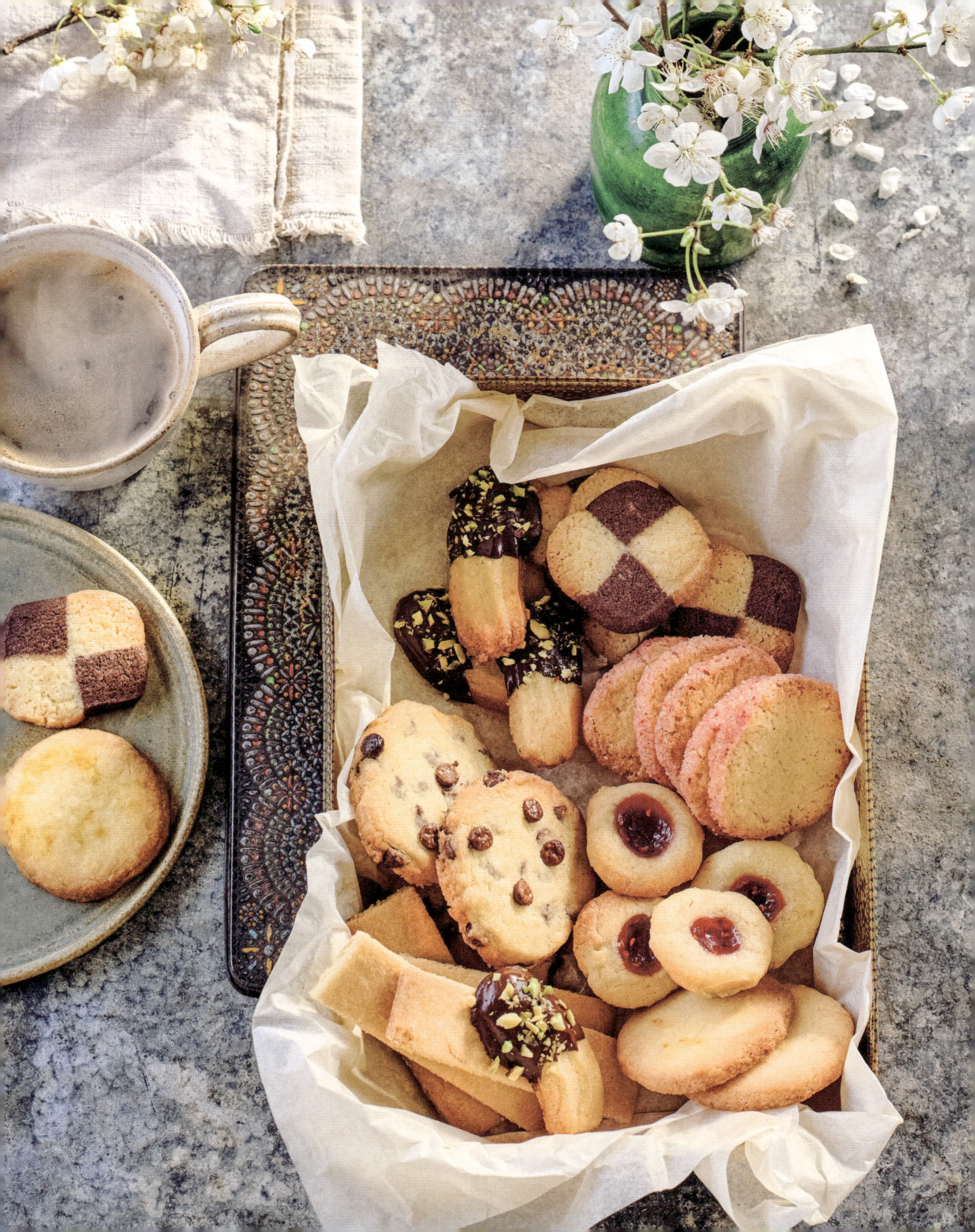

Toffee biscuits
Kolakakor

MAKES APPROX. 40

Add 3 tablespoons of golden/corn syrup to the dough when adding the sugar and proceed with the recipe. Chill the dough for at least 30 minutes, ideally longer. You may need a smidgen more flour, too.

Preheat the oven to 210°C/190°C fan/410°F/Gas 6.

On a floured surface, roll out the dough into two rectangles approx. 12 x 40 cm/5 x 16 inches and transfer to a lined baking sheet (make sure they are slightly separated from each other). Bake for around 10 minutes or until they start to go slightly brown, then remove from oven and immediately slice into little pieces – approx. 20 pieces from each log. I often add a bit of flaked sea salt on top while they are still warm.

Pink 'Brussels' biscuits
Brusselskex

MAKES APPROX. 50

Mix 4–5 tablespoons of granulated sugar (caster is too fine) with a few drops of pink food gel. Using your fingers, crumble the sugar and the gel until the sugar is completely pink.

Roll the dough into a log approx. 4–5 cm/1½–2 inches in diameter, then roll the log in the pink sugar to get it to stick all around the edge. You may need to press slightly to get it all around the log. Wrap in clingfilm/plastic wrap and chill for 30 minutes before using.

Preheat the oven to 210°C/190°C fan/410°F/Gas 6.

Slice the log into circles and place on lined baking sheets. Bake for around 7–9 minutes or until slightly golden. Cool on a wire rack.

Chequerboard cookies
Schackrutor

MAKES APPROX. 40–45

Split the dough into two equal pieces. Add 1–1½ tablespoons cacao powder to one part and mix until the dough is uniformly brown in colour. Refrigerate for about 15 minutes if the dough is quite soft.

Roll each piece into two logs, so you have two brown and two white logs, each 1 cm/½ inch in diameter. Press each roll slightly on each side to make the logs into squares, then arrange in a checkerboard pattern. If they are not sticking together, you can brush the edges with a little water. Wrap in clingfilm/plastic wrap, ensuring all sides stay square. Chill for 30 minutes.

Preheat the oven to 210°C/190°C fan/400°F/Gas 6.

Slice the log into chequerboard biscuits and place on lined baking sheets. Bake until the while bits start to go slightly golden, then remove from the oven and leave to cool on a wire rack.

Raspberry jam biscuits
Hallongrottor

MAKES APPROX. 30–35

Preheat the oven to 210°C/190°C fan/400°F/Gas 6.

After chilling the dough for 30 minutes, cut into little pieces around 20 g/¾ oz. each. Roll each piece into a ball and add to a paper petit four case. Make a deep hole in the middle with your finger. Fill the holes with jam/preserve (it is easiest to do this using a piping/pastry bag). I like to use raspberry jam, but cloudberry and other berry jams work well – you will need 150–200 g/½–⅔ cup.

Bake for around 9–11 minutes or until the pastry starts to turn golden. Remove from the oven and cool on a wire rack.

Danish Shrovetide buns

Fastelavnsboller

Danes have many versions of Lent buns, different to the more well-known Swedish kind. Many Danish bakeries sell laminated pastry or delicate choux pastry versions. At home, most people bake a yeasted dough filled with custard. I really love the choux version as a variation. Fill these with whipped cream or a mixture of pastry cream and whipped cream, add berries for a tart flavour or leave plain. I love to top with colourful icing.

1 quantity Choux Pastry Basic Batter (see page 235)

75 g/4 tablespoons raspberry jam/preserve (or other berry jam of your choice) or fresh raspberries

½ quantity Pastry Cream (see page 237)

300 ml/1¼ cups whipping cream

1 teaspoon vanilla extract or vanilla sugar

1 tablespoon icing/confectioner's sugar

TOPPING

150 g/1 cup icing/confectioner's sugar

pink food colouring

sprinkles or freeze-dried raspberries, to decorate (optional)

baking sheet, lined with baking parchment

large piping/pastry bag fitted with a large plain nozzle/tip

MAKES 8

Preheat the oven to 200°C/180°C fan/400°F/Gas 6.

Spoon or pipe out eight buns of equal generous size onto the prepared baking sheet. They will puff up slightly, so space them apart.

Bake in the preheated oven for 10 minutes, then reduce the oven to 180°C/160°C fan/350°F/Gas 4. Do not open the door for the first 20 minutes of baking time. These need around 30–35 minutes in total. Remove from the oven, pierce immediately to allow steam to escape from the pastry and cool on a wire rack.

Cut the top third off each cooled choux bun and set aside. Add a dollop of jam/preserve or some fresh raspberries to each hole, then spoon or pipe a generous amount of pastry cream into each hole. Whip the cream with the vanilla and icing/confectioner's sugar until stiff. Place in a piping/pastry bag and pipe around the top of each bun, then top with the lid.

To make the icing, mix the icing/confectioner's sugar with drops of food colouring and a little hot water until you have a thick mixture that is not too runny. Spoon some icing on top of each lid, then decorate.

VARIATION To make these with a laminated pastry, use the Basic Danish Pastry Dough (see page 236) and bake circles of pastry, split after baking, then fill and proceed as this recipe.

To make the yeast version, use the Basic Bun Dough (see page 234). Roll out and cut into squares, fill each square with pastry cream, wrap and bake, then decorate.

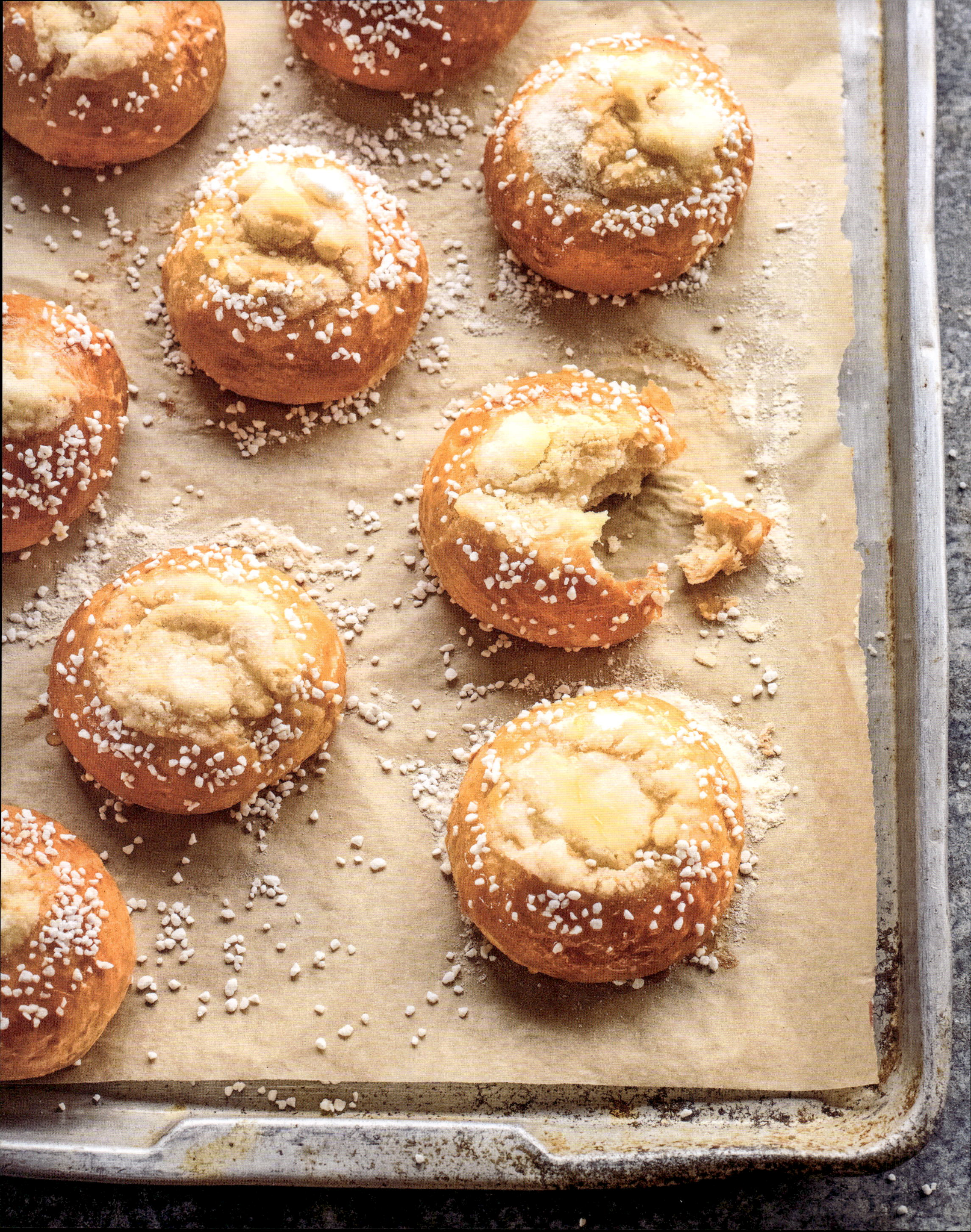

Riina's butter eye buns
Voisilmäpullat

The literal translation of these buns is 'butter eye buns' and they are a favourite in all of Finland. My colleague Riina sometimes makes these at the café.

When you make these buns, ensure the hole in the centre of the dough is quite deep or the butter will spill out (the flour added on top of the butter does help). The nibbed/pearl sugar is optional – Riina doesn't add it, but some Finns do. These are best eaten on the day of baking.

1 quantity Basic Bun Dough (see page 234)
beaten egg, for brushing
pearl/nibbed sugar, for sprinkling

BUTTER 'EYE'
a small knob/pat cold salted butter per bun (about 10 g/2 teaspoons for each bun)
½ teaspoon flour per bun
1 teaspoon caster/granulated sugar per bun

baking sheet, lined with baking parchment

MAKES 24

Prepare the dough following the instructions on page 234, then divide into 24 equal balls. Roll into buns and put on the lined baking sheet, leaving space between the buns as they will rise.

Cover with a kitchen towel again and leave to prove until doubled in size, around 20–25 minutes, depending on the warmth in your kitchen.

Preheat the oven to 200°C/180°C fan/400°F/Gas 6.

Using a finger, push a hole in the middle of each bun. Then, brush them with the beaten egg using a pastry brush.

Fill each hole with a knob/pat of cold butter, sprinkle a little flour on top of the butter and finally put a teaspoon of sugar on top of the butter and flour.

Bake in the preheated oven for 10–15 minutes until golden brown. Allow to cool, then sprinkle with pearl/nibbed sugar before eating. Best eaten on the day of baking, but can also be frozen on day of making.

Wales cake

Walesstang

This cake is a bit of a mystery because it's not very Welsh, nor has it been to Wales on any sort of holiday. Why it is sold in Danish bakeries is unclear, but it is a popular pastry made with choux dough, baked in a long piece, then decorated with cream and berries. Traditionally, it is decorated with more white icing than I use – and probably less berries – but I do think it needs the berries to cut the sweetness of the cream.

The first version of this cake dates from 1926, when it was described as a *waleskringle*. The general name for this type of baking with choux is also known as *walesbrød* (Wales bread), and you'll find versions of these at many traditional bakeries all over Denmark. The connection to Wales, however, remains a mystery.

1 quantity Choux Pastry Basic Batter (see page 235)
450 ml/2 cups whipping cream
1 tablespoon icing/confectioner's sugar
1 teaspoon vanilla extract
75 g/4 tablespoons strawberry jam/preserve
½ quantity Pastry Cream (see page 237) or 300 g/10½ oz. store-bought custard
200–250 g/7–9 oz. mixed berries, to decorate
chocolate shavings, to decorate

baking sheet, lined with baking parchment
piping/pastry bag fitted with a round nozzle/tip

SERVES 10 (MAKES TWO 30-CM/12-INCH LONG CAKES OR ONE LARGE ROUND WREATH)

Preheat the oven to 200°C/180°C fan/400°F/Gas 6.

Make the dough and pipe out, in a tight 'S' pattern, into two rectangular shapes approx. 30 cm/12 inches long and 8 cm/3¼ inches wide (they will rise as they bake). If you want to make one larger cake, pipe out a wreath in 'S' shapes all around.

Bake in the preheated oven for 35–40 minutes or until done (see the choux instructions on page 235) – do not open the oven door for at least the first 20 minutes or the cake will collapse.

When baked, remove from the oven, pierce holes at the side to let out the steam and leave to cool on a wire rack.

To assemble, whip the cream with the sugar and vanilla until stiff and spoon into a piping/pastry bag.

Split the choux cakes in half, spread over the jam and pipe pastry cream in the middle, then add the top layer (lid). On top, pipe whipping cream and decorate with mixed berries and shavings of chocolate. Eat on the day of baking.

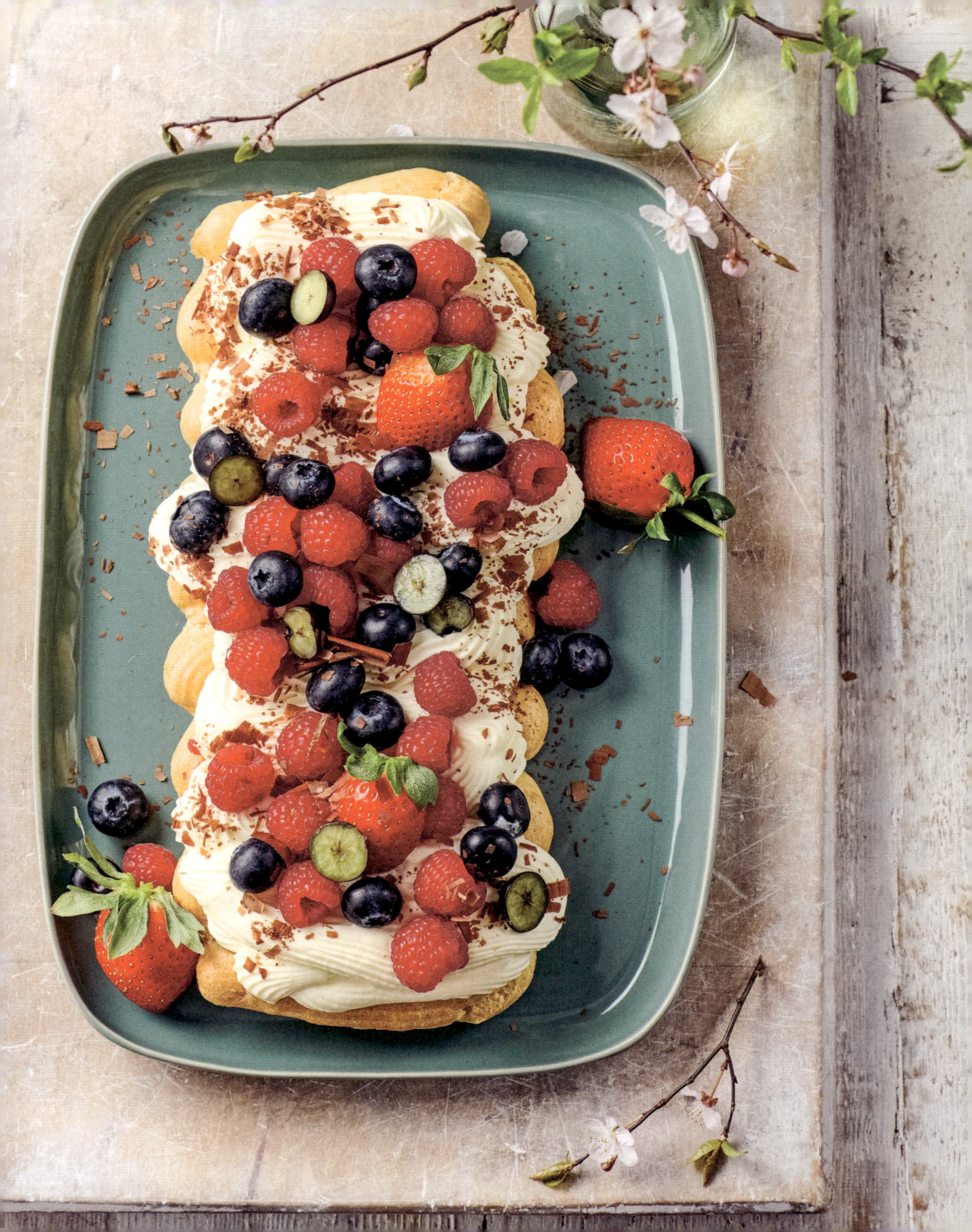

Time to catch the last few runs on the slopes, at least if you're in Norway or Sweden. In Denmark, the forests are bright green and new wildlife is busy exploring. The differences in weather from the north to the south are most apparent at these cusps of the changing seasons – with over 2,500 km/ 1,500 miles between southernmost Denmark and northernmost Norway, one is warm while the other is still bitterly cold.

With the snow still on the mountains, Norwegians make their Easter treks to the holiday homes they call *hytter*. This is family time with lots of food and reading an abundance of crime novels (it's a thing).

In Sweden, kids go door-to-door dressed up as little witches – an Eastertime version of trick-or-treating, with sweets collected in little baskets and brought home. Across Scandinavia, Easter eggs are often papier-mâché eggshells filled with our hugely popular pick'n'mix sweets, rather than the big chocolate eggs enjoyed elsewhere.

April ends with *Valborgsmässoafton* in Sweden: bonfires are lit as symbols of light triumphing over darkness and the reawakening of nature in the name of St Walpurga.

APRIL

EASTER

Across Scandinavia, a lot of our Easter traditions are shared between the countries and go back to pagan times. Easter is known as *Påsk*, a word originating from the Hebrew word for Passover, *Pesach*. By the time Christianity took hold during the Viking era, the Norse were happily mixing pagan and Christian traditions, some of which we still celebrate today.

Maundy Tuesday in Scandinavia is often also a half-day holiday, along with the holidays on Good Friday and Easter Monday, meaning most people benefit from a very long weekend off work. Many drive to their cottages and spend Easter getting their houses ready for the warmer months and meeting up with friends and family.

In the weeks before, Danish children write letters called *gækkebreve*, sweet 'teaser letters' on paper which has been carefully cut into a pattern with a little verse between the cuts. They sign their name, replacing the letters with dots and enclose a snowdrop flower (*vintergæk* – one of the first flowers we see in Denmark after winter). These letters have been popular since the 1800s. If the recipient cannot guess who sent the letter in time for Easter, the prize for the sender is a big Easter egg. If, however, the recipient guesses correctly, the egg goes to the recipient.

Easter in Norway incorporates a slightly different tradition: reading multiple crime novels (*Påskekrimmen*). Sales of such books peak just before Easter, with publishers celebrating as people stock up before heading to their cottages. This all began in 1923 with the launch of a big advertising campaign for a crime novel about two friends going to their cottage at Eastertime. Nowadays, anything from TV to magazines is full of Easter crime series, so everyone can go relax in nature and think about gruesome murders.

Sweden has Easter celebrations that are rooted in the times of witch hunts. It was thought that Maundy Thursday was when witches would fly off on their broomsticks to the *Blåkulla* (Blue Hill, also known as *Blockula*) to dance with Satan (this same belief is mirrored in Denmark's St John's Eve celebrations in June). Swedish kids dress up as *påskkärringar* (Easter witches) with bright, red-painted cheeks and a basket for collecting treats as they go door to door, trick-or-treat style.

Outside and inside Swedish houses, you will often see birch twigs decorated with colourful feathers – some people even decorate bushes or trees. The use of birch is a symbol of renewal as they bud. These birch bouquets are known as *påskris*. There is also an old Norse tradition of collecting and burning all the winter wood around this time of the year, which can be seen in the Swedish tradition of *Valborgsmässoafton* (Walpurgis' Night) on the last day of April (regardless of when Easter falls). On this day, bonfires light up Sweden and signal that spring is finally here.

As in many places across the Western world, Easter is also all about chicks, eggs and chocolate, although our Easter eggs are quite often hollow papier-mâché eggs that we fill the recipient's favourite sweets/candies. This is a holiday that is about being outside in nature (because now we can) and spending time with our loved ones – and, of course, enjoying amazing food.

For all of Scandinavians, Easter weekend culminates with a *smörgåsbord* of delicious foods: lots of eggs, fish (smoked salmon is very popular), pickled herring and often also lamb (the Swedish classic Jansson's Temptation goes well with lamb, even if it is not a spring dish at all), all washed down with the obligatory aquavit.

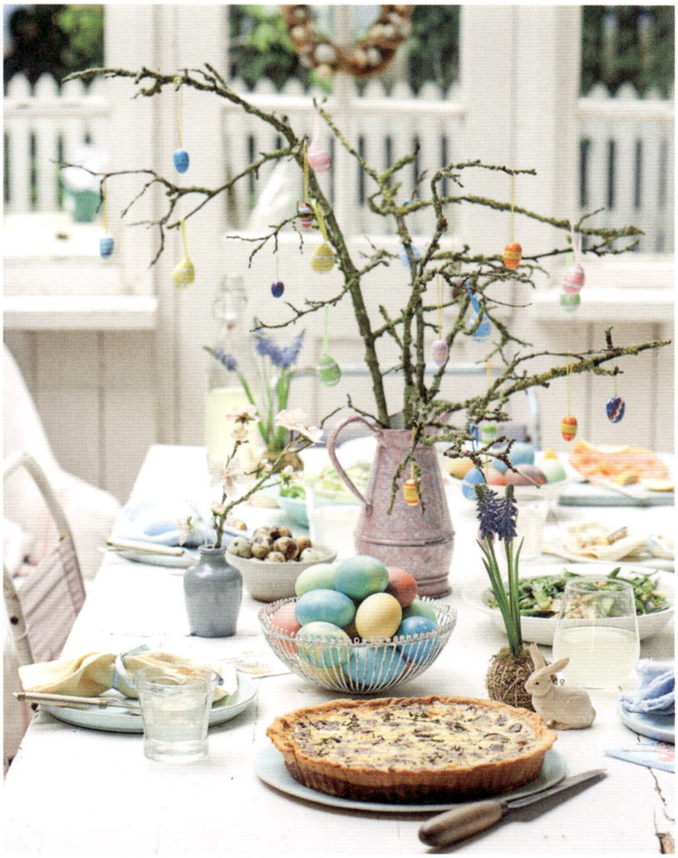
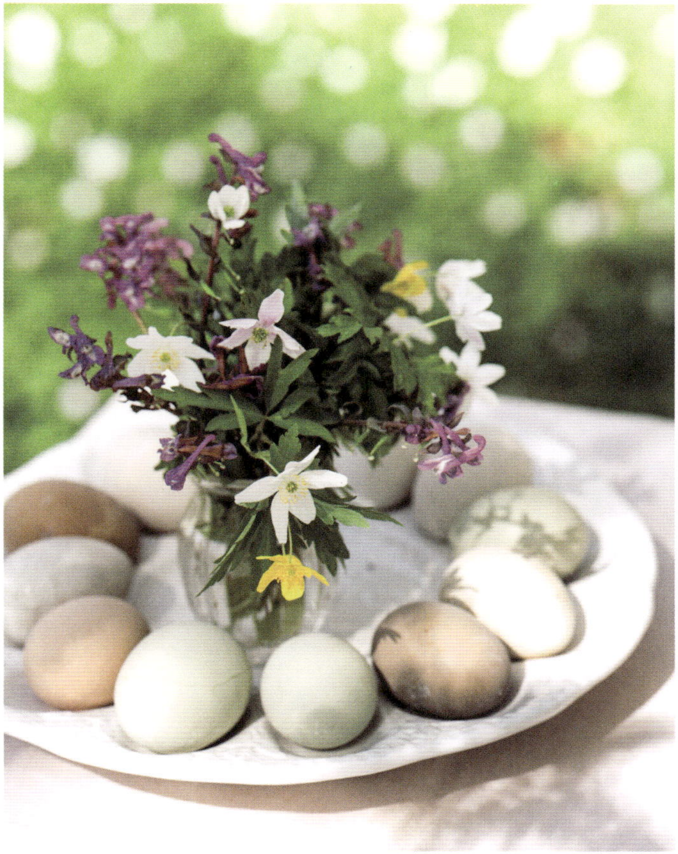
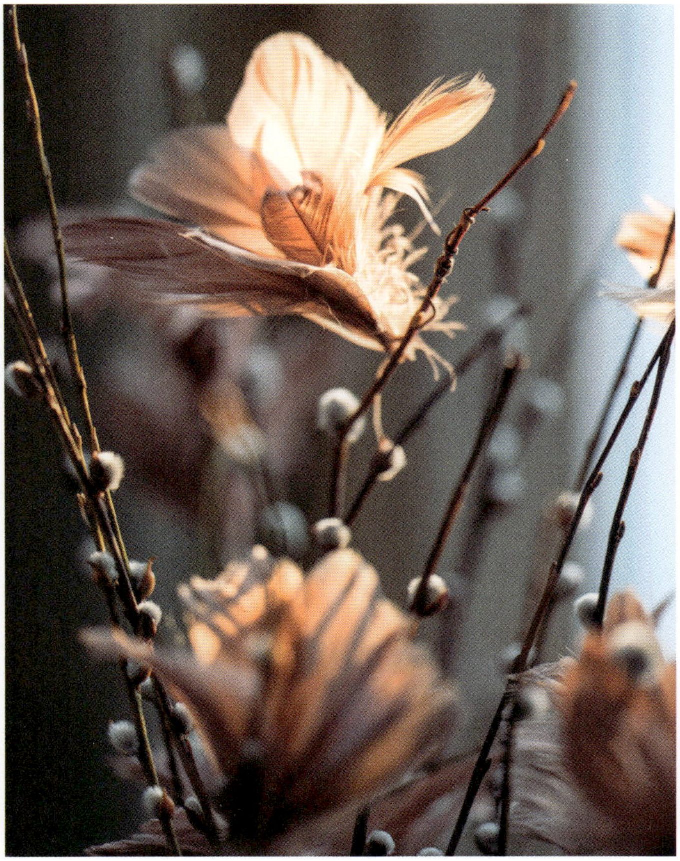
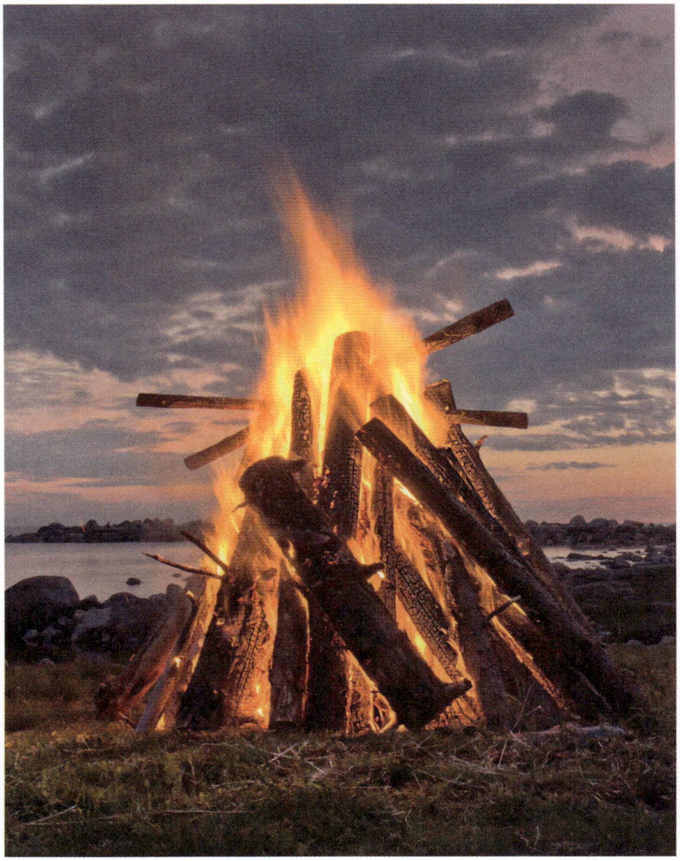

Swedish rösti with caviar & salmon

Råraka med kaviar och lax

Essentially, this is a version of the Swiss *Rösti*, except the potatoes are not parboiled first but cooked from raw and there is no added onion in *Råraka*. It takes time to cook to ensure the potatoes are cooked through properly, so a little patience is needed. Don't worry; it will come together at the end.

These differ from the *Raggmunk* (see page 95) as the only ingredients here are salt and potato – no batter. Some people serve these with bacon and lingonberry jam – like with *Raggmunk* – but quite often, these are served with roe, sour cream and even sometimes a bit of smoked salmon (which is how I prefer to eat these). This is traditionally a lighter dish served as a starter or lunch/late brunch main.

700–800 g/1 lb. 9 oz.–1 lb. 12 oz. starchy potatoes, such as Maris Piper, peeled
50 g/3½ tablespoons butter
sunflower oil
salt and freshly ground black pepper

TOPPINGS
lumpfish roe caviar or caviar of your choice (1 heaped tablespoon per person)
finely chopped red onion (1 heaped tablespoon per person)
100–150 ml/⅓–⅔ cup sour cream
finely chopped chives
100 g/3½ oz. smoked salmon (optional)
freshly squeezed lemon juice (optional)

MAKES 2 LARGE RÖSTI (SERVE 1 PER PERSON)

Peel the potatoes, then grate them into a bowl, season with salt and mix. Squeeze out as much excess liquid from the potatoes as you can – it is easiest to do this by placing the potatoes in a muslin cloth and squeezing.

Melt the butter in two frying pans/skillets and add a generous glug of oil to each pan.

Add half the potato mixture to each pan and fry over a gentle heat. Only turn over once the mixture has cooked for quite a while or else it will break – it will take around 5–6 minutes per side. Use the plate-method to turn it over to the other side (place a plate on top, flip over the frying pan/skillet and slide the potato cake back into the pan). Continue frying over a lower heat to ensure the potatoes are cooking through and then, right at the end, blast the heat up to high to crisp up on both sides.

Place the cooked potato cakes on paper towels to drain off excess fat, then arrange on plates. Top with roe caviar, chopped onion and sour cream sprinkled with chives, plus some smoked salmon, if you wish. Finish with a squeeze of lemon juice if using salmon.

VARIATIONS These potato hash are delicious for breakfast, too. Serve an updated version with avocado and either smoked salmon or fried halloumi, with lots of fresh dill on top. A poached egg also works here, and even butter-fried wild mushrooms. You can also fry these as smaller potato cakes, if you prefer.

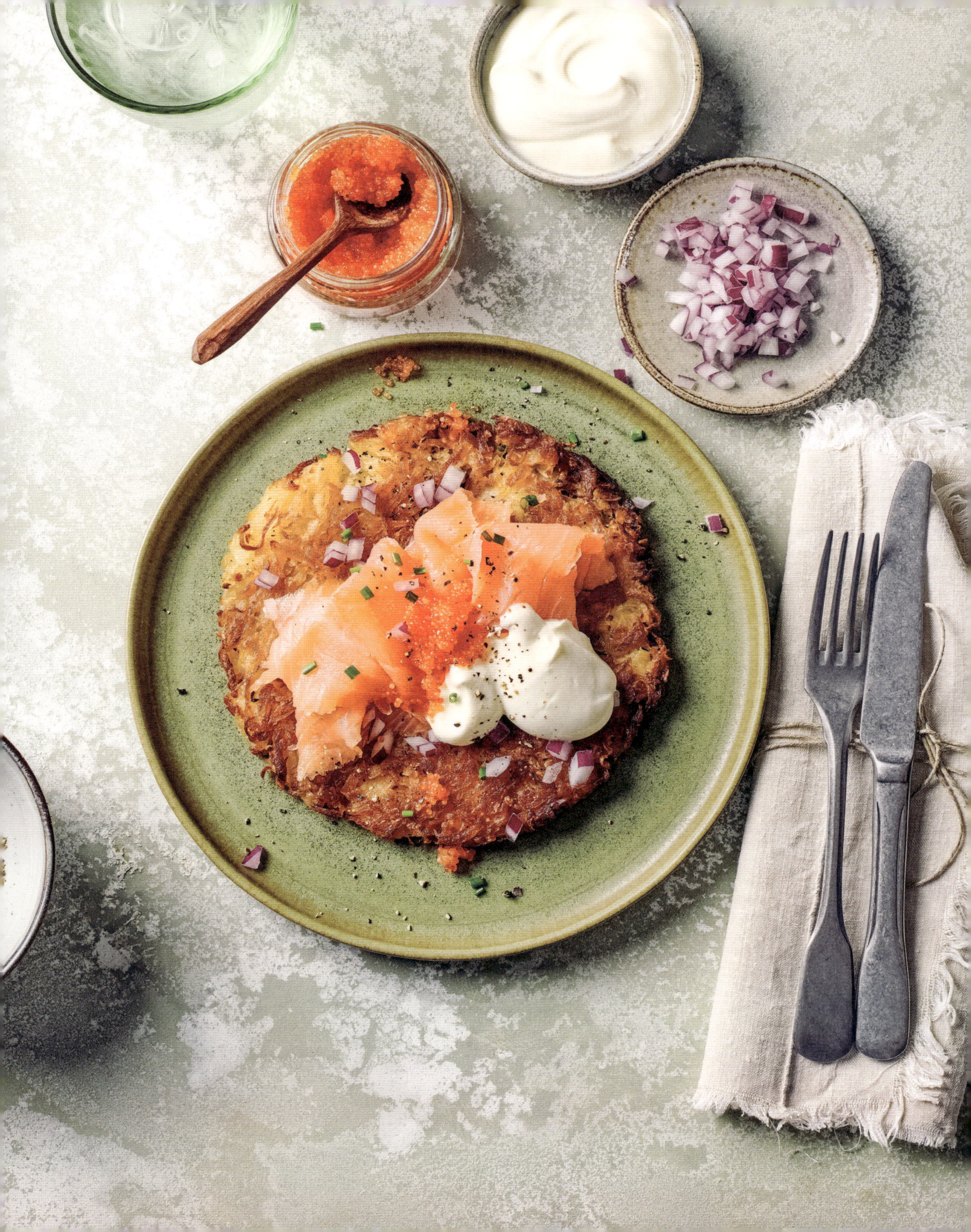

Danish breaded meatballs *Krebinetter / Karbonader*

These breaded meatballs are called *Krebinetter* in Denmark and are a proper old-school dish, traditionally accompanied by boiled new potatoes and creamed peas and carrots (see below). That's how my mother served this comfort dish, but I often add a fresh slaw or charred cabbage, potato wedges and a good dressing.

Krebinetter is also often known as *Karbonader* in Danish, with a never-ending discussion of when it's one or the other and everyone has an opinion and everyone's always right. My mother called these *krebinetter* – regionally this varies and there are differences such as whether they are in breadcrumbs or if they are pork or pork and veal. In Norway, *Karbonader* is different again (as they use beef), and Swedes may say it resembles *Wallenbergera* (and they would add egg yolk and a dash of cream).

600 g/1 lb. 5 oz. minced/ground pork (15% fat content) or half pork/half veal

1 egg (or 2, if you're double-dipping)

75 g/1 cup dried breadcrumbs (or more, if double-dipping)

a knob/pat of butter and a generous glug of oil, for frying

salt and freshly ground black pepper

SERVES 3–4

Mix the meat with salt and pepper, then shape into six equal-sized patties. These should be thicker than a beef patty for a burger, but less round than a meatball – about 1.5–2 cm/⅝–¾ inch thick, with a flat top and base.

Whisk the egg(s) in a bowl, and place the breadcrumbs in a separate bowl. Dip each patty first in egg, then cover in a good amount of breadcrumbs. My mother always double-dipped and did two coats of breadcrumbs.

Heat the butter and oil in a frying pan/skillet and fry the breadcrumbed patties until golden and crisp on all sides and the meat is cooked through (around 6–8 minutes per side, depending on thickness). Take care not to overcook as the meatballs can quickly become dry.

Serve with boiled skin-on new potatoes and the creamed peas and carrots below. Alternatively, serve with a fresh slaw.

Creamed peas & carrots *Stuvede grøntsager*

200 g/7 oz. carrots, fresh or frozen

25 g/1¾ tablespoons butter

25 g/3 tablespoons plain/all-purpose flour

200 ml/¾ cup whole milk

a dash of cream (optional)

200 ml/¾ cup vegetable stock (use water from boiling the potatoes and dissolve a stock cube in this)

200 g/7 oz. frozen peas

salt and freshly ground black pepper

grated nutmeg (optional)

finely chopped flat-leaf parsley (a small bunch is plenty)

SERVES 3–4

If using fresh carrots, cut them into small pea-sized pieces and blanch just until al dente.

In a saucepan, melt the butter, then add the flour and whisk to make a roux. Cook for a minute, then start adding the milk, followed by the vegetable stock, continuously whisking for around 5–7 minutes, allowing the mixture to thicken as you go. The mixture should be a smooth creamy sauce. For a creamier sauce, add more milk than stock or even a dash of cream. Add the peas and carrots and season to taste with salt, pepper and a little nutmeg. Just before serving, add the parsley.

VARIATIONS If you want to vary the sauce, add your own vegetables of choice – broccoli works well here. I also sometimes add chopped spring onion/scallion for a flavour lift (fry the onion slightly first if using the white bits). Fresh chervil also works well in the sauce if you're not a parsley fan.

Chicken vol-au-vents with asparagus

Tarteletter med kylling i asparges

To most Danes, this is one of the most iconic, super-retro, must-haves for Christmas and Easter lunches – although traditionally always made using canned white asparagus instead of fresh. During winter asparagus is, of course, out of season so this makes sense – although it isn't always easy to get hold of the white kind either canned or in jars in the UK, so I use fresh when I can or opt for green asparagus.

You can use pre-made vol-au-vent cases or pastry cases made from puff pastry to make this, or make your own using store-bought puff pastry. The filling is the star here, though. This chicken and asparagus mix is nice even without the pastry cases – I often have it as a side with potatoes or salad.

- 1 store-bought sheet of puff pastry, approx. 320 g/11½ oz.
- 400 g/14 oz. blanched green asparagus or tinned/jarred white asparagus (reserve some liquid – it gives great flavour mixed with the chicken stock)
- 400 g/14 oz. cooked chicken meat (⅔ white meat)
- 40 g/3 tablespoons butter
- 50 g/6 tablespoons flour
- 400 ml/1¾ cups chicken stock
- 100 ml/⅓ cup plus 1 tablespoon milk
- 100 ml/⅓ cup plus 1 tablespoon cream
- fresh thyme sprigs, leaves stripped
- a few drops of white wine vinegar
- salt and freshly ground black pepper
- parsley, chervil or pea shoots, to garnish (optional)

- 10-cm/4-inch cookie cutter or round cutter
- 10-hole muffin tray, lined with baking parchment, plus 10 circles of baking parchment
- baking beans or rice for baking blind

SERVES 4–5 AS A STARTER, OR MORE IF PART OF A SMÖRGÅSBORD

First make the pastry cases. Preheat the oven to 220°C/200°C fan/425°F/Gas 7.

Cut out 10 rounds of pastry using the cookie cutter and carefully add to the lined muffin holes. Prick the bases several times with a fork. Add a second piece of baking parchment on top of each, pressing it gently into the pastry case, and line with baking beans to weigh down the pastry.

Bake in the preheated oven for 10–12 minutes, then remove the beans and second lining paper, and return to the oven for a further 10 minutes, or until golden and baked through (the final baking time may vary).

To make the filling, chop the asparagus into small pieces and chop or shred the chicken. Melt the butter in a saucepan, then add the flour to make a roux and cook for a minute. Start adding the stock, little by little, stirring to combine and thicken the sauce as it simmers. When all the stock has been added, add the milk and cream. Simmer for a few minutes, then turn down the heat and season well. Stir in the thyme leaves. Add a dash of vinegar to lift the flavour of the sauce. Add the asparagus and chicken and stir to combine. Spoon the filling into the pastry cases just before serving.

Serve warm, garnished with herbs or pea shoots, if using, as a starter or as part of a *smörgåsbord*.

VARIATIONS Prawn and asparagus also work really well together. For vegetarians, make a creamed mushroom and fresh thyme filling.

Scandinavian fishcakes *Fiskefrikadeller*

There's a fish shop near our wooden house on the West Zealand coast where they make huge delicious fishcakes – just one makes a whole lunch. I often make these at home in London when I am longing for the Danish seaside, fir trees and blue sky. Danish fishcakes are quite plain (often eaten with our remoulade sauce). Norwegian fishcakes (*fiskekaker*) are quite similar, but often include nutmeg.

½ onion, finely chopped or grated (ideally blended with the cream)
75 ml/⅓ cup single/light cream
400 g/14 oz. cod (or haddock, pollock or similar white fish, if preferred), skinned and boned
1 generous teaspoon flaked salt
1 egg
2–3 tablespoons plain/all-purpose flour (this can really vary depending on the fish)
1 tablespoon cornflour/cornstarch
generous amount of butter and a dash of oil, for frying
salt and freshly ground black pepper

MAKES 7–8 FISHCAKES

Blend the onion with the cream and set aside (this avoids onion pieces in the fishcakes).

Place the fish and flaked salt in a food processor and pulse well until blended. It's important to salt and process the fish first.

Add the onion, cream, egg and flour (start with 2 tablespoons flour, but you might need to add a bit more later) and process until well combined. Add the cornflour/cornstarch and season. Chill the mixture for 1 hour.

Heat up a large frying pan/skillet and add a very generous knob/pat of butter and a glug of oil. Using a tablespoon and the palm of your (wet) hand, shape egg-sized balls from the fish mixture and add to the pan. Squash the fishcakes down gently to give them slightly flatter surfaces.

Fry for 2–3 minutes on each side until golden brown and crisp on both sides. You may want to cook one first and assess if the mixture is firm enough to hold together – if not, add a bit more flour. You don't want them to fall apart, but adding too much flour isn't nice either.

Serve warm with a side of remoulade and buttered rye bread (or even new potatoes for dinner). Also goes well with herby mayo and a green salad.

Danish remoulade *Remoulade*

50 g/1¾ oz. each carrot, cauliflower and pickled gherkins
1 tablespoon capers
1 small shallot, chopped
150 ml/⅔ cup mayonnaise
100 ml/⅓ cup crème fraîche or sour cream
½ teaspoon medium curry powder
1 teaspoon ground turmeric (optional, for colour)
½ teaspoon Dijon mustard
1 teaspoon white wine vinegar
2 tablespoons caster/granulated sugar
salt and freshly ground black pepper

SERVES 4

This is a classic Danish condiment that got its name from the French salad but it has evolved to be the same thing in name only. Danes add remoulade to just about everything, from beef to fish, and enjoy it with fries too.

Finely chop the carrot, cauliflower and gherkins. Mix all the ingredients together until well combined. I like a chunky remoulade, so I chop all the ingredients by hand; for a quicker result and smoother finish, you can pulse a few times in a food processor (but make sure it still has bits; it shouldn't be smooth).

Leave in the fridge for 30 minutes before using, to allow the colour and flavour to develop. Store any leftovers in the fridge and use within 5 days.

NOTE Store-bought remoulade is very sweet – if you're used to this taste, add more sugar to taste.

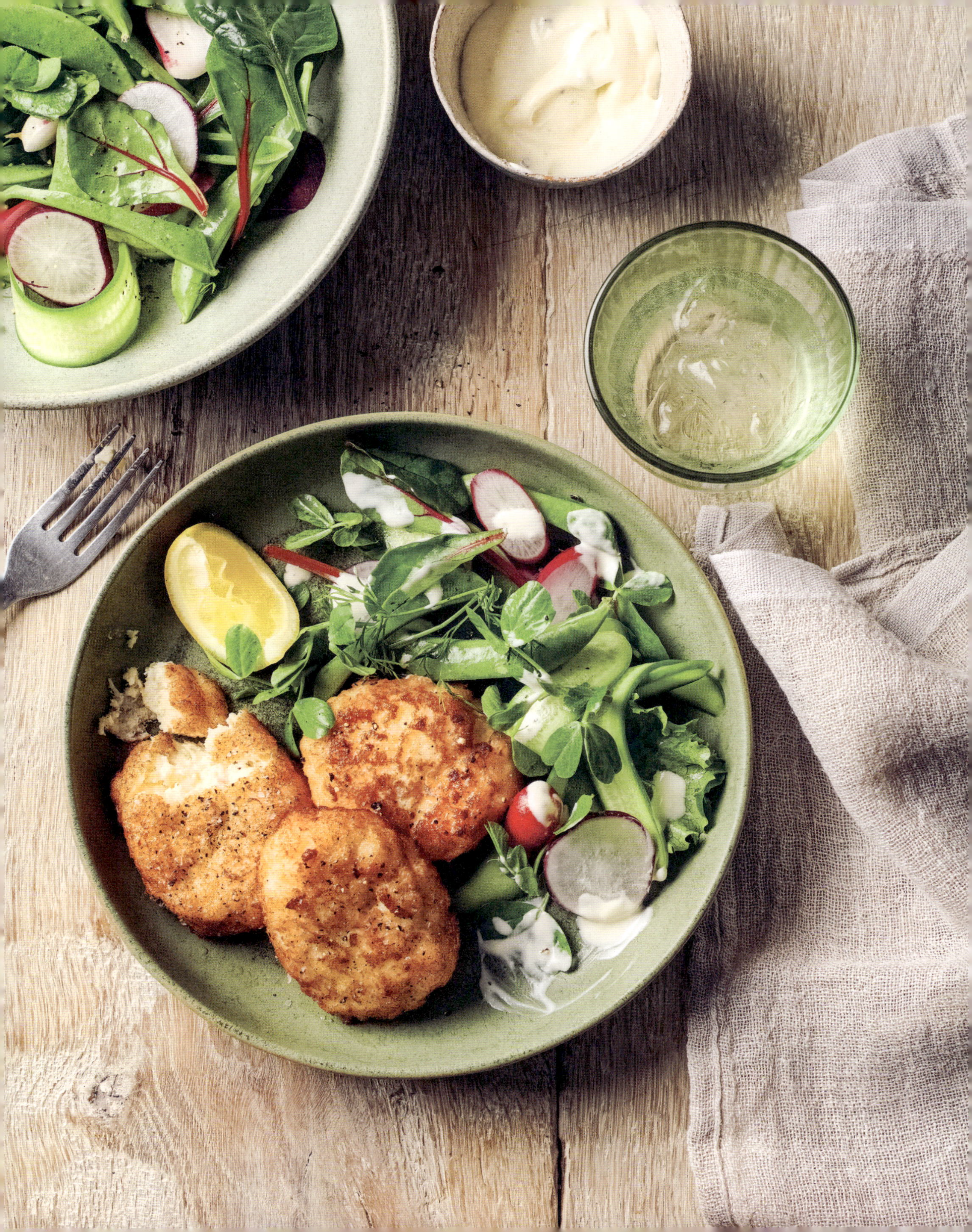

74 APRIL

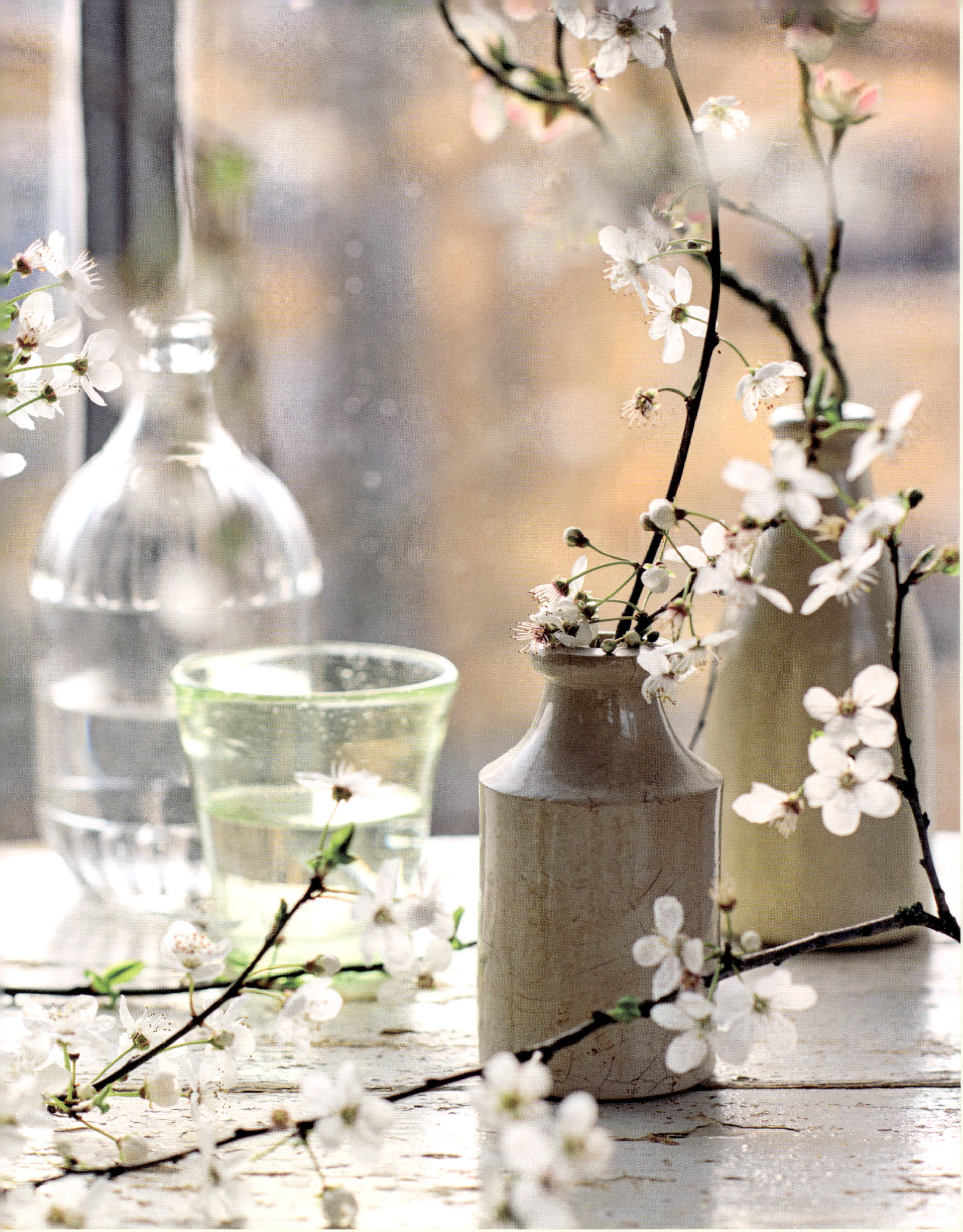

Danish pastries

Wienerbrød

Danes are fiercely proud of the *Wienerbrød*, as we call it (literally, 'Vienna bread'). This is because this method of making pastry was brought to Denmark back in the day by visiting bakers from Austria and so the name stuck, even if everyone else calls them Danish pastries). There are many different kinds to make – I've included four different suggestions here, but do experiment (and read the notes below). Laminated pastry takes a bit of practice to get the feel of just how the butter needs to roll between the layers. Do persist and don't lose hope as it will come together.

Poppy-seed pastry
Tebirkes

1 quantity Basic Danish Pastry Dough (see page 236)
1 quantity Almond Filling (see page 236)
beaten egg, for brushing
white poppy seeds (each pastry needs approx. 1 tablespoon poppy seeds)

Cut the dough into two pieces, then roll each to a long rectangle approx. 65 x 30 cm/26 x 12 inches – the dough will be quite thin, around 3–4 mm/⅛ inch. Tidy the edges with a pizza cutter. Add the almond filling in the middle of each long piece, lengthways, then fold the long edges of the dough on top of the filling. Cut each long piece into eight pastries (16 in total) and transfer to lined baking trays to rise for an hour.

Brush with beaten egg, then liberally sprinkle white poppy seeds on top (black works too, if you don't have white). Bake in the preheated oven for 18–20 minutes or until golden. Leave to cool before serving.

NOTES All Danish pastries are baked in an oven preheated to 210°C/190°C fan/400°F/Gas 6, but you may need to adjust a bit as ovens do vary.

Choose baking sheets with a slight lip as the butter melts during baking.

I've written these recipes assuming you want to make one type of pastry, i.e. using the basic dough for one kind. You can, however, split the dough into four equal parts and make all four kinds in one go, giving you a total of 16 pastries, four of each.

Custard or jam crowns
Spandauer

1 quantity Basic Danish Pastry Dough (see page 236)
1 quantity Almond Filling (see page 236)
1 quantity Pastry Cream (see page 237) or 150 g/½ cup raspberry jam/preserve
beaten egg, for brushing
70 g/2½ oz. chopped hazelnuts
100 g/¾ cup minus ½ tablespoon icing/ confectioner's sugar, to decorate

Roll the dough to a square approx. 40 x 40 cm/16 x 16 inches and, using a knife or pizza cutter, tidy the edges so the sides are straight. Cut into 16 pieces, each 10 x 10 cm/4 x 4 inches. Place on a lined baking tray.

Add 2 tablespoons of almond filling to the middle of each piece, then take each corner and press it into the middle of the pastry, over the filling. Press down with your fingers to make a slight well, then leave to prove for an hour.

Once proved, add a good dollop (2–3 tablespoons) of the pastry cream to the hole in the middle (raspberry jam is sometimes used instead of pastry cream). Brush with beaten egg and sprinkle with chopped hazelnuts. Bake in the preheated oven for about 15–18 minutes or until golden and baked through. Leave to cool.

Make the icing by mixing the sugar with a few drops of hot water. Decorate with a circle of thick icing on the top.

Rhubarb & custard
Rabarber og vaniljecreme

400 g/14 oz. rhubarb, cut into 5-cm/2-inch pieces
150 g/¾ cup caster/granulated sugar
1 quantity Basic Danish Pastry Dough (see page 236)
flour, for dusting
1 quantity Pastry Cream (see page 237)
beaten egg, for brushing
icing/confectioner's sugar, for dusting

To prepare the rhubarb, place the cut pieces in a saucepan with the sugar and 50 ml/3½ tablespoons water. Bring to the boil and simmer for 5 minutes, then leave to cool completely before using.

Roll the dough to a square approx. 40 x 40 cm/16 x 16 inches and 4–5 mm/¼ inch thick. Using a knife or pizza cutter, tidy the edges so the sides are straight. Cut into 16 pieces, each 10 x 10 cm/4 x 4 inches. Place on a lined baking tray and leave to prove for around an hour.

Dust the base of a cup 4–5 cm/1½–2 inches in diameter with a little flour. Press down in the middle on each piece to create a dip and fill with pastry cream, then add rhubarb on top (don't add too much of the liquid). Brush the pastry with beaten egg.

Bake in the preheated oven for about 15–18 minutes or until golden and baked through. When cooled, dust with icing/confectioner's sugar.

VARIATION Use different berries instead of rhubarb or even leave plain with pastry cream only.

Custard & cinnamon
Overskåren

½ quantity Basic Danish Pastry Dough (see page 236)
1 quantity Cinnamon Remonce (see page 236)
beaten egg, for brushing
100 g/¾ cup minus ½ tablespoon icing/ confectioner's sugar, to decorate

Cut the dough into two pieces, then roll each to a long rectangle approx. 40 x 20 cm/16 x 8 inches and 3–4 mm/⅛ inch thick. Tidy the edges with a pizza cutter. Add the remonce in the middle of each long piece, lengthways. Fold over the dough on top from both sides towards the middle, covering the remonce, but ensuring the dough does not double up too much. Press down along the middle to create a slight channel down the length of the dough (this is where the pastry cream will go after rising).

Leave to rise for an hour, then press a channel along the middle of the pastry again. Pipe the pastry cream along the middle, in a line 4–5 cm/1½–2 inches wide.

Brush with beaten egg, then bake in the preheated oven for 24–26 minutes or until golden and baked through. Leave to cool completely.

Make the icing by mixing the sugar with a few drops of hot water, then pipe two long, thick lines of icing down each pastry on either side of the pastry cream. You can serve these cut up or in long sharing pieces. If serving individually, cut each long piece into four pastries.

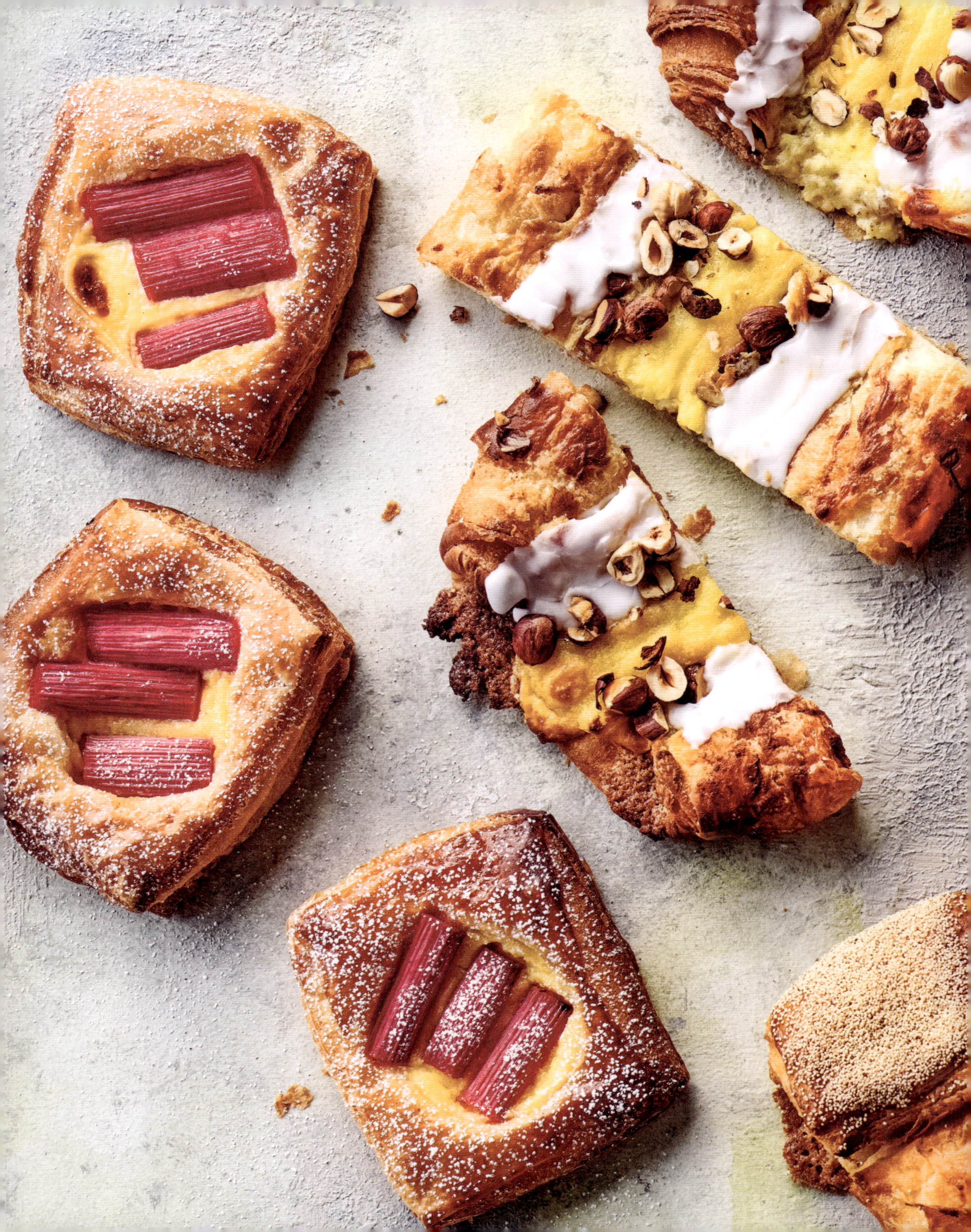

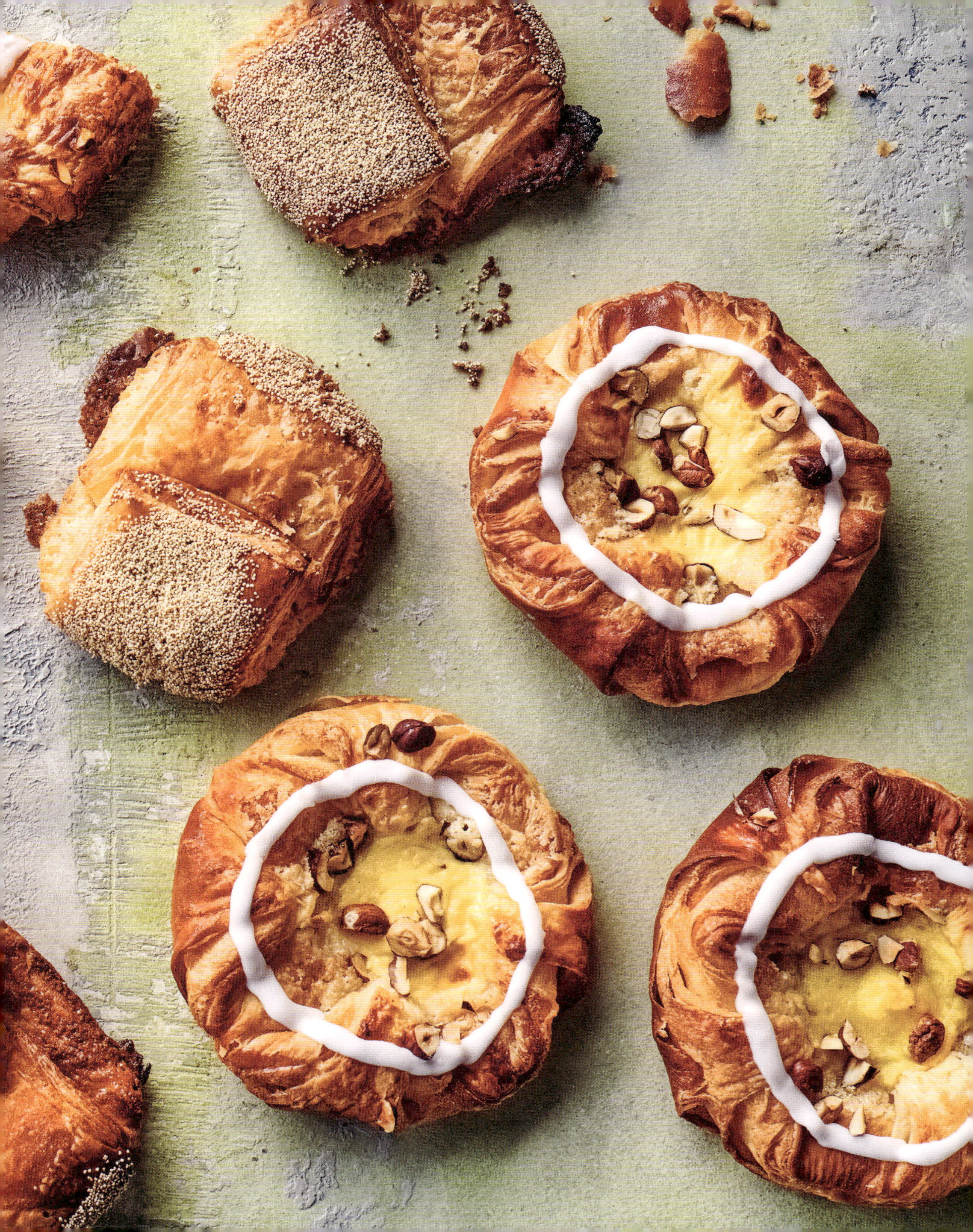

Sweet Funen 'foccacia'

Brunsviger

Funen (known as Fyn in Danish) is the island right in the middle of Denmark. It is a place of beautiful scenery, rich culture, and the home of Hans Christian Andersen and the *Brunsviger* – a bread-like cake topped with lashings of brown sugar and butter. If the people of Fyn had an official cake, this would be it. It's hard to explain the appeal of this huge bun – it isn't the prettiest thing, but what it lacks in looks it makes up for in taste. Think of it as like a focaccia, but topped with sugar and butter, and baked in the oven with all the delicious melty bits collecting in the holes. It is also often used as a base for making the traditional birthday cake known as *Kagemand*. Eat on the day of baking.

1 quantity Basic Bun Dough (see page 234)
plain/all-purpose flour, for dusting

TOPPING
175 g/1½ sticks butter, softened
225 g/1 cup plus 2 tablespoons dark brown soft sugar
4 generous tablespoons golden/corn syrup
a dash of vanilla extract
¼ quantity Pastry Cream (see page 237) (optional)

35 x 25-cm/14 x 10-inch baking pan with sides, greased and lined with baking parchment

MAKES ABOUT 12 GENEROUS SLICES

To make the topping, whisk the softened butter with 200 g/1 cup of the sugar, the syrup and vanilla extract until you have a very soft, spreadable mixture.

Tip out the dough onto a floured surface and knead it through. Roll the dough out to roughly the size of the baking pan and transfer to the pan. Stretch the sides to fit the entire baking pan. Prod shallow holes all over the dough with your fingers. The deeper the holes, the more hiding places for the topping, which is the best bit.

Spread over the topping with a spatula (blast quickly in the microwave if it needs loosening up) so that every bit of dough is covered. Smear on the Pastry Cream at this point, if using. Scatter over the remaining dark brown soft sugar.

Cover with clingfilm/plastic wrap and leave to rise for another 20 minutes.

Preheat the oven to 200°C/180°C fan/400°F/Gas 6.

Remove the clingfilm. Check if you need to re-poke some of the holes, then bake in the preheated oven for around 20–25 minutes, or until baked through. The topping should be sticky and shiny. Baking times may vary, so do keep an eye on it. Remove from the oven and leave to cool. Cut into slices and serve. This cake is best enjoyed the same day it is made.

TIP I sometimes add date syrup to my filling. Entirely untraditional, but it's delicious.

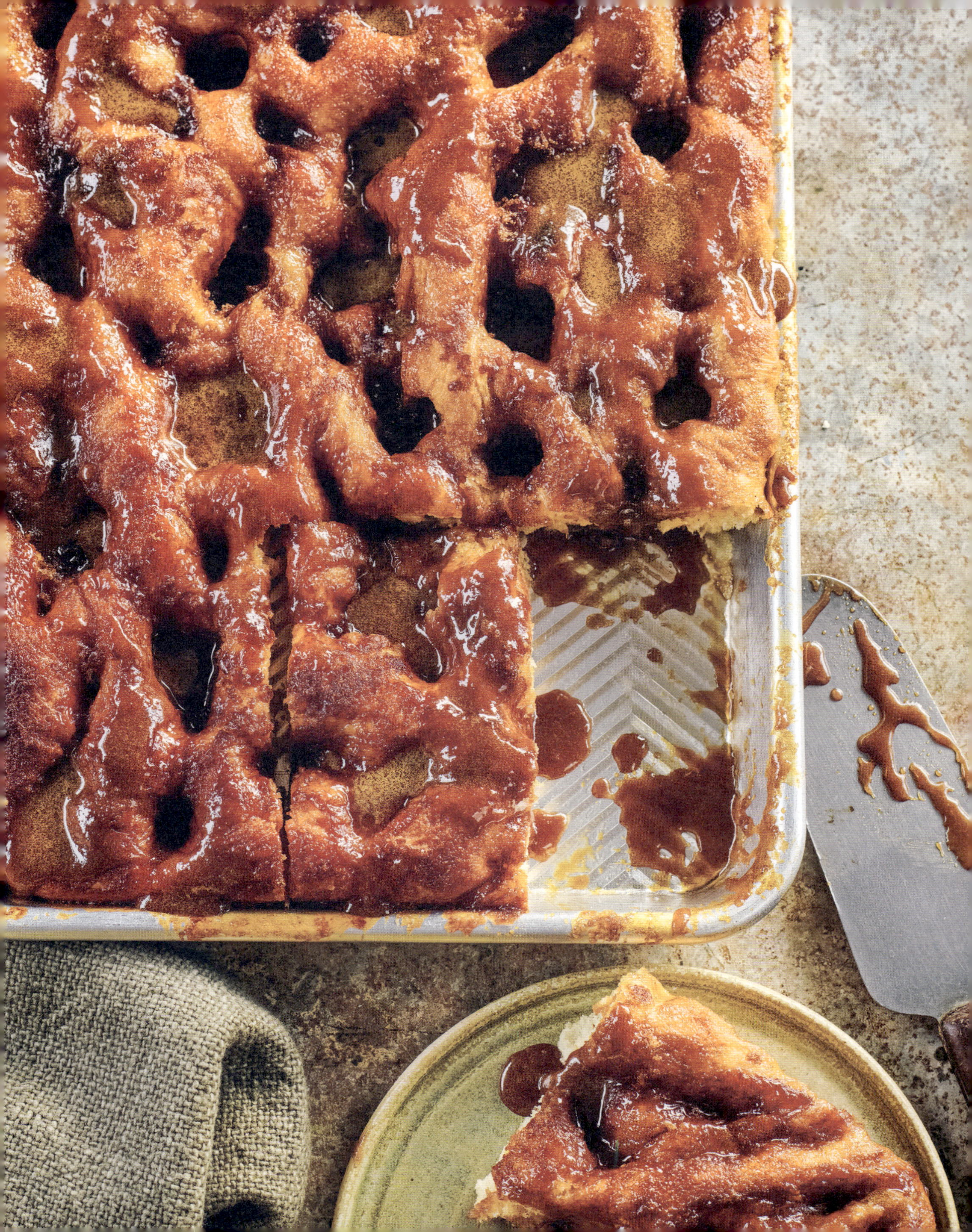

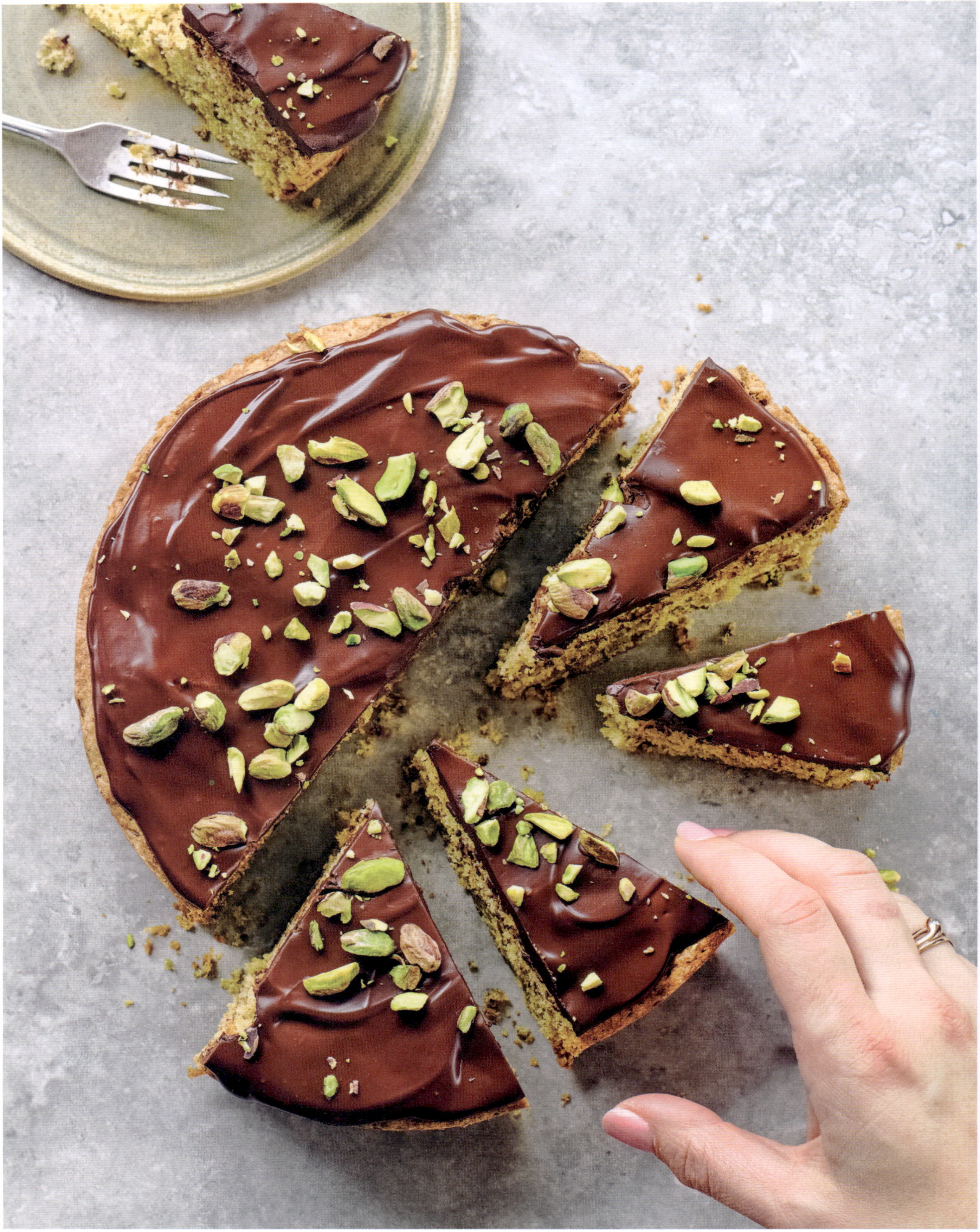

Pistachio cake

Mazarin med pistasche

Across the Nordics, you will find cakes named *mazarin* in various guises, supposedly named after a 17th-century French-Italian cardinal. Traditionally, a *mazarin* cake is made with marzipan (or ground almonds), but I have adapted this one to be made with pistachios. It's a simple cake and always served cooled (or even cold), never warm out of the oven, so you can easily make it the day before.

If you prefer a more traditional *mazarin* cake, change the pistachios to ground almonds and add 2-3 teaspoons of almond extract to the batter.

200 g/7 oz. shelled pistachios
175 g/1½ sticks butter, softened
200 g/1 cup caster/granulated sugar
1 teaspoon vanilla extract or vanilla sugar
4 eggs
75 g/½ cup plus 1 tablespoon plain/all-purpose flour
50 g/½ cup cornflour/cornstarch
a pinch of salt
½ teaspoon baking powder

TOPPING
120 g/4 oz. chocolate (60% cocoa solids is fine)
20 g/1½ tablespoons butter
chopped pistachios, to decorate

25-cm/10-inch round baking pan, greased

SERVES 6-8

Preheat the oven to 175°C/155°C fan/350°F/Gas 4.

In a food processor, whizz the pistachios until finely ground.

In a stand mixer, cream together the butter and sugar, then add the ground nuts, vanilla and the eggs, one by one, ensuring the mixture is incorporated after each addition of egg. Sift the dry ingredients into the mixture and fold in, then pour into the prepared baking pan.

Bake in the preheated oven for around 35 minutes or until a skewer inserted into the centre comes out clean. Cool completely in the pan before turning out onto a serving plate, upside down.

For the topping, melt the chocolate in a bowl set over a pan of hot water, then add the butter and stir to mix. Spread thinly over the top of the cooled cake. Decorate with chopped pistachio nuts.

This cake is best eaten once completely cooled. I also love it served with a dollop of vanilla whipped cream (or crème fraîche) and some fresh raspberries.

With the snow finally gone, May is the month of awakenings for both nature and people. The sun has returned with its light – and the lakes and seas are slowly warming up. While the first day of May for most Scandinavians is a day off, when I was growing up it was the first day we were allowed to swim in the sea by our little wooden house. While it was a mostly bitterly cold affair, with a dip lasting just a few minutes accompanied by screams of pure joy (and warm towels), it signalled the start of the magical Scandinavian summer. By the middle of May, as the Norwegians are celebrating their Constitution Day, everything turns green and comes fully alive – as if by magic.

Late in May is the time for the very first new potatoes to be harvested in Denmark and the southern parts of Sweden (a bit later the further north you go). Asparagus makes its presence felt majestically, along with the first fresh dill, salad leaves and rhubarb.

MAY

NORWAY DAY

For the past two decades, I've attended the Norwegian Constitution Day celebrations held in London, where I live. As part of our huge Nordic community here, we're fortunate to have easy access to the different cultural celebrations of our friends that we wouldn't ordinarily have back home. I do think Norwegians win the prize for having the most elaborate and festive national day of all of the Nordic countries, hands down – for sure, it's the happiest one. Every year on *Syttende mai* (17th May), the entire country (and Norwegians living overseas) spends the day celebrating and feeling patriotic. If you're anywhere near a Norwegian person, it is impossible not to be swept away by armies of happy people greeting each other and waving Norwegian flags all day long.

In 1814, after centuries under both Swedish and Danish rule, Norway finally acquired its own constitution on 17th May. As they were still officially in a union with Sweden, Norwegians were not actually allowed to celebrate this for many years, but by the 1860s, parades started to appear and 17th May as known today began to take shape.

Syttende mai is very much about parades. Every town and village has a parade featuring every imaginable club, from schools and scouts to veterans and cultural societies. Those who are left line the streets, waving flags and hoping to spot people they know.

This is also the day when any Norwegian who owns national dress will wear it. The *bunad*, as the outfit is known, is unique to every region in terms of designs and patterns. As the clothes are so special, the only other times they are worn is when there's a wedding or an important occasion, such as meeting the king. These suits and dresses are elaborately hand-sewn out of wool. On warmer 17th Mays, they can become quite hot (not to mention itchy) – particularly after a day of eating non-stop, when many hit the dance floor in their *bunads* (a practice known as *bunadsboogie*, which doesn't need a translation).

A typical celebration begins with a Champagne breakfast with family or friends. It starts early (around 7am), so people can get to the parades in time and not be hungry. A *koldtbord* (the Norwegian *smörgåsbord*) is usually served, consisting of scrambled egg, air-dried lamb, prawns/shrimp, salmon, roast beef, cheese, fruit salad, *rømmegrøt* (sour-cream porridge), fresh bread and lashings of wine. It's one of the most abundant meals of the year (and bigger than Christmas). Later on, hotdogs and ice cream are enjoyed, *ad libitum*, by everyone, along with waffles served with brown cheese (caramelised whey). This is a day for overindulging in all the Norwegian favourite foods. The end of the day is marked with a big dinner and maybe a little dance to one of the many live bands playing.

It's hard not to be very enamoured with all things Norwegian on this special day. The people's love of their country is so passionately genuine and rooted in such immense pride of everything that makes them as unique as they are. For those of us who can't join as a real Norwegian, we can aim to be one of the *Norgesvenner* – friends of Norway. Essentially, this is a non-Norwegian who loves Norway and has had that love recognised by Norway. Whilst possibly tongue in cheek at times, the honour is often bestowed on famous people who have visited Norway many times, spoken well of the country and probably given some sort of indication that they *may* like to live in Norway some day. Many *Norgesvenner* include politicians, artists, writers, singers and other famous people – and once you get the title it's hard to shake. Just ask Bruce Springsteen, 50 Cent and Steven Van Zandt.

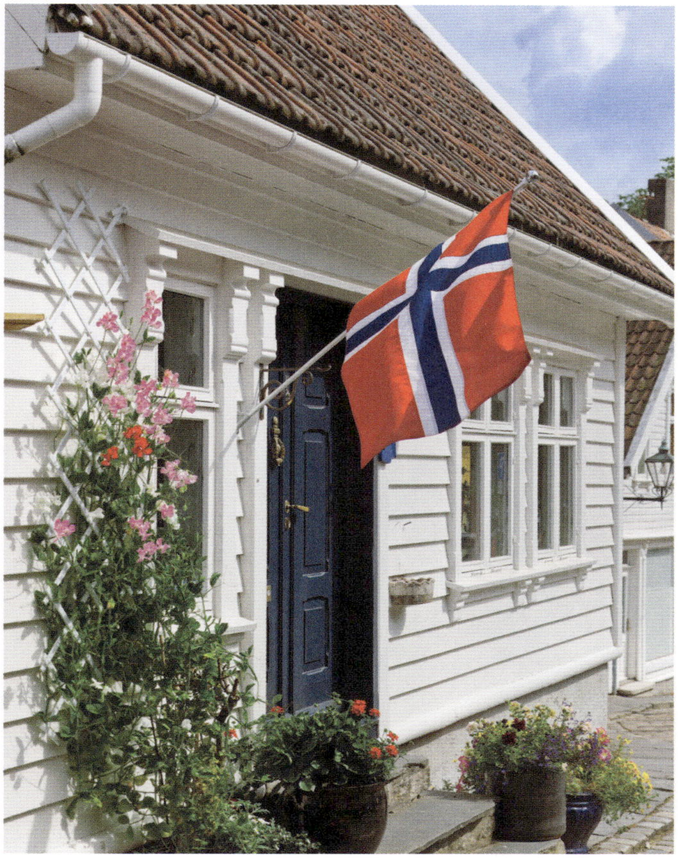

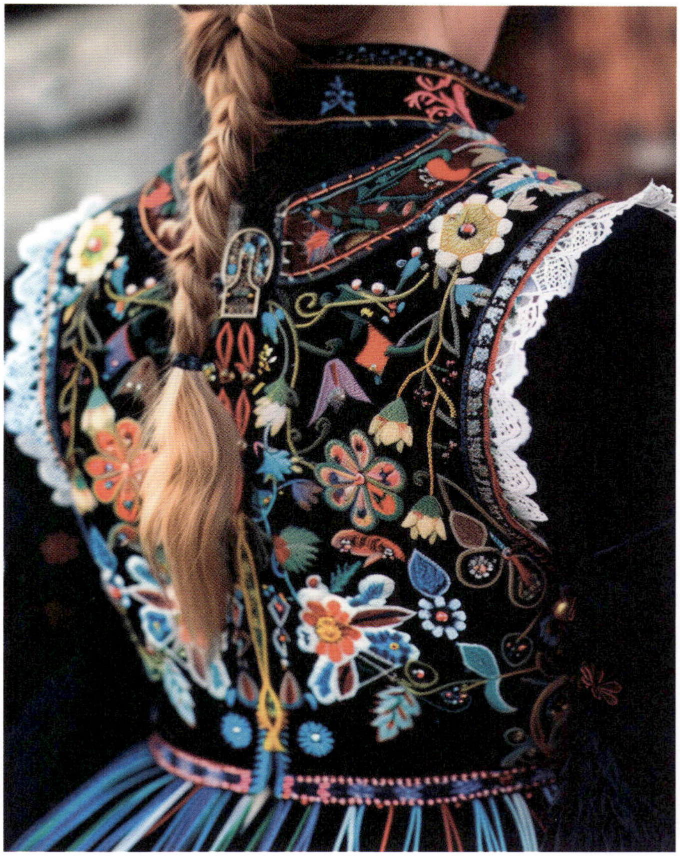

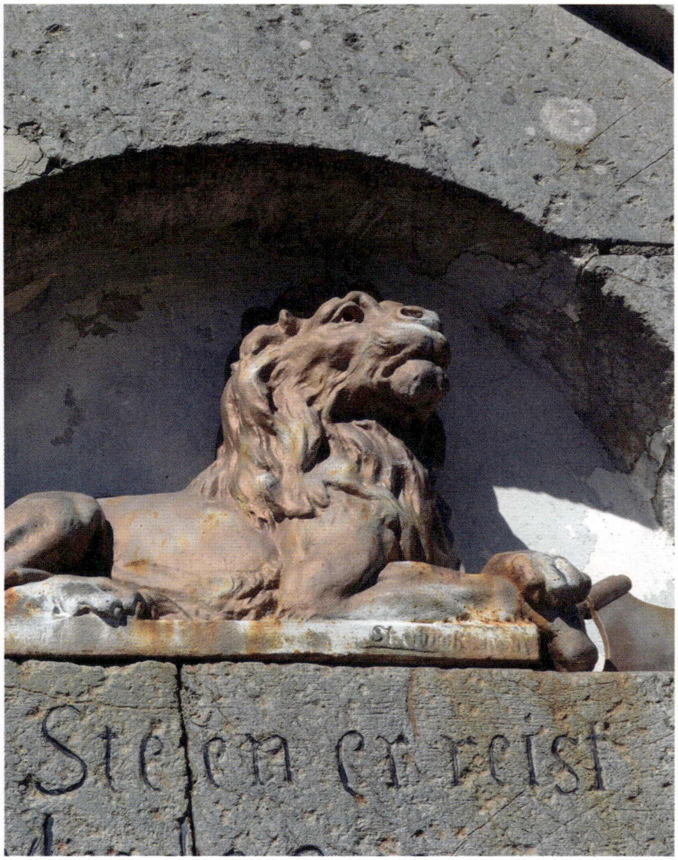
Stenen er reist

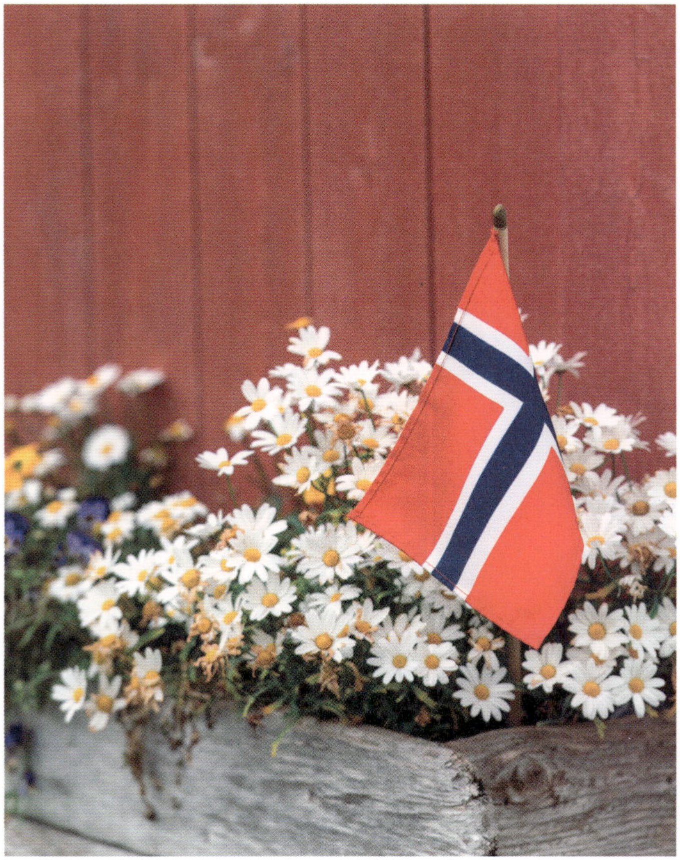

Eight open sandwiches

Otte smørrebrød

These recipes are made to serve two people with one large piece each in the style we call *højtbelagt* – toppings piled high. You could split each recipe into four and make a large selection if serving these at a lunch where you want more variety for people to choose from.

Open sandwiches are always eaten using cutlery, except when being served as larger canapés at standing events. You can make each of these recipes into eight pieces instead of two, which will give you the size for the 'hand delivery' version, or *snitter* as we say in Danish. Just cut the bread to size before assembling.

Smoked salmon & egg
Røget laks med æg

If you were to serve salmon on its own on an open sandwich, you would probably usually choose a softer and white bread, but as this one is served with a light egg mayo, a more robust rye bread works well. This is always popular in ScandiKitchen – and I love the fresh fennel on top.

2 slices of rye bread, or 4 smaller slices (or softer bread if preferred), buttered
3 hard-boiled/hard-cooked eggs
2–4 tablespoons mayonnaise, to taste
½ teaspoon Dijon mustard
115 g/4 oz. smoked salmon
very thinly sliced fennel, to taste
very thinly sliced red onion, to taste
salt and freshly ground black pepper
pea shoots and dill sprigs, to garnish
lemon wedge, to serve (optional)

Chop the boiled eggs and put in a bowl with the mayonnaise and mustard. Season with a bit of salt and some black pepper, then mix.

Spread the egg mayo on top of the buttered bread, ensuring you go right to the edges, but also creating height. Arrange the salmon neatly on top, then add the fennel and onion.

Garnish with pea shoots and dill sprigs, taking care to maintain the height of the open sandwich. Squeeze over a bit of lemon juice before serving (optional).

Pickled herring with beetroot
Marineret sild med rødbedesalat

This is the most popular herring open sandwich we make at ScandiKitchen. It is not the most traditional, but a Swedish *smörgåsbord* often includes both pickled herrings and a beetroot salad, and the two go together so well.

2 slices of dark rye bread, or 4 smaller slices, buttered
200 g/7 oz. Scandinavian Beetroot Salad (see page 35)
2 hard-boiled/hard-cooked eggs, halved
100 g/3½ oz. pickled onion herring (drained weight)
3 tablespoons chopped chives
freshly ground black pepper
micro herbs, to garnish

Spread the beetroot salad on top of the buttered bread. Add the halved eggs on top of the beetroot salad, then add the pickled herring (it's important to ensure it is well drained).

Top with the chopped chives, season with black pepper (salt won't be needed) and garnish with micro herbs.

Egg & prawns
Æg og rejer

There's always a discussion about whether prawns/shrimp should be served on dark rye or white bread. Many feel that if served with sliced boiled/cooked egg, then it should go on rye – but if on its own then it should go on white bread. Except sometimes we break these (unwritten) rules. You do you: it will taste great, regardless of what bread you use.

2 slices of rye bread, or 4 smaller slices, buttered
4 hard-boiled/hard-cooked eggs
4–6 tablespoons mayonnaise, blended with some fresh dill and chives, salt and pepper
100g/3½ oz. cooked small prawns/shrimp
a handful of cress
salt and freshly ground black pepper
micro herbs, to garnish
grated lemon zest and a squeeze of juice, to serve

Using an egg slicer, slice the boiled/cooked eggs and arrange them neatly across the bread (at our cafe, we sit two whole eggs onto one large open sandwich in two rows).

Pipe or arrange a generous amount of herby mayonnaise down the middle. Arrange the prawns to one side of this, then, on the other side, add a generous amount of cress, all the way along (using the mayo to make it stick).

Season with salt and pepper, garnish with micro herbs, then finish with some grated lemon zest and a squeeze of lemon juice to serve.

Dill-marinated carrot & avocado
Dillmarineret gulerod med avocado

A veggie favourite at the café. You can keep it veggie or make it vegan – either way, the delicious tang of the make-ahead dill-marinated carrots makes for a wholesome lunch option.

2 slices of rye bread, or 4 smaller slices, buttered (either white or rye bread work well)
1 avocado, sliced
dill sprigs and toasted seeds, to garnish
crispy kale chips to serve (optional)

CARROTS (MAKE AHEAD)
4 carrots
2 tablespoons olive oil
2 tablespoons apple cider vinegar
1 teaspoon liquid smoke, such as Hickory (available online)
3 tablespoons freshly chopped dill
1 teaspoon soft brown sugar
a few black peppercorns
½ teaspoon mustard seeds
salt and freshly ground black pepper
a pinch of paprika
a sheet of dried nori or a pinch of dried seaweed flakes (optional)

Start by making the marinated carrots. Cook the whole carrots in boiling water until al dente (no more or they will be mushy and impossible to slice), then add to cold water to stop the cooking process. Set aside to cool.

Using a peeler or mandolin, shave long strips of carrot lengthways, trying to keep each slice intact. Add the rest of the marinated carrot ingredients to a food bag, then add the carrot slices. Try to remove the air, then seal and place in the fridge to marinate for at least 12 hours.

Arrange the sliced avocado on the buttered bread, then add rolled-up carrot slices – this will give the open sandwich height, rather than just laying the carrot slices flat. Decorate with toasted seeds of your choice and some dill and crispy kale chips (store-bought or you can crisp some up in the oven in a jiffy – just add kale and a bit of oil).

This is also good with some cream cheese on the base.

Cauliflower on rye
Smørrebrød med blomkål

Not one of the traditional toppings for an open sandwich – then again, there are very few veggie and vegan open sandwiches in the traditional repertoire. This one is my go-to again and again: I love the combo of miso with the crunchy, just-cooked cauliflower.

- 2 slices of rye bread, or 4 smaller slices, buttered
- 4 tablespoons mayonnaise, mixed with 3 sprigs of finely chopped tarragon leaves
- 6 cherry tomatoes, halved
- 25 g/3 tablespoons toasted hazelnuts, crushed slightly
- micro herbs, to garnish

CAULIFLOWER
- 1 tablespoon miso paste
- 1 tablespoon oil
- 250–300 g/9–10½ oz. cauliflower (keep any inner leaves – they taste great)
- salt and freshly ground black pepper

Start by making the miso cauliflower. Preheat the oven to 160°C/140°C fan/320°F/Gas 3.

Mix the miso and oil together with 2 tablespoons water and season. Cut the cauliflower into florets and mix with the miso. Place on a baking sheet and roast in the preheated oven until done – about 15 minutes, depending on the size of your pieces (you want the cauliflower to retain some crunch). Allow to cool.

Spread the tarragon mayonnaise over the buttered bread and arrange the cauliflower on top, then add the tomatoes and toasted hazelnuts. Season with salt and pepper, and garnish with micro herbs.

Meatball sandwich
Köttbullemacka

Probably the most popular Swedish open sandwich that people make at home. It's also super-easy and really delicious. Meatballs (store-bought, if you don't have time to make your own) work well paired with beetroot salad on thick, buttered crusty bread. This sandwich has looked the same since forever: true nostalgia.

- 2 slices of crusty bread, buttered
- 115 g/4 oz. Scandinavian Beetroot Salad (see page 35, enough to generously fit the base of the bread slices)
- 10 small Swedish Meatballs (see page 96), or use fewer and slice them if they are larger
- pickled cucumber, to taste
- 6 cherry tomatoes, halved (or thicker tomato slices, hidden under the beetroot)
- salt and freshly ground black pepper
- micro herbs, to garnish

Spread the beetroot salad on the buttered bread. Arrange the meatballs on top. Add the pickled cucumber and tomatoes, season and garnish with micro herbs.

Roast beef
Roastbeef

Traditionally, roast beef in Denmark is served on green leaves, but I really feel that it needs something else under it. However, if you want to be traditional, leave out the celeriac salad.

2 slices of dark rye bread, or 4 smaller slices, buttered
enough Simple Celeriac Salad (see page 182) to cover the base of each open sandwich, or green leaves
170 g/6 oz. rare roast beef (we use thick-cut steak, cooked rare, then cooled and sliced; leftover roast beef also works)
2 tablespoons horseradish cream (store-bought is fine) or freshly grated
4 tablespoons Danish Remoulade (see page 72)
pickled cucumber slices and pickled red onion, to taste
crispy onions
salt and freshly ground black pepper
micro herbs, to garnish

Arrange the celeriac salad or leaves on top of the buttered bread. Arrange the slices of beef on top.

Add the horseradish cream, remoulade, pickled onion, pickled cucumber and a few rings of crispy onion. Season with salt and pepper, and garnish with micro herbs.

Chicken & bacon on rye
Hønsesalat

The classic combo of chicken and bacon is just perfect on a slice of dark rye bread. Vary the filling here as you fancy – mushrooms or no mushrooms, asparagus in the summer. If I have some chicken skin left over, I crisp it up in the oven and add as a crunch topping.

2 slices of rye bread, or 4 smaller slices, buttered
4–5 slices of streaky/fatty bacon
a few salad leaves to cover the base
6 cherry tomatoes, halved
micro herbs and crispy chicken skin, to garnish

CHICKEN MIXTURE
100 g/3½ oz. mushrooms, sliced
100 g/3½ oz. asparagus, blanched, or 1 jar white asparagus, drained (100 g/3½ oz. drained weight)
200 g/7 oz. cooked chicken, chopped (leftovers from the Sunday roast work well)
50 g/3½ tablespoons crème fraîche
50 g/3½ tablespoons mayonnaise
1 teaspoon Dijon mustard
1 teaspoon dried tarragon
a squeeze of fresh lemon juice
2 tablespoons chopped chives
salt and freshly ground black pepper

Fry the bacon until crisp, then set aside to drain on paper towels and allow to cool.

To make the chicken mixture, fry the mushrooms in the pan you used for the bacon until cooked (the bacon fat gives great flavour). Transfer to a bowl.

Roughly chop the asparagus and add to the mushrooms with the cooked chicken and all the remaining chicken mixture ingredients. Mix, taste and season.

To assemble, add some salad leaves to the buttered bread, then top with a generous amount of the chicken mixture. Arrange the bacon and tomatoes on top, and garnish with micro herbs and crispy chicken skin.

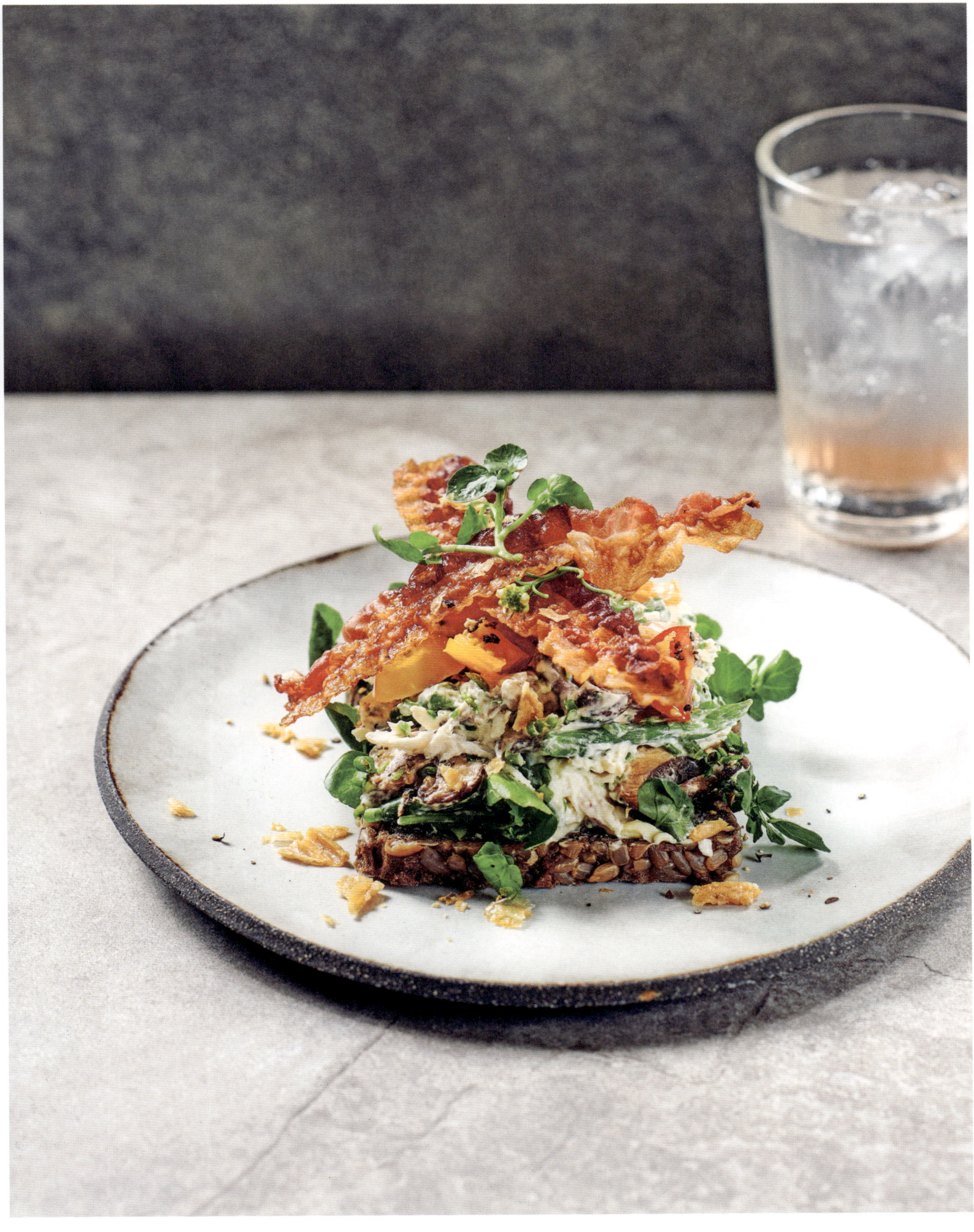

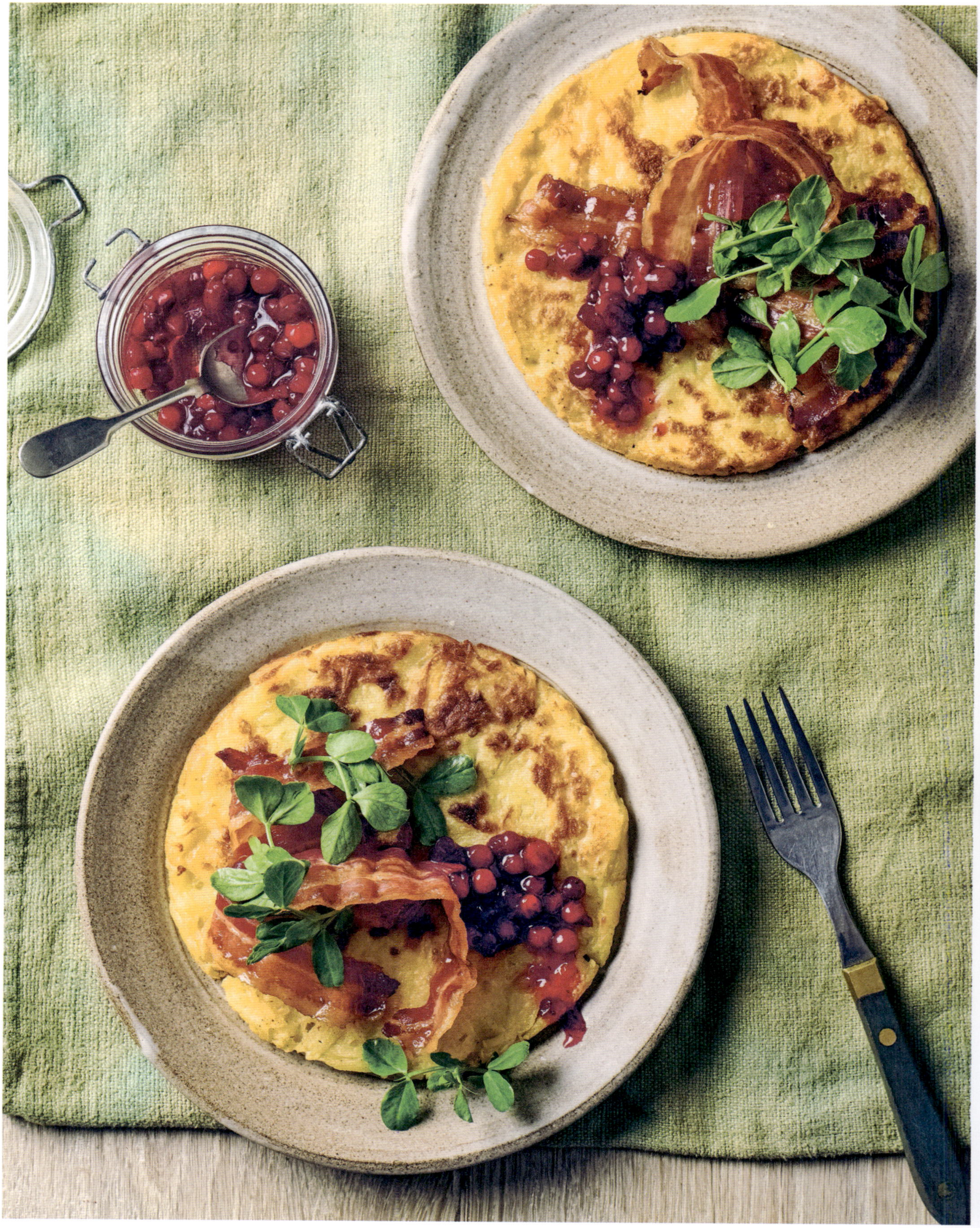

Potato pancakes with bacon & lingonberry

Raggmunk

Raggmunk is a Swedish potato pancake that most resembles a meeting between a pancake and a *rösti*, often served with fried pork belly slices and lingonberry jam. It's a light lunch or dinner dish dating back to the early 1900s and is a perfect example of Swedish *husmanskost*: working man's food.

Ragg refers to the crispiness and *munk* is a doughnut – these were often made in a munkpan, which used to be commonplace in Swedish kitchens. These days, no special pan is needed – just make them in a regular frying pan/skillet. I get three to four American-sized pancakes from this amount of batter.

At home, I don't actually serve these with thick pork belly slices as I much prefer streaky/fatty bacon. The lingonberry is a wonderfully tart addition – you can substitute with cranberry jelly if you can't get hold of lingonberry. Serve with a side dish of green salad leaves or just on its own with the jam.

500 g/1 lb. 2 oz. floury potatoes (such as Maris Piper)
120 g/1 cup minus 1½ tablespoons plain/all-purpose flour
1 egg
300 ml/1¼ cups whole milk
1 teaspoon salt
leaves from a sprig of thyme (optional)
4–6 slices of streaky/fatty bacon
butter and a glug of neutral oil, for frying
salt and freshly ground black pepper
lingonberry jam/preserve, to serve
pea shoots, to garnish

SERVES 2–3

Peel the potatoes, then coarsely grate them into a bowl. Squeeze out as much excess liquid from the potatoes as you can – it is easiest to do this by placing the potatoes in a muslin cloth and squeezing.

To make the batter, whisk the flour and egg together, then add the milk as you whisk. Season and add the thyme leaves, if using, and potato. Leave the batter to rest for 30 minutes before using.

Preheat the oven to 120°C/100°C fan/250°F/Gas ½.

Heat a frying pan/skillet with a knob/pat of butter and a small glug of neutral oil. You can either make larger or smaller pancakes – I get around four smaller (American pancake-sized) from this batch. Make sure that when you add the mixture, the potato is spread out and not too thick or it will not cook through as evenly.

Fry the potato pancakes until done. It will take around 8–10 minutes for the potatoes to be cooked through, so lower the heat and take care not to overcook the exterior. I usually prefer to finish these in the oven on a low heat. Meanwhile, fry the bacon and keep warm. To serve, top each pancake with bacon, add a spoonful of lingonberry jam/preserve and garnish with some pea shoots.

VARIATIONS You can make this with potato and add carrots or parsnips for a bit of variation – or leave out the potato entirely and just use root veg (carrots, parsnips, celeriac/celery root). For a veggie version, omit the bacon and serve with a dollop of herby crème fraîche (chopped chives, parsley and chervil work well here). For a pescatarian version, these are delicious with smoked or cured salmon.

Swedish meatballs *Köttbullar*

I often wonder if the search for the perfect Swedish meatball is never-ending. There are as many recipes as there are people who make them, and just when I think I'm entirely happy with mine, I change my mind and start adding things. Remember that homemade *köttbullar* are never the same as processed ones you buy (or eat at that very well-known furniture store) and while there is a time and place for buying meatballs, making them yourself is worth it. Homemade meatballs take time and patience, but they are wholesome and so amazing served with a creamy homemade mash, stirred lingonberries and some pickle on the side. Comfort food 101.

1 onion, finely chopped or grated
250 g/9 oz. minced/ground pork
250 g/9 oz. minced/ground beef (minimum 15% fat content)
30 g/1 oz. breadcrumbs
50 ml/3½ tablespoons cream
100 ml/⅓ cup plus 1 tablespoon meat stock
1 egg
1 teaspoon ground allspice
½–1 teaspoon ground pepper
a good dash of Worcestershire sauce (or soy sauce)
salt
butter and oil, for frying
mashed potato, to serve

CREAM GRAVY (GRÄDDSÅS)
300 ml/1¼ cups meat stock
1 tablespoon plain/all-purpose flour
a good glug of single/light cream
salt and freshly ground black pepper

STIRRED LINGONBERRIES (RÅRÖRDA LINGON)
250 g/9 oz. frozen lingonberries (available in some speciality food stores and online)
100 g/½ cup caster/granulated sugar

SERVES 4

In a frying pan/skillet, melt some butter and fry the grated or chopped onion until caramelised.

Add the meats to a food processor, season with salt and mix for a minute. In a separate bowl, mix the breadcrumbs, cream, stock and egg together.

Add the egg mixture to the meat, then add the onion and pulse until combined (don't overmix, but do ensure no larger onion bits remain). The mixture should be sticky, but mouldable. Leave the mixture to rest for 20–25 minutes before using.

Heat a frying pan/skillet with a small knob/pat of butter or oil. Shape one small meatball. Fry until done and then taste. Adjust the seasoning as necessary and fry another meatball to test it until you get it just right.

Shape the individual meatballs in your hands – it helps if your hands are slightly wet. Each meatball should be around 2.5 cm/1 inch in diameter, or larger if you haven't got time. This mixture will make around 30 meatballs.

Melt a knob/pat of butter in the same frying pan/skillet with a dash of oil and add a few meatballs – make sure there is plenty of room for you to swirl the pan round and help turn them so they get a uniform round shape and do not stick. You'll probably need to cook them in several batches. Cooking time is usually around 5 minutes per batch. Keep in a warm oven until needed.

When the meatballs are done and in the oven, keep the pan on a medium heat to make the gravy. Ensure you have enough fat in there, if not, add a little more butter to the pan. Add the tablespoon of flour and whisk, then add a splash of stock and whisk again as you bring it to the boil. Keep adding stock until you have a good creamy gravy, then add a good glug of cream and season well. The gravy should be light brown in colour.

To prepare the lingonberries, simply add the sugar to the frozen berries and stir. Leave for a while, then stir again, until the sugar dissolves and the berries have defrosted. Store any leftovers in the fridge. If you can't get lingonberries, use lingonberry jam/preserve instead.

Serve with mashed potatoes and, if you wish, quick pickled cucumbers.

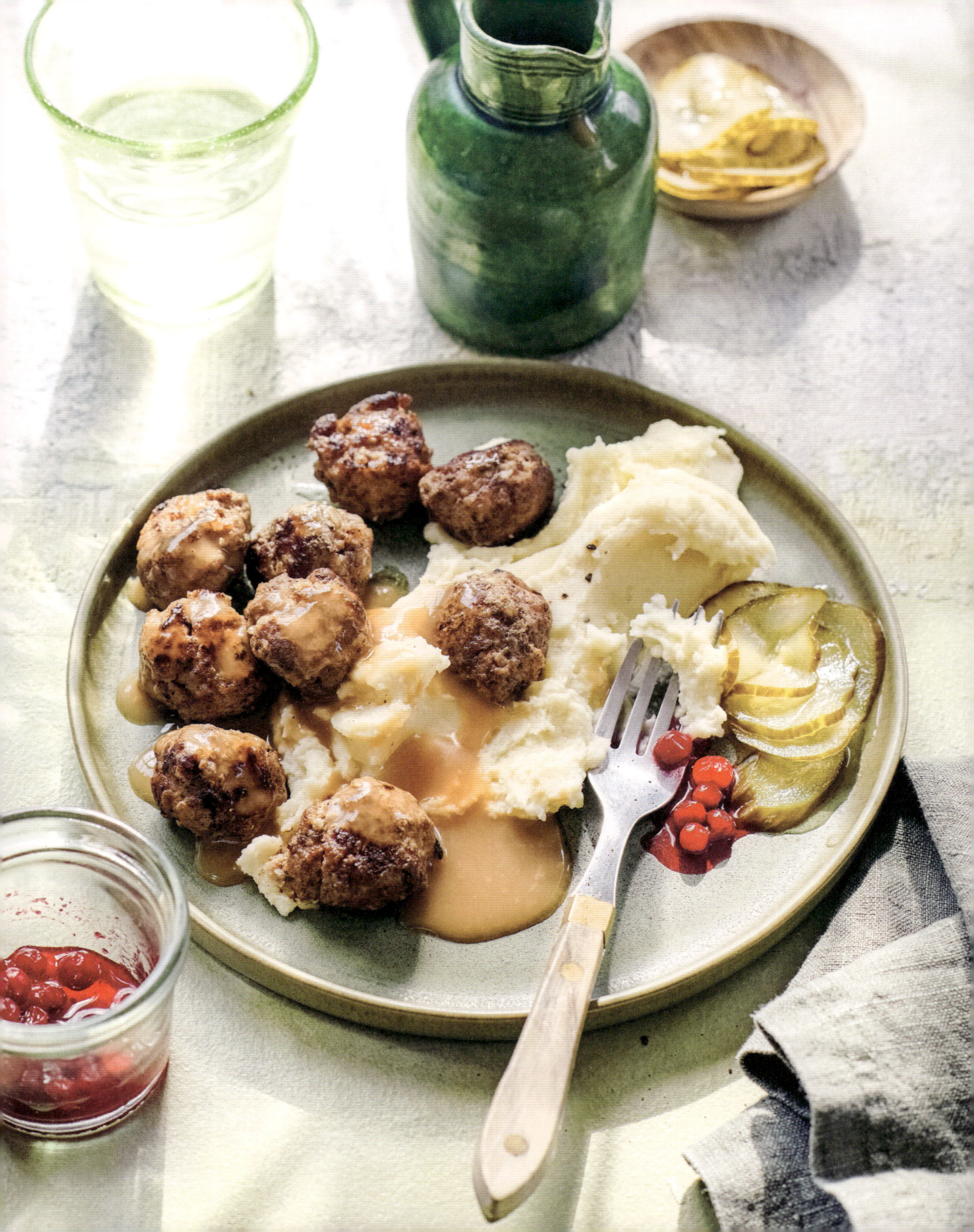

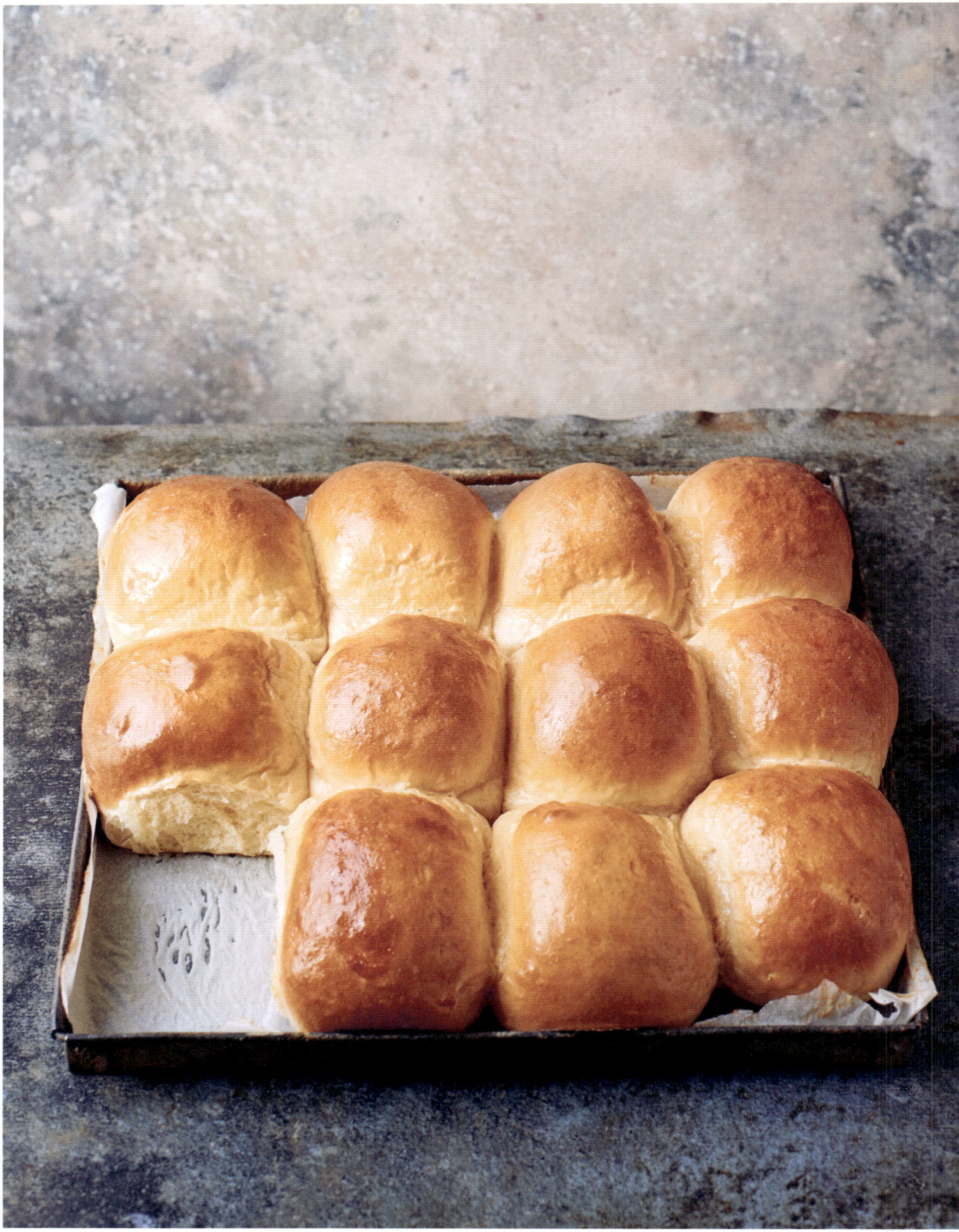

Toasted wheat buns

Hveder

There is a Danish tradition of eating these rolls on the eve of *Store bededag* ('Great Prayer Day'), a religious observance on the fourth Friday after Easter. We buy these in the afternoon and toast them – despite these being fresh rolls – and enjoy with a good load of *tandsmør* (literally 'tooth butter' – enough butter so that you can see the indent of your teeth when you take a bite).

I bake these brioche-style rolls quite often and use them for both lunches and breakfast rolls – they are simply too nice to just eat once a year.

25 g/1 oz. fresh yeast
200 ml/¾ cup whole milk, heated to 35–36°C/95–97°F
100 ml/7 tablespoons finger-warm water
40 g/3¼ tablespoons caster/granulated sugar
approx. 600 g/4¼ cups strong bread, flour, plus extra for dusting
1 teaspoon salt
1 teaspoon ground cardamom
100 g/7 tablespoons butter, softened
1 egg, plus extra for brushing

25 x 35-cm/10 x 14-inch baking pan, greased and lined with baking parchment

MAKES 12 ROLLS

Add the fresh yeast, milk and water to a stand mixer fitted with a dough hook. Mix until the yeast has dissolved. Add the sugar and stir again, then slowly add half the flour, little by little. Add the salt, cardamom, softened butter and the egg and keep mixing. Slowly add the remaining half of the flour. You may not need all the flour or you may need a bit more: keep mixing until you have a uniform springy dough.

Leave the dough to rise, covered, for around 40–45 minutes or until doubled in size.

Turn the dough out onto a lightly floured surface and divide the dough into 12 equal pieces. Place on the prepared baking sheet, spaced about 1–2 cm/⅜–¾ inch apart – when they rise, they will touch and stick together, giving them the traditional look. Cover and leave to rise again for 20–25 minutes under a kitchen towel.

Preheat the oven to 200°C/180°C fan/400°F/Gas 6.

Brush each bun lightly with beaten egg and bake in the preheated oven for around 15 minutes, or until baked through. If the buns start browning too quickly, turn the oven down to 180°C/160°C fan/350°F/Gas 4. Cool on a wire rack.

Norwegian custard buns *Skoleboller*

Every Norwegian has a fond space in their hearts and memories for *Skoleboller* – translated as 'school buns'. They became popular in the 1950s, named because people used to put these into their kids' lunch boxes. You'll find versions of these buns all over Norway (some with slightly different names, such as *Skolebrød*). Make sure you poke a big enough hole in the middle to contain a good amount of pastry cream.

1 quantity Basic Bun Dough (see page 234)
plain/all-purpose flour, for dusting
½ quantity Pastry Cream (see page 237) or 300 g/10½ oz. store-bought custard (make sure it is suitable for baking as not all types are)
1 egg, for brushing
150 g/¾ cup minus ½ tablespoon icing/confectioner's sugar
100 g/1½ cups desiccated/shredded dried coconut

2 baking sheets, lined with baking parchment

MAKES 24 BUNS

Dust the work surface with flour and turn out the dough. Knead the dough with your hands and work in more flour if needed. Cut the dough into 24 equal-sized pieces. Roll out so the buns are round and uniform in size and place on the prepared baking sheets, well-spaced out.

Leave for about 10 minutes to rest, then prod a large hole in the middle of each one and flatten slightly so you end up with a hole around 4 cm/1½ inches in diameter. Add a large tablespoon of the pastry cream or custard to each one.

Leave for another 15 minutes to rise, then brush the sides of the buns with the beaten egg.

Preheat the oven to 180°C/160°C fan/350°F/Gas 4.

Bake in the preheated oven for around 10–12 minutes or until baked through and golden around the sides.

When the buns have cooled slightly, make the icing by mixing the icing/confectioner's sugar with a little hot water until you have a syrup-like consistency. Carefully brush the icing around the edges of the buns (I use a pastry brush for this), then scatter the coconut on top (try not to get too much on top of the custard, the coconut is just for the edges). Leave to set before serving.

VARIATION In Sweden, the same buns are known as *Vaniljbullar* (vanilla buns). There, instead of the icing and coconut, the just-out-of-the-oven buns are brushed with a little melted butter and dipped in caster/granulated sugar.

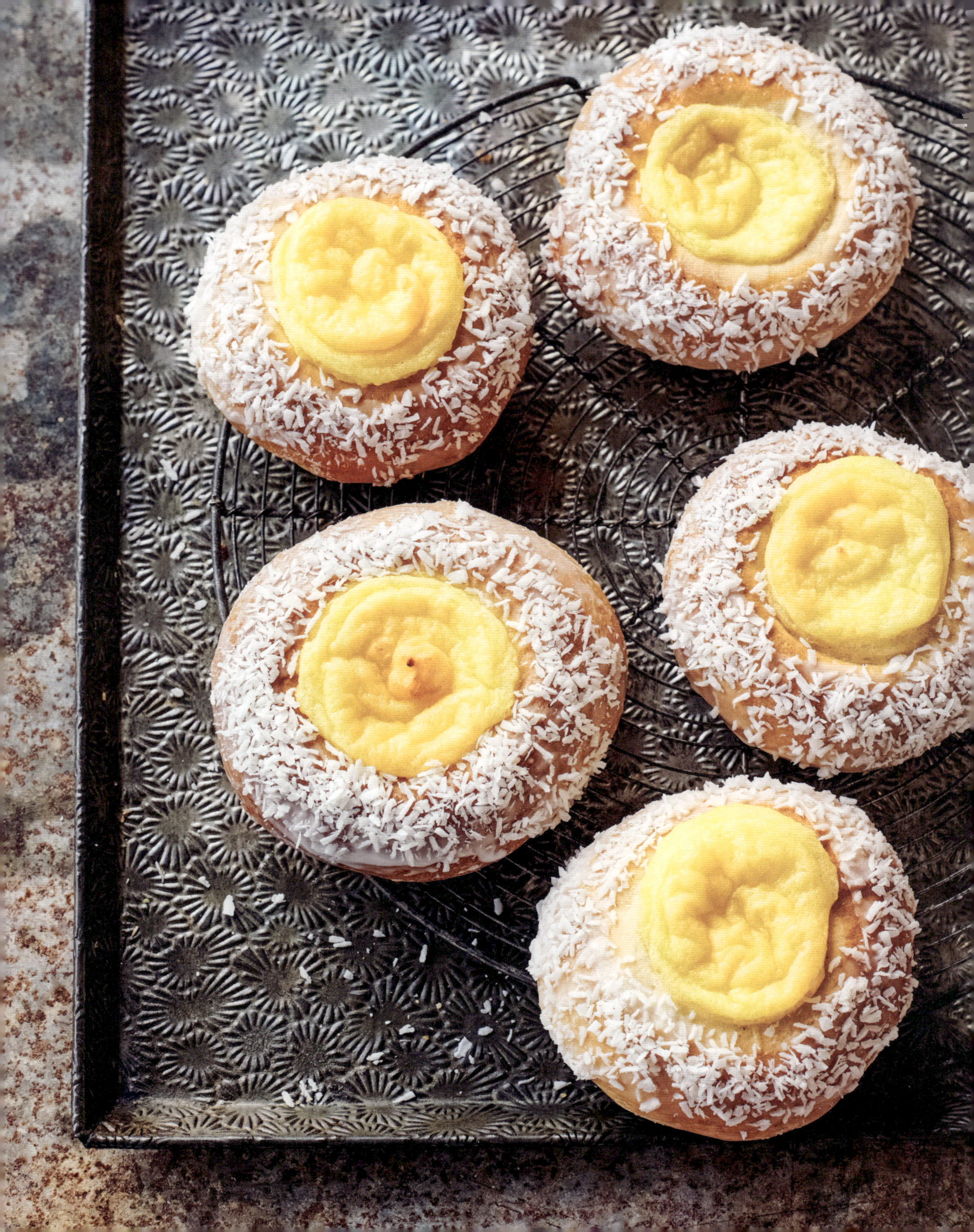

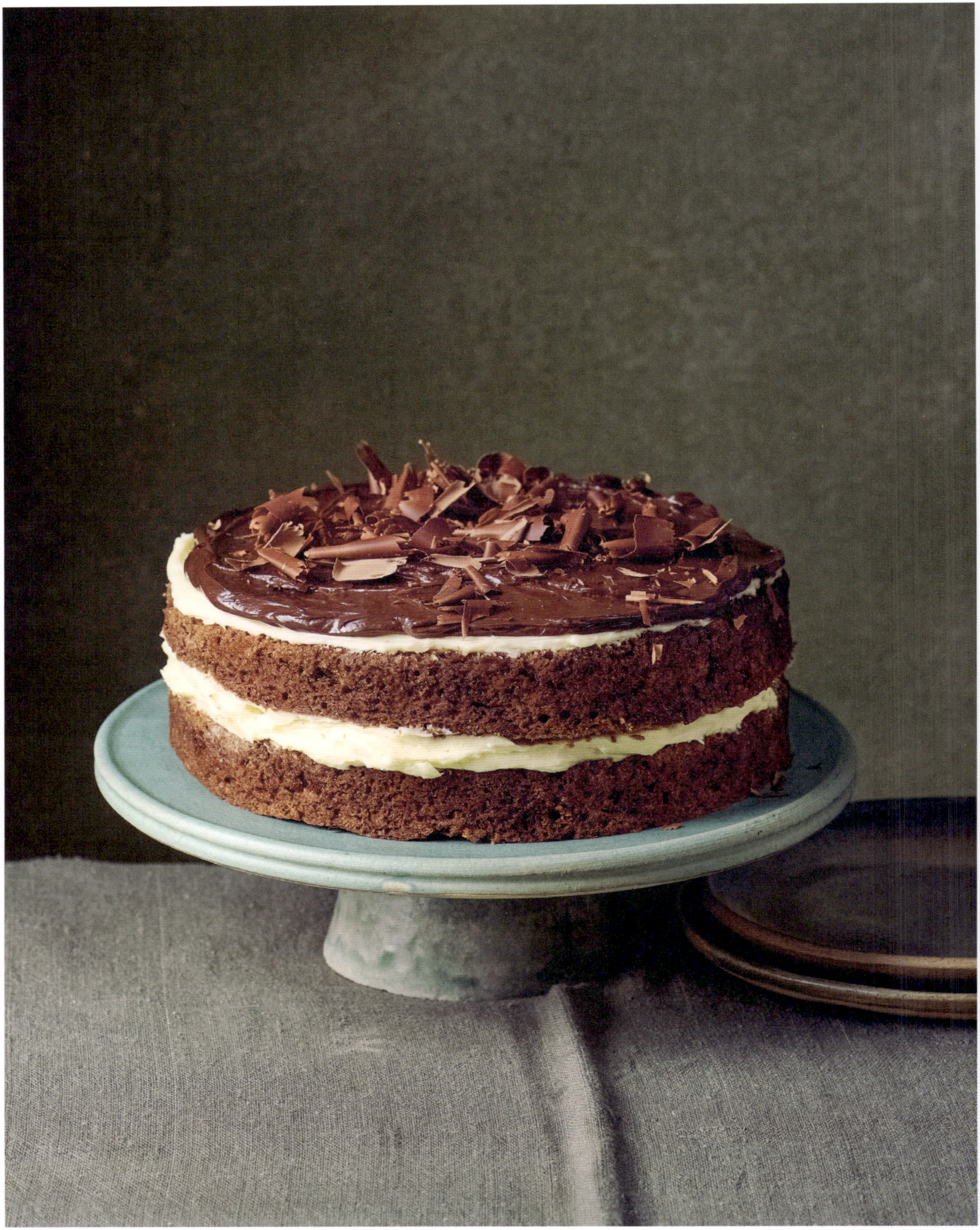

Syrup cake

Sirupslagkage

Many might argue this cake reminds them of Christmas, likely because of the warm gingerbread flavours, but I just love it and make it all year round – even in the summer. It is quite a firm cake with good bite and a very buttery filling. My grandmother Inger used to make a version of this when we were kids and it brings back such fond memories of the old house in the Danish countryside where so much of my early childhood was spent. If you prefer a fruitier flavour, try a layer of orange marmalade or apricot jam/preserve under the buttercream.

75 g/5⅓ tablespoons butter, softened
75 ml/5 tablespoons golden/corn syrup
50 g/¼ cup dark brown sugar
75 g/⅓ cup plus 2 teaspoons caster/granulated sugar
200 g/1½ cups plain/all-purpose flour
1 teaspoon vanilla sugar or extract
2 teaspoons ground cinnamon
1 teaspoon ground cardamom
1 teaspoon ground cloves
1 teaspoon ground ginger
½ teaspoon salt
1 teaspoon bicarbonate of soda/baking soda
1 egg
200 ml/¾ cup buttermilk or natural/plain yogurt
chocolate shavings, to decorate

BUTTERCREAM FILLING
125 g/9 tablespoons butter, softened
125 g/¾ cup plus 2 tablespoons icing/confectioner's sugar
1 teaspoon vanilla sugar or extract
dash of milk
½ egg yolk (optional – omit if you don't love the idea of raw egg)

CHOCOLATE GLAZE
75 ml/5 tablespoons double/heavy cream
75 g/2½ oz. dark/bittersweet chocolate
a pinch of sea salt flakes, to taste
1 teaspoon butter

2 x 20-cm/8-inch round baking pans, lined with baking parchment

SERVES 8

Preheat the oven to 200°C/180°C fan/400°F/Gas 6.

In a stand mixer, cream together the butter, syrup and sugars.

Mix all the dry ingredients together.

Add the egg to the mixer and whisk until incorporated, then add the buttermilk. Sift in the flour mixture and fold with a spatula until all incorporated. Don't over-mix or the cake will feel too dense. Pour the batter into the prepared cake pans.

Bake in the preheated oven for around 30 minutes or until a skewer inserted into the centre comes out clean – the exact time will depend on your oven. Remove from the oven and leave to cool.

To make the buttercream filling, cream the butter in a mixer fitted with the paddle attachment, then add the icing/confectioner's sugar, the vanilla and a dash of milk. Keep whisking – this is quite a firm buttercream. For extra richness, add ½ egg yolk – but this is entirely optional.

To make the glaze, bring the cream to boiling point (use a microwave if you wish), then add the chocolate and stir until melted. Add a pinch of sea salt flakes and the butter. Stir again and allow to cool.

To assemble, place one of the cakes on a serving plate and spread most of the buttercream filling across the base, then add the top layer of cake. Spread the remaining buttercream across the top of the cake. Once the chocolate glaze has cooled down and is less runny, spread over the top of the cake. Allow to set, then decorate the top with chocolate shavings before serving. Sometimes I serve the cake with fresh berries on the side.

When the land of winter turns into the almost mythical land of the midnight sun, you can be sure that we blossom. The further north you go, the bigger the contrast – and in some places, June means that the sun simply doesn't set at all. While eternal daytime can mess with your circadian rhythm, most of us don't complain (where else can one catch up with the gardening or enjoy a round of golf at 11pm?).

The contrast between Scandinavia's winter and summer is everything. For those near the Arctic Circle, where these extreme seasons of light and dark are not a novelty, they will tell you that the darkness is tougher than the 24-hour daytime, with its lack of natural vitamin D. In fact, they usually report that the summer months make them feel incredibly alive.

June is also the month of Sweden's Midsummer celebrations. School is out and many people either leave for southern Europe or move to their summer cottages to enjoy an abundance of strawberries that taste better than any other in the world, more of those exquisite new potatoes, freshly caught fish and so much dill on everything.

JUNE

MIDSUMMER

Because Midsummer dominates the entire month of June, with all its beautiful daylight and flowers, both Denmark's Constitution Day and Sweden's National Day can feel like a slight afterthought (especially if compared to Norway, see page 86).

Denmark's Constitution Day, known as *Grundlovsdag*, falls on 5th June. It's a celebration of the anniversary of the 1849 signing of the Danish Constitution, establishing Denmark as a constitutional monarchy. In 1915, it was the day women finally got the vote. Today, it's also Father's Day. Although not a public holiday, many people get half a day off work. The streets are lined with flags and there are many political speeches and rallies, as well as patriotic celebrations – but it's mostly a calm affair. Denmark is a very proud country – proud of the flag, of the landscape, of its history – and certainly Danes walk a little taller on this day.

It's easy to assume that Sweden's national day is *Midsommar* given the enthusiasm for celebrating it. However, the official National Day is earlier, on 6th June. It used to be known as Swedish Flag Day, but in 1983, after much debate, it was decided that it should be the new National Day. However, it only became a public holiday in 2005. On this day, new Swedes are welcomed into the country and the royals wave the blue-and-yellow flag at Skansen in Stockholm.

Midsommar is one of the biggest celebrations of the year, particularly for Sweden. The official date is 23rd June, although in Sweden and Finland the date moves to the nearest Friday, as it's a public holiday. Denmark and Norway also celebrate at this time, but as *Sankt Hans Aften* (St John's Eve).

The longest day of the year was incredibly important in the pagan calendar. It was a day of healing, fertility and warding off evil, as well as hopes for a good harvest. The Vikings would visit sacred wells and light bonfires. Today, the Midsummer symbol of Sweden is a huge phallic pole (a long stick with two rings near the top) decorated with flowers and greenery. In Norway and Denmark and parts of Finland, bonfires are lit as the sun never sets.

In Sweden, people wear flower crowns and long, flowing summer dresses (some don traditional dress). The flower crowns are a huge part of Midsummer, as people sit outside creating beautiful garlands together. Later, people gather to raise the pole and dance around it, hand in hand, singing traditional songs. We play games (*kubb*, a throwing game dating back to the Vikings, is very popular) and the party will go on until very late.

Whether celebrating at home or with a picnic in a field, the food is always the same: sour *Matjes* herring, lots of new potatoes with dill, cured or smoked salmon, meatballs, beetroot salad and good cheese and bread. Some bring *smörgåstårta* sandwich cakes (see page 118) and maybe even a vegetable tart. Just as essential are strawberries, eaten all day long, as this is when they're at their finest. Everything is washed down with a solid amount of aquavit. On Midsummer night, it's traditional to pick seven different kinds of wildflowers and put them under your pillow before going to bed to dream of the person you will marry (a great alternative to dating apps).

In Denmark and Norway, *Sankt Hans Aften* is more muted and largely focused around the bonfires. In Denmark, these feature effigies of witches to ward off evil (although quite sinister too). As we watch the witch burning to a crisp, we sing songs about how much we love Denmark. Kids bake campfire twist bread on the embers and people may be tempted to a Midsummer's night swim.

From the dancing and the ancient traditions to the seasonal food and togetherness, Midsummer across Scandinavia is truly spellbinding and enchanting. It's something to be experienced – from the togetherness to the perfect light and old traditions – and it's always a night to remember.

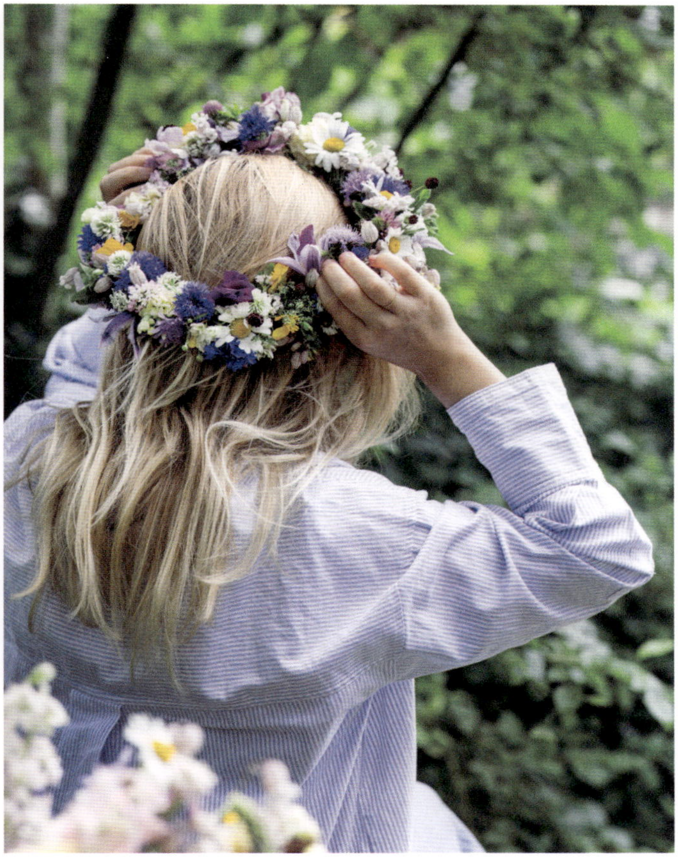
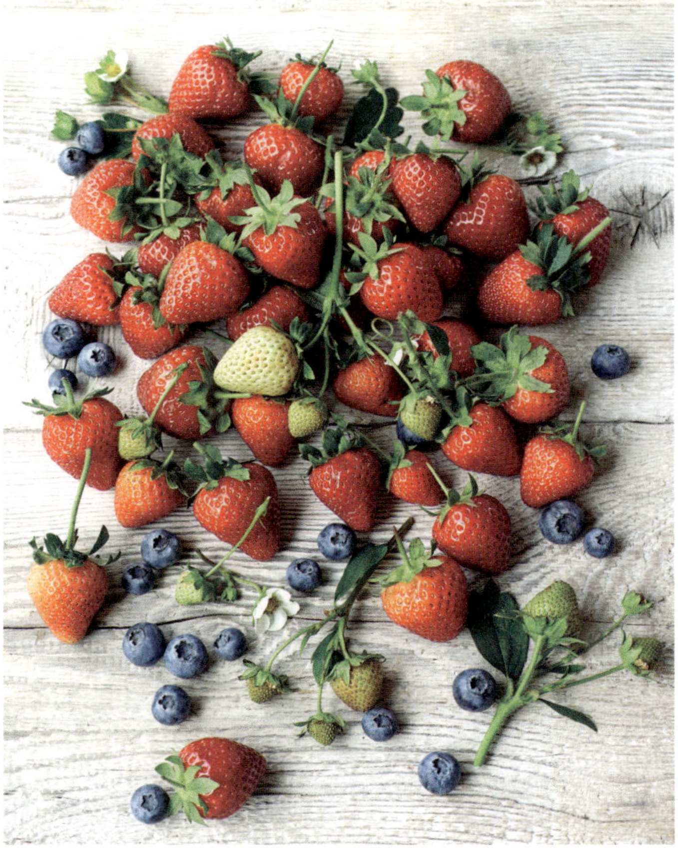
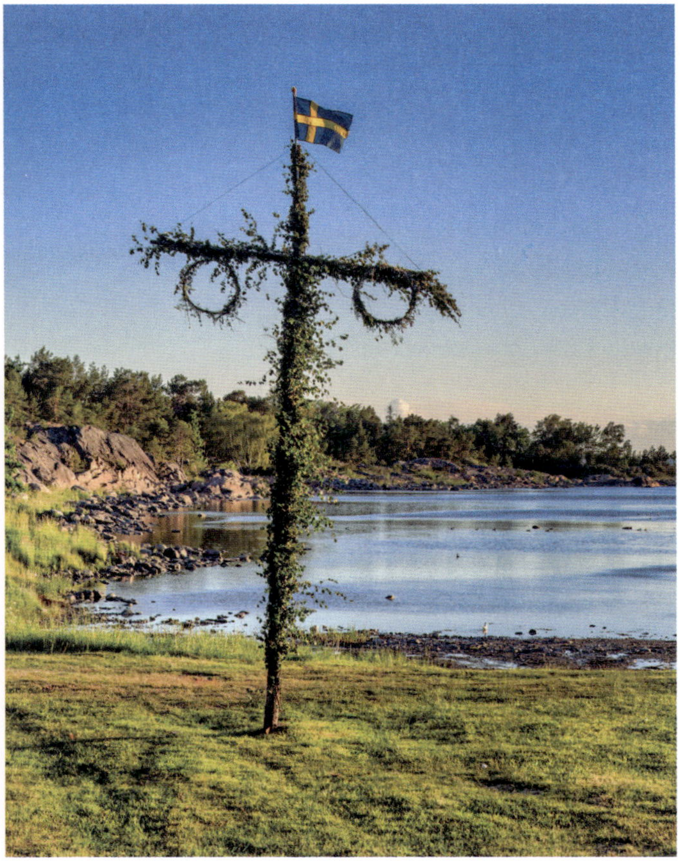
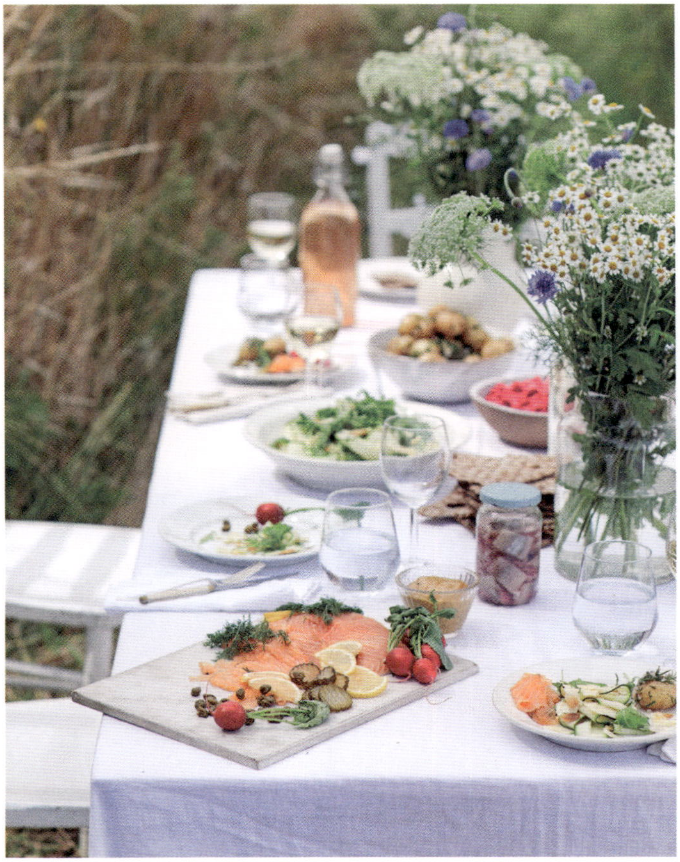

Asparagus, pea & dill tart

Aspargestærte med ærter

This is a delicious summery tart to serve alongside your summer picnic or *smörgåsbord*. Use the shortcrust pasty as a base, or even store-bought puff pastry, if you prefer a more buttery taste. As the seasons change, you can vary the fillings to suit your weekly vegetable stash, although avoid vegetables that go quite wet when cooked as these can make the result watery.

1 quantity Shortcrust Pastry (see page 235) or 320 g/11½ oz. store-brought – I also sometimes use puff pastry

FILLING
a bunch of asparagus, stalks trimmed (approx. 200 g/7 oz.)
10 g/⅓ oz. dill, chopped weight (rough stalks removed)
60 g/⅔ cup grated hard cheese, such as Västerbotten or Cheddar
3 eggs
250 ml/1 cup cream
100 ml/⅓ cup plus 1 tablespoon whole milk
a pinch of paprika
100 g/¾ cup peas (frozen are fine)
salt and freshly ground black pepper

25-cm/10-inch diameter tart pan

baking parchment

baking beans

SERVES 6–8 AS A SIDE, 4 AS A MAIN

Preheat the oven to 200ºC/180ºC fan/400ºF/Gas 6.

Roll out the pastry and use it to line the base and sides of the tart pan. Cover the base with baking parchment and place the baking beans on top. Blind bake in the preheated oven for around 12–14 minutes, then take it out from the oven and remove the baking beans and baking parchment. Return uncovered to the oven and bake for a further 5 minutes.

In the meantime, lightly blanch the asparagus in boiling water.

Whisk together all the remaining filling ingredients, except the peas.

Arrange the asparagus on the pastry base and add the peas. Pour the filling over and return to the oven, turning the heat down to 180ºC/160ºC fan/350ºF/Gas 4 at the same time. Bake for around 20–25 minutes or until the custard has set – I start to keep an eye on it after 15 minutes. It's better to lower the heat and cook for a little longer to avoid overcooking the custard filling.

I often like to decorate the top with fresh pea shoots and more dill. Serve with a side salad or as part of a summer *smörgåsbord*.

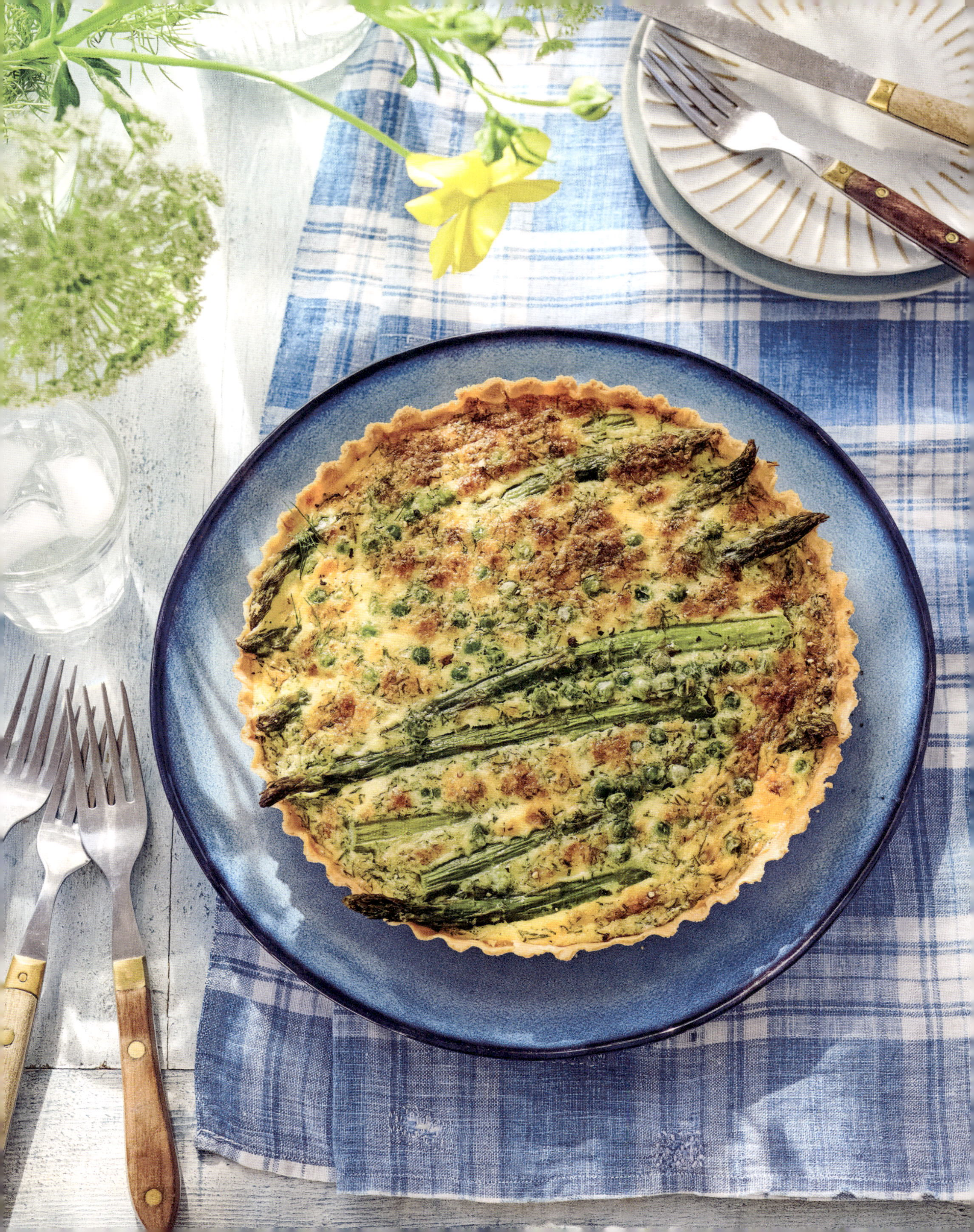

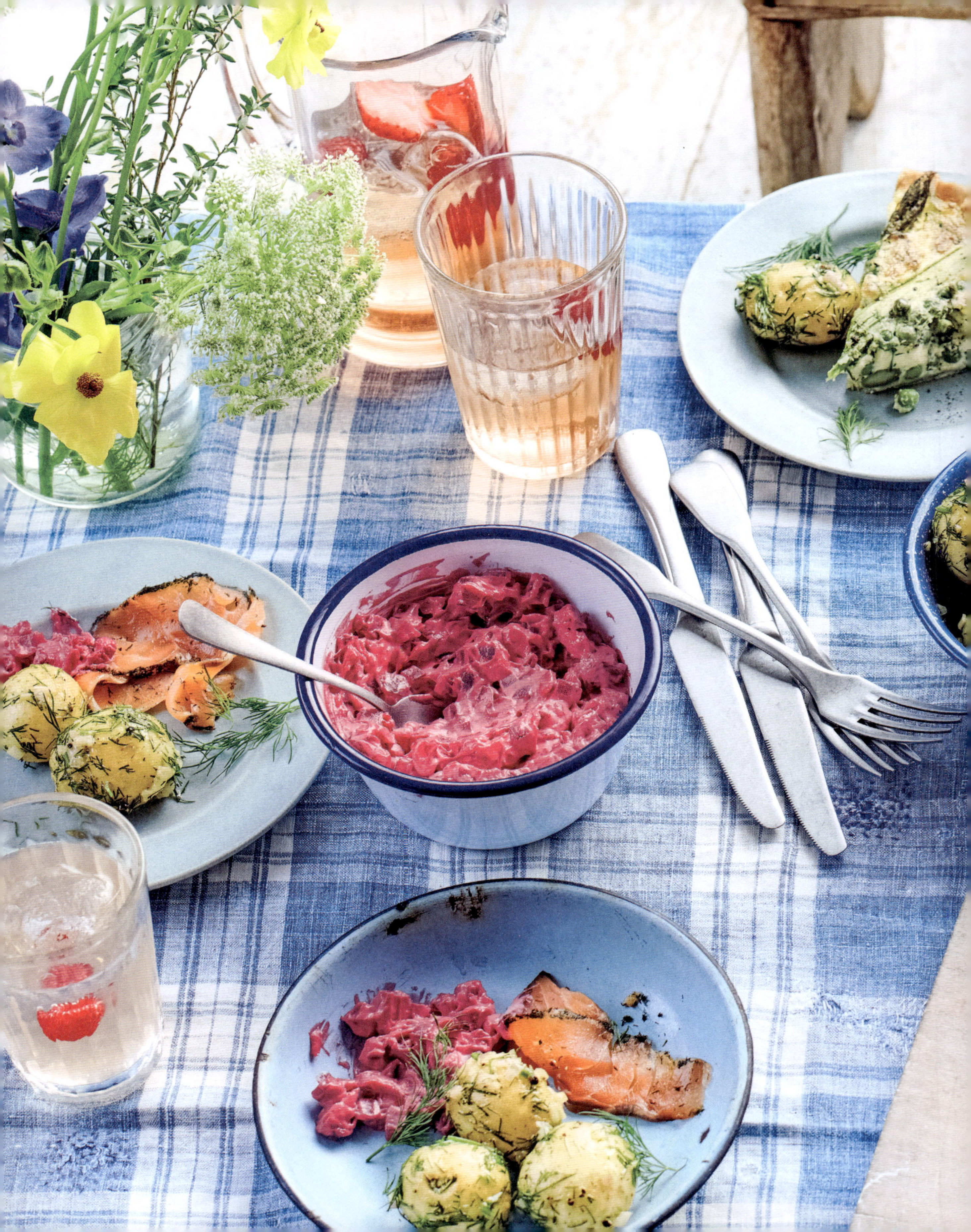

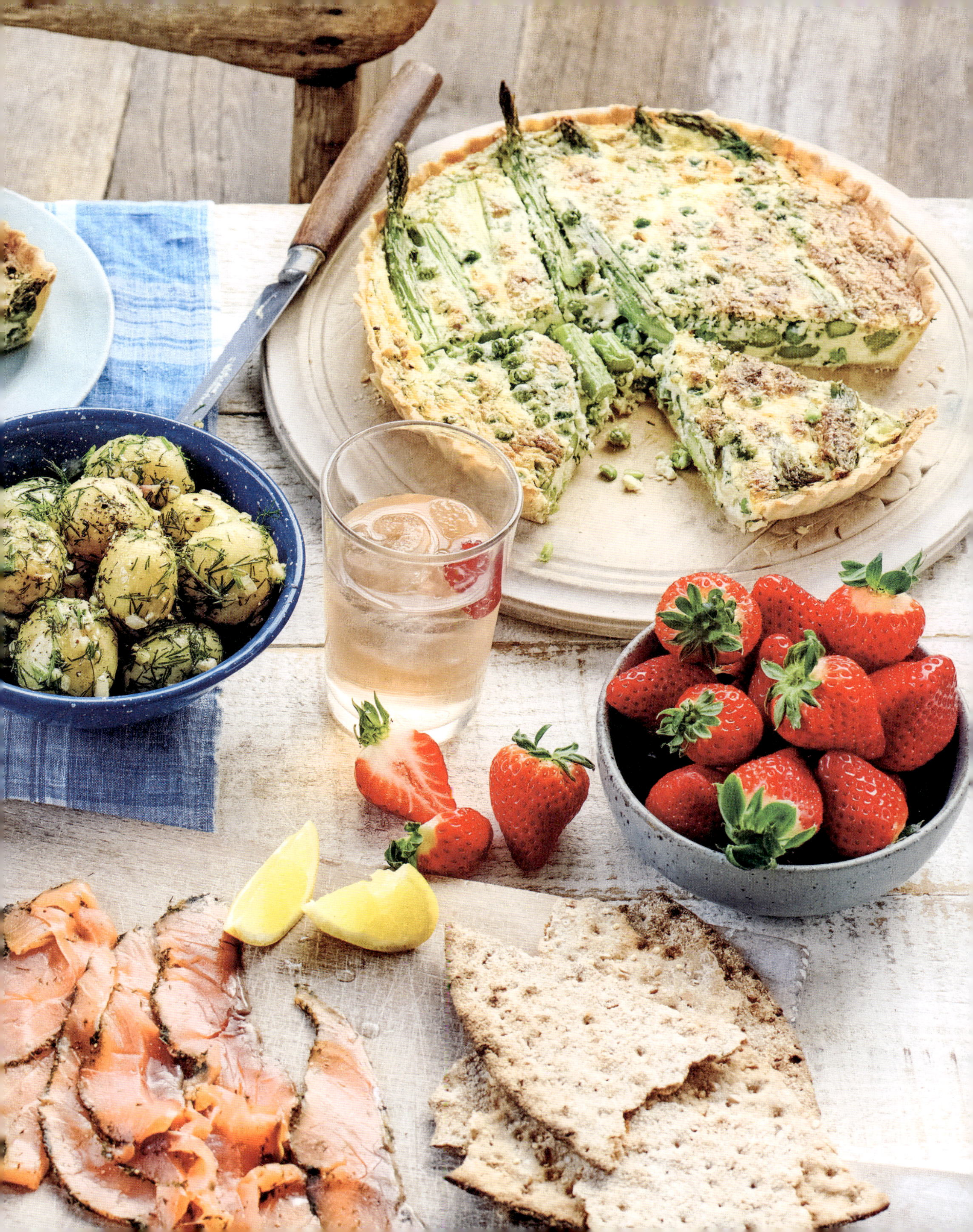

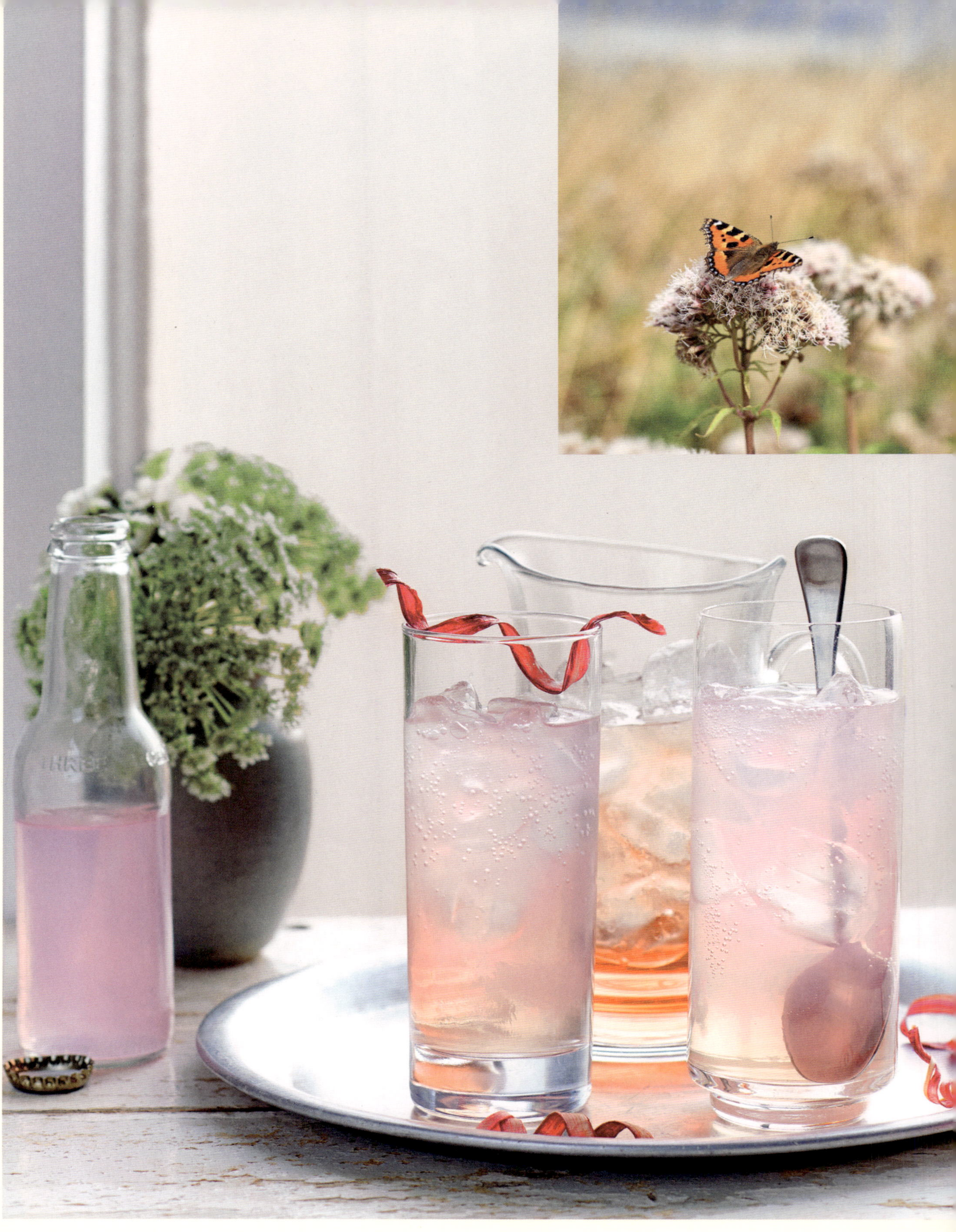

JUNE 113

Midsummer plate

Midsommartallrik

One of my most treasured days of the year is inviting friends over to celebrate Midsummer and I often make this plate to start. It looks so pretty set on the table where each person is seated. I've suggested all the traditional midsummer things we eat: herring, salmon, new potatoes and so on – but vary to your own taste and decorate with fresh herbs and maybe a few edible flowers to complete your edible wreath.

1 boiled/cooked egg
50 g/1¾ oz. smoked or cured salmon
3–4 pieces of pickled Matjes herring or plain onion herring
2–3 cold, boiled new potatoes, halved
3 teaspoons red lumpfish roe caviar
2 cherry tomatoes, halved
1 radish, thinly sliced
2 tablespoons sour cream
pea shoots, dill or other small leaves, such as baby spinach, to garnish
a few edible flowers, if available
crispbread and butter, to serve

SERVES 1 (SCALE UP AS REQUIRED)

Cut the egg into quarters and arrange on the plate in four places around the edge of the plate. Do the same with salmon, herring pieces and potatoes, creating a midsummer wreath of food as you go. Decorate with caviar, cherry tomatoes, radish slices, dollops of sour cream, pea shoots, leaves and dill sprigs.

Serve with crispbread and butter as a starter or light lunch.

Midsummer aquavit cocktail
aka 'The Jon-Anders'

Midsommar cocktail

Jon-Anders, our lovely friend who's an esteemed expert on aquavit, came up with this cocktail for our midsummer party. It's based on the Paloma cocktail, but we just call it 'The Jon-Anders'.

50 ml/3½ tablespoons aquavit (Jon-Anders prefers aged aquavits like Linie, but I use OP or even a clear one)
5 ml/1 teaspoon freshly squeezed lime juice
20 ml/4 teaspoons rhubarb cordial
sparkling grapefruit soda, to top up (Jon-Anders prefers Three Cents)
candied rhubarb, to garnish (optional)

SERVES 1

Add the aquavit, lime and rhubarb cordial to a tall glass of ice, then top with grapefruit soda to taste. Garnish with candied rhubarb twirls or a fancy straw.

TIP Aquavit is an acquired taste and can be quite potent to the uninitiated. If you're not used to the strong taste of caraway and dill in an alcohol, start with a lower amount of aquavit and increase the rhubarb cordial, to taste.

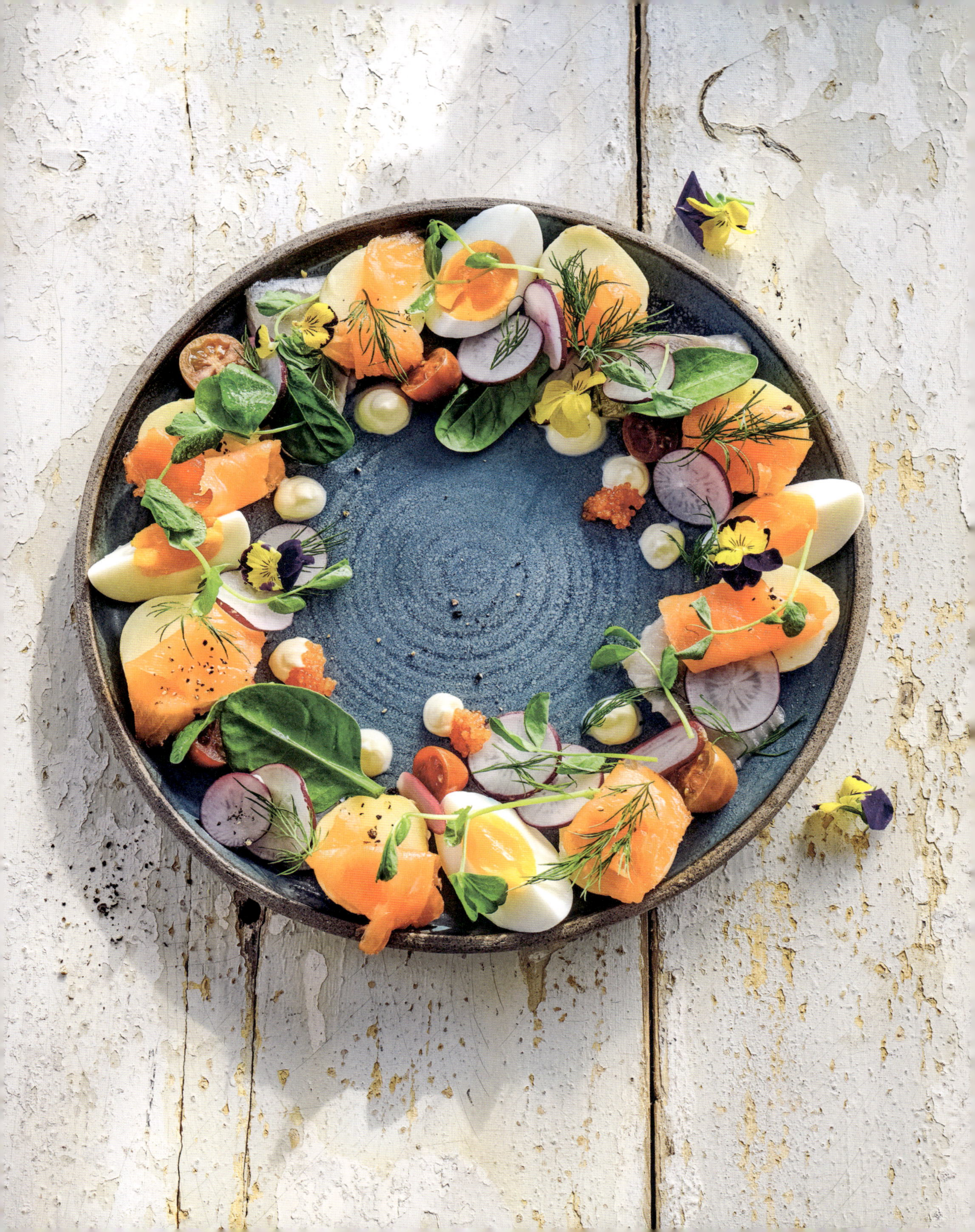

Cured salmon with dill

Gravad lax

Cured salmon is an essential part of a *smörgåsbord* in Sweden. It isn't hard to cure your own salmon, it just takes time. To make good *gravad lax*, invest in a good middle piece of salmon fillet, or even a whole side (leave the skin on). The most important thing is the freshness and quality of the fish, as well as the balance of the curing ingredients used. Dill is the traditional herb to use, but punchy flavours such as fennel and coriander/cilantro also work, or you might want to try beetroot/beets, citrus or even maple syrup.

1-kg/2¼-lb. piece of salmon fillet (middle bit, if available)
50 g/¼ cup salt
80 g/6 tablespoons white sugar
2 teaspoons white peppercorns, crushed
2 tablespoons gin, vodka or aquavit (optional)
2 bunches of dill (around 60 g/2 oz.)

DILL & MUSTARD DRESSING
2 tablespoons Swedish mustard (I like Slotts Skånsk, but if you can't get Swedish, go for a good Dijon mustard)
4 tablespoons finely chopped dill
1 tablespoon white wine vinegar
1 teaspoon sugar (if using Dijon, you may need to add a bit more sugar)
100 ml/⅓ cup plus 1 tablespoon rapeseed or other neutral oil
salt and freshly ground black pepper

SERVES 10

I always freeze the salmon for 48 hours below -18°C/0°F. Freezing kills most parasites, if any are present, so I think it's good practice to do this. Check with your fishmonger.

Defrost the salmon in the fridge before using. Once defrosted, check for bones by running very clean fingers across the fleshy side and using tweezers to pick out any stray bones you find. Cut the salmon across the middle into two equal pieces.

Mix together the salt, sugar and white peppercorns. Rub the alcohol (if using) and a bit of water over the fleshy sides, then rub in the salt, sugar and pepper mixture. Ensure all the flesh is covered.

Chop the dill (including stems) and place on top of one of the pieces on the flesh side. Place the other piece on top, flesh-side down, and wrap the fish tightly in clingfilm/plastic wrap. Place the salmon in a plastic bag and transfer to the fridge. Turn the bag over several times a day for the following 2–3 days to ensure the cure is even. It is ready when the flesh changes to slightly translucent.

Unwrap the fish and discard the herb filling (it's fine if some dill remains, but it should be mostly clear of rougher stalks).

Place the salmon skin-side down on a board and carve into thin slices, cutting through the fish with the knife held at a slight diagonal so that the skin is left behind. The fish will keep for several days stored in the fridge.

To make the dressing, whisk the mustard, dill, vinegar and sugar in a bowl with a good pinch of salt and pepper. Add the oil carefully as you whisk: start by adding a few drops, then begin steadily adding a thin stream of oil. It should emulsify the dressing as you continue to whisk. If you add it too quickly it may split. Keep whisking until you have a good, creamy consistency. Add a little bit more oil if it is too thick.

Serve the cured salmon drizzled with the dressing.

Breaded plaice & new potatoes

Fiskefilet med nye kartofler

When asked, Danes will often say that one of their favourite dishes is a form of fish and chips: fried flat fish with potatoes in some form. We make this when staying at our summer house. The fish in our local waters in Storebælt are flat fish – including plaice, dab and flounder – and the local fishmonger always has small fillets of these available, sold by the kilo.

Serve with new potatoes tossed in parsley and butter, or homemade fries or wedges. And always with a good dollop of Danish remoulade on the side. The fish can also be served as an open sandwich, either hot or just slightly warm. Butter a slice of rye bread, add the fish, then top with remoulade and a bit of lemon.

4 pieces of fillets of plaice or other flat fish
1 egg, lightly beaten
60 g/1⅔ cups panko breadcrumbs
butter and olive oil, for frying
buttered new potatoes or fries, green salad and lemon wedges, to serve (optional)
Danish Remoulade (see page 72), to serve

SERVES 4

Preheat the oven to 100°C/80°C fan/210°F/Gas ¼.

Rinse the fish and pat dry with paper towels. Prepare two wide shallow dishes, with the beaten egg in one and the breadcrumbs in the other. One by one, dip the pieces of fish first in the egg, then roll in the breadcrumbs to evenly coat on both sides and set aside.

In a large frying pan/skillet, heat up a good knob/pat of butter and a glug of oil. When hot, add the fish, skin-side down, and fry for 1 minute over a medium heat, then turn over and fry for a further 1–2 minutes, or until cooked through and the breadcrumbs are golden all over. You will probably need to fry in batches of 2–3 fillets, depending on the size of your pan.

Transfer the cooked fish to the warm oven until ready to serve alongside potatoes or fries and a green salad. Add lemon wedges for squeezing over and a generous spoonful of remoulade.

Swedish sandwich cake *Smörgåstårta*

The literal translation of 'sandwich cake' doesn't do justice to this dish. It is so much more than that: a big, bold sharing sandwich that can be the centrepiece of any festive *smörgåsbord*. *Smörgåstårta* tends to get a bad rap as many are still made to look more like Liberace's dream lunch than a stylish sandwich on a summer buffet table. The origin of the *Smörgåstårta* is said to be from 1950s America, and somehow the recipe travelled to the Nordics. Today, it is popular in Sweden, Iceland and Finland. You can make *Smörgåstårta* with meat, veg or fish. A good basic rule for choosing fillings is if you would eat this as a stand-alone sandwich, it can work as a sandwich cake.

9 thick square slices of white bread, exactly the same size, crusts cut off, buttered
120 g/½ cup full-fat cream cheese
120 g/½ cup mayonnaise
2–3 whole cucumbers

FIRST LAYER
150–200 g/5½–7 oz. mix of cooked prawns/shrimp and crayfish tails
1 shallot, finely chopped
1 tablespoon crème fraîche
1 tablespoon mayonnaise
squeeze of fresh lemon juice
finely chopped dill and chives
salt and freshly ground black pepper

SECOND LAYER
3 hard-boiled/cooked eggs
1 heaped tablespoon mayonnaise
1 heaped tablespoon crème fraîche
¼ teaspoon Dijon mustard
100 g/3½ oz. smoked salmon
squeeze of fresh lemon juice

GARNISH SUGGESTIONS
small prawns/shrimp
2 slices of smoked salmon
2 radishes, thinly sliced
4–5 cherry tomatoes
4–5 peas in pods
3–4 asparagus tips, lightly blanched
pea shoots and sprigs of fresh dill

mandolin slicer (or use a metal cheese planer and some patience)

SERVES 8–10

Make up the first layer by mixing all the ingredients together. To make the second layer, chop the eggs and mix with the mayo, crème fraîche and mustard. Season to taste and set both layers aside.

To assemble, place three slices of buttered bread on a serving tray (it's hard to move after assembly). Spread a good quantity of the first layer across the bread, as evenly as you can. It should be a nice thick layer that is not runny. Add three more buttered bread slices on top.

Add the second layer of small pieces of salmon drizzled with lemon juice. Then add the egg mayo, then add the last layer of bread. Carefully press down and secure the 'cake'. Some people prefer to cover and refrigerate it at this point to let it set, but you don't have to.

Make sure the sides are neat and straight (trim them, if necessary). Mix the cream cheese with the mayonnaise until smooth. Using a spatula, spread the mixture around the side of the sandwich and a thin layer on top. The straighter the sides of your base sandwich, the less mayo mix needed. You only need enough to have a covering that is sticky enough to hold the thin cucumber slices in place (too much becomes sickly). The leaner your filling and mayo spreading, the nicer the *smörgåstårta*.

Using a mandolin slicer, carefully slice the cucumbers thinly lengthways. Begin at one short end and start covering the sandwich with the cucumber slices, adding a new slice every 1.5 cm/⅝ inch, and continue until almost midway at the top. Then repeat from the other side. At the end, place two or three slices of cucumber on top to close the gap. You might need to use your fingers to press the slices down to make them stick better. At the end, cut any edges from the base to tidy.

To decorate the top, use your choice of prawns/shrimp, rolls of salmon, sliced radish and cherry tomato in a line on the top, and then add the opened pea pods, asparagus, pea shoots and dill. Refrigerate until ready to serve. Eat on the day of making.

TIP The fillings should all work together, and less is more when it comes to decoration.

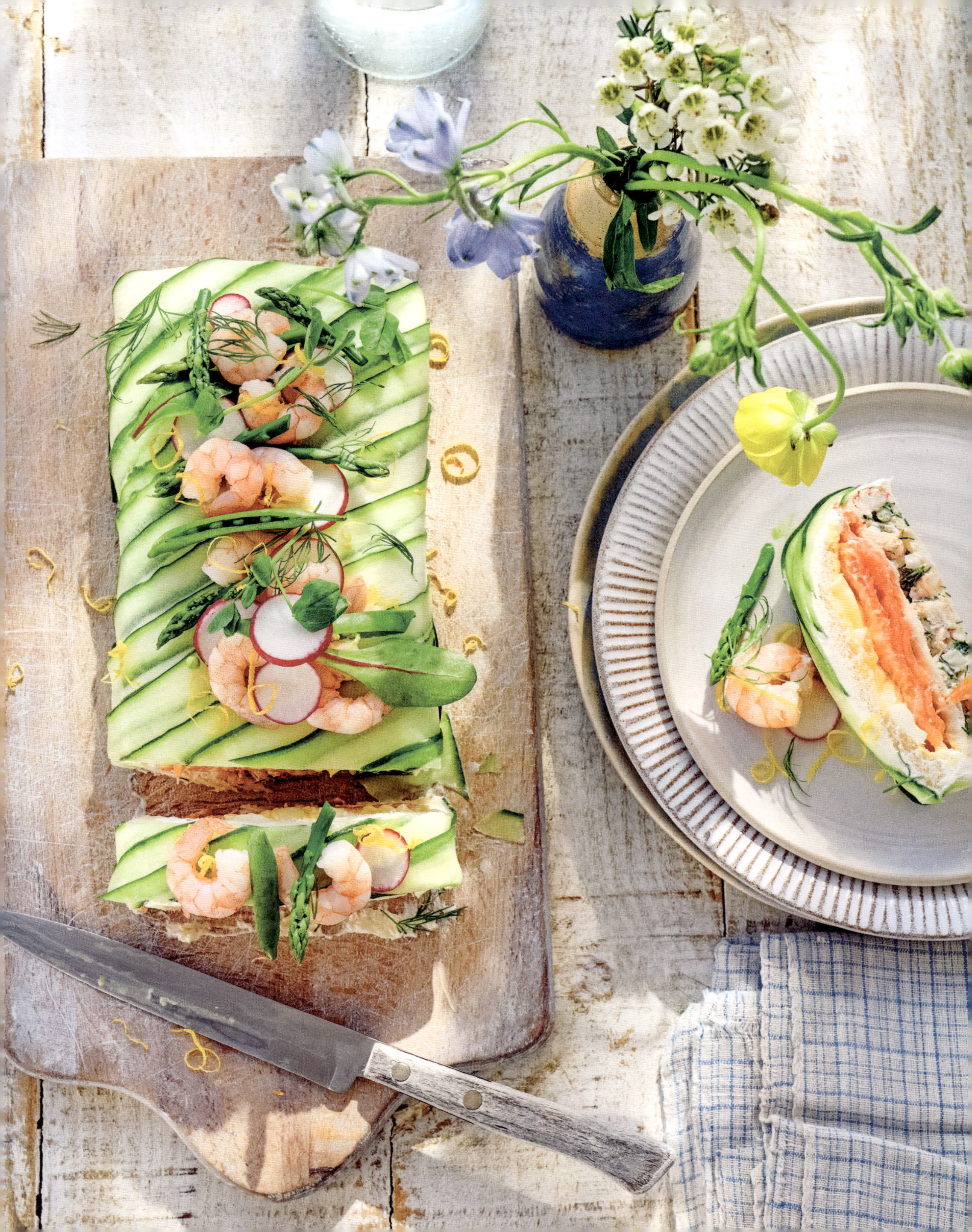

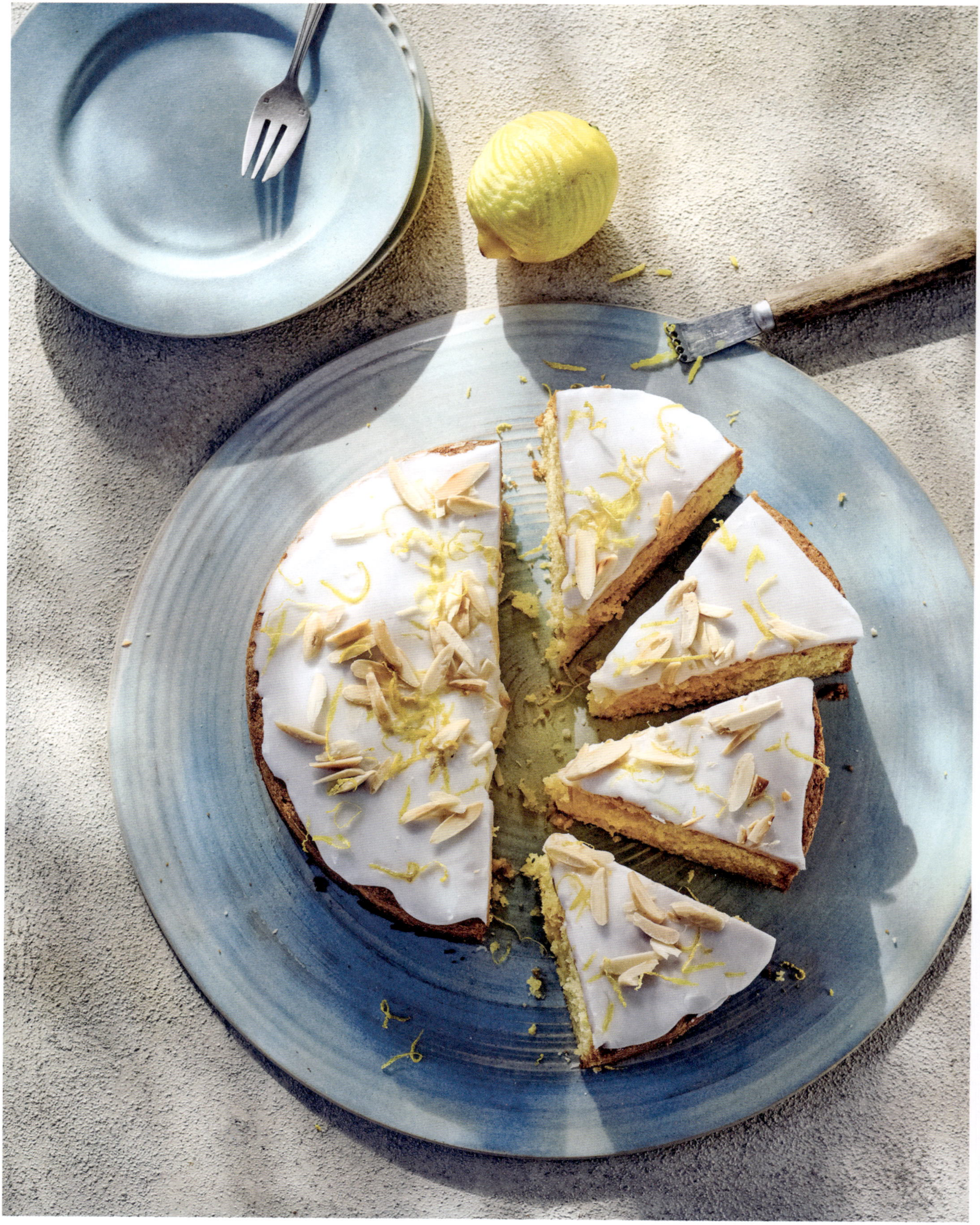

Danish lemon cake *Citronmåne*

Most Danes will remember this cake from their childhood. The name translates as 'lemon moon' and the cake got its name because it was always sold in half circles and was made famous by a supermarket cake producer in the 80s. Most of the time, we'd have the store-bought supermarket version as kids, so to be fair, that is where the nostalgia lies for me.

Over time, I found that this cake wasn't quite punchy enough, so I started adding lemon juice to the topping after baking (as often done on lemon drizzle loaves). Doing it this way means you can keep the icing less lemony overall, providing a sweet contrast to the tart cake. You may need more or less lemon juice, depending on the size of your lemons and taste preference.

200 g/1¾ sticks butter, softened

200 g/1 cup caster/granulated sugar, plus 20 g/5 teaspoons for the lemon syrup

100 g/3½ oz. Marzipan (see page 237 or use store-bought with a minimum 50% almond content)

seeds from 1 vanilla pod/bean or 1–2 teaspoons vanilla extract

4 eggs

200 g/1½ cups plain/all-purpose flour

2 teaspoons baking powder

a pinch of salt

grated zest and freshly squeezed juice of 1 good-sized lemon

ICING

150 g/1 cup icing/confectioner's sugar

1–3 tablespoons hot water

1–2 teaspoons freshly squeezed lemon juice

toasted chopped almonds and lemon zest, to decorate

round 23-cm/9-inch springform cake pan, lined with baking parchment

SERVES 8, GENEROUSLY

Preheat the oven to 190°C/170°C fan/375°F/Gas 5.

In a stand mixer or using a hand-held electric whisk, cream together the butter and sugar until pale and fluffy. Grate the marzipan into the mixture, add the vanilla and mix again. Add the eggs, one at a time, ensuring you incorporate fully between each addition and scraping down the sides of the bowl if necessary.

Combine the flour, baking powder and salt. Sift into the cake mixture and fold in with a spatula until combined. Add the lemon zest and half the juice and fold again. If the mixture seems too thick, you can add a bit more lemon juice.

Pour the mixture into the prepared pan and bake in the preheated oven for around 30–35 minutes or until a skewer inserted into the middle comes out clean (baking time depends on your oven and it may need a bit longer).

As soon as the cake is baked, remove from the oven and using a fork, prick some small holes across the top in random places. Mix juice from the remaining half of lemon (reserve a little for the icing) with a bit of sugar (allow to dissolve) to make a lemon syrup and pour over the top of the cake for extra lemon flavour – hold back a bit if the lemon is on the larger side.

Transfer the cake to a wire rack and leave to cool completely.

To make the icing, put the icing/confectioner's sugar in a bowl and add 2 tablespoons of hot water and 1 teaspoon of lemon juice, mixing in well. Add additional teaspoons of water or lemon juice slowly until you get to the consistency of thick, runny honey: spreadable, but not so liquid that it runs off the cake. If the icing becomes too runny, add a bit more sugar. Spread over the cooled cake and decorate with chopped almonds and lemon zest.

Swedish strawberry cake

Jordgubbstårta

To say that we Scandies are obsessed with strawberries during the summer season is an understatement. Those berries grown in that fresh Nordic air, when they finally pop out to greet us, are the sweetest most delicious berries.

Traditionally the Swedish strawberry cake can be made in many ways. Most often, it is round, with three layers and decorated with only berries and whipped cream – or berries, whipped cream and pastry cream (which is the version I prefer as I think the balance of the pastry cream makes it nicer). This version is made with just two layers of vanilla cake, in a larger rectangle, for a sharing cake on the buffet table. The filling is half-cream, half-pastry cream and full of chopped strawberries.

The top is decorated using a piping/pastry bag and some firmly whipped cream and a bit of patience – but you can, of course, also just spread whipped cream on top and decorate with cut or whole berries.

6 eggs

180 g/1 cup minus 1½ tablespoons caster/granulated sugar

1 teaspoon vanilla sugar or vanilla extract

180 g/1⅓ cups plain/all-purpose flour

a pinch of salt

1 teaspoon baking powder

25 g/1¾ tablespoons butter, melted and cooled

TO DECORATE

approx. 400–500 g/14–18 oz. strawberries

400 ml/1¾ cups whipping cream

2 tablespoons icing/confectioner's sugar

2 teaspoons vanilla extract

70 g/3½ tablespoons raspberry jam/preserve

½ quantity Pastry Cream (see page 237)

25 x 35-cm/8 x 14-inch cake pan, lined with baking parchment

piping/pastry bag fitted with a nozzle/tip

SERVES 8 GENEROUSLY

Preheat the oven to 180°C/160°C fan/350°F/Gas 4. You will need to make two layers, but you can bake them one at a time (unless you have two identical cake pans).

Beat together the eggs and sugar on high speed in a stand mixer fitted with a whisk attachment until the mixture reaches ribbon stage. Add the vanilla.

Combine the flour, salt and baking powder in a separate bowl. Sift into the egg mixture, little by little, carefully folding in using a figure-of-eight movement until incorporated. Pour the cooled melted butter down the side of the bowl and fold carefully again, trying not to knock out the air.

Pour half the mixture into the prepared cake pan. Bake in the preheated oven for about 6–8 minutes or until light golden brown. Remove from the oven and allow to cool slightly before removing the baking parchment and re-lining for the second layer. Repeat to bake layer two.

When both bases have cooled, tidy up the edges, ensuring two identical rectangles.

Chop three-quarters of the strawberries into 1–2-cm/½–¾-inch pieces. Slice the remaining strawberries.

Whip the cream with the icing/confectioner's sugar and vanilla until stiff. Place the first cake layer on your serving plate and spread the jam/preserve across.

Fold one-third of the whipped cream into the pastry cream and spread over the jam. Scatter the chopped strawberries across, then add the top layer of cake. Using a piping/pastry bag, pipe dollops of cream all over the top layer to cover, and decorate with sliced strawberries.

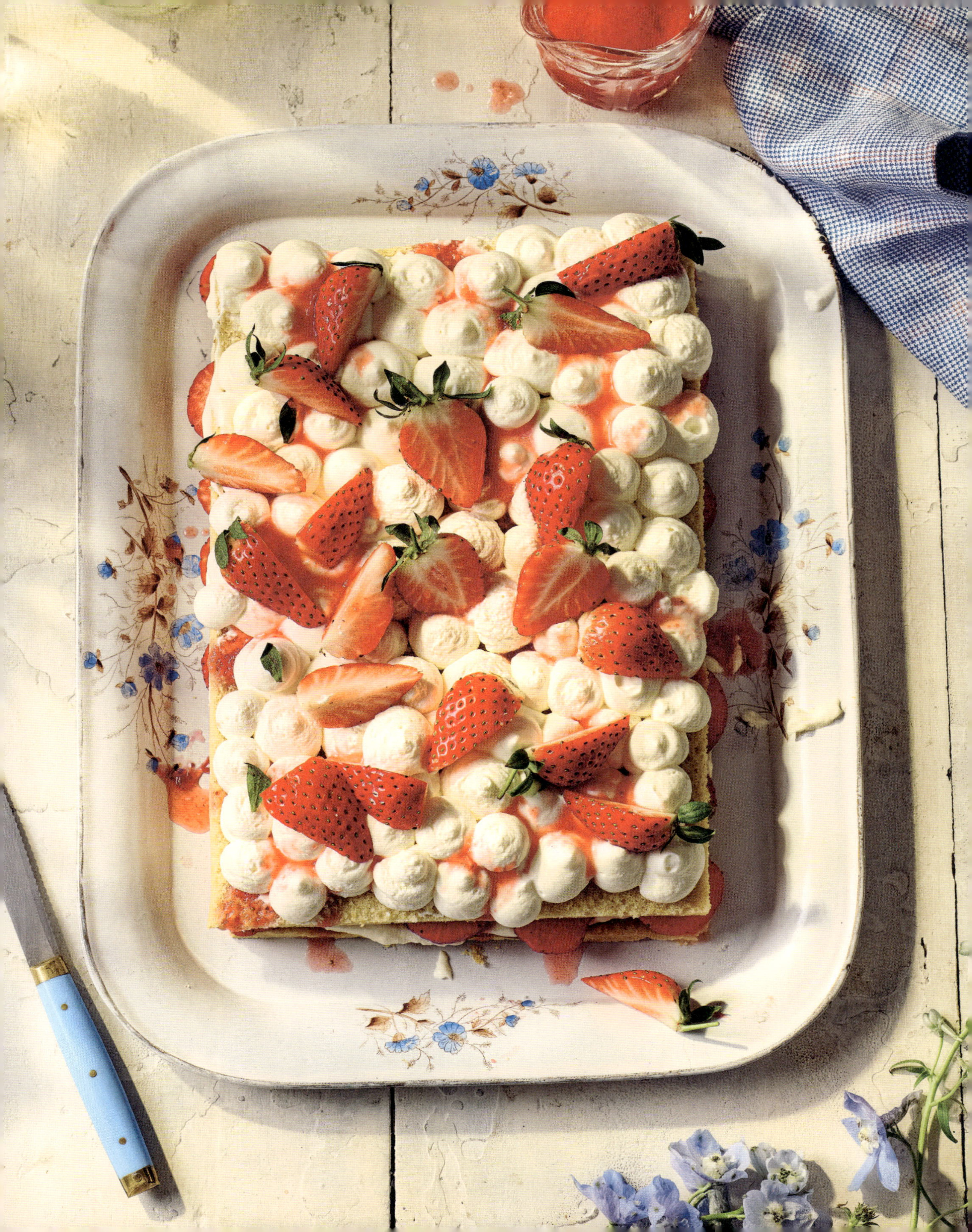

By the time July comes around, we've forgotten that winter exists. As temperatures reach the low 30s (or mid 80s in Fahrenheit) in the south (a little cooler in the north), we don our bathing suits and enjoy our lakes and beaches to the fullest. We picnic, barbecue and maximise our outdoors time while trying not to be eaten alive by the ruthless insects known as 'midges'. Factories and workplaces tend to reduce their operations to allow people a long break. Our coastlines are almost festival-like in mood, as people party, sunbathe and rejuvenate.

Tomatoes are ripe and we buy paper bags of sugar peas in their pods from roadside honesty stands and eat them raw, like the most delicious candy. Wild strawberries are in abundance – children thread them on pieces of string to enjoy. The meadows around our beaches and forests stand in full bloom with poppies, wild cornflowers, sea thrift, ox-eye daisies and wild bluebells. In the north, those in the know will start to visit their secret cloudberry patches in the hope of hitting this shortest of harvest seasons, picking as much as they can to make enough jam and syrup to last all of the coming winter. Impossible to cultivate, these bulbous, bright-orange berries are the treasures of the Arctic in the height of the summer.

JULY

THE SUMMER COTTAGE

Midsummer gives way for full summer by early July. As everything blooms and school holidays are in full swing, many prepare for the customary three weeks off work known as the *industriferien* ('the industry holiday'). Not much gets done during this time and many workplaces and factories run with skeleton teams to allow people to take a proper break from day-to-day life.

For many people, the holiday is when they spend time at their summer cottages. While it sounds extravagant to have two houses, this is quite a normal thing across the Nordics. Summer cottages are mostly only built for summer use and not made for full-time living during the winter months. Being small, not insulated and often remote makes a summer house an affordable option for many.

A Dane would refer to their house simply as *sommerhus*. To a Norwegian it's a *hytte* and to a Swede it's a *stuga*. Most of these houses are built of wood and located far from towns, near seas, lakes or fjords, offering a welcome escape from daily life and a chance to spend more time in nature. In fact, to many people, the more basic and remote, the better.

The summer cottage lifestyle is not a new thing: many are passed down from parents and grandparents and often form a big part of both our children's and our parents' childhoods. More often than not, these summer cottages are shared in the same family across siblings and generations.

While most have running water and flushing toilets (especially in Denmark, as it's small and well connected), some cottages in Norway and Sweden's remote areas do not, which is all part of their charm (for some). Lack of phone signal can also be a bonus, forcing not just kids but also parents to take a proper step back from being online

all the time. The cottages are rarely big – usually just one or two bedrooms, with kids sharing in bunks. It's a place for mismatched crockery, old flea-market finds and a spice rack that still holds a jar of paprika from 1998. Everything is centred around spending time together in one open-plan space.

Time at a summer cottage is never about being indoors, it's about exploring nature. The storage shed of any respectable cottage will be well stocked with, for example, hiking gear, fishing rods and stuff for boating (plus a selection of blow-up beach balls that are all full of holes). The important Norwegian term *friluftsliv*, meaning 'open-air living', is valued across all the Nordic countries. We move from the inside to the outside in the summer and spend as many hours as we can feeling calmer and more connected to the land and each other. It feels very mindful and purposeful at the same time. *Friluftsliv* was introduced by the playwright Henrik Ibsen in 1859, when he discussed the value of spending time in remote locations for spiritual and physical wellbeing.

To me, food is a very important part of our annual summer weeks at our little wooden cottage. Our family is large, so we spend time planning meals, picking up fresh fish or meat and hoping that we can forage enough blackberries to make a crumble to feed everyone. Every memory is centred around our kitchen and my mother would always be taking full charge of the delegation of tasks (someone always had to scrub the darn potatoes). Every meal, from breakfast to lunch and dinner, is enjoyed outside. Every moment of precious daylight is spent running, swimming, chatting and playing games. I feel as if the summer months are all about collecting as much daylight as possible for our souls to store up and preserve, to help us when the darkness returns.

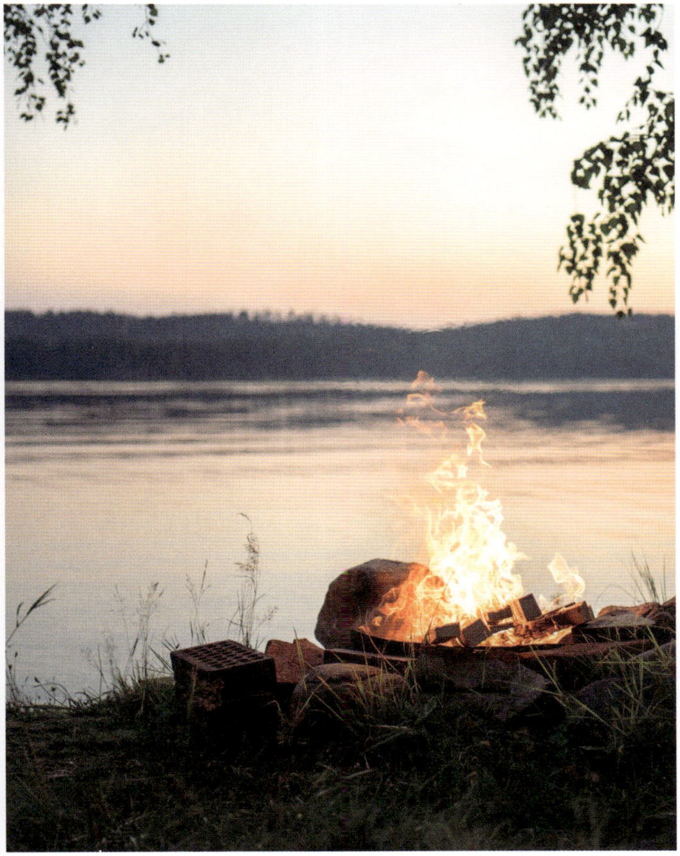

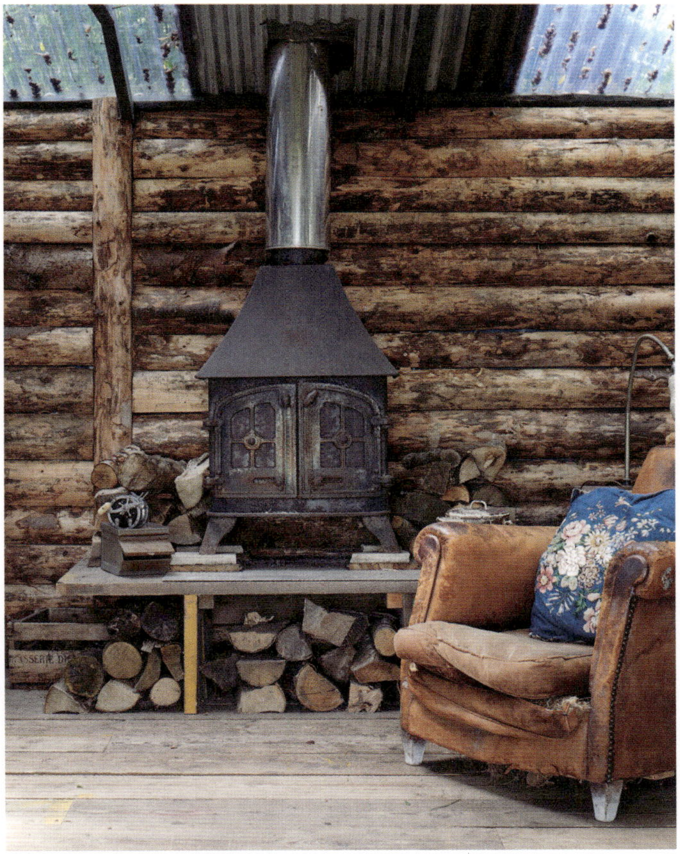

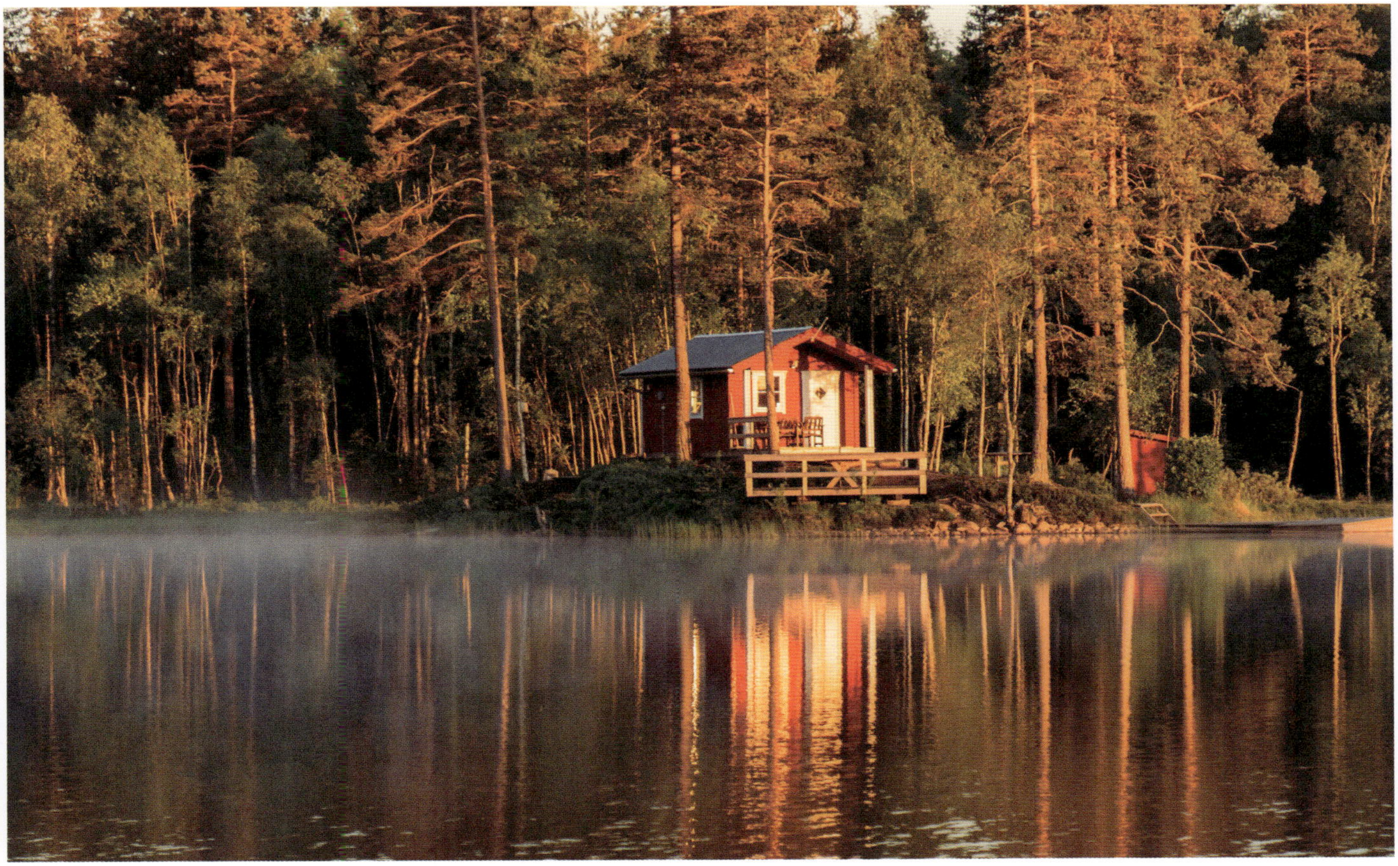

Hot-smoked trout & dill potato salad

Varmrökt laxöring sallad

A simple go-to summer salad which uses up leftover cooled new potatoes. Vary the vegetables as your fridge dictates, and you can also change up the fish from trout to hot-smoked, cured or smoked salmon. What brings this dish together is the freshness of the ingredients and the tang from the dill dressing.

- 3–4 cooked, cooled new potatoes, sliced (more if they are on the small side – 150 g/5½ oz. in total)
- 1 quantity Dill Dressing (see page 132)
- 50 g/1¾ oz. green beans, blanched and cut into bite-sized pieces
- 50 g/1¾ oz. green asparagus, blanched, cut into bite-sized pieces
- 6–7 cherry tomatoes, halved
- 1 small Gem lettuce or similar crisp leaves
- 170–200 g/6–7 oz. hot-smoked trout
- 1 small shallot, sliced into rings
- pea shoots or dill sprigs, to garnish

SERVES 2

Coat the potatoes with some of the dressing and set aside.

Arrange the vegetables, leaves and potatoes on one large plate or two individual plates. Flake over the fish. Finish with the shallot rings, pea shoots or dill sprigs. Pour over the remaining dressing and serve.

TIP Try adding a cut boiled/cooked egg for a more substantial dish.

Green salad with grandma dressing

Salat med mormordressing

'Grandma dressing' is something that all Danes know how to make. Essentially, it's a bit of cream, whisked with lemon juice and seasoning, then poured over fresh summer green salad leaves. When talking about traditional comfort food, you will often hear Danes mention *Mormormad* – literally 'grandma food'. Even if all you have is a head of salad leaves, this dressing just works. Simple and tasty.

- 1–2 Gem lettuce or other green salad leaves
- 2 baby cucumbers, sliced thinly lengthways
- a handful of fresh green peas, plus 6–8 sugar snap peas in the pod, open halfway
- 3 thinly sliced radishes, pea shoots or other herby topping, to garnish

DRESSING
- 100 ml/⅓ cup plus 1 tablespoon whipping cream
- 1 teaspoon sugar
- 2–3 tablespoons freshly squeezed lemon juice, to taste
- salt and freshly ground black pepper

Gently whisk the dressing ingredients together to combine and season to taste.

Arrange the vegetables in a serving bowl. Drizzle with some dressing just before serving. Garnish with radishes, pea shoots or herbs. Serve the remaining dressing on the side.

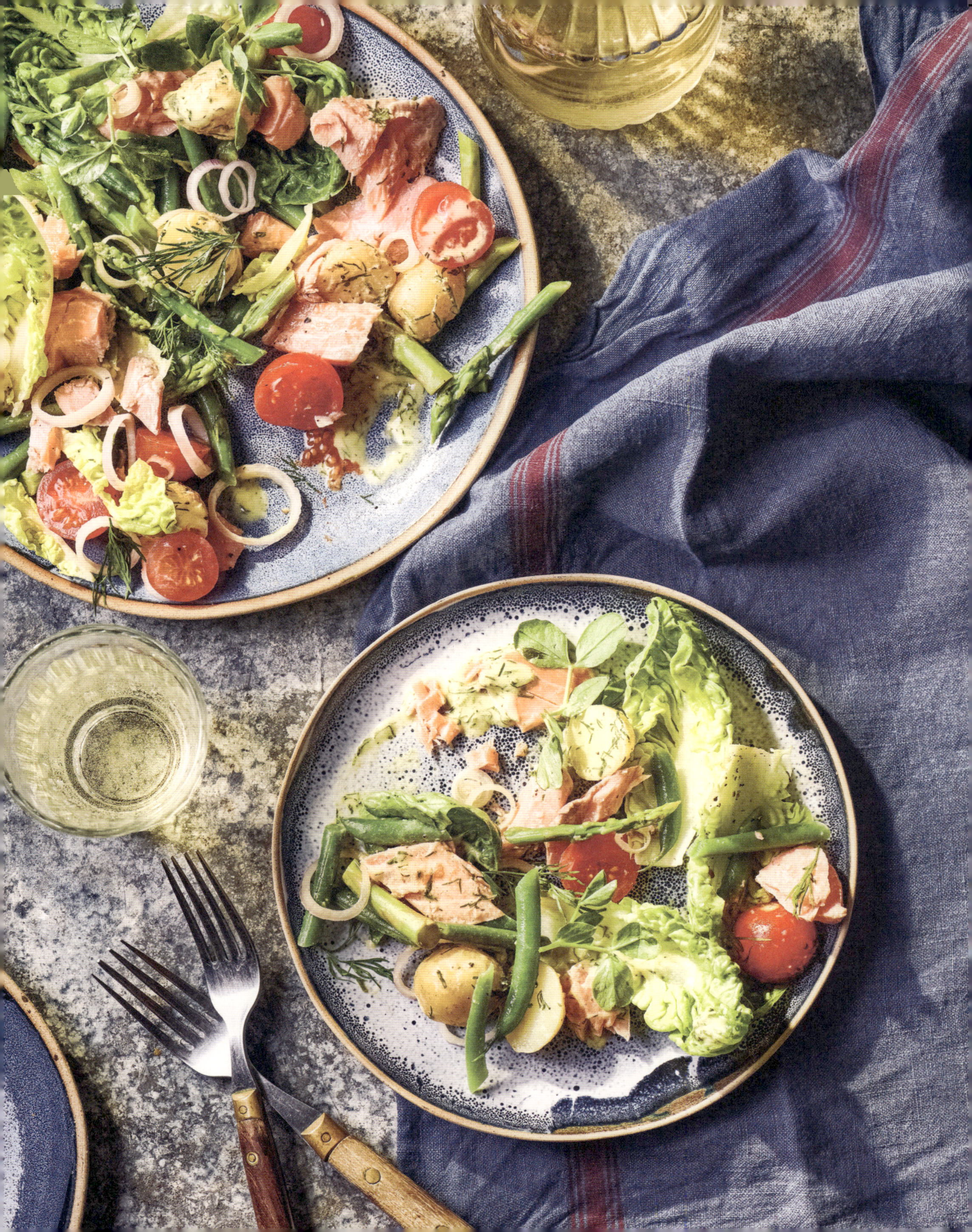

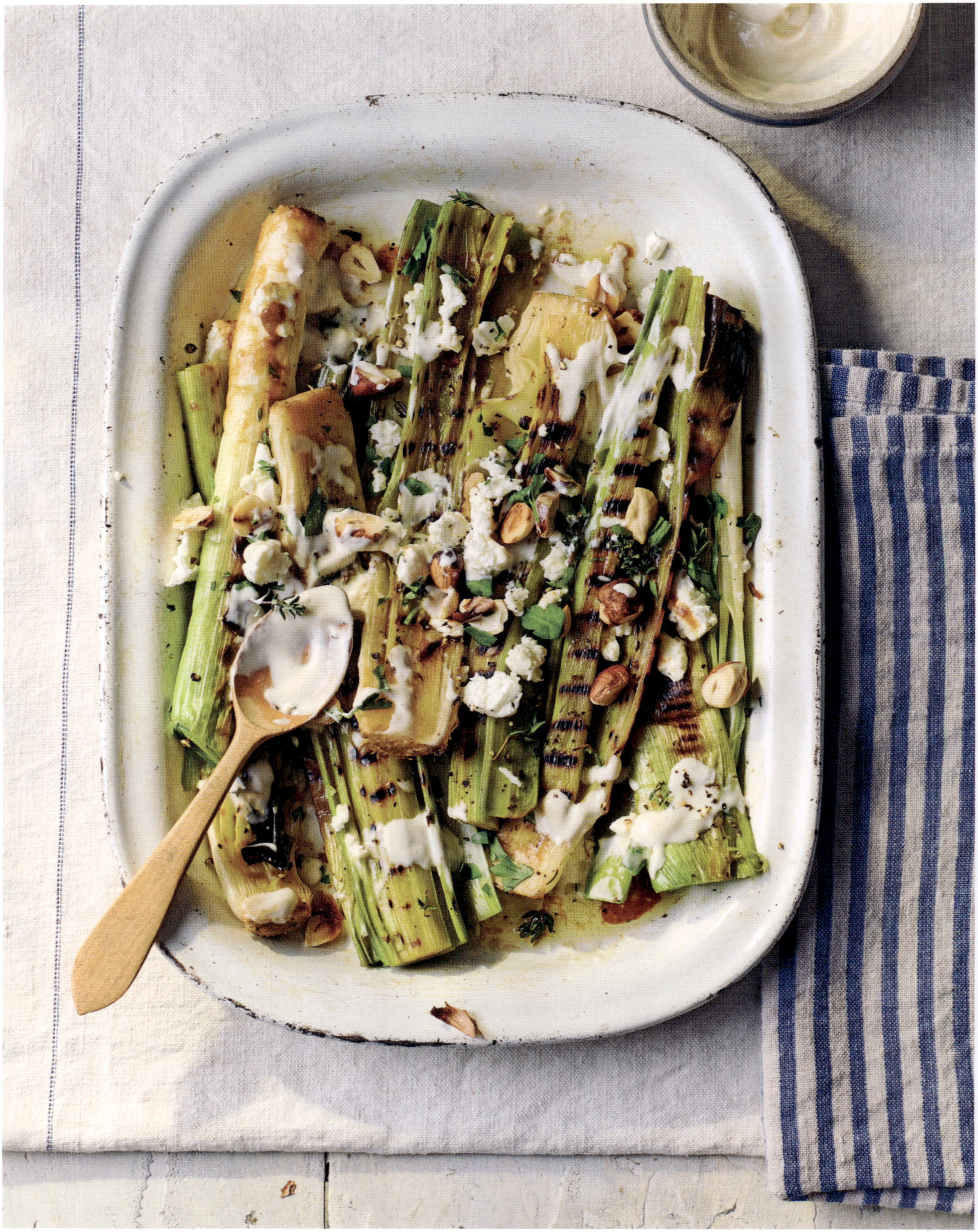

Pan-roasted leeks with hazelnuts

Smørstegte porrer med hasselnødder

This is a side I make so often at home. I just love leeks that are soft, crispy and buttery all at the same time. I serve this in the roasting pan, adding the dressing and the nuts just before serving. The cooking time varies depending on the size of the leeks – do test before serving and leave in the pan over the heat for a bit longer if not quite cooked through.

20 g/1½ tablespoons butter
olive oil
8 leeks, green bits cut off and halved lengthways
2 sprigs of fresh thyme
1 teaspoon brown sugar
50 g/1¾ oz. feta cheese or goat's cheese
30 g/1 oz. toasted hazelnuts, roughly chopped
2 tablespoons freshly chopped flat-leaf parsley
salt and freshly ground black pepper

DRESSING
3 tablespoons Greek yogurt
2 tablespoons freshly squeezed lemon juice
1 tablespoon tahini

SERVES 4

Melt the butter in a large pan that fits all the leeks in one single layer (tightly packed is fine, as long as it's a single layer) and add a small glug of oil, too. Add the leeks, cut side down, season with salt and pepper, add the thyme and sprinkle the brown sugar over.

Cook over a medium heat for around 8 minutes until the leeks start to char. Turn the leeks over and cook for another 7–8 minutes over a low heat. Keep checking to see if the leeks are tender– if in smaller pieces, they will need less cooking time.

To make the dressing, mix the yogurt with the lemon juice and tahini. Add water, as needed, to make a smooth, pourable dressing. Season with salt and pepper and taste – it might need a little more lemon juice to contrast with the sweet leeks.

Serve the leeks in the pan, with the feta or goat's cheese crumbled across the middle, dressing poured over and toasted hazelnuts on top. Finish with the chopped parsley.

Three potato salads
Tre kartoffelsalater

We are the potato people. Especially when summer comes around, we Scandinavians become obsessed with all things new potato – potato salad, potatoes with butter, cold potatoes, hot potatoes ...

Potato & dill
Potatis med dill

This potato salad is the perfect one for a summer picnic. The dressing is tangy and fragrant and keeps well, even when the potatoes are served cold.

75 ml/⅓ cup sunflower oil or other neutral oil
2 tablespoons white wine vinegar
1 tablespoon Dijon mustard
1 tablespoon sugar
1 large or 2 small shallots, very finely chopped
20–g/¾-oz. bunch of fresh dill, finely chopped
salt and freshly ground black pepper

You can use slightly warm potatoes or cooled ones straight out of the fridge, but dress just before serving for best results. For the dressing, whisk the oil, vinegar, mustard and sugar until the sugar has dissolved, then fold in the shallot and dill. Season to taste, then toss the dressing with the potatoes and ensure they are evenly covered.

Creamy potato salad
Kartoffelsalat

This creamy potato salad works well at both picnics and barbecues. If you prefer something creamier, increase the mayo; or for a tangier salad, up the yogurt.

6–7 spring onions/scallions, sliced
75 g/2½ oz. chopped pickled cucumber
10 radishes, sliced
100 g/½ cup Greek yogurt
100 g/½ cup mayonnaise
1 teaspoon Dijon mustard
20–g/¾-oz. bunch of chives, chopped
salt and freshly ground black pepper
crispy onions (store bought), for topping
pickle juice or lemon juice (optional)

Mix everything together (except the crispy onions and a little of the chives) and leave in the fridge for a few hours for the flavours to mingle before serving. Toss the potatoes with the dressing and top with the remaining chives and some crispy onions on top. If you need more zing, add pickle juice or lemon juice.

Dill pesto
Dillpesto

I love using dill in a nut-based pesto. This is a potato salad with slightly bitter notes. You can vary the notes depending on your taste, and certain nuts will result in a slightly sweeter pesto – I make this using anything from walnuts to pine nuts.

50 g/1¾ oz. hazelnuts
20-g/¾-oz. bunch of fresh dill
15-g/½ oz. bunch of fresh parsley
50 g/1¾ oz. spinach
25 g/⅞ oz. Parmesan or Västerbotten cheese
1 tablespoon freshly squeezed lemon juice (or more, to taste)
125 ml/½ cup oil
salt and freshly ground black pepper

In a small food processor, combine all the ingredients except the oil and seasoning and pulse well. Add the oil and seasoning and pulse again. Fold with either warm or cold potatoes.

All dressings are sufficient for 1 kg/ 2 lb. 4 oz. cooked new potatoes.

ALL SERVE 4–6 AS A SIDE

Three herring dressings
Tre forskellige sild

No *smörgåsbord* at any time of the year is complete without pickled herring. Whilst you can pickle your own fish, most people don't (me included). I use a good plain herring and then simply make dressings to fit the season and taste. Nordic pickled herrings come in a sweeter brine than Dutch, Scottish or Eastern European pickled herring, so I recommend you try to buy a plain onion herring from Scandinavia. Drain it, make a dressing and leave to mingle for a little while and you're good to go. Experiment with herbs and vegetables and fruit – whatever takes your fancy.

Always serve dressed herring at the beginning of the meal along with a shot of chilled aquavit (if you're so inclined).

Roe herring
Skärgårdssill

This is a Swedish favourite.

50 ml/¼ cup mayonnaise
100 ml/½ cup crème fraîche or sour cream
3 tablespoons finely chopped chives
3 tablespoons finely chopped dill
½ spring onion/scallion, finely sliced (both white and green bits)
50 g/1¾ oz. red lumpfish roe, plus extra to garnish
a squeeze of fresh lemon juice

Mix all the ingredients in a bowl, then season to taste. Stir in the drained herring. Serve with extra roe spooned on top.

All dressings are for 250 g/ 9 oz. pickled herring (drained weight – standard size for most ABBA herring, which is the easiest brand to find outside Scandinavia).

ALL SERVE 2–3 AS PART OF A SMÖRGÅSBORD

Mustard herring
Senapssill

Probably the most popular dressing of them all.

2 tablespoons grainy sweet mustard
1 teaspoon Dijon mustard
1 tablespoon caster/granulated sugar
2 tablespoons white wine vinegar
2 tablespoons double/heavy cream
1 tablespoon crème fraîche
1 small shallot, finely chopped
100 ml/7 tablespoons vegetable oil
2 tablespoons freshly chopped dill
1 tablespoon freshly chopped chives
salt and freshly ground black pepper

In a bowl, mix all the ingredients together (except the oil and herbs). Slowly pour in the oil while whisking continuously so that the sauce emulsifies. Add the herbs, then add the drained herring.

Saffron pickled herring
Saffranssill

Swedes love anything saffron for Christmas, but I love saffron all year round.

150 ml/¾ cup crème fraîche
50 ml/¼ cup mayonnaise
0.4 g (standard jar size) saffron strands
1 tablespoon hot milk
1 apple, chopped into small pieces
a pinch of paprika
1 small garlic clove, crushed
a few drops of freshly squeezed lemon or orange juice, to taste (I really like orange and saffron, but lemon is fine)
2 tablespoons freshly chopped chives, to garnish

Grind the saffron using a pestle and mortar, then dissolve in the hot milk, to bring out the colour and flavour. Mix all the ingredients together and add the drained herring. Serve with chopped chives on top.

JULY 133

Brunch dishes

Brunch opskrifter

Brunch is huge across Scandinavia. We love a *smörgåsbord* of options on our table – plenty of smaller plates, enjoying a bit of everything. If you visit Copenhagen, many cafés offer tapas-style brunches, where you choose four or five small options from a large menu (for yourself), in a pick'n'mix style that is delivered on a board. It's a grazing style brunch, perfect for lazy *hyggelige* weekend mornings with family or friends.

A typical Danish brunch at home has some form of oat-based bowls or granolas with yogurt or skyr and fresh berries, when available, or compotes; some form of eggs; maybe some mini sausages or streaky/fatty bacon or some smoked salmon. There'll certainly be sliced cheeses fresh rolls, rye bread and pastries, and maybe a cheeky weekend cocktail. Nordic people drink more coffee than anyone in the world, so no brunch is complete without a pot of very strong filter coffee.

Did you know that breakfast is called *frukost* in Sweden and Norway, but *frokost* in Danish means lunch, not breakfast? It does get confusing! (The Danish word for breakfast is *morgenmad* – and the word for brunch in all the languages is… brunch.)

Overnight oats
Køleskabsgrød

We make this at ScandiKitchen – it's Riina's recipe and is so wholesome. Vary the berries as you like, or use compotes. Store-bought caramel is fine (or use the recipe on page 38).

200 g/1 cup Greek yogurt
250 g/1 cup oat milk
80 g/1 cup porridge/rolled oats
20 g/2 tablespoons chia seeds
1 grated apple
1 teaspoon vanilla sugar
1 teaspoon freshly squeezed lemon juice

SERVES 4

Mix all the ingredients together and let sit overnight in the fridge.

Serve with berries or apple compote, some salted caramel (see page 38) and some of the seed granola (see opposite).

Cinnamon bun French toast
Fattiga kanelbullar

It's rare, but it happens: leftover cinnamon buns. Not surprisingly, these make excellent French toast – I love serving with a vanilla syrup on top.

3 eggs
a pinch of salt
½ teaspoon ground cinnamon
50 g/heaping ⅓ cup plain/all-purpose flour
a small pinch of bicarbonate of soda/baking soda
125 ml/½ cup whole milk
4 Cinnamon Buns (see page 194), sliced horizontally
butter, for frying
Greek yogurt and fresh berries, to serve

SERVES 4

Mix the eggs with the salt, cinnamon, flour and bicarbonate of soda/baking soda. Gradually pour in the milk and stir to a smooth batter. Place the bun slices in a bowl and pour the batter over. Mix to ensure all pieces are generously coated. Cover and leave for 10 minutes to soak through.

Heat some butter in a frying pan/skillet, then fry the pieces of bun until cooked through and golden on both sides, adding more butter as needed. Arrange two on each plate, top with yogurt and berries. Vanilla or maple syrup goes well on this, too.

Jon-Anders' Nordic Bloody Mary
Bloody Mary med aquavit

What's a Scandi breakfast without a bit of dill? This is such a lovely twist on the traditional Bloody Mary – and with the hot sauce, it has a bit of a kick, too.

50 ml/1¾ oz. dill aquavit, from Aalborg Aquavit (see note)
a squeeze of fresh lemon juice
a few drops of tabasco (Jon-Anders prefers Mexican hot sauce)
a pinch of celery salt
a pinch of freshly ground black pepper
a few drops of Worcestershire sauce, to taste
a dash of sherry (optional)
tomato juice, to taste
celery sticks and sprigs of dill, to decorate (optional)

SERVES 1

Add all the ingredients except the celery and dill to a tall glass with ice, stir and taste. Serve immediately, decorated with celery and dill, if using.

NOTE If you cannot get this particular dill aquavit, you can flavour vodka with fresh dill (takes 2–3 days). Jon-Anders likes to add a small piece of horseradish to this, too. Remove both the dill and horseradish before using.

Seed granola
Granola med frø

50 g/3½ tablespoons coconut oil
2 tablespoons honey
2 tablespoons maple syrup
1 teaspoon vanilla extract
1 tablespoon dark brown sugar
1 teaspoon ground cinnamon
100 g/1 cup jumbo oats
50 g/1 cup coconut chips
200 g/7 oz. mixed seeds (such as pumpkin/pepita, sunflower, sesame and linseed/flaxseed)

SERVES 8–10

Our family's favourite breakfast topping (and also one we use at ScandiKitchen), this contains no nuts, but you can use a mixture of whatever nuts and seeds you like, just as long as the overall quantity stays the same.

Preheat the oven to 170°C/150°C fan/340°F/Gas 4. In a baking pan, combine the oil, honey, maple syrup, vanilla, sugar and cinnamon and pop in the oven to melt. Once hot, add the oats, coconut and seeds and mix. Return to the oven and bake for 5 minutes, then stir – repeat this three times. Remove from the oven and leave to crisp up. Store in an airtight container.

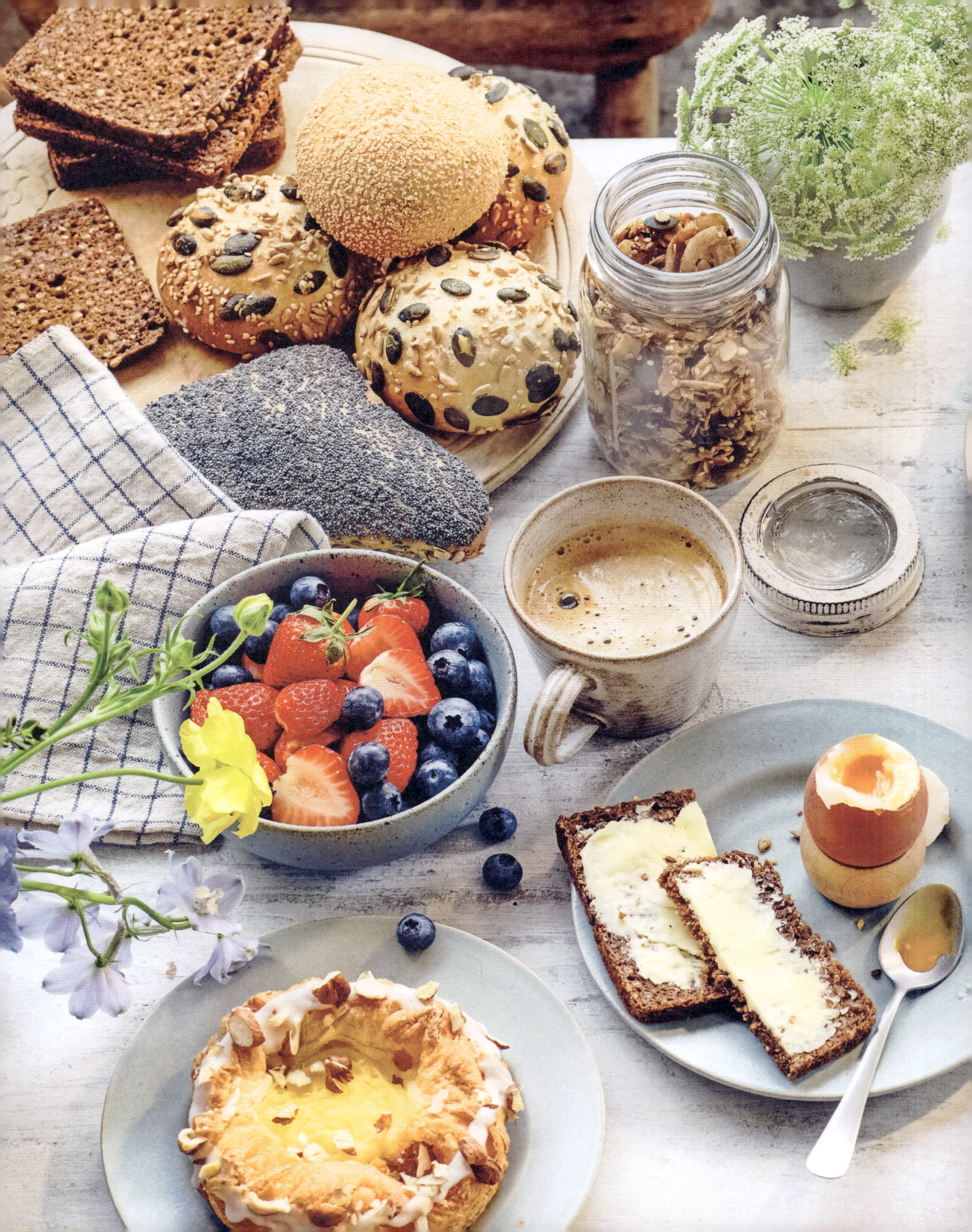

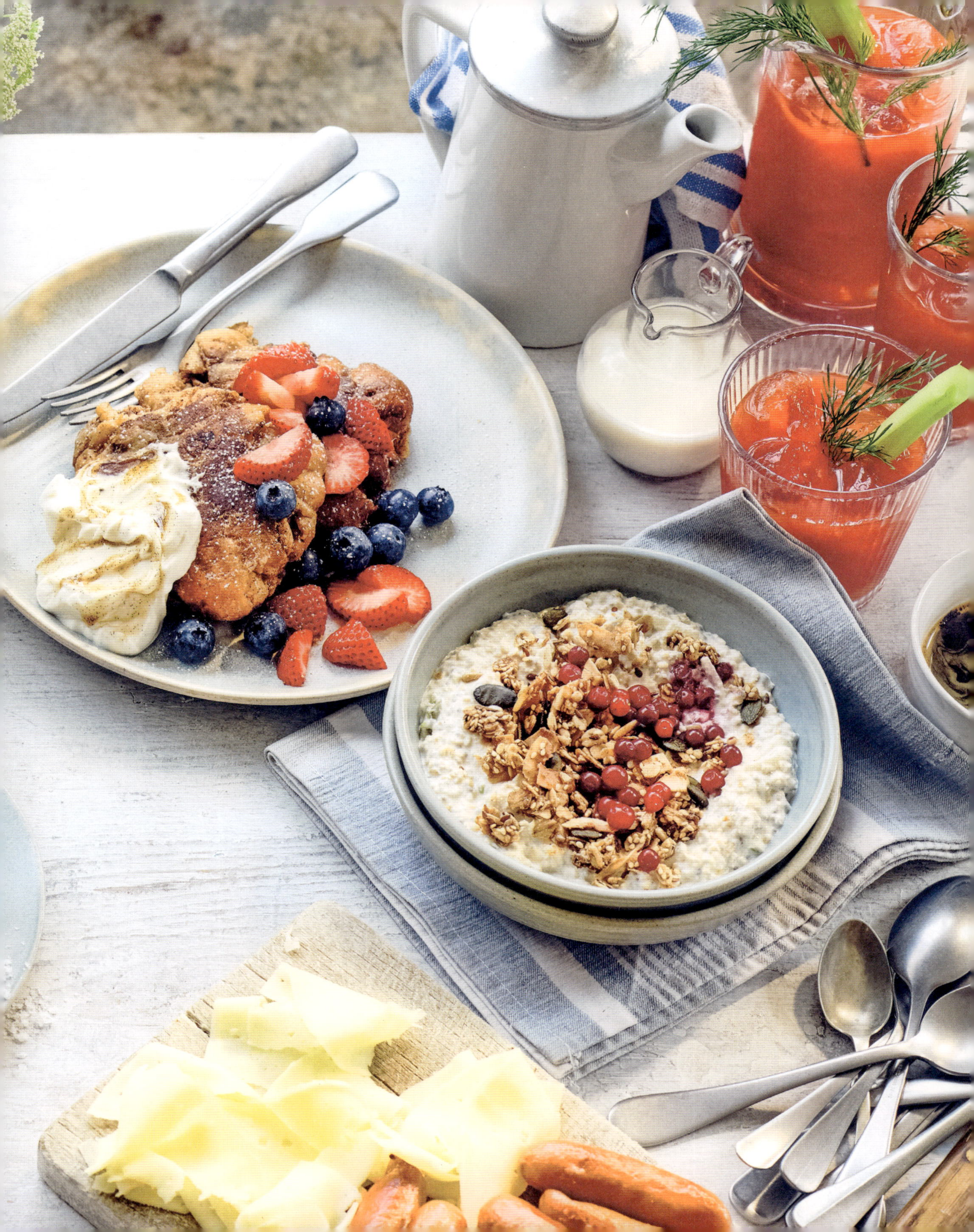

Danish brunch rolls

Rundstykker

Every baker in Denmark makes many varieties of these delicious brunch rolls, and a weekend breakfast/brunch in Denmark is one of my great joys: lots of rolls, toppings, sides and plenty of strong filter coffee, ending with a sweet pastry.

This batch makes 12 rolls. If I've got family over and I'm making brunch rolls for a big weekend breakfast, I often double the recipe and make all three toppings (eight of each topping). Essentially, the difference is only the toppings and shaping. If you do not have spelt flour, simply replace with white bread flour – it works just as well.

25 g/1 oz. fresh yeast
350 ml/1½ cups lukewarm water
1 tablespoon caster/granulated sugar
3 tablespoons neutral oil
150 g/1 cup light spelt flour
350 g/2½ cups white bread flour
2 teaspoons salt
milk, for brushing
seeds, according to the topping you wish to add (see method)

MAKES 12

NOTE To replicate *rundstykker* buns exactly like those in the Danish bakeries, you need to add a baking enzyme to the dough. It is absolutely possible to do at home, however, most of us don't really do this nor happen to have enzymes in our cupboards (unless we are quite serious about baking). For this reason, I've chosen to make a recipe without these additives, but as close to the real things as is possible without it.

In a stand mixer fitted with a dough hook, combine the yeast, lukewarm water and sugar and mix until dissolved. Add the oil. Add the spelt flour, then add the white flour, little by little. You may not need all of it – you want to end up with a sticky dough. Add the salt only after a few minutes of kneading. Once your dough is done, leave to rise, covered, until doubled in size – around 45 minutes. Turn out onto a floured surface and knead again.

TOPPING ONE: RUNDSTYKKE
Roll into 12 neat rolls. Brush each roll with a little milk and dip into a bowl of white poppy seeds (use black if you can't get hold of white poppy seeds) so that the top is completely covered.

TOPPING TWO: MIXED SEEDS
Roll into 12 neat rolls. Brush each roll with a little milk and dip into a bowl of mixed seeds – equal parts pumpkin/pepita, sesame and sunflower – so that the top is completely covered.

TOPPING THREE: SKAGENSLAPPER
Put sunflower seeds in one bowl and black poppy seeds in another. Roll out the dough and cut into 12 triangles. Brush each side with milk and dip one side in poppy seeds and the other in sunflower seeds, ensuring that a good amount of seeds stick to the roll.

Place the seeded rolls on a baking sheet lined with baking parchment and leave to rise for a further 25 minutes.

Preheat the oven to 250°C/230°C fan/500°F/Gas 9 and add a baking sheet to preheat. Turn on the steam function if your oven has this; a heatproof bowl of water placed at the bottom of your oven also works.

When the rolls are ready to bake, slide the baking parchment off the baking sheet and onto the really hot oven sheet. Immediately turn the oven down to 240°C/220°C fan/450°F/Gas 8 and bake for 8 minutes, then turn the steam function off (or remove the water tray). Continue baking until done, around 4–5 minutes (the rolls should sound hollow when you tap underneath). Remove from the oven and allow to cool. These rolls freeze well.

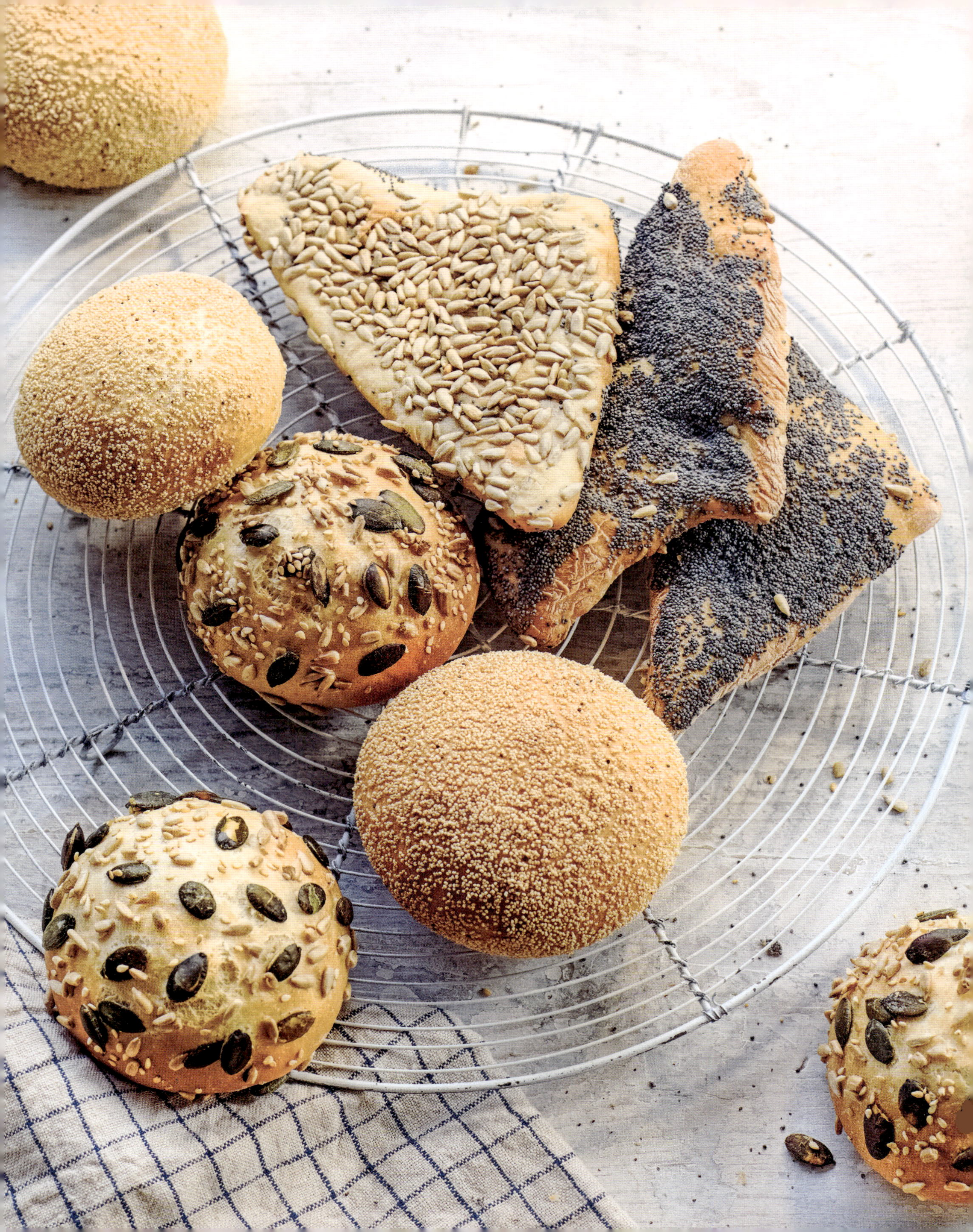

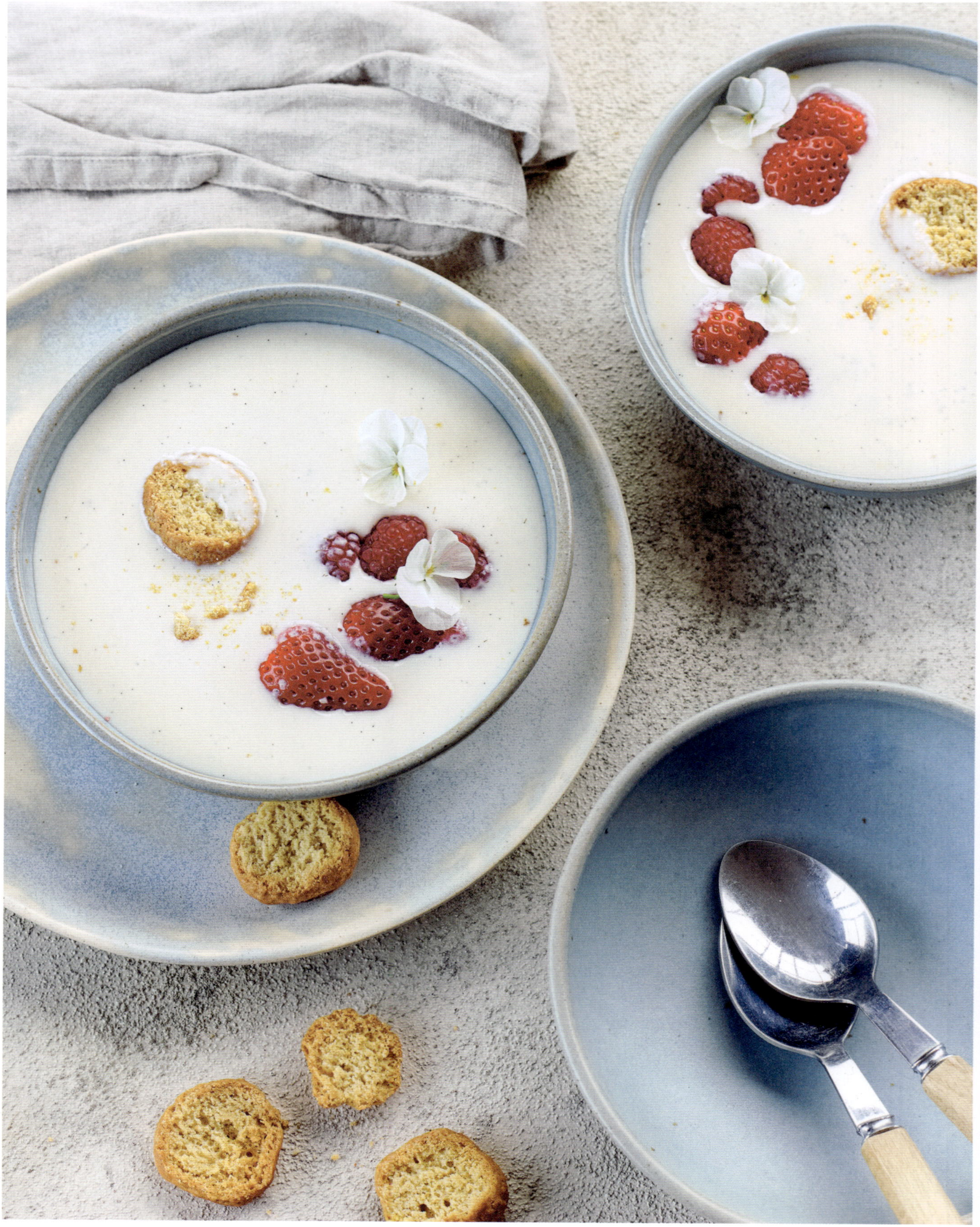

Danish midsummer soup with cardamom biscuits

Koldskål

This recipe is hard to explain to those not familiar with it. Is it a soup? Well, yes, it is – on account that it's liquid and you eat it with a spoon. Is it a dessert? Also, yes. *Koldskål* means 'cold bowl' which really doesn't sound that great (nevertheless, it really is). To Danes, this dish is summer in a bowl. It's dinners on the terrace at the wooden summer house and it's a sign that the long evenings are here. It's quickly whipped up using egg, sugar, lemon and buttermilk and a bit of yogurt. If you can't be bothered to make the little biscuits, use an alternative such as amaretti instead – or even just some berries and crunch of your choice.

Homemade *koldskål* needs to be eaten on the day you make it, on account of the raw egg yolk. You can omit the egg (but it does add a certain texture to the soup).

2 egg yolks (pasteurised, ideally)
60 g/5 tablespoons caster/granulated sugar
freshly squeezed juice from ¼ lemon
zest from ½ lemon
seeds from 1 vanilla pod/bean
150 ml/⅔ cup Greek or natural/plain yogurt
1 litre/4 cups buttermilk
fresh berries, to serve

KAMMERJUNKER BISCUITS
170 g/1¼ cups plain/all-purpose flour
1 teaspoon baking powder
75 g/5⅓ tablespoons butter, cold and cubed
50 g/¼ cup light brown sugar
1 egg
1 teaspoon vanilla extract
½ teaspoon ground cardamom (optional)
1 teaspoon lemon zest
1 teaspoon almond extract
2 teaspoons cream

SERVES 4

To make the biscuits/cookies, combine the flour with the baking powder. Add the cold cubed butter and rub in until you have a sandy result. Add the sugar, then all the other ingredients and mix again until you have an even dough. Wrap in clingfilm/plastic wrap and chill in the fridge for 20 minutes.

Preheat the oven to 200°C/180°C fan/400°F/Gas 6. Line a large baking sheet with baking parchment.

Roll the dough out and cut into 35–40 small pieces, then roll them into balls and place them on the lined baking sheet. Bake in the preheated oven for 8 minutes. Remove and cut each biscuit across the middle so you end up with two flat halves, taking care not to burn yourself as the biscuits will be quite hot.

Turn the oven down to 170°C/150°C fan/340°F/Gas 4. Place the biscuits back on the lined baking sheet and return to the oven. Bake for a further 7–8 minutes or until golden and crisp. Allow to cool on a wire rack. Store in an airtight container.

To make the soup, whisk the egg yolks with the sugar until very pale in colour – this reaction, in a way, 'cooks' the egg slightly. Add the lemon juice and zest and vanilla and whisk again. Add the yogurt and the buttermilk and combine, then taste to see if it needs a bit more sugar or lemon.

Refrigerate the soup until ready to serve (best enjoyed on the day of making). Serve the soup cold, with the little biscuits alongside or scattered on top and some fresh berries.

Prinsesstårta log

Prinsesslängd

This is a version of the famous Swedish princess cake – usually it's a green dome, but sometimes I like to change the colour of the marzipan 'lid'. In Sweden, different colour domes often also have different fillings – there are a few too many variations to mention here (and each has a different name). Never being a stickler for rules, I personally vary the fillings and colour based on occasion and season. I have used white marzipan for weddings, pink for christenings and yellow for birthdays… I flavour the cake with different berries in the summer, different jams in winter, and sometimes give the cream a bit of a lemon lift (or even elderflower). These cakes are usually round, but I make them in longer logs as they can sometimes be neater and prettier cut into slices.

- 50 g/3 tablespoons raspberry jam/preserve
- 50 g/2 oz. fresh raspberries
- ⅓ quantity Pastry Cream (see page 237) or 200 g/7 oz. store-bought custard mixed with some whipped cream to keep it firm (in which case, increase the whipping cream by 100 ml/7 tablespoons)
- 250 ml/1 cup whipping cream
- 1 teaspoon vanilla extract
- 1 tablespoon icing/confectioner's sugar
- 200 g/7 oz. light pink marzipan (available in speciality shops)
- fondant roses, to decorate

LAYER CAKE BASE
- 4 eggs
- 120 g/⅔ cup minus 1 tablespoon caster/granulated sugar
- 1 teaspoon vanilla sugar or vanilla extract
- 120 g/1 cup minus 1½ tablespoons plain/all-purpose flour
- a pinch of salt
- 1 teaspoon baking powder
- 20 g/1½ tablespoons butter, melted and cooled

baking tray with sides (large enough to cut out two pieces of cake each 8 x 25 cm/3¼ x 10 inches), lined with baking parchment

piping/pastry bag

SERVES 6–7

Preheat the oven to 180°C/160°C fan/350°F/Gas 4.

To make the cake, beat together the eggs and sugar on high speed in a stand mixer or using a hand-held electric whisk. Beat until the mixture reaches ribbon stage. Add the vanilla.

Combine the flour, salt and baking powder in a separate bowl. Sift into the egg mixture, bit by bit, carefully folding in using a figure-of-eight movement until incorporated. Pour the cooled melted butter down the side of the bowl and fold carefully again, trying not to knock out air.

Pour the mixture onto the baking tray. Bake in the preheated oven for about 5–7 minutes or until light golden brown. Remove from the oven and allow to cool before cutting to size (two pieces, each approx. 8 x 25 cm/3¼ x 10 inches) and discarding any untidy edge bits.

Place the first cake layer on your serving plate, then spread the jam/preserve and the raspberries (mash them if you wish) over the cake. Pipe the pastry cream across the base (if using custard and whipping cream, whip the cream with the vanilla and sugar to firm peaks and mix approx. 100 ml/7 tablespoons of the cream with a generous dollop of vanilla custard – it needs to be firm enough to stay between the layers).

Add the top layer of cake. Using a palette knife, spread the whipped cream all across the top in a dome shape, keeping it very neat.

Roll out the marzipan (use a little icing/confectioner's sugar if it is sticky). It needs to be larger than the cake base with 3–4 cm/1½ inches on each side to allow it to wrap. Carefully, in one confident move, transfer the marzipan across the cake. You only get one chance to do this so make it count!

Little by little, carefully pull down the marzipan at the edges. This is the stage that takes time. Work your way around the log, pulling the marzipan towards the base. Once it is all covered, trim off the excess marzipan. Decorate with fondant flowers to serve.

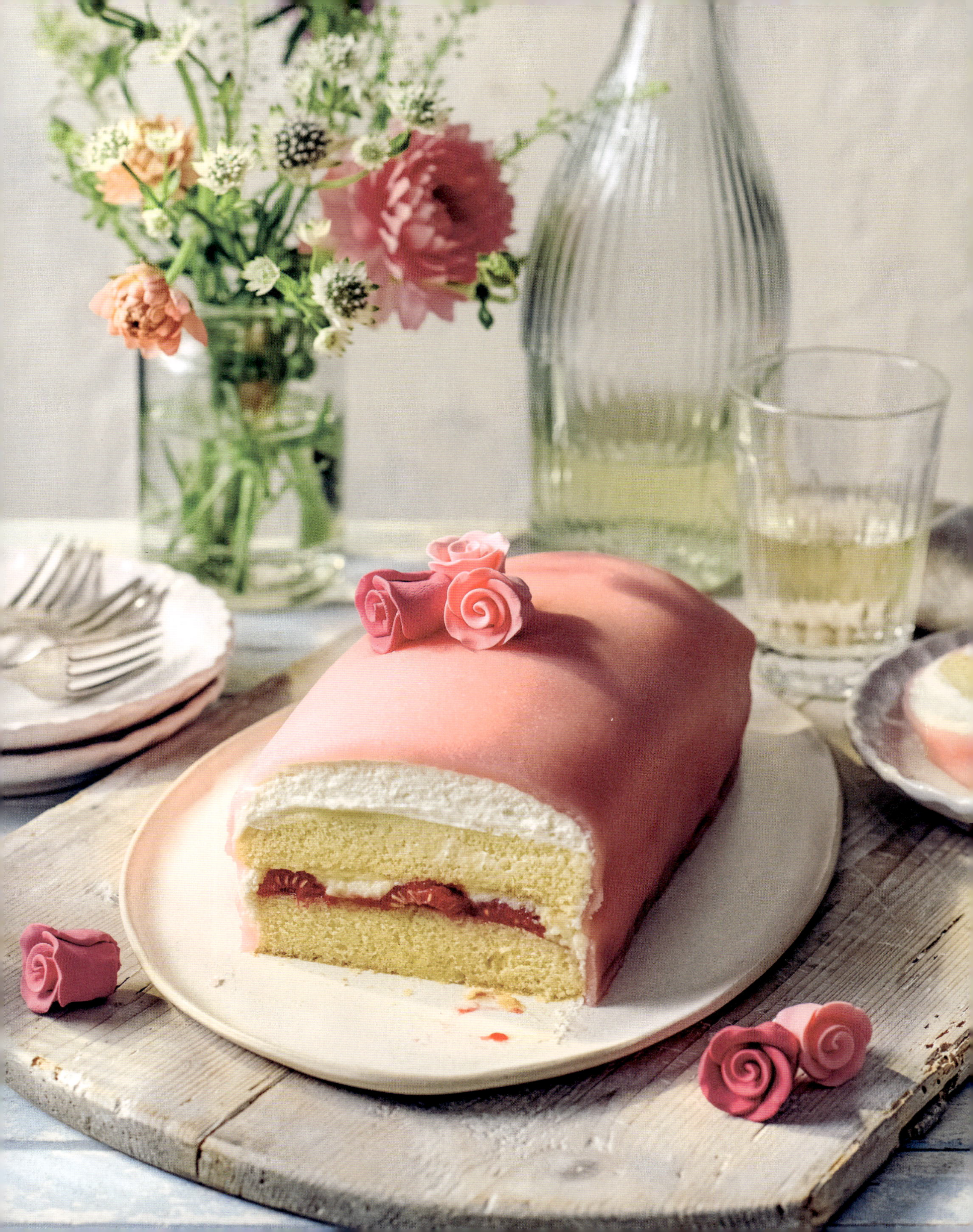

As the harvest approaches and bales of hay lie in the fields (Norwegians call them 'tractor eggs', which I've always loved), school starts again for the kids. Many families return to their main homes, leaving the wilds of the Scandinavian countryside behind. The last bits of summer and light tease us into thinking we still have time left as the leaves start to fall from the trees around us – a gentle reminder of the snowflakes to come.

August is the time to forage for wild raspberries and blackberries. Lingonberries are in the shrubs, as are wild blueberries, turning our fingers purple as we pick them (these berries, also known as bilberries, are small and have purple flesh all the way through). Wild chanterelle mushrooms blanket the forests and we brush them clean to fry in butter and serve on lightly toasted bread. We harvest plums, cherries and currants – and the first of this season's apples are ready. August is the month when most of nature's treasures bloom across our magnificent peninsula.

In Sweden and Finland, crayfish season is in full swing, with outdoor parties catching the last of the warm rays (and crustaceans), accompanied by quite a lot of song and aquavit.

AUGUST

THE CRAYFISH PARTY

The noble folk of the 1800s had a thing for all things crustacean – particularly so in Sweden, where crayfish were plentiful and easy to catch. The love of crayfish and shellfish in general persists, despite the arrival many years ago of a pest which wiped out many of the wild crayfish stocks across northern Europe. As supplies started to become scarce, the Swedish government decided to impose a strict one-month season in August when crayfish could be caught in their waters

Given that Swedes love having rules for things (the more rules, the calmer the Swede in general), legislation became tradition. Even after the crayfish fishing rules were relaxed, many Swedes simply carried on following the old laws – so much so that today, the start of the August crayfish season is a huge event with parties across the land and a lot of people won't ever entertain the thought of eating crayfish 'out of season'). Rules are rules, even when the rules are not rules anymore.

To host a traditional *kräftskiva* crayfish party, you need live crayfish – a lot of crayfish, in fact, as most attendees will get through around 700 g/1½ lb each (a lot of shell but not much meat). For this reason, most people buy their crayfish rather than fishing (strictly in season), as cooking crayfish at home requires not only the crayfish but also the space to store the live crayfish until it's time to cook them in large stockpots. This is easy-ish for two or three people, less so for a party of ten and more. For some people, it's a relief that much of the crayfish available nowadays is pre-cooked, frozen and imported from places such as Spain and China – with crayfish from Swedish waters the gourmet (and expensive) option.

Into the stockpot goes the crayfish in a solution of dark beer, water, salt, sugar and lots of crown dill (dill that has been left to flower). It takes only 5–7 minutes to cook them, after which the crayfish is left in the brine overnight to chill until serving. This resting period is what gives the crayfish a strong dill flavour.

Wherever possible, crayfish parties take place outside, as they are one of those last times in late summer where the weather is still gentle enough to be able to do so. There are long communal tables, man-in-the-moon lanterns and crayfish bunting, and everyone wears paper bibs and crayfish hats. Most Swedes will claim to be expert crayfish peelers. As a newcomer, you will find that Swedes slurp loudly while sucking on the belly – the aim of this is to suck the brine from the shell, as it tastes good. The louder the slurping, the better. Rest assured this is entirely normal behaviour at a *kräftskiva*.

The party table, with the cold, dill-infused, bright red crustaceans in bowls in the centre, also features lots of bread – most often, crispbread and a crusty variety. There will be Västerbotten cheese (akin to a strong Cheddar). Alongside, we serve salads and dips. Aquavit is poured in large quantities, traditionally a sip per claw (although it would be unwise for any newbies to attempt this, as aquavit is a powerful alcoholic drink that has been known to make grown men sing *Dancing Queen* at the top of their voice while picking a fight with a tree).

A *kräftskiva* is a lovely, messy affair and a fitting ode to the humble crayfish and to the last of the summer sun. As the Scandinavian summer starts to fade, I can't think of a better way to spend an evening.

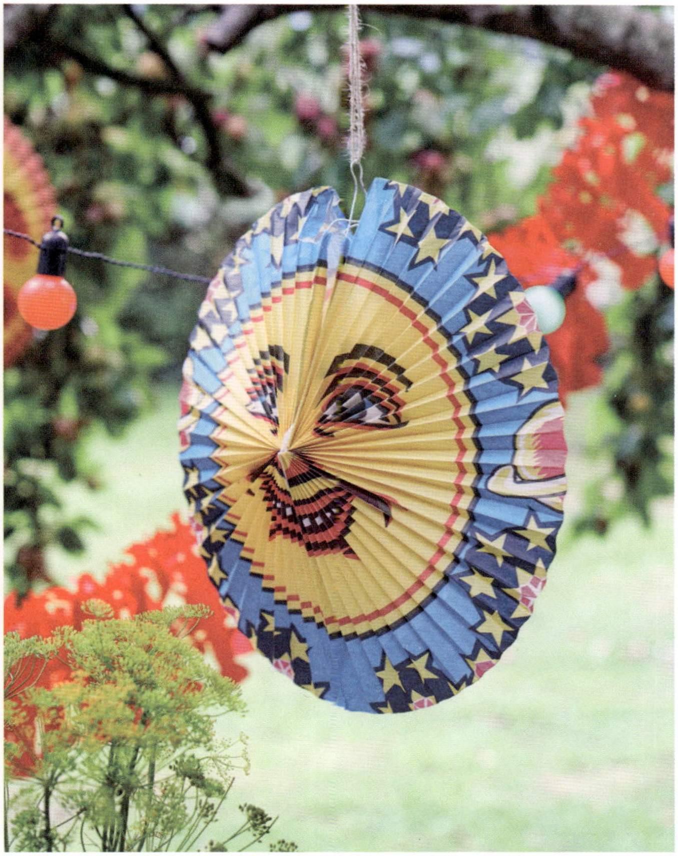

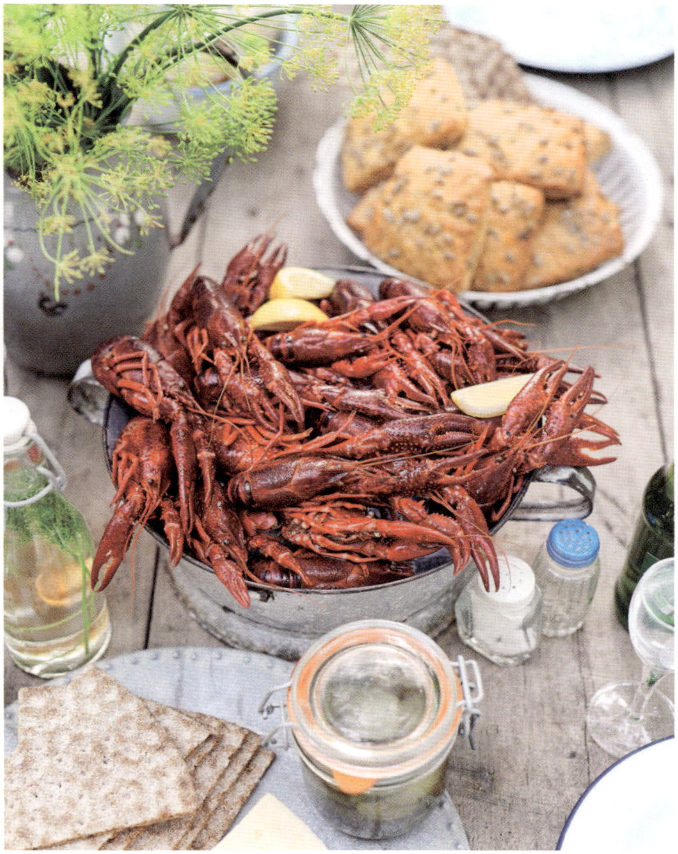

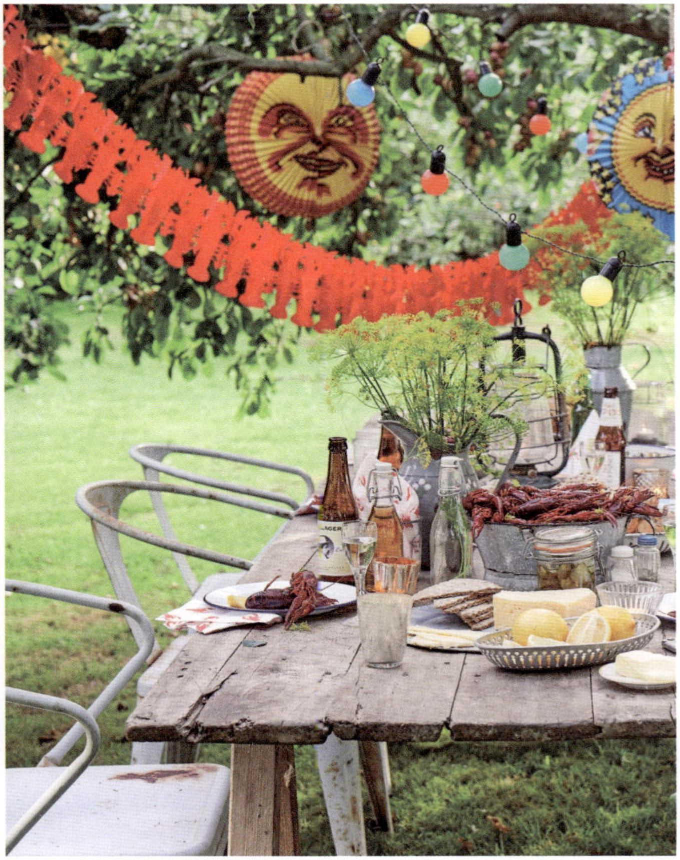

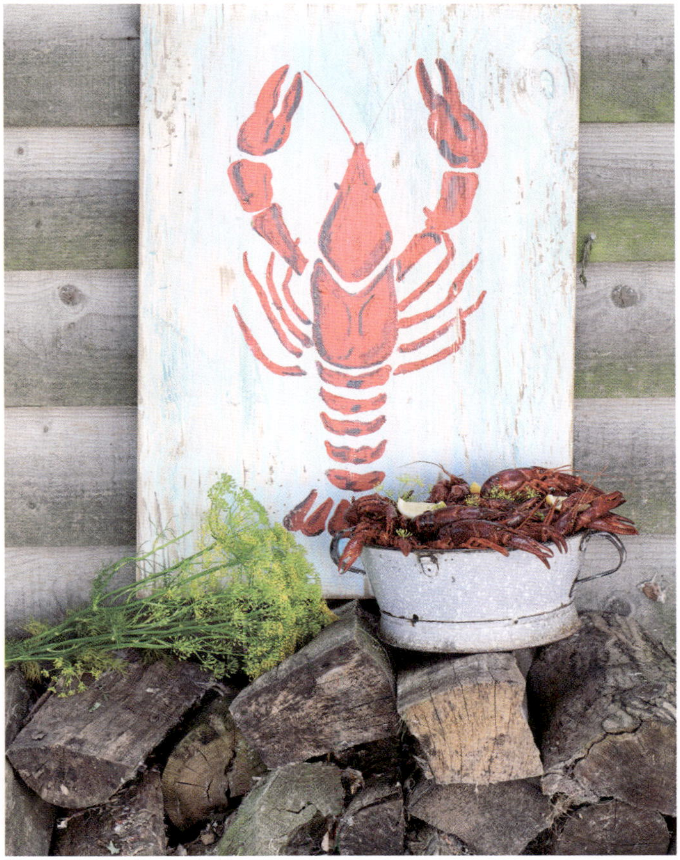

Danish omelette with bacon *Æggekage*

A few weeks before my mother passed away, we were chatting about old, simple Danish dishes. She mentioned the Danish omelette – we call it *æggekage*, which literally means 'egg-cake' – cooked in bacon fat and served with buttered rye bread. I admitted to her that I had never cooked it, which surprised her. She also said I am not allowed to call it an omelette, because it's not – and it's not a frittata, either. It's even simpler.

That evening we cooked *æggekage* together (with extra-crispy bacon, of course) as we drank red wine and talked about old times. That was the last meal she cooked for me and since she's been gone, I now make this dish all the time. It's in those little moments that life happens – and it's often the least expected things we remember people by when they're gone.

oil, for frying
6–8 slices of streaky/fatty bacon
6 eggs
100 ml/7 tablespoons whole milk
½ teaspoon salt
1 tomato, sliced
freshly chopped chives
rye bread, buttered, to serve
tomato ketchup, to serve

SERVES 2

In a non-stick frying pan/skillet – I use a 20-cm/8-inch pan for this recipe – heat a little oil to fry the bacon. Fry until you have cooked it the way you like your bacon – for me, it has to be crispy. Set the bacon to one side on a piece of paper towel.

Crack the eggs into a bowl and break up with a fork. Add milk and salt and whisk again. Turn the heat to low and add the egg to the pan. Wait for it to cook – it will, eventually. You can add a lid on top to speed it up a bit. The whole thing will take around 10–15 minutes over a low heat, but look for the top to be set as that means it is ready.

Before the egg sets, add slices of tomato on top and finish the cooking. Place the bacon on top and garnish with chives. Serve in the pan on the table and cut into triangles. Serve with buttered rye bread on the side, and maybe a dash of ketchup.

TIP This dish is very easy to scale up if serving more people (allow three eggs per person).

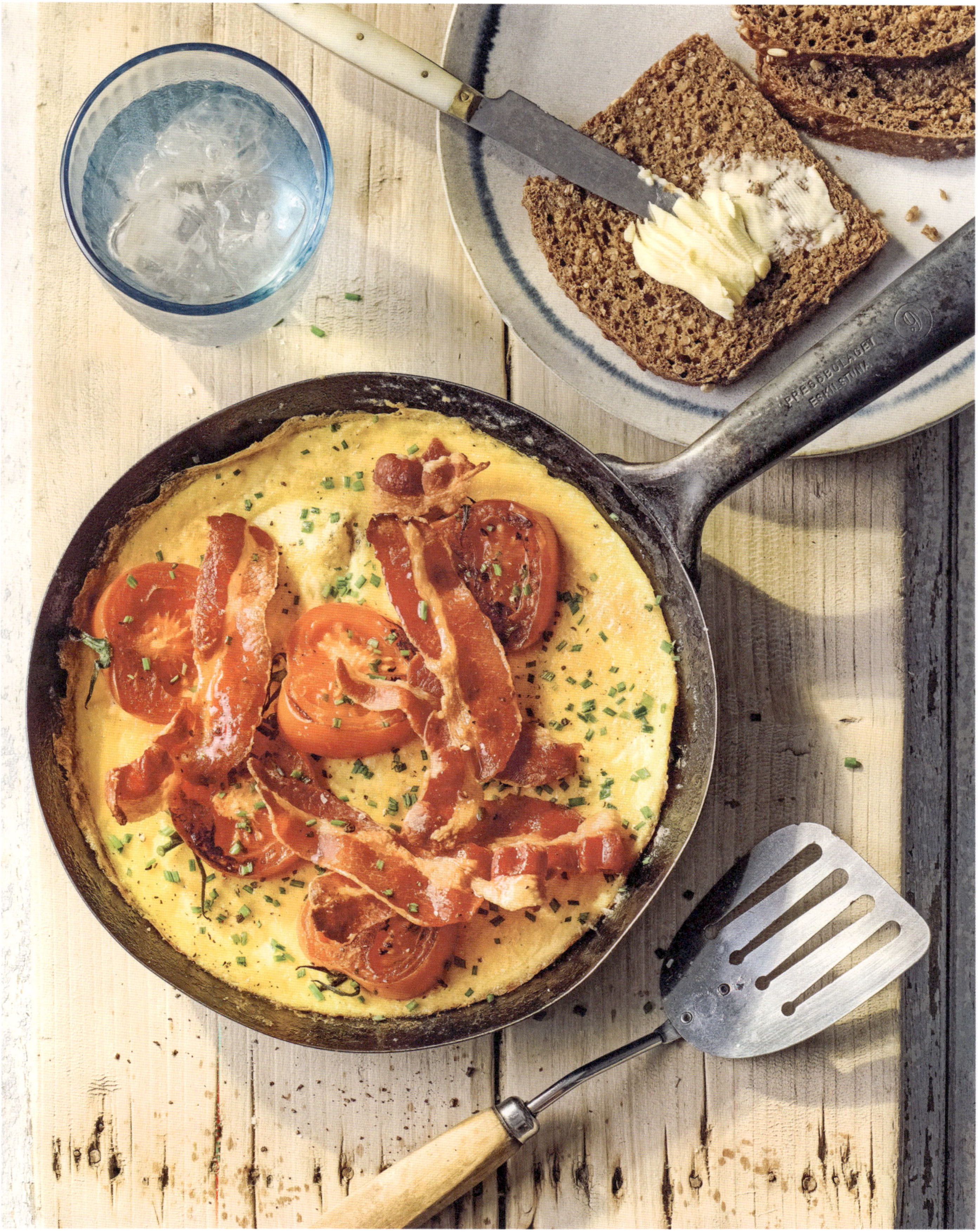

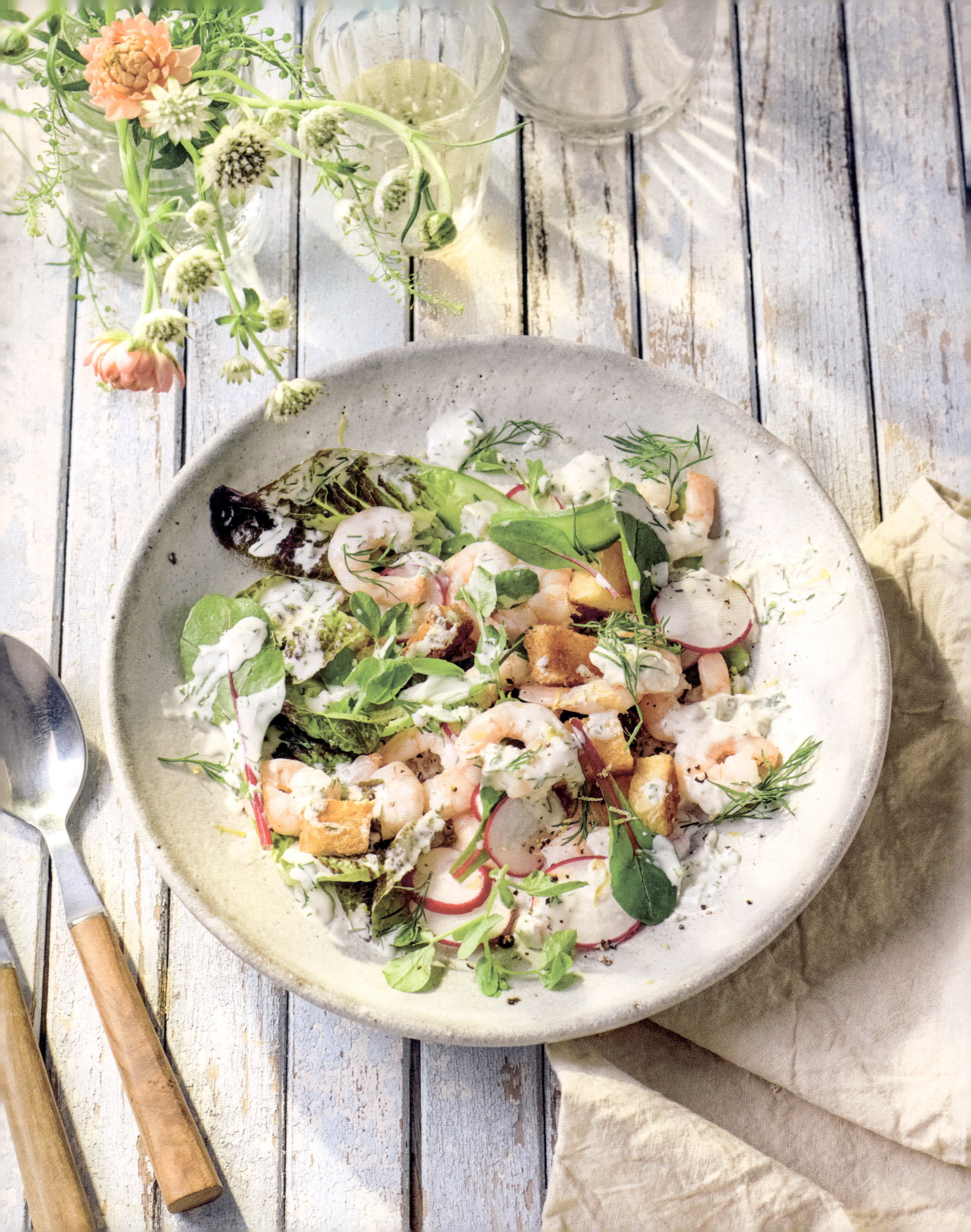

Toast skagen salad
Toast skagen salad

Few starters are more iconic in Scandinavia than *Toast Skagen*. I prefer a lighter version but with a nod to my childhood (where this dish reigned supreme at dinner parties in the 80s and 90s). The best prawns to buy are cooked North Sea prawns that you peel yourself, or cooked prawns in brine. If using supermarket prawns, good-quality frozen prawns beat the chilled ones, in terms of taste.

- a knob/pat of butter and 1 teaspoon oil, for frying
- 2 slices of brioche or soft white bread, cut into small croutons
- 1 Gem lettuce, leaves washed
- 10 cherry tomatoes, halved
- 1 baby cucumber, sliced thinly lengthways
- 1 avocado, peeled, stoned and sliced
- 1–2 radishes, thinly sliced
- 200 g/7 oz. fresh cooked prawns/shrimp
- pea shoots and dill sprigs, to garnish

DRESSING
- 1 small shallot, finely chopped
- 3 tablespoons mayonnaise
- 2 tablespoons crème fraîche
- 3 tablespoons freshly chopped dill
- 2 tablespoons freshly chopped chives
- ½ teaspoon horseradish sauce
- 1 teaspoon lemon zest
- freshly squeezed lemon juice, to taste
- dash of milk (optional)

SERVES 2

Mix the dressing ingredients together. Add a dash of milk if necessary to make an almost spoonable dressing.

Melt the butter and oil in a pan and fry the croutons, toasting them gently until crisp.

Arrange the leaves and vegetables in a serving bowl, then top with the prawns, croutons, pea shoots and dill. Drizzle over a little dressing and serve the rest on the side.

Jonas' midweek fish
Lax i ugn

This is my husband Jonas' go-to midweek dish. You can vary this in many ways: change the veg, swap out herbs, use anything from salmon to cod or haddock. There is no pre-cooking and it goes with anything from pressed potatoes to rice and salad.

- 400 g/14 oz. salmon or white fish fillets, skin left on if you wish
- 1 leek, white bits only, finely sliced
- 200 ml/¾ cup crème fraîche or sour cream
- 200 ml/¾ cup whipping cream
- 20 g/¾ oz. dill, chopped
- 20 g/¾ oz. chives, chopped
- 1 tablespoon fresh lemon juice
- 1 teaspoon Dijon mustard
- 1 teaspoon lemon zest
- 100 ml/7 tablespoons fish stock
- salt and freshly ground black pepper
- 1 handful of breadcrumbs or grated Västerbotten or Cheddar cheese

SERVES 2

Preheat the oven to 190°C/170°C fan/375°F/Gas 5.

Select an ovenproof dish that fits the fish with room for the sauce to reach about halfway up the fish. Add the leek to the dish and place the fish on top. Mix together the remaining ingredients (except the breadcrumbs or cheese) and pour over the fish. Scatter the breadcrumbs or cheese on top.

Bake in the preheated oven for approx. 15–20 minutes – check the internal temperature of the fish has reached 60°C/140°F as cooking time depends on the thickness of the fish. This cooking time will only just cook the finely sliced leek – if you prefer it softer (or if using, for example, fennel or other harder veg), fry them in butter for 5–10 minutes first.

TIP You can use frozen fish (increase cooking time and lower temperature slightly, and always use a thermometer to check the internal temperature as above; it will continue to cook for a while after you remove from the oven and you don't want to risk overcooking fish).

Västerbotten tart *Västerbottenpaj*

Västerbotten cheese has been made in a place called Burträsk in northern Sweden since 1872. It's truly fantastic and cannot be made anywhere else (despite cheesemakers trying), and if you can get hold of it, I highly recommend making this cheese tart. *Västerbottenpaj* is served as part of a *smörgåsbord* either during Midsummer or at a crayfish party, or simply served in slices for lunch or as a starter. It works really well if you serve with a dollop of crème fraîche and red fish roe.

1 quantity Shortcrust Pastry (see page 235)
3 eggs
100 ml/⅓ cup plus 1 tablespoon whole milk
250 ml/1 cup double/heavy cream
½ teaspoon paprika
250 g/9 oz. Västerbotten cheese, grated
salt and freshly ground black pepper

25-cm/10-inch loose-based tart pan

baking beans

MAKES 1 LARGE TART

Preheat the oven to 180°C/160°C fan/350°F/Gas 4.

Roll out the chilled pastry and line the tart pan evenly. Prick the base with a fork a few times, then line the pastry with baking parchment and fill with baking beans. Blind bake in the preheated oven for about 12–14 minutes. Remove the beans and baking parchment and bake for a further 5–6 minutes.

Meanwhile, mix together all the filling ingredients except the cheese.

Once the case is part baked, remove from the oven and scatter the cheese across the base, then pour the egg mixture over.

Return to the oven for about 15–20 minutes. The filling will puff up quite a bit towards the end and will turn golden on top. It's done when the middle is set, so do keep an eye on it. If your oven tends to run a little hot, turn down the heat a bit as you don't want to overcook the filling – it needs to be just set. Leave to cool before removing from the pan and slicing.

NOTES If you cannot get hold of Västerbotten cheese, I have made this with three-quarters Cheddar and one-quarter good Parmesan or pecorino.

This dish goes very well with *romsås*, a caviar sauce. To make this, mix together one small jar of red lumpfish roe with 3 large tablespoons of crème fraîche and leave to set. Just before you serve the tart, stir the *romsås* again. Alternatively, if you can get real bleak roe (*löjrom*) – a pricy Arctic caviar – serve the tart with a spoonful of crème fraîche, chopped red onion and a spoonful of this delicious caviar on top.

Fried pork belly with parsley sauce

Stegt flæsk med persillesovs

Denmark's national dish is not – surprisingly – open sandwiches or *Frikadeller* meatballs, but this fried pork belly dish. It is little known outside our borders and is most certainly old school and the food of the working people. Still, time after time, *stegt flæsk* is voted the Danes' favourite meal.

While some people prefer to cook the belly pieces in the oven, I think you get the best flavour when fried in a pan. I agree this is not a dish for those trying to cut back on the fat, as the slices need to be done to a crisp.

500 g/1 lb. 2 oz. pork belly slices
salt
butter and oil, for frying

FRESH PARSLEY SAUCE
20 g/1½ tablespoons butter
3 tablespoons plain/all-purpose flour
approx. 500 ml/2 cups milk (if I have some stock, I replace 100 ml/7 tablespoons milk with stock for flavour)
a pinch of grated nutmeg
30-g/1-oz. bunch of flat-leaf parsley, finely chopped
a few drops of white wine vinegar or freshly squeezed lemon juice
salt and freshly ground black pepper

SERVES 4

Cut the pork belly into thin 5–7-mm/¼-inch thick slices (you can put the slices between sheets of baking parchment and beat flatter with a rolling pin). If the slices are quite long, cut them in half. Salt the pork slices liberally on both sides and leave for an hour.

In a frying pan/skillet, melt a knob/pat of butter and a small glug of oil. Add the pork slices and fry over a medium heat, turning the slices frequently. They are done when they have gone crispy – this can take a little while. When done, drain the pork pieces on paper towels. Taste – you may need a little more salt.

To make the sauce, melt the butter in a saucepan, add the flour and cook into a roux. Start adding the milk to thicken the sauce, little by little, as you keep whisking. Leave to simmer for a few minutes until the sauce is your desired thickness, then season with salt and pepper and nutmeg. Add all the parsley and the vinegar or lemon juice and heat through.

Great served with buttered boiled new potatoes and seasonal veg.

Freja's buttermilk crescent rolls *Kærnemælkshorn*

Freja from our café shared this recipe with me – her grandmother Inger's recipe for buttermilk crescent rolls. Among Freja's favourite childhood memories are Farmor Inger's ready supply of these warm rolls, fresh out of the oven. Of course, enjoyed with copious amounts of butter and slices of good Danish cheese. Freja says that Inger always made a big batch and froze ahead, which is excellent advice. Take frozen rolls out a few hours before you need them (and pop in the oven for a few minutes to warm through).

200 ml/¾ cup buttermilk
25 g/⅞ oz. fresh yeast
1 teaspoon honey
50 g/3½ tablespoons very soft butter
1 egg
500 g/3½ cups bread flour, plus extra for dusting
1 teaspoon fine salt

TO DECORATE
beaten egg, for brushing
40 g/½ cup sunflower seeds

baking sheet(s), lined with baking parchment

MAKES 16

Heat the buttermilk in a pan with 100 ml/7 tablespoons water to finger-warm temperature. In a stand mixer, add the fresh yeast and the buttermilk mixture, along with the honey. Mix until the yeast has dissolved.

Add the butter and egg and start adding the flour – you may not need all the flour, so start with about two-thirds and keep kneading. Add the salt once you have added three-quarters of the flour. Knead the dough until it is elastic and lets go of the sides of the bowl, adding more flour as necessary. You may need a little more or less than specified in the recipe. Leave to prove until doubled in size – this usually takes around 45 minutes.

On a floured surface, knead the dough, then split into two equal pieces. Roll the first piece of dough out to a circle, around 30 cm/12 inches in diameter, then cut into eight slices, like a pizza. To make a little horn shape, gently roll from the longer side, in towards the middle tip – a bit like a croissant shape. Repeat with the remaining pieces and with the second piece of dough, giving you a total of 16 rolls/horns (or make 12 if you prefer larger rolls – just bake for a little longer). Leave to rise under a kitchen towel for another 20 minutes.

Preheat the oven to 220°C/200°C fan/425°F/Gas 7.

Brush each roll with beaten egg and scatter some sunflower seeds onto each horn. Bake in the preheated oven for around 10–12 minutes or until baked through. Enjoy warm with butter and cheese. These rolls freeze well – just take out of the freezer a few hours before you wish to eat them.

VARIATIONS You can add more sunflower seeds to the dough for a healthier version if you wish. If you cannot get hold of buttermilk, you can use half sour cream/half milk – or whole milk with a few drops of lemon juice added (leave for 15 minutes before using).

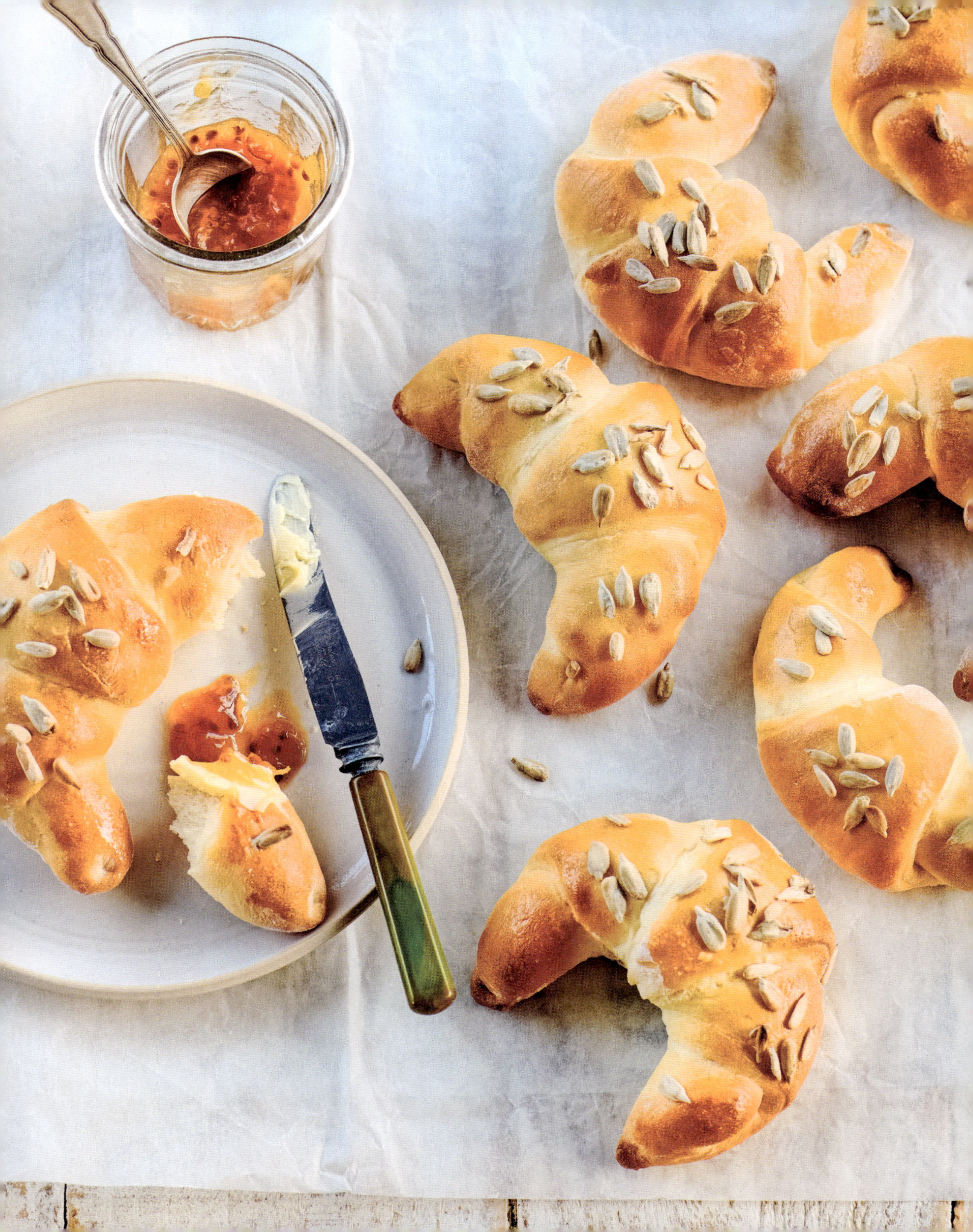

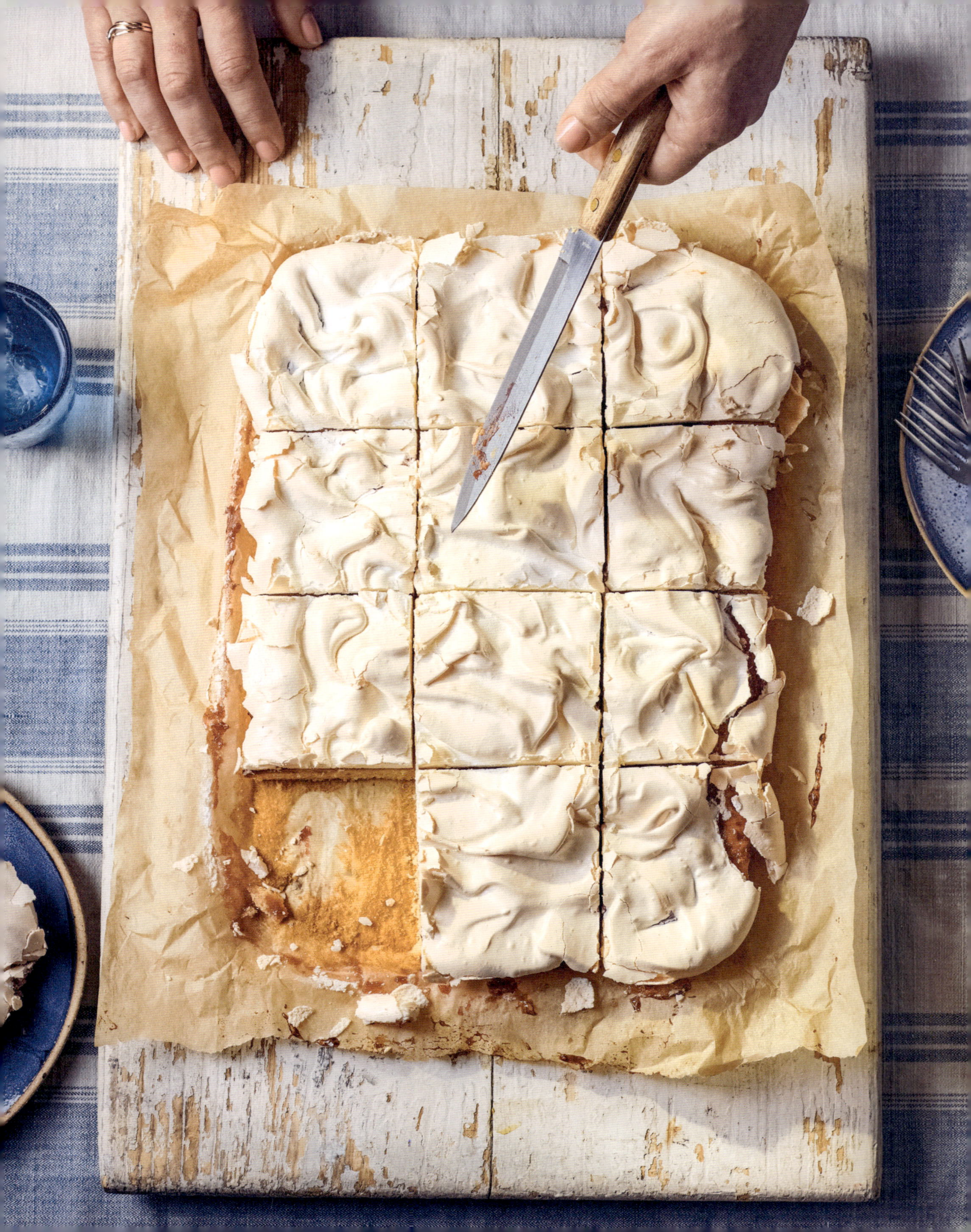

Grandad's beard

Bedstefars skæg

The reason this Danish home bake classic is called Grandad's Beard is because the soft-baked mallow on top risks sticking to your upper lip when you eat it. It's not a difficult cake to make, but because the mallow is that soft it should be eaten on the day it is baked or else it weeps and goes too soft. Use whatever jam/preserve or marmalade you like – I like love any sort of berry or even rhubarb or apple compote.

200 g/1¾ sticks butter, softened
200 g/1 cup caster/granulated sugar
4 egg yolks (you'll need the whites for the meringue)
350 g/2⅔ cups plain/all-purpose flour
1 teaspoon vanilla sugar or vanilla extract
2 teaspoons baking powder
250 ml/1 cup whole milk
200 g/⅔ cup jam/preserve of your choice (raspberry is traditional)

MERINGUE
4 eggs whites
½ teaspoon vinegar
220 g/1 cup plus 1 tablespoon caster/granulated sugar
1 teaspoon vanilla extract (optional)

25 x 35-cm/10 x 14-inch cake pan, lined with baking parchment

MAKES 12 GENEROUS PIECES

Preheat the oven to 195°C/175°C fan/375°F/Gas 5.

In a stand mixer with a paddle attachment, cream the butter and sugar, then add the egg yolks, one by one.

Sift the flour with the vanilla sugar and baking powder (if you're using vanilla extract, just add this to the wet mixture instead). Fold the flour into the egg mixture with the milk.

Pour the batter into the prepared cake pan and bake in the preheated oven for 15 minutes.

Meanwhile, make the meringue mixture. In a stand mixer fitted with the whisk attachment, whisk the egg whites until soft peaks form, then add the vinegar and start to add the sugar, a spoonful at the time, taking care to whisk well before adding more sugar. Once all the sugar is added, whisk on high speed for 4–5 minutes until you have hard peaks. Add the vanilla extract if using.

Remove the cake from the oven – the top should be just set, if it's still too wobbly, give it a few more minutes. Add a layer of your jam/preserve of choice. Spread the meringue mixture on top and cover completely.

Return to the oven with the temperature turned down to 180°C/160°C fan/350°F/Gas 4 and bake for around 12–14 minutes until the topping has browned slightly and is set.

Eat on the day of making, as the meringue goes soft quickly.

The green finally gives way to brown and orange hues, contrasting with the deep blue waters of the fjords and seas. In the far north, the moose- and game-hunting season begins. In Lapland, the Sámi people start to herd the reindeer from their summer grazing pastures towards the winter areas. The last of the potatoes are dug up, sea buckthorn starts to fruit and we're still enjoying wild mushrooms. Mostly, though, we try to work out what to do with all those apples.

In Sweden, everyone's right to access the land (enshrined in Swedish law as *Allmänsrätten*, with similar legislation in Norway and Denmark) opens up huge areas that might otherwise be closed off. We forage and hike freely, as long as we do so responsibly. However, don't expect anyone to ever tell you their spots for foraging – those are usually a closely guarded secret.

SEPTEMBER

HIKING AND FORAGING

September brings autumn into focus as things start to feel calmer after the busy months of summer. It's a perfect time for both hiking and foraging nature's treasures across the landscape.

No one loves a good hike more than Norwegians. There's a famous saying: *'Ut på tur, aldri sur!'*, which roughly translates to 'out on a hike, never grumpy' (it sounds better in Norwegian as it rhymes). This is about the intention of the hike: to generate a smile and a good mood.

Weekends and holidays for Norwegians often involve long, strenuous hikes, for which appropriate equipment is essential. This includes physical maps (you're unlikely to have any phone reception, as Norway's landscape is vast and very little of the land is urbanised – imagine the UK with only 5 million people in it). In Norway, you can go for a hike and see no other people for days, if you so choose.

Scandinavians are practical and we tend to dress for the weather. When on a hike, this means layering, proper footwear, waterproofs and finishing off with the all-time favourite Norwegian item, the all-weather jacket, often so bright it can be seen from space.

Another essential item to bring is a practical backpack. It will hold sticking plasters, the maps, a flask of coffee, a fresh orange and a *Kvikk Lunsj* chocolate wafer bar. Some people bring a second flask of hot water and hotdog sausages, because you never know when that need for a hotdog will take over. Finally, dress yourself with a wide, bright smile: this is the only time where we break the rule of not chatting to strangers. Other hikers must be greeted with a jolly *'hei-hei!'* as you hurry past them with purpose.

When it's impractical to go for a long hike, Norwegians tend to go on purposeful urban walks. The rules are the same as on a long hike, although there's less call for a map and you can just stop for hotdogs or coffee along the way – although the purpose of the walk must be to go for the walk itself. These are often known as *søndagsture* ('Sunday walks'), which to a Norwegian can also mean something that is quite easy to do (as in 'How was that hike you did to the top of Mont Blanc?' 'Like a *søndagstur!*').

One thing that's fun to do when out on a hike is to look for wild fruits, berries and other edible plants. At the height of the Nordic Food Revolution about a decade ago (when eating ants and moss became popular), foraging became fashionable. Not because it was something we had to rediscover, but because it suddenly became popular to show how we could reconnect with the land, nature and the food we put on our plates.

Before it was trendy, foraging wasn't really a purposeful thing we did, merely a practical way to get into nature and pick some good stuff along the way – wild berries, mushrooms, girolles and nettles, and maybe stealing apples from the garden next door. Nowadays, there's a bit of a foraging subculture – as there is in most places – of people walking around looking for obscure herbs and finding pride in picking things from the side of the road to use in a new dish. However, most Scandinavians don't go foraging with any sort of planned purpose.

That said, the Nordic Food Revolution has absolutely reignited our pride in the landscape and we are most certainly eating more local and, when we can, opting for wilder, more organic options. Foraging in Scandinavia is no different to foraging anywhere else. Firstly, no one is going to share with you where the good patches are (that's rule number one of foraging: never tell anyone else anything). Secondly, research is essential (nobody likes a poisonous mushroom), as is making good friends with local foragers.

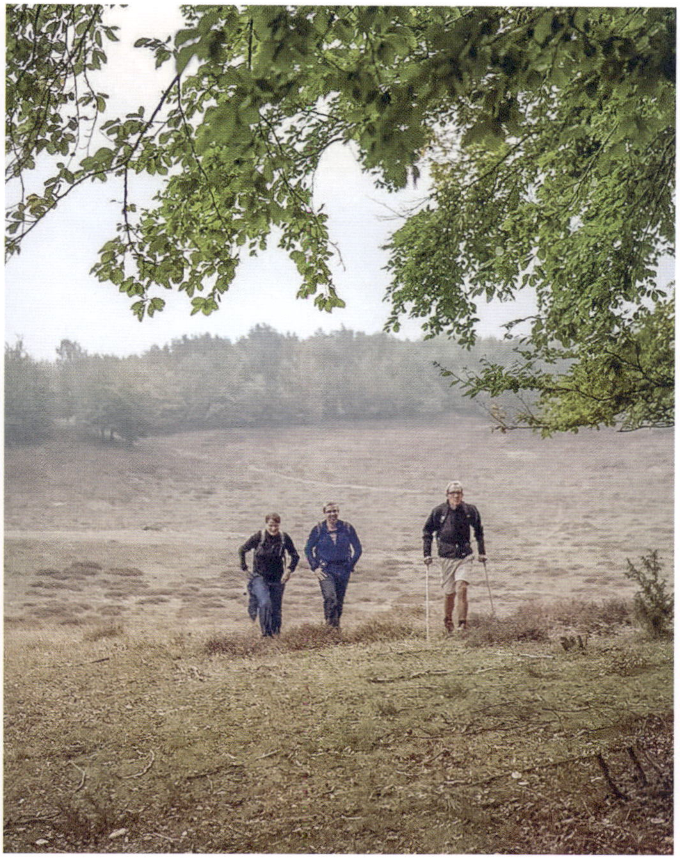
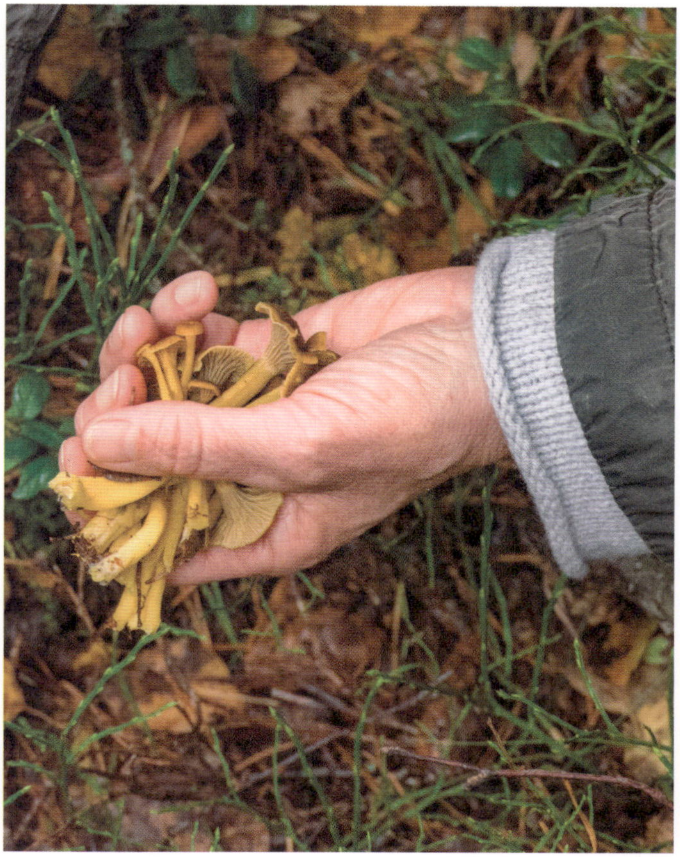
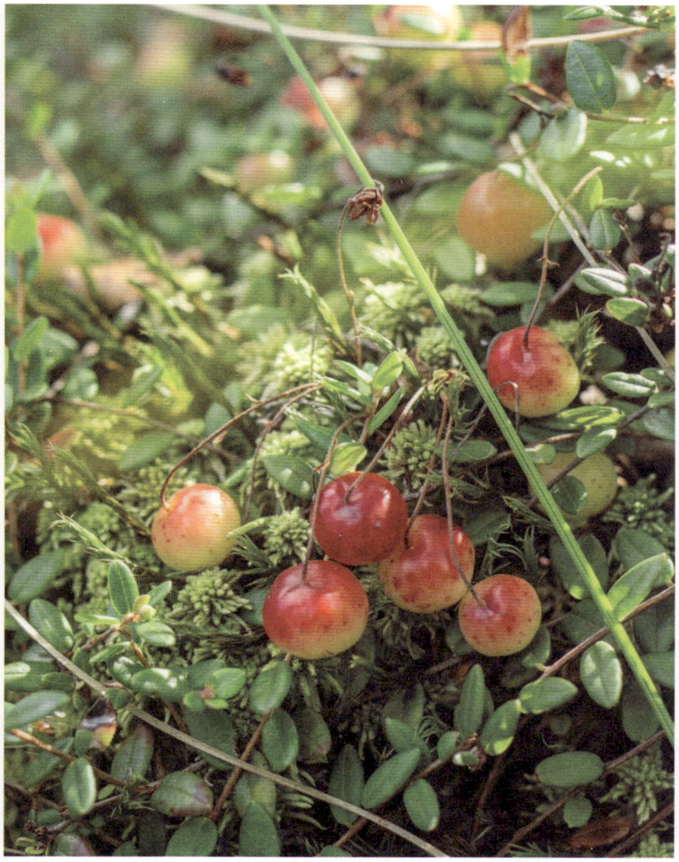
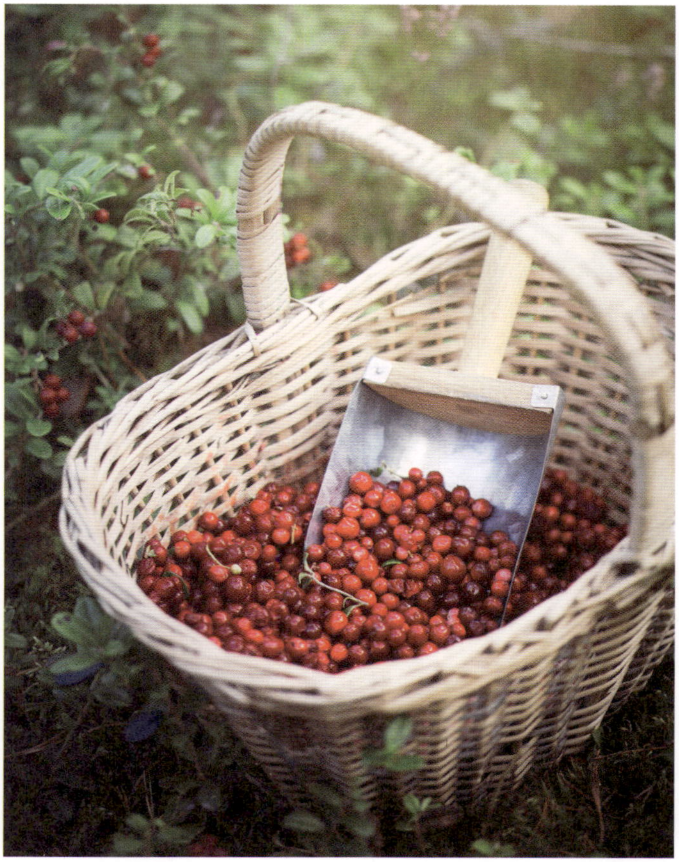

Riina's salmon chowder *Lohikeitto*

Riina manages ScandiKitchen's operations and hails from Finland. She is also a great cook and this is her recipe for *Lohikeitto*, a traditional Finnish salmon chowder. It's one of those dishes that is so simple to make that you might think the result would be simple too – but far from it. It's a one-pot wonder that, with just a few minutes' prep and a short, no-effort cooking time, makes a really delicious light midweek meal.

Lohikeitto has a long history in Finland. It was a meal prepared by families living along the thousands of lakes – and the soup has a warm place in the heart of the Finns today as a nostalgic working man's meal.

30 g/2 tablespoons butter
1 large leek (200 g/7 oz.), sliced into half moons
180 ml/¾ cup dry white wine (optional)
400 g/14 oz. potatoes, peeled and cut into 2-cm/¾-inch cubes
2 carrots (200 g/7 oz.), peeled and cut into half moons
2 bay leaves
850 ml/3½ cups fish stock
500 g/1 lb. 2 oz. side of salmon, skin removed, boned and cut into 2-cm/¾-inch chunks
150 ml/⅔ cup double/heavy cream
a big handful of fresh dill, chopped
salt and freshly ground black pepper
buttered rye bread, to serve (optional)

SERVES 4

Warm the butter in a large pan over a medium-high heat. Once melted and bubbling, add the leeks and sauté until they are soft.

Add the white wine, if using, and cook for 2 minutes.

Add the potatoes, carrots, bay leaves and fish stock. Cook for 15 minutes or until the potatoes and carrots are al dente. Add the salmon chunks and cream and give it a gentle stir. Let it simmer for 5 minutes until the salmon is just cooked. Finish with a large handful of chopped dill and generous grinds of salt and pepper.

Serve immediately with buttered rye bread on the side, if you wish.

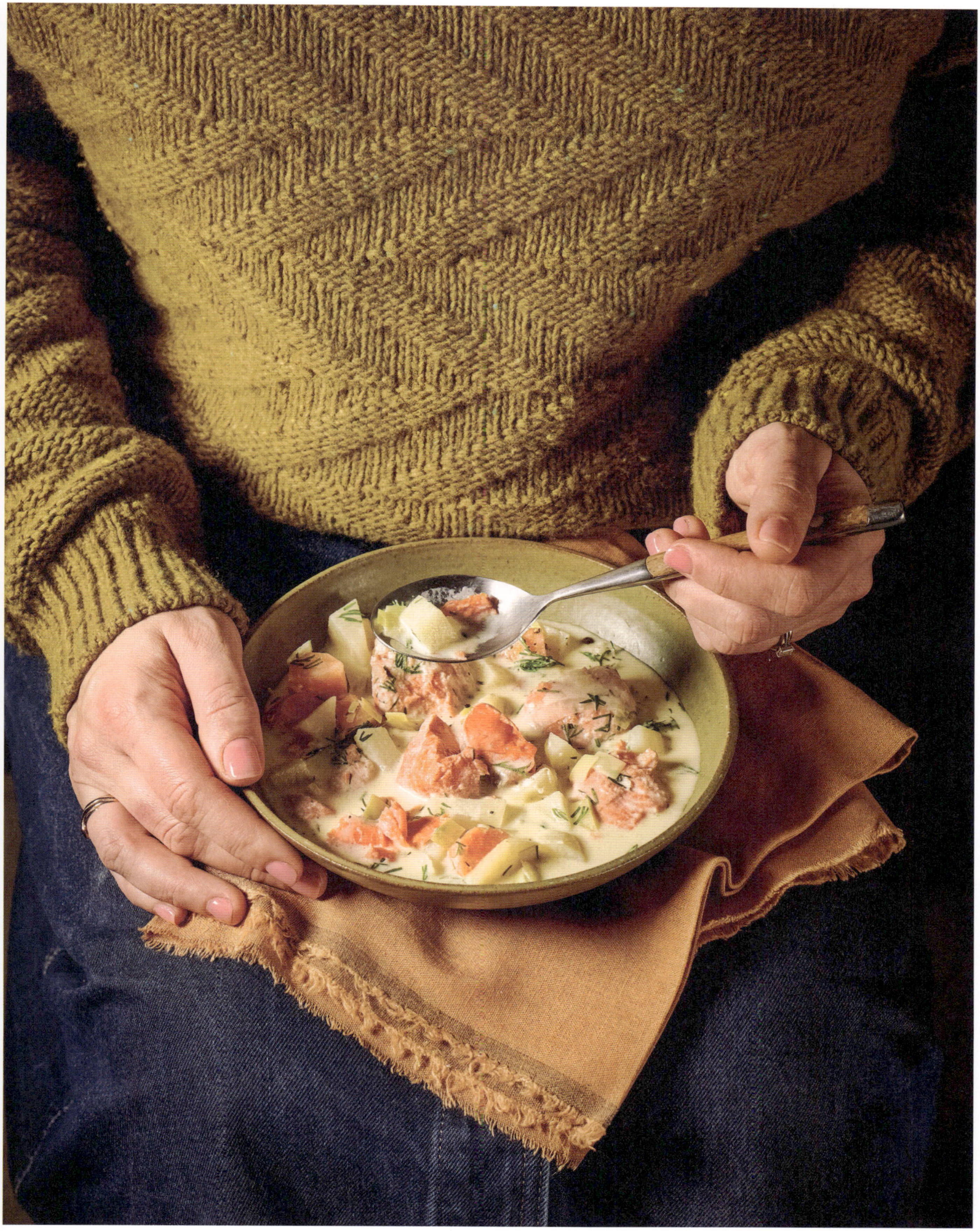

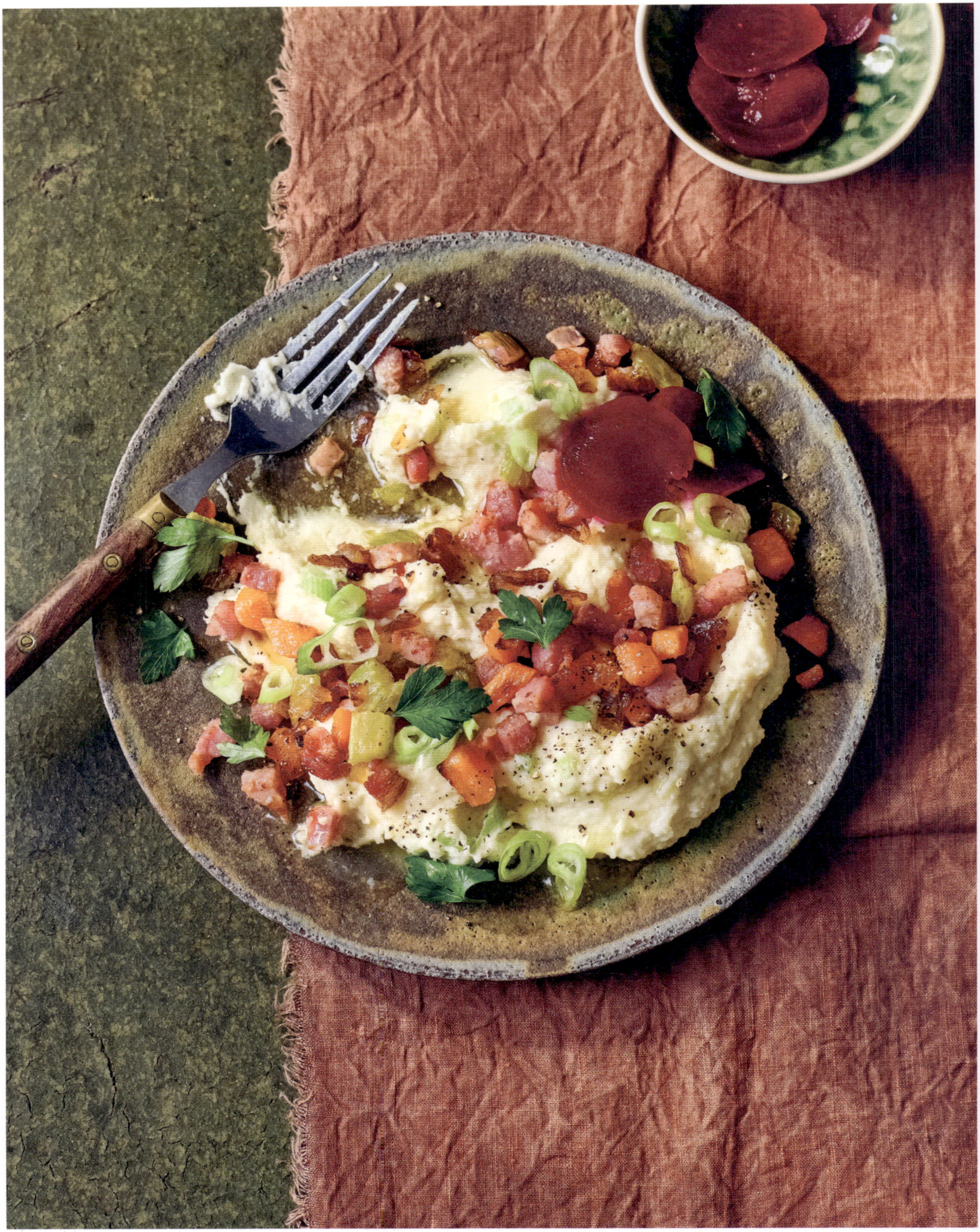

Hunka hunka burning love

Brændende kærlighed

Okay, so this is not really called *hunka hunka burning love* (I just love Elvis) – it's just *Burning Love*. Why that name? Nobody really knows – but as it's an old Danish farmer's dish, some say it's because mash and bacon are real comfort foods, full of love and good warm-belly feelings. This is a super-simple dish, and, like *Lohikeitto* on the previous pages, one to add to your Nordic midweek meal repertoire.

The original version is mashed potato with fried bacon pieces on top – that's it. When I make this at home, I like to add a bit more flavour and so I tend to make a parsnip and potato mash and I add some veg to the meat to bulk it out a bit. You can vary as you prefer.

butter and oil, for frying
50 g/1¾ oz. shallots, chopped
50 g/1¾ oz. carrot, chopped
1 stick celery, chopped
2 spring onions/scallions, chopped, white and green parts separated
150 g/5½ oz. lardons or pancetta pieces (smoked or unsmoked)
freshly chopped parsley, to garnish

POTATO & PARSNIP MASH
250 g/9 oz. potatoes, peeled
250 g/9 oz. parsnips, peeled
50 ml/3½ tablespoons cream
50–100 ml/3½–7 tablespoons milk
1 bay leaf
½ onion, leave in one piece but peeled
a sprig of thyme
a pinch of grated nutmeg
25 g/1¾ tablespoons butter
½ teaspoon horseradish cream (optional)
½–1 teaspoon Dijon mustard, to taste
salt and freshly ground black pepper

SERVES 2

To make the mash, boil the potatoes and parsnips in a pan of water until tender, then drain and set aside.

While the veg are cooking, bring the cream and milk to boiling point in another pan. Turn off the heat, add the bay leaf, onion, thyme and a grating of nutmeg, then leave to infuse.

Heat a frying pan/skillet over a medium heat and add a glug of oil or butter and add the chopped shallots, carrot, celery and white parts of the spring onions/scallions. Leave to fry without browning too much for around 6–7 minutes, then add the bacon pieces and cook until crispy and golden.

Mash the warm potatoes and parsnips with the butter, then start adding the warm milk (discard the bay leaf and onion). You may not need all the liquid, depending on the type of potato – or you may need a splash more. Season to taste with salt and pepper, horseradish cream and mustard, then finish with the sliced spring onion/scallion greens.

Serve big dollops of mash with the bacon mixture on top and add a sprinkling of freshly chopped parsley on top. Don't drain the bacon mix, as the butter from the frying of the bacon is spooned over the mash when serving. Good served with pickled beets on the side.

Norwegian lobscouse

Lapskaus

Lobscouse is a stew that comes in many shapes and sizes, using different meats and all linked to Northern Europe's extensive history of shipping – indeed, Denmark's version is called *Skipperlabskovs* ('Captain's lobscouse'). I prefer how the Norwegians make their *Lapskaus*: full of delicious root vegetables. It's thought that the dish has strong links to the English port city of Liverpool (where scouse is still made and the inhabitants are called Scousers) and nearby Wales. Given the city's strong historical maritime links, it's not surprising that Nordic sailors would have taken the recipe home with them.

If you want to make the more traditional Danish version, simply increase the quantity of potatoes, leave out the root vegetables and use chives instead of parsley at the end.

butter and oil, for frying

800 g/1 lb. 12 oz. chuck steak, cut into 2-cm/¾-inch pieces

2 medium onions, chopped

700 ml/3 cups beef stock

2 bay leaves

800 g/1 lb. 12 oz. potatoes, cut into 2-cm/¾-inch pieces

500 g/1 lb. 2 oz. mixed root veg (such as celeriac/celery root, parsnip, carrot, turnip), peeled and cut into 2-cm/¾-inch pieces

1 leek, sliced (optional, but it adds a nice flavour)

½ tablespoon cornflour/cornstarch, for thickening (optional)

a handful of freshly chopped flat-leaf parsley

salt and freshly ground black pepper

crusty bread, to serve

SERVES 4–6

In a flameproof casserole dish, melt a knob/pat of butter with a glug of oil, add the steak and fry until browned. Remove the meat with a slotted spoon and set aside.

Add the onions to the dish and fry over a lower heat until caramelised (approx. 15 minutes) – you may need to add a little more oil.

Add the meat back into the pan, then add the stock and bay leaves, season, then cover the dish. Reduce the heat to a simmer and leave for 2 hours. From time to time, skim off any impurities that collect on the surface of the stock.

Once the meat has started to fall apart when you press it (this may take a little more than 2 hours of cooking, so if it feels tough, just increase the cooking time), add the potatoes, root veg and leek (if using). Season, cover and leave to simmer again until the veg is just cooked through – around 30–40 minutes.

If the mixture is still really thin, dissolve the cornflour/cornstarch in a little water and add to thicken. This is not a thick sauce, but almost broth like – so you should not need to add much cornflour, if any.

Finally, add the parsley to serve. Enjoy steaming hot in bowls, with some crusty bread on the side. Norwegians love adding lingonberries on top, but this is optional – I don't think it always needs it.

Leftover hash

Pyttipanna

This is the ultimate Scandi leftover dish. In Sweden and Norway it's *Pyttipanna* and *Pyttipanne* respectively – both meaning pieces in a pan; in Denmark it's *Biksemad* – mixed-together food. We're nothing if not logical in our naming of some dishes.

Use any leftover meat you like (roast pork is great – as is ham, beef or even sausage), and always use cold, cooked potatoes that are quite firm or else they will start to fall apart in the pan. Traditionally, only potatoes are used – not the root vegetables I list – but I do feel they elevate this super-simple dish a bit. You can, of course, leave out the root veg, if you prefer.

50 g/3½ tablespoons butter, plus extra as needed

oil, for frying

1 onion, chopped

200 g/7 oz. of each root veg (celeriac/celery root, turnip, carrot, parsnip), all cut into 5-mm/¼-inch pieces

2 sprigs of fresh thyme

400 g/14 oz. potatoes, firm cold and cooked, cut into 1-cm/½-inch pieces

300 g/10½ oz. cooked meat, cut into small pieces

salt, freshly ground black pepper and Worcestershire sauce, to serve

a small bunch of fresh parsley, chopped, to serve

TO SERVE

1–2 fried eggs per person (served on top of the potato mix)

pickled beetroot/beet slices

tomato ketchup

SERVES 2–3

In a frying pan/skillet, melt half of the butter and a glug of oil. Add the onion and cook for about 5–7 minutes, then add the small pieces of root veg and the sprigs of thyme and continue to cook for another 8 minutes.

Add the potatoes and more butter – yes, I know, but butter makes the world go round and it also makes potatoes taste really nice as they crisp up. Keep an eye on the pan as you turn the heat up a bit to help crisp up the potatoes. Lastly, add the meat and allow to heat through, then season well with salt, pepper and a few drops of Worcestershire sauce and add the freshly chopped parsley just before serving.

Great served with fried eggs, pickled beetroot/beets and tomato ketchup.

MAKE IT VEGGIE Instead of the meat, fry 300 g/10½ oz. mixed sliced mushrooms in a separate pan. I prefer dry-frying using this method. Add the mushrooms to a hot pan and allow to cook – don't worry, it will happen even with no oil. Keep the heat on and eventually – it might take 5 minutes or more – the mushrooms will release all the water. Allow this to evaporate, then add a knob of butter and season and take off the heat. Add the mushrooms to the *Pyttipanna* instead of the meat.

168 SEPTEMBER

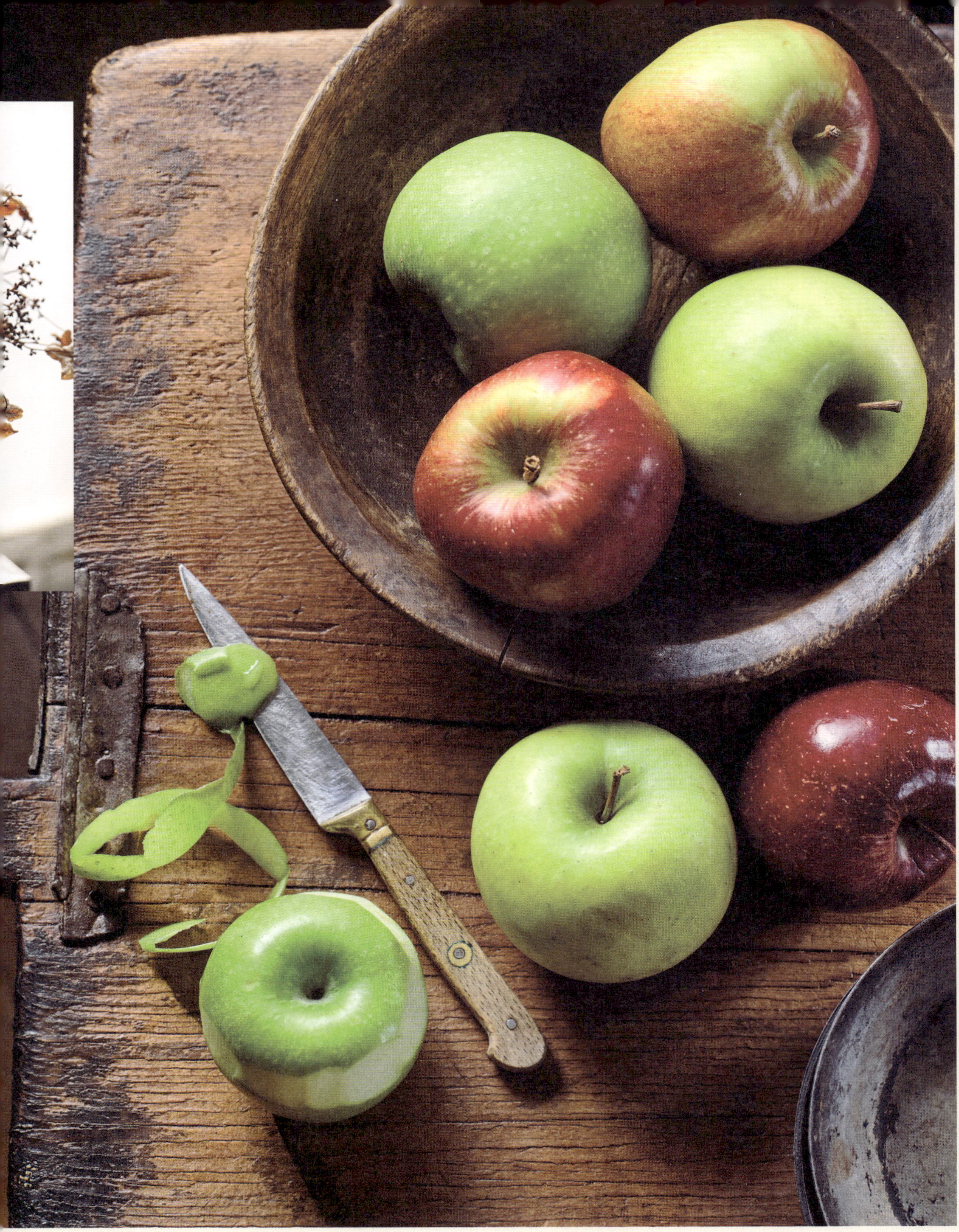

Upside-down apple cake with custard

Æblekage

I have a thing for pastry cream, as you might have guessed from reading my books. When I was pregnant with my youngest, I had an even bigger craving for custard and apple than normal, so I baked many kinds of cakes featuring these ingredients in some form or another. The force was very strong.

Layer this cake with apples, then pastry cream and then cake batter (upside down). You can also bake it the other way up – adding the batter, then custard and apples – it works well, too, but it is a little harder to tell when the cake it done because the custard stays soft. When turning the cake out, drizzle with some syrup (I like maple) and add toasted flaked/slivered almonds or pearl sugar before serving.

40 g/3 tablespoons butter
150 ml/⅔ cup milk
3 eggs
180 g/1 cup minus 1½ tablespoons caster/granulated sugar
200 g/1½ cups plain/all-purpose flour
2 teaspoons baking powder
1 teaspoon vanilla sugar or vanilla extract
a pinch of salt
½ quantity Pastry Cream (see page 237)
flaked/slivered almonds or pearl/nibbed sugar, to serve (optional)

APPLE MIXTURE
35 g/2½ tablespoons butter
25 g/2 tablespoons caster/granulated sugar
50 g/¼ cup dark brown sugar
2 generous teaspoons ground cinnamon
4 Granny Smith apples or other tart apples, peeled, cored and cut into 1–2-cm/½–¾-inch pieces
a pinch of salt

23-cm/9-inch springform cake pan, lined with baking parchment
piping/pastry bag (optional)

MAKES 10 SLICES

Preheat the oven to 190°C/170°C fan/375°F/Gas 5.

To make the apple mixture, place the butter and sugars in a saucepan and melt with the cinnamon. Add the apples and a pinch of salt, then stir to coat the apples evenly. Take the pan off the heat (the apples will cook in the oven).

To make the cake batter, melt the butter, then mix with the milk and leave to cool down a little.

Whisk the eggs and sugar in a bowl until light and airy. Combine the dry ingredients, then sift into the egg mixture. Add the milk and butter mixture, then fold until all the ingredients are evenly incorporated.

Tip the apple mixture into the base of the prepared cake pan, then add the pastry cream (it is easiest to do this using a piping/pastry bag or a plastic bag with a hole cut in the corner). Add the cake batter on top.

Bake in the preheated oven for around 35–40 minutes (or until done – baking time can vary by oven). You might need to turn the heat down a little towards the end to stop the top from going too brown.

Leave the cake to cool down in the pan. To serve, turn it upside down on a plate and remove the baking parchment. I sometimes like to sprinkle flaked/slivered almonds or pearl/nibbed sugar on top before serving.

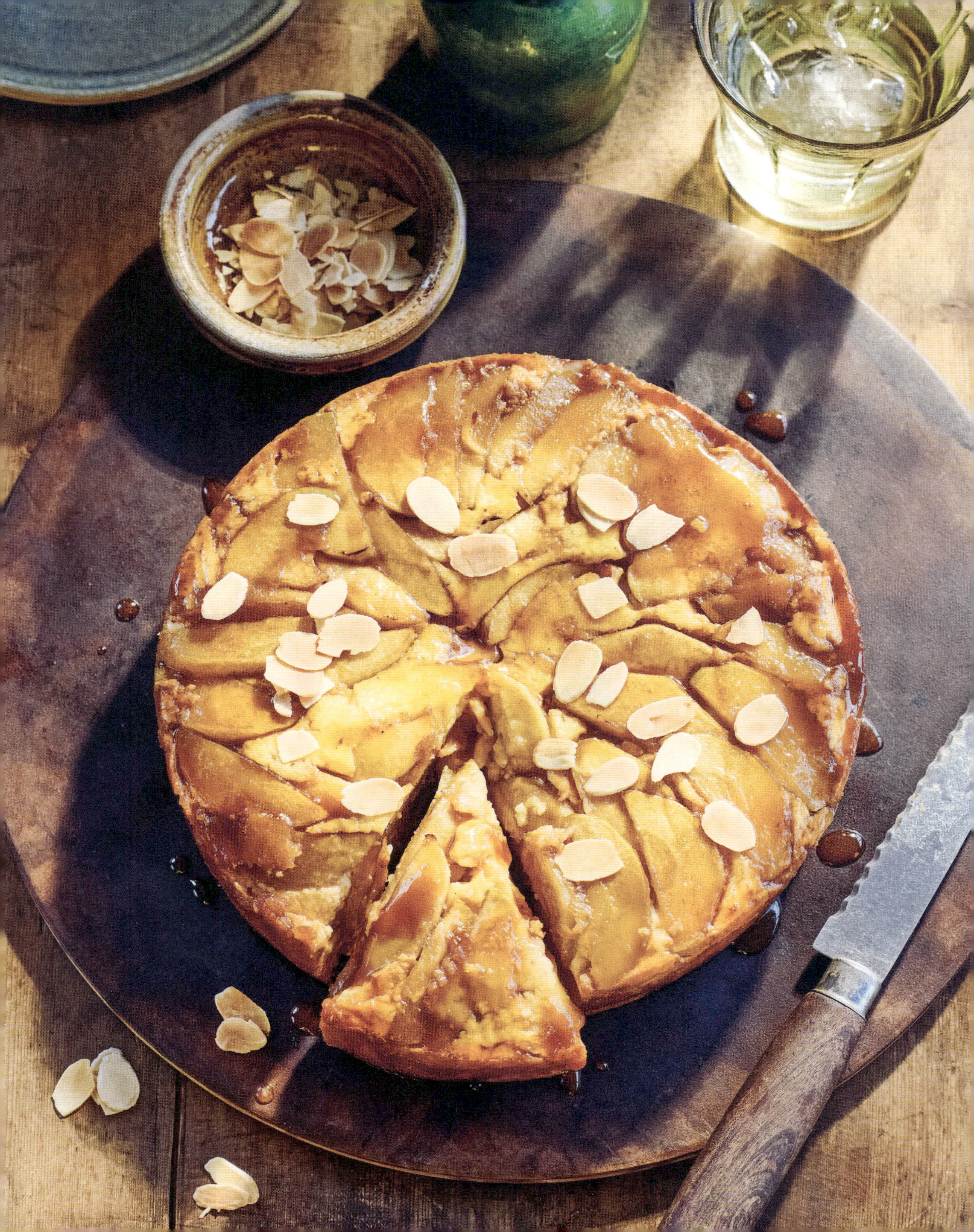

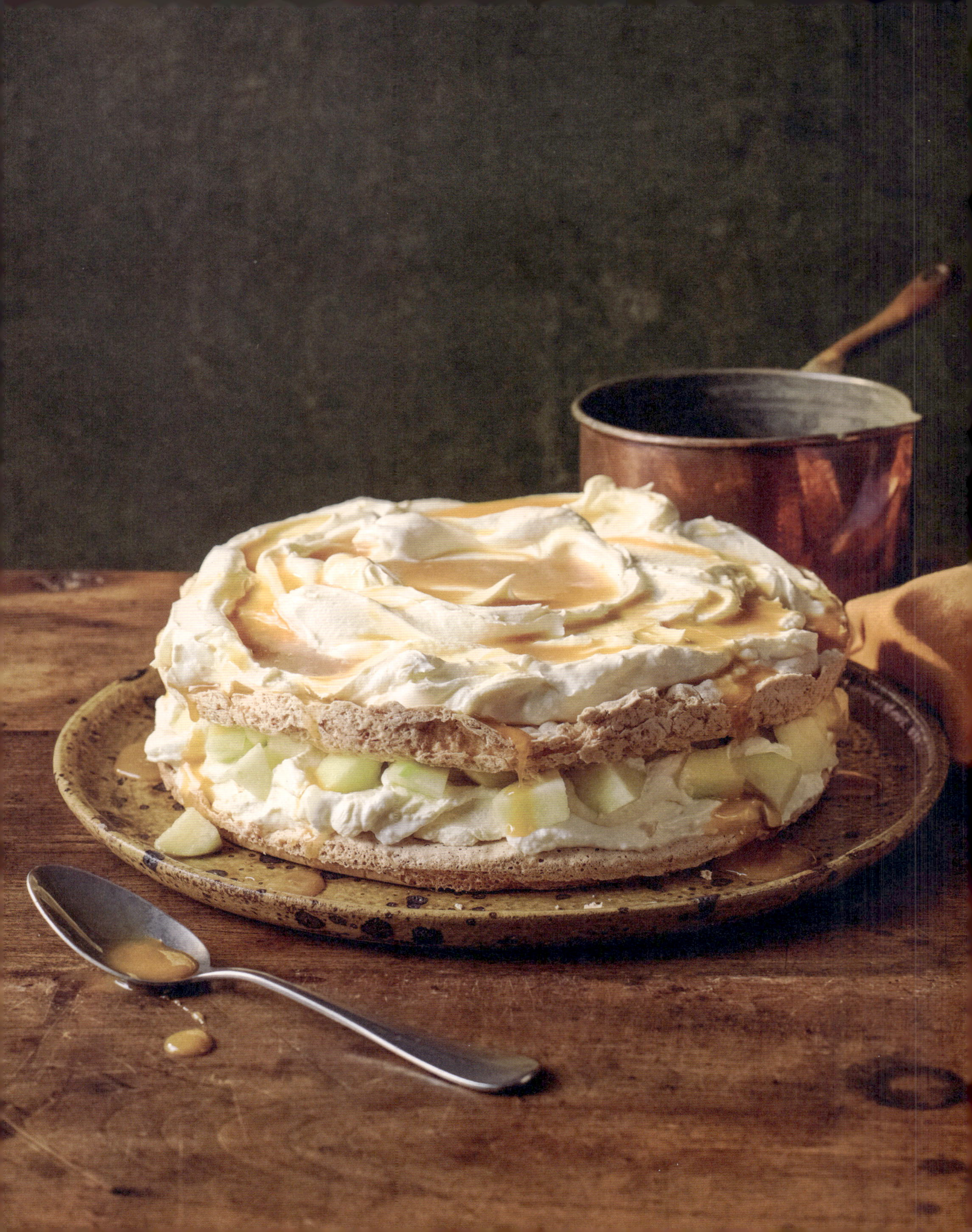

Faeroese apple cake

Føroysk súreplakaka

The beautiful Faroe Islands are between Shetland and Iceland. As a remote territory of less than 55,000 people across 18 islands, not much of their food culture travels, except this cake, which has been popular on the islands since the mid 90s. This version is based on a recipe from a Faroese lady called Ella, who got it from her sister-in-law Jóhanna.

Ella and Jóhanna both use chopped almonds in the meringue, but some recipes use desiccated/shredded coconut (which is what I have done). Use whatever you prefer: both options are lovely. It's unusual to use finely chopped raw apple in a cake, but somehow, the sweet meringue with the filling of fresh, creamy apple and salted caramel on top works so well.

It's a little tricky to style this cake. I drizzle on the caramel only just before serving. Eat on the day of making.

4 egg whites
200 g/1 cup caster/granulated sugar
1 teaspoon vanilla extract or vanilla sugar
75 g/1 cup desiccated/shredded dried coconut

FILLING & TOPPING
100–150 g/3½–5½ oz. Salted Caramel (see page 38 or shop-bought)
4 Granny Smith apples or similar tart apples (Pink Lady is also great)
300 ml/1¼ cups whipping cream
1 teaspoon vanilla extract
1 tablespoon icing/confectioner's sugar
200 ml/¾ cup crème fraîche

SERVES 6–8

Preheat the oven to 170°C/150°C fan/340°F/Gas 4.

Draw two 25-cm/10-inch circles on two pieces of baking parchment and place on baking sheets.

To make the meringue layers, whisk the egg whites until stiff, then start to add the sugar one spoonful at a time, whisking on high speed as you go. Add the vanilla and whisk for 5–6 minutes on full speed until the meringue mixture is thick and has firm peaks. Fold in the coconut, carefully.

Split the mixture between the baking parchment circles and carefully spread out to fit inside the lines exactly. Bake in the preheated oven for 35 minutes, then turn off the oven. Leave the oven door ajar and allow the bases to cool down completely in the oven.

If making the salted caramel, do this now and allow to cool completely.

To serve, peel and core the apples and chop into bite-sized pieces.

Place the cream in a bowl with the vanilla and icing/confectioner's sugar and whip until almost stiff, then add the crème fraîche and whip for a little longer until you have a thick mixture.

Mix the apples with around two-thirds of the whipped cream (reserve the rest for topping).

Add one meringue layer to a serving tray, add all the apple mixture and half the salted caramel. Top with the second meringue, then spread the remaining cream over the top and drizzle over the remaining salted caramel. Serve immediately.

Danish beer loaf

Ølkage

In Denmark this is called Beer Cake, but it's more like a soda bread – although with no dairy at all. Because of the spices in this loaf, it's often served around Christmastime, but I absolutely love this loaf and make it all year round. It's super-easy to put together. It looks like a dark rye bread when it is baked, but it is sweet and fragrant – and irresistible, with a spread of delicious, cold butter on top.

400 g/3 cups plain/all-purpose flour
1 teaspoon bicarbonate of soda/ baking soda
1 teaspoon ground ginger
1 teaspoon ground cloves
2 teaspoons ground cinnamon
½ teaspoon cacao powder
½ teaspoon fine salt
300 g/1½ cups dark brown muscovado sugar
250 ml/1 cup stout

1-litre/2-lb. loaf pan, lined with baking parchment

MAKES 10 SLICES

Preheat the oven to 190°C/170°C fan/375°F/Gas 5.

Mix together all the dry ingredients (apart from the sugar) in a bowl, then add the sugar. Add the stout and stir until smooth.

Pour the batter into the prepared loaf pan and bake in the preheated oven for around 1 hour or until baked through and a skewer inserted into the centre comes out clean.

Allow to cool, then serve in slices with a nice thick layer of butter. Keeps moist for several days.

NOTE I use Guinness as this is the stout I tend to have in my house, but you can use different beers or stouts.

Danish jam slices

Hindbærsnitter

Any Dane will tell you that getting a raspberry slice from the local baker was a big, sweet treat for a kid. Essentially, it is sweet shortcrust pastry with a middle layer of jam (raspberry is traditional), a thick layer of icing on top and colourful sprinkles.

1 quantity Sweet Shortcrust Pastry (see page 235)
200 g/⅔ cup raspberry jam/preserve (or whatever flavour you like)
300 g/2 cups plus 2 tablespoons icing/confectioner's sugar
1–3 tablespoons hot water
sprinkles, to decorate

2 baking sheets, lined with baking parchment

MAKES 12–16 SQUARES

Preheat the oven to 180°C/160°C fan/350°F/Gas 4.

Split the pastry in half and roll into two 30-cm/12-inch squares, around 4 mm/⅛ inch thick. Put on the baking sheets and prick the surfaces with a fork to prevent air bubbles forming during baking. Bake in the preheated oven for 10–12 minutes or until slightly golden, then cool on a wire rack.

On one of the cooled pastry sheets, spread the raspberry jam/preserve in an even layer. Slide the other piece of pastry on top so that it sits exactly on top of the base. Handle delicately, as the pastry can break quite easily. Mix the sugar with enough hot water to form a smooth paste. Spread on top of the pastry to evenly cover, top with sprinkles and leave to set.

Using a very sharp serrated knife, cut the edges off the pastry to make straight sides. Cut into small equal pieces (it is easier to cut after a little time because the jam will soften the pastry quite quickly).

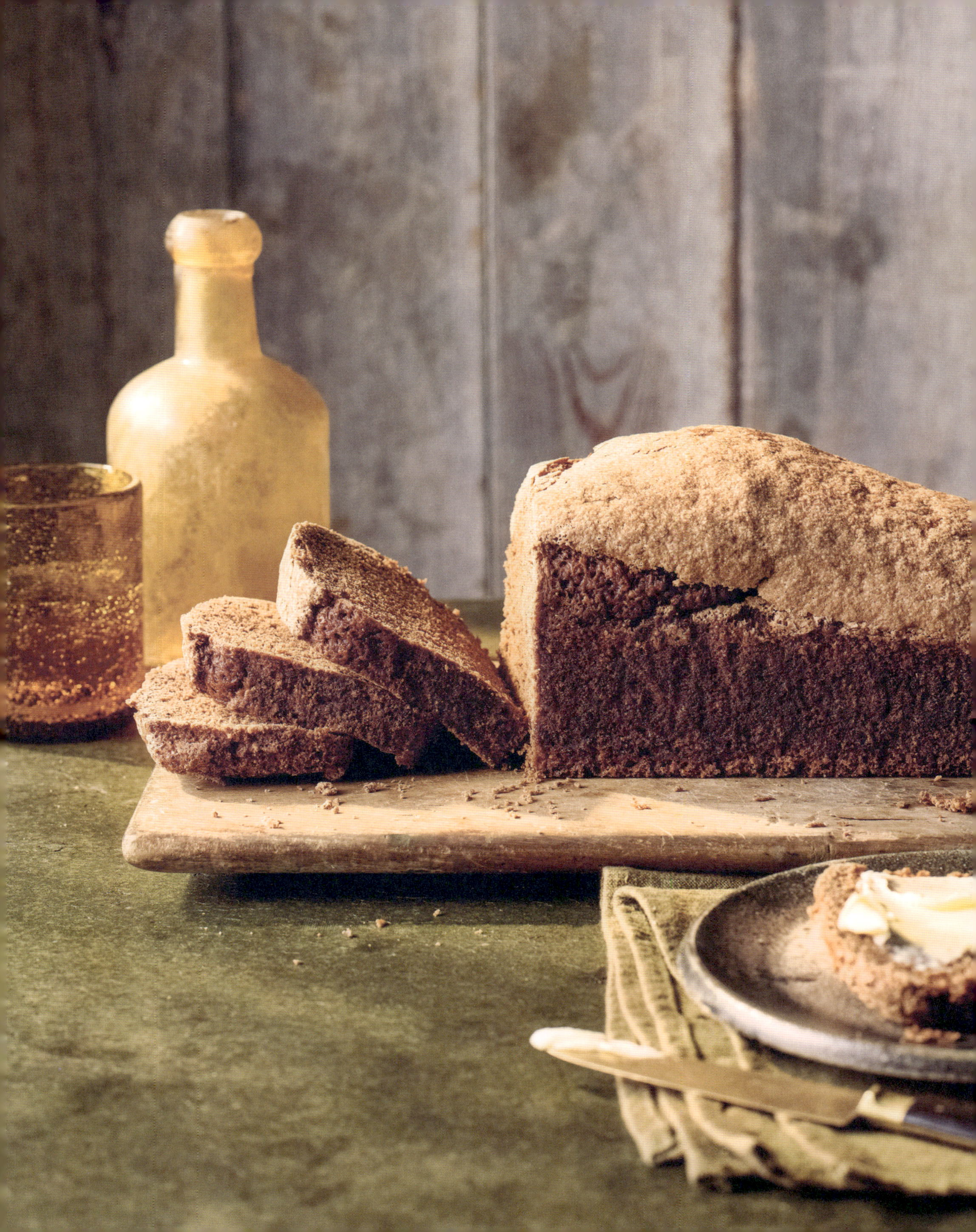

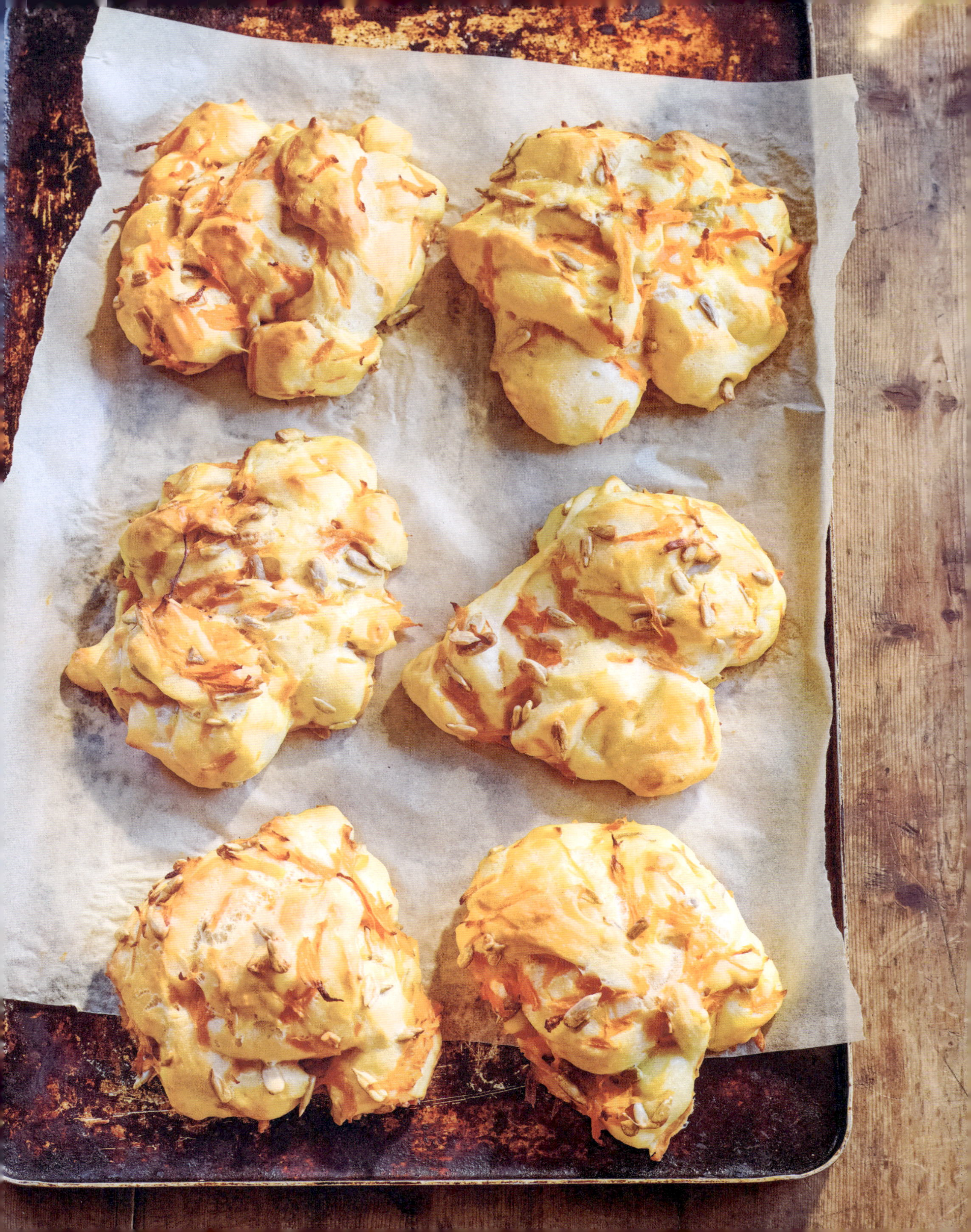

Danish carrot rolls
Gulerodsbrud

Brud in Danish means 'break' and these rolls are essentially 'carrot breaks', the 'break' meaning the dough is roughly chopped together into a mass, which gives these rolls their unusual, messy look. Pretty, they're not – tasty, they are. I love baking these for packed lunches. Grated carrot in bread is so delicious and naturally sweet. If you prefer a less sweet roll, you can reduce the sugar or replace with a bit of honey. You can halve the recipe for a smaller batch (or freeze any extras on the day of baking), or replace the carrot with courgette/zucchini to mix things up a bit.

a few drops of freshly squeezed lemon juice
250 ml/1 cup whole milk
50 g/1¾ oz. fresh yeast or equivalent of active dry yeast granules
50 g/¼ cup caster/granulated sugar
800 g/5¾ cups approx. white bread flour
75 g/5⅓ tablespoons butter, softened
1 teaspoon fine salt
2 eggs
250–300 g/9–10½ oz. grated carrot
100 g/¾ cup sunflower seeds

2 baking sheets, lined with baking parchment

MAKES 16

Add the lemon juice to the milk and wait 10 minutes, then add 250 ml/1 cup lukewarm water and heat until finger-warm (maximum 36°C/97°F).

Add the yeast and warm milk mixture to a stand mixer and add the sugar. Mix until dissolved, then add the flour little by little. You may not need all the flour, so start with 700 g/5 cups and add more as needed. Add the softened butter and mix it in. Add the salt. Mix the dough until you have an elastic, uniform dough, then roll into a ball and cover.

Leave dough to rest until double in size. This will take around 45 minutes in a normal temperature room (longer if cooler, shorter if warmer).

Knead the dough and make a well in the middle. Crack the eggs into the well, then add the grated carrot and sunflower seeds. This next bit is messy: 'close' the dough into a ball by stretching the dough around and over the top, packing the filling inside. Using a dough scraper or wide bladed knife, cut and mix the dough until it starts to stick together – the egg might spill a bit, but just keep using the scraper to add it back and chop some more.

Once it more or less hangs together, but is still looking like a mess, start cutting pieces of dough – you will get around 16 buns. They will be very uneven in shape and look, but this is part of the eventual appeal.

Place eight buns on each lined baking sheet – they will rise, so give them plenty of space. Cover and leave to rise for 30 minutes.

Preheat the oven to 240°C/220°C fan/475°F/Gas 9. Turn on the steam function if your oven has this; a heatproof bowl of water placed at the bottom of your oven also works.

Add the buns to the preheated oven, turn down the heat to 220°C/200°C fan/425°F/Gas 7 and bake until done – around 13–15 minutes, depending on your oven. If you tap on the base of the bun, it should sound slightly hollow; this means they're done.

These rolls are best eaten on the day they are baked. You can freeze them, but for best result, do so as soon as they have cooled down.

VARIATION Replace the sunflower seeds and carrots with 200 g/1⅓ cups chocolate chips for *chokoladebrud* – chocolate chip break rolls.

I always feel that October is the 'in-between month' – not quite cold enough for winter, but there is nothing left of anything green (and we're not yet allowed to play Christmas music). The leaves are brown and the winds and serious rain have set in. Now, we wait: for the snow, for the cold, for the darkness to return once again. Up north, the first snow has started to settle.

October is a month of immense beauty in Scandinavian nature, and you can enjoy it as long as you're dressed for it (as all Scandinavian mothers will tell you, 'there's no such thing as bad weather, only bad clothes'). This is a great month for getting in a last few long hikes on the milder days. While it's not as light or as warm as our summers, the immense colour palette of nature would thrill even the most reluctant walker.

And we're still enjoying all those apples, pears, squash and pumpkins as Halloween comes around.

OCTOBER

FIKA & HYGGE

We love days for things in Scandinavia: 4th October is Cinnamon Bun Day and there are few things more comforting than a big, soft, fluffy cinnamon bun. For most, it is peak *fika* and *hygge* all in one.

Those two words are these days at the forefront of people's minds when talking about Scandinavia. A decade ago, most people outside our borders wouldn't have known what either meant, but both have become synonymous with Scandinavian culture. However, as with all things that ride a wave of popularity, sometimes meaning can get a little lost in translation.

Fika

All Scandinavians practise this, but the Swedes have the best word: *fika*. In fact, a Swede will use this word several times a day. *Fika* means to take a break and eat something, usually sweet, with a cup of coffee (or whatever else you fancy, as long as it's not alcohol, but it's usually coffee).

In a nutshell, it means to stop, eat something and chat with someone else. It's your coffee break at work (twice a day), it's a break at school, a break in a meeting or even an evening *fika* at home. The word is both a noun and a verb: you can *fika* with someone, but equally you can take a *fika*. You can do it with family, friends and coworkers – and even go on a *fika* date. In terms of cultural relevancy, *fika* is more than a coffee break but not a formal event. It's an important part of how the day is structured and the kind of people the Swedes are. Everyone does it.

As Scandinavians are huge coffee drinkers, *fika* is about maximising coffee intake throughout the waking hours (we drink more coffee than anyone else in the world). Alongside, people will opt for some sort of *fikabröd* ('*fika* bread'), which describes a whole range of possible options – the most famous of which is the cinnamon bun. Alternatively, it could be soft bread with butter and cheese, a slice of cake or a muffin.

Fika is a twice-a-day reminder to stop what we're doing and talk to other humans for 15 minutes – something many of us have become bad at in the past decades as we feel more and more chained to our desks.

Hygge

At the height of the *hygge* wave a few years ago, items such as *hygge* hairbands and *hygge* socks were being touted as essential items in the pursuit of this feeling. Now that the *hygge* hype seems to have moved on, we can try to reclaim it for what it really is. It is a very important word and state of being, especially to Danes and Norwegians.

Hygge simply means to appreciate the moment you're in, while you're in it.

As with *fika*, most Danes will use the word in many forms throughout the day. We use it as an affirmation – 'This is a *hyggelig* dinner', 'What a *hyggelig* trip to the park', 'Let's *hygge* together in front of the telly', etc. (*hyggelig* literally means '*hygge*-ly'). Voicing our feelings means the *hygge* becomes shared and often special. While one can of course *hygge* alone, it is most often done with others – and quite often (but not always) there is some sort of food or drink involved. From a bottle of wine with friends to a bowl of snacks on the table or a cup of coffee and a bun, all these moments can be where real *hygge* is found. Candles can help, but are by no means essential, as you can just as easily *hygge* in a tent, sharing a packet of potato chips while listening to the rain outside. At Christmastime, everything becomes about *julehygge* (Christmas *hygge*), just as at Easter it's about *påskehygge* (Easter *hygge*).

What *hygge* is *not* is mobile devices or other interruptions to the space you're sharing at that moment. In order to *hygge*, you need to be present and affirm that you're doing it (*hygge*-ly). You don't need *hygge* pants, *hygge* candles or anything else labelled *hygge* to feel present and appreciate a shared moment.

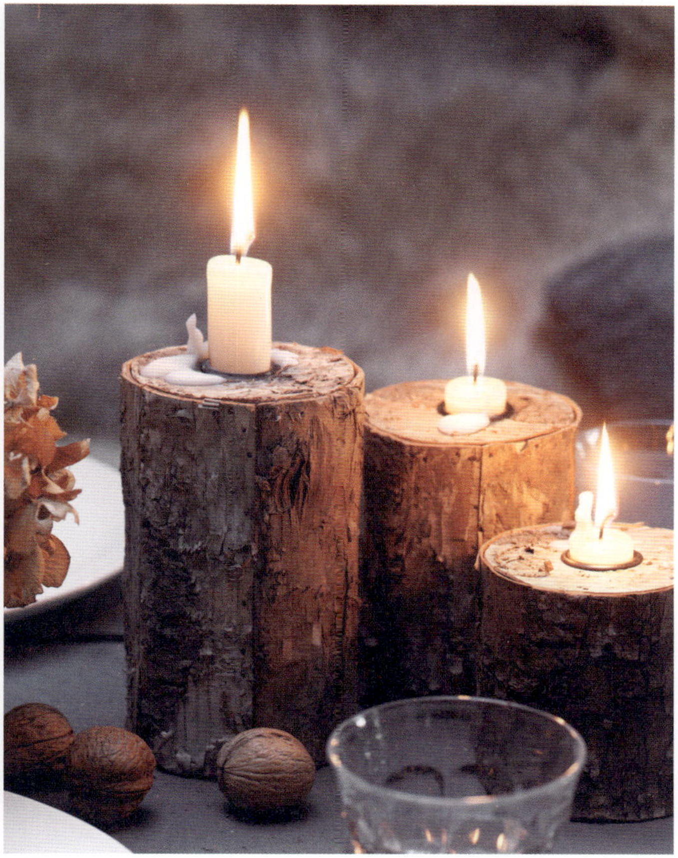
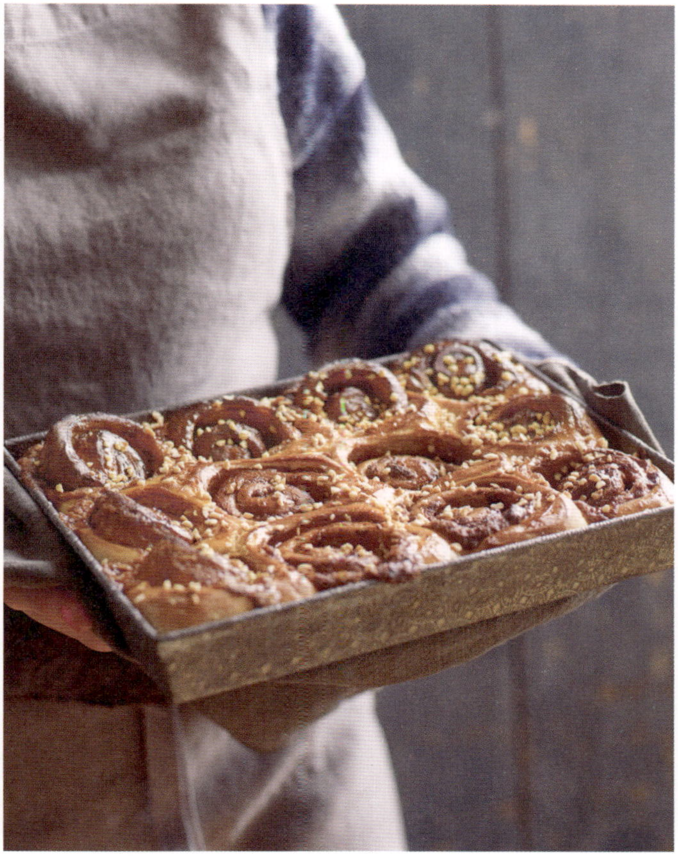
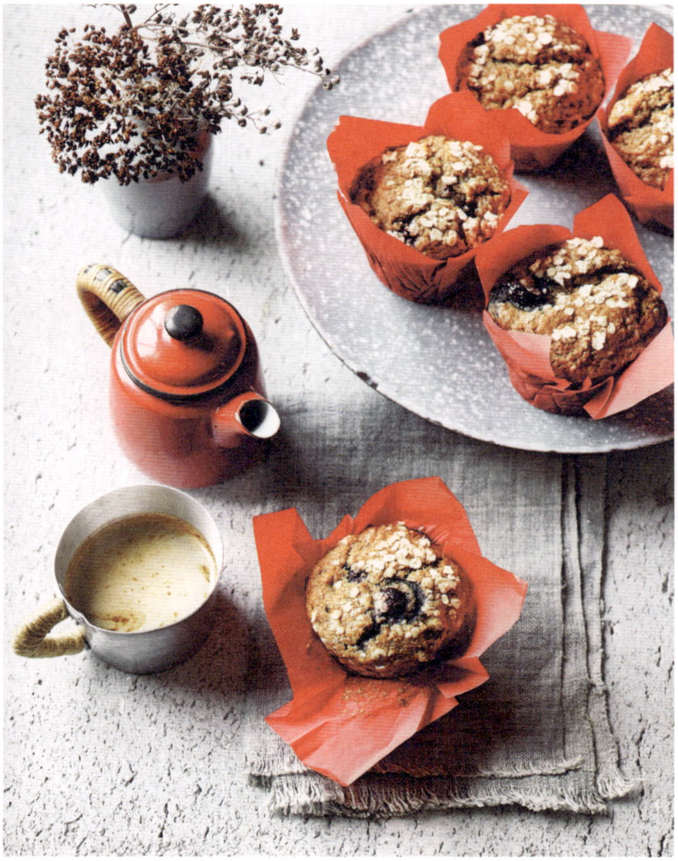
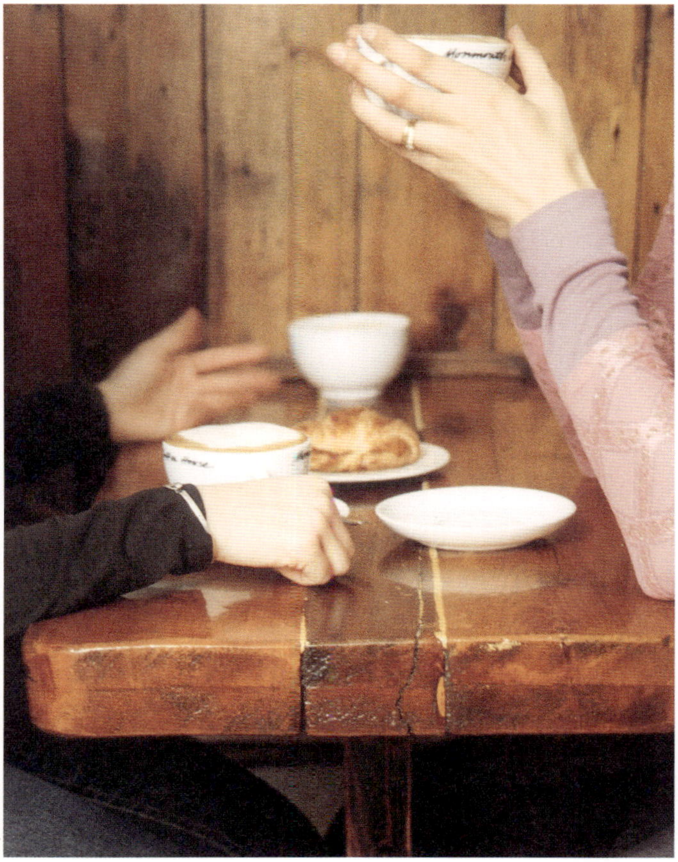

Roasted beets with dill
Rødbeder med dill og feta

An inexpensive and quick side dish to make. You can, of course, roast or boil fresh beetroot for this but I often make this after coming home from work and needing to fix dinner in a jiffy, so I just use pre-cooked beetroot from the supermarket. The nuts can be varied, based on what is hiding in your cupboard – hazelnuts and walnuts are earthy, pecans also work well, as do flaked/slivered toasted almonds.

250-g/9-oz. packet cooked beetroot/beets
1–2 tablespoons runny honey
a knob/pat of butter
a glug of oil
50 g/1¾ oz. feta cheese, crumbled
10 g/⅓ oz. fresh dill, chopped
25 g/¼ cup toasted hazelnuts, roughly chopped
rocket/arugula leaves, to serve
pea shoots, to garnish
salt and freshly ground black pepper

SERVES 2 AS A SIDE

Preheat the oven to 200°C/180°C fan/400°F/Gas 6.

Cut the beetroot/beets into quarters, then add to an ovenproof dish and drizzle with the honey and a small knob of butter. Season. Roast in the preheated oven for around 15–20 minutes until slightly caramelised.

On a serving plate, arrange the rocket/arugula leaves, then add the beetroot. Scatter over the feta, dill and hazelnuts. Garnish with pea shoots and serve immediately. I rarely add any dressing but if the beets have gone a little dry, I sometimes add a drizzle of good extra virgin olive oil.

VARIATIONS No dill? Parsley works, as do chervil and tarragon. If you want to roast your own beetroot/beets, I find it easier to pre-boil them on the stove, then peel and cut before roasting.

Simple celeriac salad
Nem knoldselleri salat

This is a great healthy side salad. Raw celeriac/celery root is underused, I think. This is similar to the French salad *céleri rémoulade* (not the same as Danish remoulade). I love using this as a base for an open sandwich with beef or as a side to dishes where I may otherwise use a Danish remoulade, such as fried fish.

300 g/10½ oz. celeriac/celery root (grated weight)
a small bunch of flat-leaf parsley, chopped
100 g/7 tablespoons crème fraîche
2 tablespoons olive oil
4 teaspoons white wine vinegar
1 generous tablespoon honey
1 teaspoon Dijon mustard
1 tablespoon capers, chopped
salt and freshly ground black pepper
25–35 g/1 oz. lightly toasted pecans (or other nuts – blanched almonds also work well)

SERVES 2–3 AS A SIDE

Peel the celeriac/celery root and grate.

Mix all the other ingredients (except the nuts) in a bowl. Taste to check if the balance is right – it should taste a bit vinegary but not too powerful, so adjust as necessary. Finally, add the grated celeriac and mix with the dressing. Sprinkle the nuts on top.

VARIATION If you want to dress this salad up, add a grated apple (mix this with a bit of lemon juice before adding or it will go brown quickly).

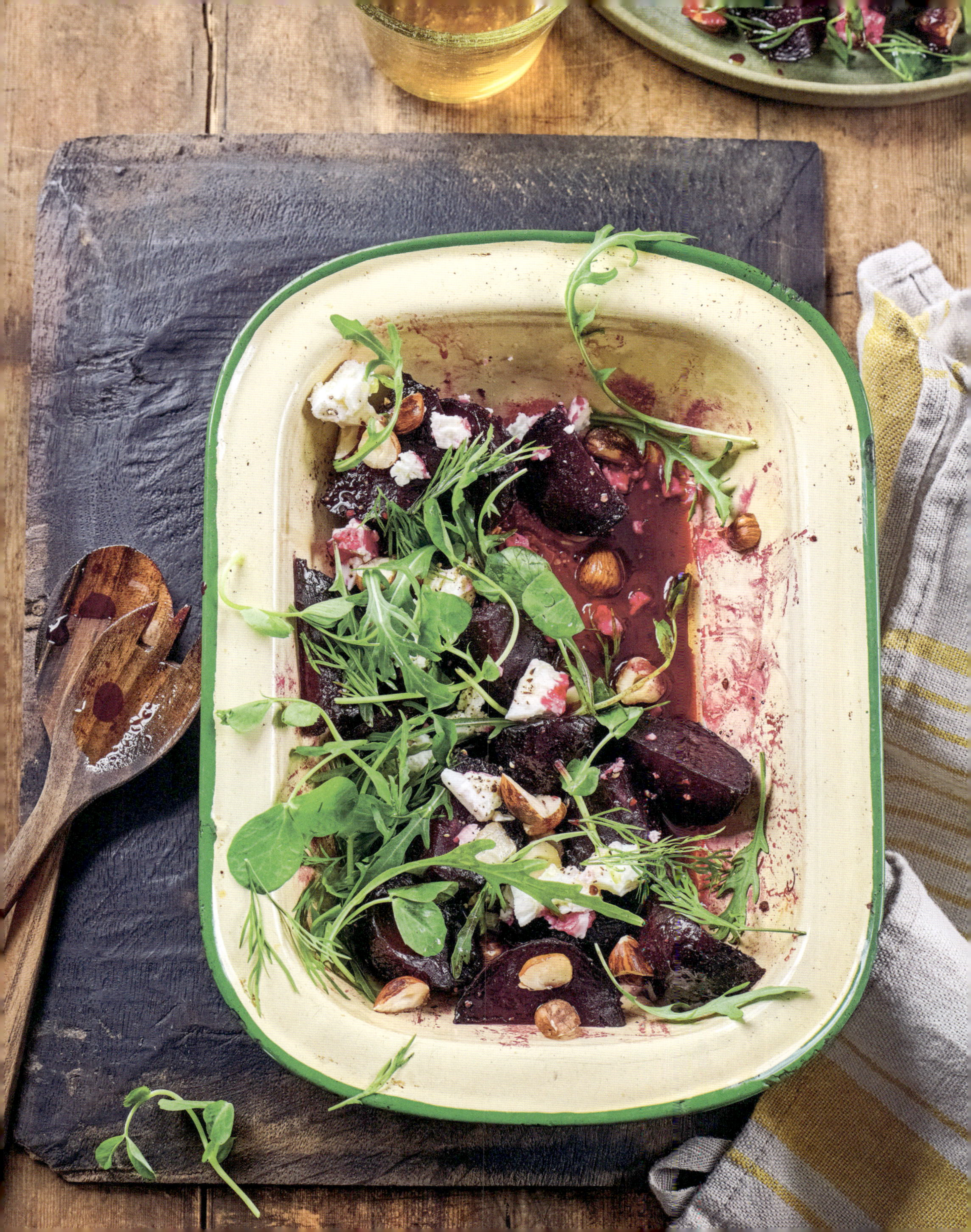

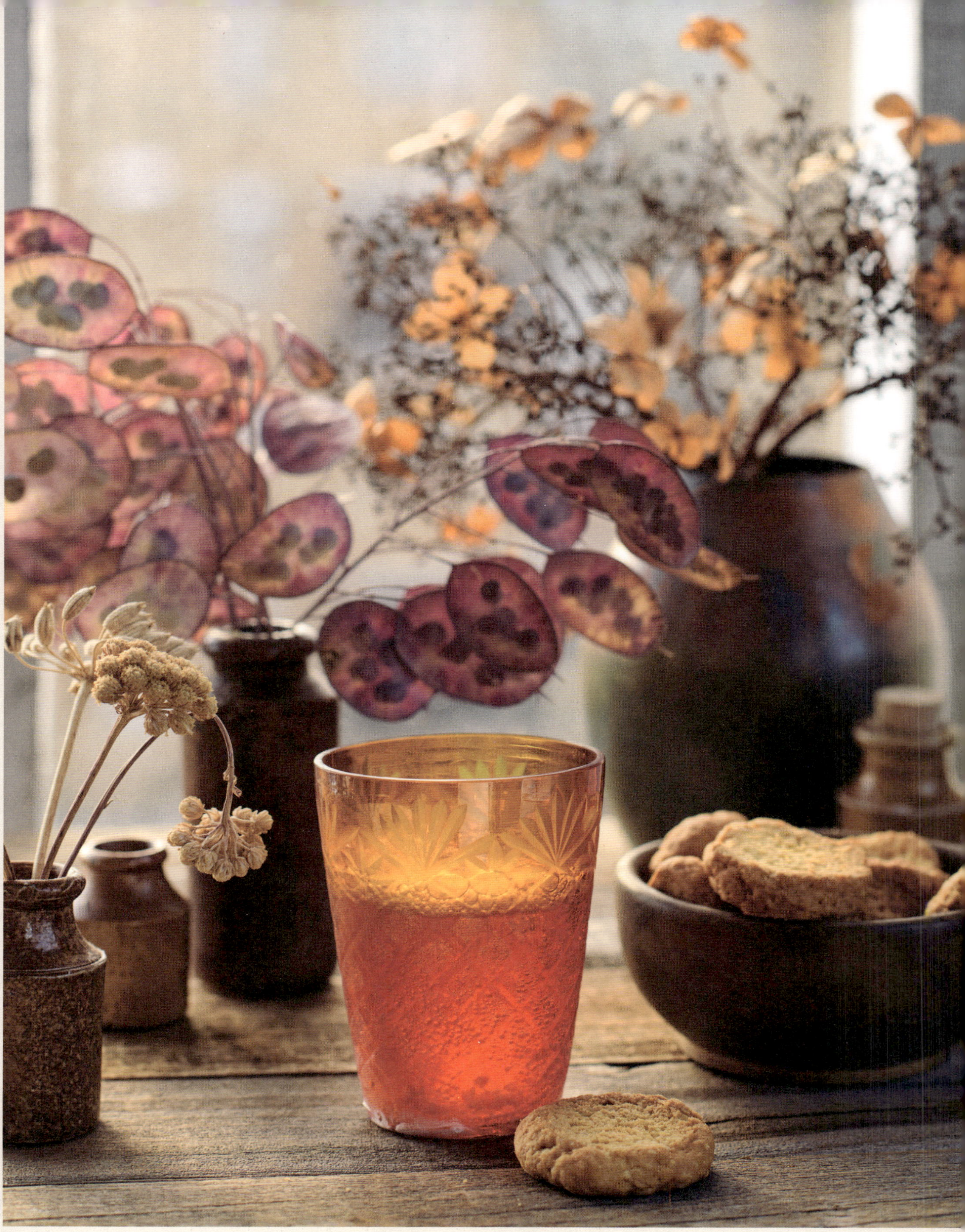

OCTOBER 185

Quick pork tenderloin pot — *Mørbradgryde*

This is a midweek dinner dish we were served as children growing up in Denmark. There are countless variations on a theme when it comes to *Mørbradgryde* – the name means 'tenderloin pot'. Some people add sausage, some bacon, some both; some favour no mushrooms, some go overboard. Either way, this is ready in the time it takes to boil a pot of rice or some potatoes.

Tenderloin pork is still a reasonably inexpensive meat and one fillet in this dish – with a bit of what you have in the cupboards and veg drawer – can feed a family of four. Whatever you do, don't leave this to stew for long: pork tenderloin is a meat so lean that it is best when it is *just* cooked through.

a glug of oil and a knob/pat of butter, for frying
1 pork tenderloin fillet, approx. 500–600 g/1 lb. 2 oz–1 lb. 5 oz.
1 onion, chopped
1 medium carrot, chopped into 5-mm/¼-inch pieces
1 celery stick, chopped into 5-mm/¼-inch pieces
100 g/3½ oz. bacon or pancetta, chopped
200 g/7oz. mushrooms, sliced
1 tablespoon tomato purée/paste
100 ml/⅓ cup plus 1 tablespoon wine – either red or white will do
1 teaspoon paprika
1–2 bay leaves
½ teaspoon dried thyme
150 ml/⅔ cup stock
1 x 400-g/14-oz. can chopped tomatoes
200 ml/¾ cup double/heavy cream
1–2 tablespoons cornflour/cornstarch (optional)
salt and freshly ground black pepper
freshly chopped parsley, to serve

SERVES 4

In a flameproof casserole dish, heat a glug of oil and a knob/pat of butter. Slice the tenderloin, add to the casserole and brown on all sides, then remove from the dish and set aside.

Add the chopped onion and leave to caramelise, then add the carrot and celery. Add the bacon and sliced mushrooms and leave to cook for a few minutes. Add the tomato purée/paste and then the wine. Cook for a few more minutes to allow the alcohol to evaporate, then add the paprika, herbs, stock and chopped tomatoes.

Add the cream and check the thickness of the sauce – if you prefer a thicker sauce, dissolve the cornflour/cornstarch in a bit of water, add to the dish and bring to the boil to thicken.

Add the pork back into the dish, cover and simmer for 5 minutes to ensure the pork slices are just cooked through. Adjust the seasoning and dress with parsley just before serving. Goes well with new potatoes, rice or a fresh green salad.

NOTE If you need to bulk out this dish a bit, add a can of butter beans, drained, when you add the meat for the last 5 minutes – they add lots of goodness and fibre.

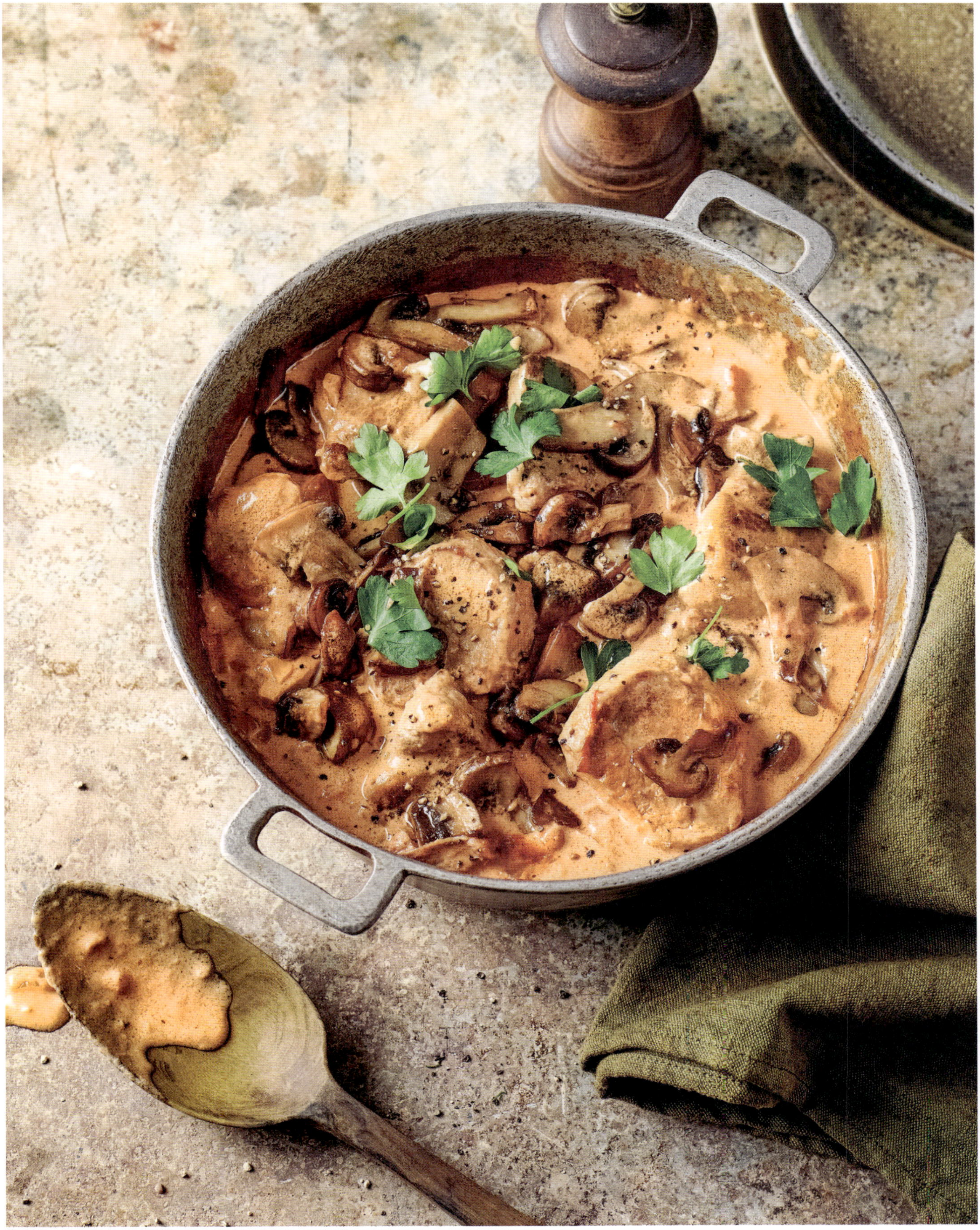

Swedish beef stew

Kalops

The Swedish name of this dish apparently comes from the English word 'collops', meaning small slices of meat – and apparently that word originated from Swedish itself. Few people would use the word in English today, though. A version of this is also served in Finland as *Palapaisti*.

I am a big fan of stews and even more so, of slow cooking less fancy meat for hours and hours to bring out the full flavours. Serve this with boiled potatoes and sliced pickled beetroot on the side. Perfect on a cold day.

a knob/pat of butter and a glug of oil, for frying
1 kg/2lb. 4 oz. braising/chuck steak, cut into 4–5-cm/1½–2-inch pieces
2 onions, sliced
100 g/3½ oz. lardons or streaky bacon, cut into pieces
1 celery stick, chopped
3 large carrots, 1 chopped and 2 sliced
200 ml/¾ cup red wine
4 bay leaves
10 whole allspice berries
1 litre/4 cups meat stock
2–3 tablespoons cornflour/cornstarch
a splash of milk
salt and freshly ground black pepper

SERVES 4

Melt a knob/pat of butter in a large pan and brown the beef on all sides, then using a slotted spoon, set the beef aside on a plate.

Add a glug of oil if needed, then add the sliced onions and fry for around 10 minutes under a lid and allow to caramelise. Remove the lid and add the bacon, celery and chopped carrot. Add the wine and cook off the alcohol for a few minutes, then add the bay leaves, allspice and stock.

Bring to the boil, then slow to a simmer and cook, covered, for 2 hours. After 2 hours, remove the lid and add the sliced carrots. Cover and cook for 1 hour – by then, the meat should be falling apart.

Mix the cornflour/cornstarch with a splash of milk, then add to the stew and bring to the boil for a few minutes to thicken the stew.

Season well and serve with boiled potatoes and pickled beetroot.

White loaf with white poppy seeds

Franskbrød

While this loaf may not be fancy, it's the bread that you'll see in every Danish bakery. It's a white sandwich loaf – you can make this with or without a loaf pan, without or without poppy seeds (blue or white). You can sweeten it up a bit if you prefer that, or you can add seeds for a healthier option (100 g/3½ oz. per loaf).

This recipe makes two loaves. I only ever use compressed, fresh yeast, but you can use the live-action yeast granules too (stay clear of the quick action stuff).

You can also cold rise this dough in the fridge overnight. In that case, reduce the yeast by at least half and let the dough come to room temperature before continuing the recipe.

The name *franskbrød* means French loaf (but I don't think it's ever been to France, even on holiday…). Best on the day of baking, but freezes well, too.

650 ml/2¾ cups whole milk
25 g/⅞ oz. fresh yeast
2 tablespoons honey or sugar
1 kg/7 cups white bread flour, plus extra for kneading
50 g/3½ tablespoons softened butter
1½ teaspoons fine salt
beaten egg or milk, for brushing
25 g/¾ cup white poppy seeds, for topping

2 x 1.5-litre/3-lb. bread pans, lined with baking parchment, or a large baking sheet, lined with baking parchment

MAKES 2 LOAVES

Heat the milk to 32–35°C/90–95°F, then pour into a stand mixer, add the yeast and mix. Add the honey or sugar. Once it has dissolved, start adding the flour little by little, then add the softened butter (it will mix in). Add the salt and keep kneading until you have a uniform dough – around 5 minutes.

Leave to rise until doubled in size – this will depend on how warm your kitchen is. Time matters less than the size of the rise (usually 1–1½ hours).

Knock the dough out onto a floured surface and knead. Split into two pieces and shape into loaves.

Put the bread, smoothest side up, to the lined bread pans. Alternatively, put on a lined baking sheet, ensuring the loaves are not too close together. Leave to rise for another 30–40 minutes.

Preheat the oven to 220°C/200°C fan/425°F/Gas 7. Turn on the steam function if your oven has this; a heatproof bowl of water placed at the bottom of your oven also works.

Just before you pop the bread in the oven, brush with beaten egg or milk, and dust a generous amount of poppy seeds on top. Score the top four or five times at an angle (or one score down the middle lengthways, if using a bread pan).

Pop into the preheated oven and bake for 5 minutes on full heat, then turn down to 200°C/180°C fan/400°F/Gas 6 for the remaining baking time. Total baking time is around 30 minutes, but this varies by oven – the bread is done when the internal temperature reaches 92°C/198°F.

Remove from the pan and leave to cool on a wire rack.

Tosca tart

Toscatærte

The original Swedish Tosca cake is a vanilla-almond-based sponge with a delicious mixture of caramel and almonds on top. It has been popular for decades and is an old-school favourite. The name is a nod to Tuscany (Toscana) and in turn a nod to Puccini's opera *Tosca*. The topping is, essentially, based on a Florentine topping.

In Denmark, we also make a Tosca tart – also known as *Nøddemazarin* (nut frangipane), which is confusing as it is not the same as the Swedish Tosca cake. Instead, this tart has a pastry base, a frangipane middle and the topping, while similar to the Swedish caramel-almond topping, uses a mixture of nuts.

1 quantity Sweet Shortcrust Pastry (see page 235)

dark/bittersweet chocolate, melted, for decorating (optional)

ALMOND FILLING

125 g/1⅛ sticks butter, softened

100 g/½ cup caster/granulated sugar

200 g/7 oz. Marzipan (see page 237)

1 teaspoon vanilla extract

2 eggs

50 g/heaping ⅓ cup plain/all-purpose flour

a pinch of salt

NUT TOPPING

75 g/5⅓ tablespoons butter

50 g/¼ cup sugar

2 tablespoons golden/corn syrup

4 tablespoons whipping cream

2 tablespoons plain/all-purpose flour

a generous pinch of sea salt flakes

125 g/1¼ cups roughly chopped nuts (I use a mixture of flaked/slivered almonds, hazelnuts, pecans and pistachios, but traditionally it would be just almonds)

26-cm/10-inch tart pan

baking parchment and baking beans

SERVES 8–10

Preheat the oven to 200°C/180°C fan/400°F/Gas 6.

Roll out the shortcrust pastry and place in the tart pan (you may have pastry left over – freeze for later use). Bake blind (add baking parchment and baking beans on top to weigh down the pastry) in the preheated oven for 10 minutes, then remove the beans and paper and bake for a further 5 minutes, then remove from oven.

Meanwhile, make the almond filling. In a stand mixer, cream together the butter and sugar, then grate in the marzipan. Add the vanilla and mix again, then add the eggs one at a time and beat. Sift in the flour and salt and fold until incorporated.

Spread the filling onto the pasty base and place back in the oven for 15 minutes (at this point the cake should be browned and set enough to hold the nut mixture – too wet and it will collapse).

Meanwhile, make the nutty caramel topping. In a heavy-based saucepan, melt the butter and sugar, then add all the other ingredients except the nuts. Bring to boiling point and leave to simmer for a minute or so. Add the nuts and spread this mixture carefully over the cake, then place back in the oven for around 8–10 minutes until the top is golden and crusty. Remove from the oven earlier if it looks done. Take care not to overcook the caramel on too high a heat or it may set quite hard.

Allow to cool completely before eating. Decorate with melted dark chocolate piping, if you wish.

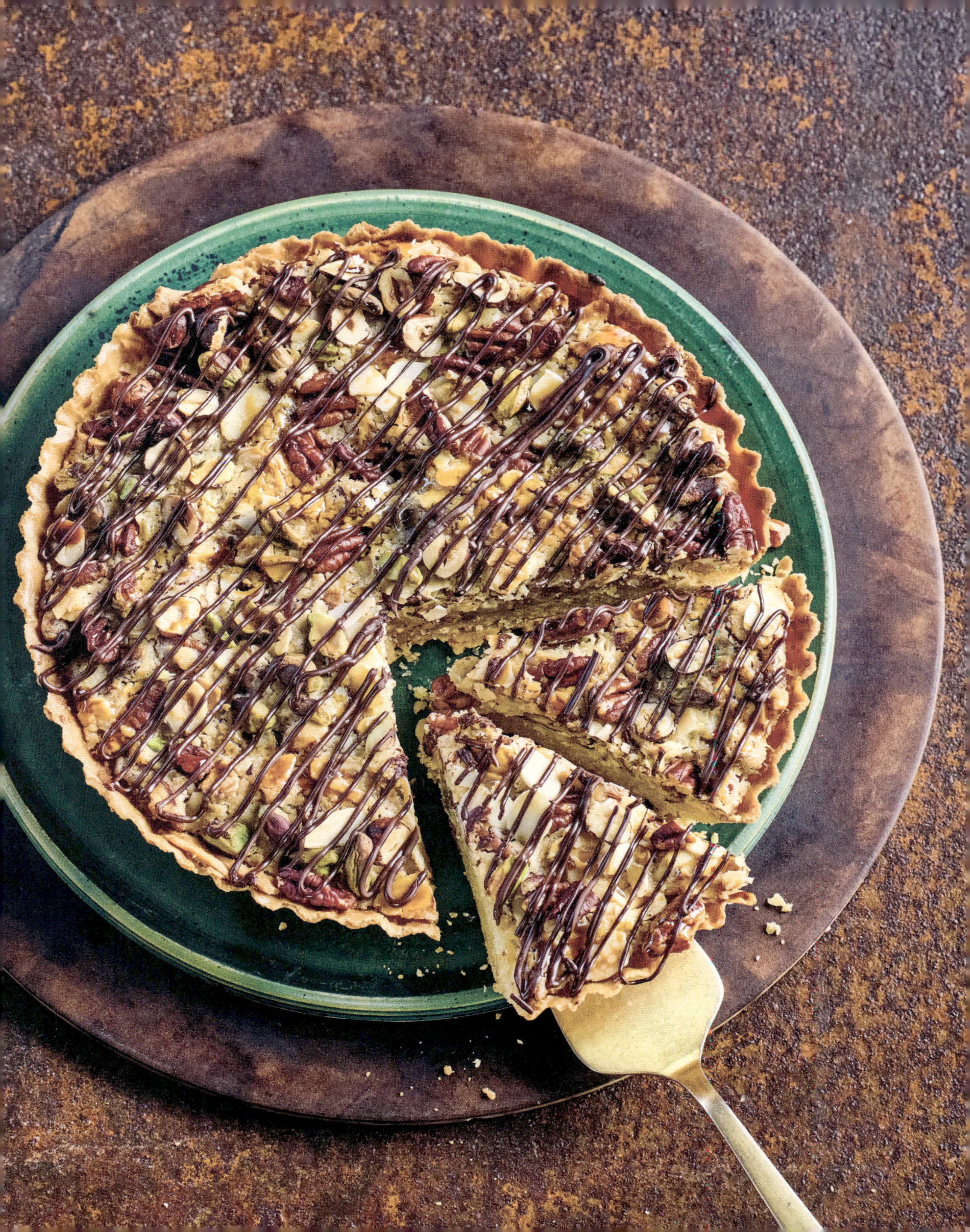

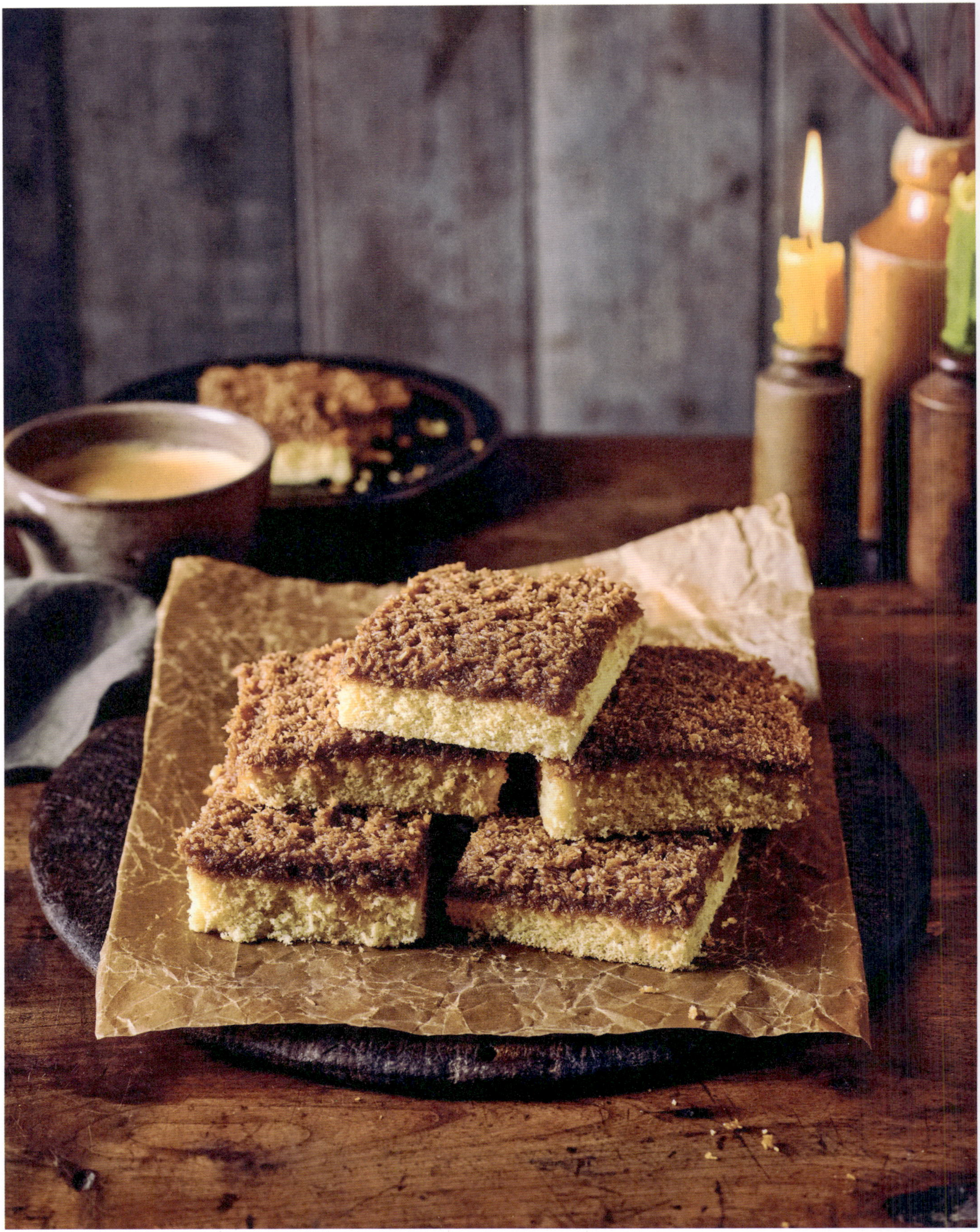

Danish dream cake

Drømmekage

This is a delicious cake and probably in the top three favourite cakes of the Danes, maybe even the overall favourite.

The story of this cake is that a young girl from a town called Brovst in Jutland baked this at a competition in the early 1950s – it was her grandmother's recipe and was then known as *Østergårdskage*. It then became popular all over Denmark by the name 'Dream Cake from Brovst', marketed as a recipe by the flour company which judged the competition (although the company never credited the girl). As a final twist in the story, this is similar to an American cake from the early 1940s called a 'Lazy Daisy Cake', so the origins of the *Drømmekage* may be from further afield than a small farm in Jutland.

Traditionally this is made in a sheet pan (see below), but you can make as a round cake too (use a cake pan with a diameter of at least 26 cm/10 inches) – baking time will need adjusting, too.

50 g/3½ tablespoons butter
200 ml/¾ cup milk
4 eggs
250 g/1¼ cups caster/granulated sugar
275 g/2 cups plain/all-purpose flour
1 tablespoon baking powder
2 teaspoons vanilla sugar or vanilla extract
a pinch of salt

TOPPING
100 g/7 tablespoons butter
150 g/2 cups desiccated/shredded dried coconut
250 g/1¼ cups dark brown sugar
75 ml/⅓ cup whole milk
a pinch of salt

25 x 35-cm/10 x 14-inch cake pan, lined with baking parchment

MAKES 12–16 PIECES

Preheat the oven to 190°C/170°C fan/375°F/Gas 5

To make the cake batter, melt the butter and mix with the milk, then leave to cool a little.

In a stand mixer, whisk the eggs and sugar until light and airy. Combine the dry ingredients, then sift into egg mixture, add the milk and butter, then fold together until incorporated.

Pour into the prepared cake pan and bake in the preheated oven for approx. 20 minutes or until a skewer inserted into the centre comes out almost clean.

While the cake is baking, prepare the topping by combining all the ingredients together in a saucepan over a low heat, until the sugar and butter have melted.

Remove the cake from oven and pour the topping all over. Return the cake to the oven for 5 minutes to caramelise slightly. Allow to cool before slicing and eating.

Big cinnamon buns

Stora kanelbullar

Is there anything as Swedish as big, warm, fragrant cinnamon buns? I think not. The stickiness of the bun, the sweet pearl/nibbed sugar, and the cardamom and cinnamon melting with the sweet bun – divine!

This batch is made using a slightly different knot than in my other books, but the recipe is, essentially, the same, so if you prefer making more buns, rather than large buns, just go smaller and use your preferred twirling of the dough.

Add the nibbed sugar after baking: as soon as the buns are done, brush with a warmed syrup (I love date syrup but any syrup will do), then add your sugar. Immediately, cover the hot tray of buns with a very damp tea towel and leave until cooled. This will prevent your buns forming a crust.

1 quantity Basic Bun Dough (see page 234)
flour, for dusting
1 beaten egg, for brushing
60 ml/3 tablespoons golden/corn syrup, for brushing
nibbed/pearl sugar, to decorate

FILLING
150 g/1¼ sticks butter, softened
150 g/¾ cup caster/granulated sugar
75 g/⅓ cup plus 2 teaspoons dark brown sugar
20 g/3½ tablespoons ground cinnamon
1 teaspoon vanilla sugar or vanilla extract
a pinch of salt

2 baking sheets, lined with baking parchment

MAKES 14–16

To make the filling, whip the butter with the sugars, spices and salt until spreadable and soft.

Dust a tabletop with flour and roll out the dough to a very large rectangle, approx. 90 x 30 cm/35 x 12 inches.

Spread the filling all over, then fold the dough over itself so you end up with two layers of filling. The dough is now approx. 30 x 30 cm/12 x 12 inches. Gently roll the dough out a little more to around 50 x 30 cm/20 x 12 inches. Using a knife or pizza slicer, cut the dough into 14–16 long pieces, slicing from one short edge to the other.

To knot the bun, take one piece of dough and gently stretch it, being careful not to tear it. Twist the dough twice around your four fingers, then wrap the rest of the dough around the middle bit, as you remove from your fingers, ensuring the end bit is tucked underneath. Repeat with the rest of the dough.

Place the buns on the lined baking sheets and leave to prove for a second rise for 20–25 minutes.

Preheat the oven to 220°C/200°C fan/425°F/Gas 7.

Brush the buns with beaten egg and bake in the preheated oven for around 10–13 minutes or until baked through – the baking time may vary by oven. If the buns are browning too quickly, you can turn the oven temperature down a bit.

As soon as you remove the buns from the oven, immediately brush all over with warmed golden/corn syrup and add a generous amount of nibbed/pearl sugar on top. Cover with a damp kitchen towel and leave it on top until the buns cool down (this will prevent a crust from forming).

TIP Too many buns? Freeze on the day of baking.

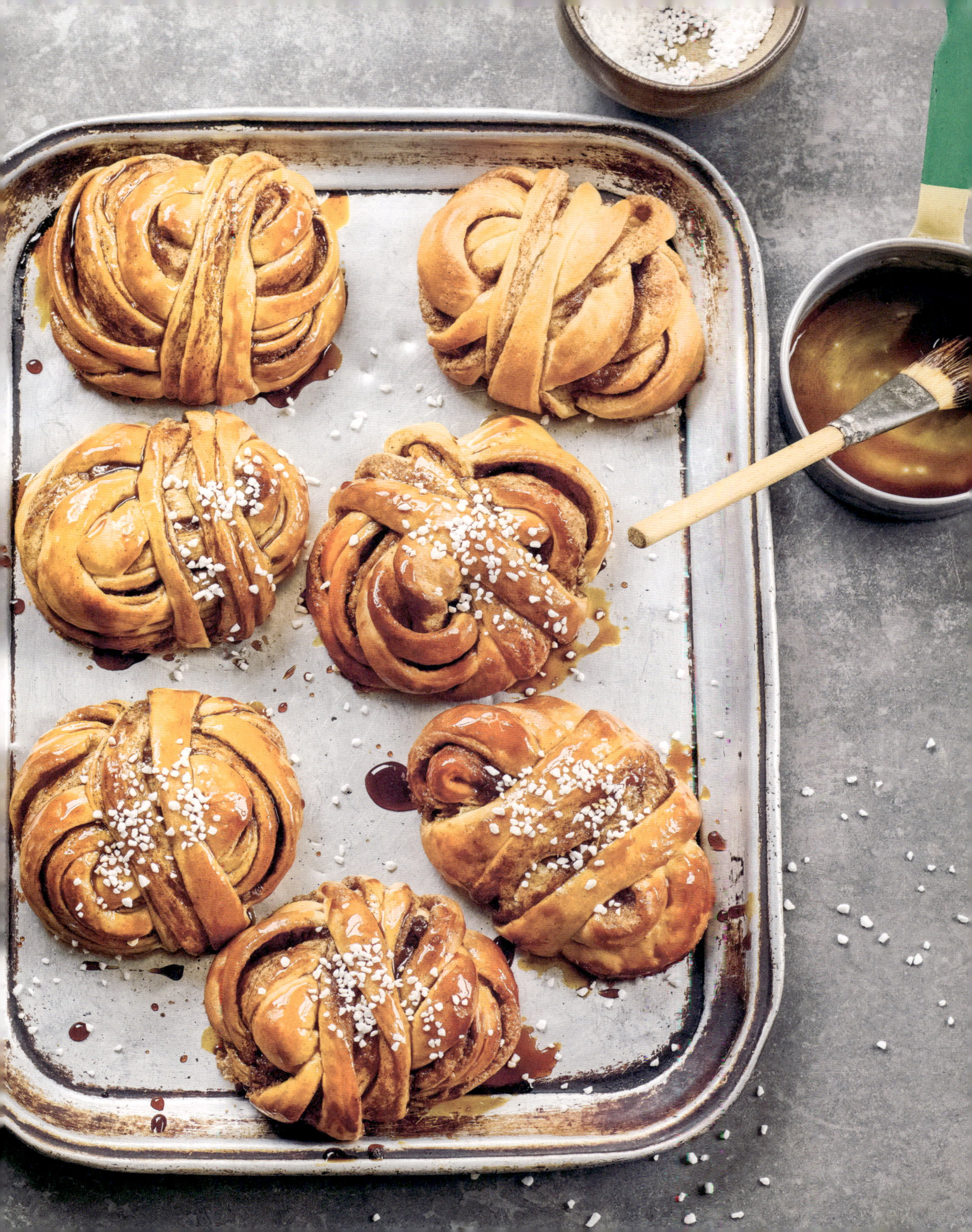

In Sweden, November starts with All Saints Day – a public holiday in Sweden, where we remember those no longer with us and light candles by their graves. Darkness once again firmly covers the peninsula, quickly lulling us into our own long hibernation. Everything slows down and we prepare for the year to come to an end and for the long polar nights to begin in the north. The sun will not rise again for many weeks.

By the time it all starts feeling a little too much to bear, Christmas sets in and we prepare for Advent Sundays and weekends with family and friends. Christmas markets begin and we make the mulled wine we call *glögg* for the season ahead. Suddenly, our dark towns are replaced by millions of twinkling Christmas lights and candles in the windows – and so the gloom lifts.

NOVEMBER

ADVENT

Even though Christmas isn't until the following month, November plays a big part in Scandinavia's preparations for the festivities. Perhaps it also helps us to find some high points as the darker days firmly set in and the temperatures drop dramatically.

The Vikings always celebrated the end of the year, the longest and darkest time. The season of *jól* (where the English word 'yule' comes from) meant that the end of the year was approaching and the days would start to become lighter on the other side. The season varied in length, but lasted from around mid-November to mid-January. The long-bearded Norse god Odin bears many names, two of which are Jólfuðr (Norse for 'Yule father') and Jólnir ('the Yule one'), a sort of pagan version of Santa Claus, though less jolly – he would apparently go from house to house checking that people had put out hay for his eight-legged horse Sleipnir and in return, would leave gifts.

King Haakon the Good is often credited with the Christianisation of Norway following a visit to England and subsequent decree that *jól* and Christmas should be celebrated at the same time. The only way he could sell this change to the Viking chiefs was to promise them that the celebrations would happen as long as the ale lasted (in other words, more time to party). Probably due to this close connection with *jól* (and we still call it *jul*), Christmas in Scandinavia has always been about a celebration of the winter season rather than one day of exchanging gifts. Today, *jul* begins on the last Sunday of November, which is the start of Advent, and counts down the four Sundays before Christmas itself.

The Advent weekends tend to be celebrated with family and friends. Usually, the mulled wine we call *glögg* is served alongside festive biscuits or other traditional bakes. *Glögg* is traditionally a red wine warmed with festive spices, including cinnamon, orange, clove, ginger and cardamom, although there are many variations (some even made with white wine). It's served warm in little cups with a few raisins and flaked/slivered almonds (some soak the raisins in brandy beforehand, which feels extra warming). There are few tipples that create Christmas-is-coming ripples in my soul as much as a warm glass of *glögg* on a cold day.

When it comes to Christmas and baking, there are so many more different bakes than space to mention in this book. The most famous of all the Scandinavian Christmas biscuits is the Swedish ginger biscuit (*Pepparkakor*): thin and crispy, with a soft undertone of Christmas spices. This is the same dough you can use to make gingerbread houses. At a Danish house, you will be served two different types of ginger biscuit at Christmas: *Pebernødder* (a variation of the German *Pfeffernüssen*) and the *Brunkage*, full of spices, almonds and candied orange, made in logs and sliced very thinly before baking. We make a lot of butter cookies, too – the most famous of which is the vanilla ring (*Vaniliekranse*). There are also the crumbly *Jødekager* (literally Jewish biscuits) with a cinnamon topping, made popular in Denmark in the 1850s as the Jewish bakeries introduced us to more spices. In my own house, we often like to add a little touch of saffron flavour to a pistachio biscotti (although not traditionally a Scandinavian biscuit) as using saffron is always a big thing during Christmas time for us.

At Swedish and Norwegian *glögg* parties, you will most likely also be served *lussebullar*, saffron-flavoured yeast buns, while in Denmark you will be served *æbleskiver* – pancake balls dipped in icing/confectioner's sugar and jam/preserves.

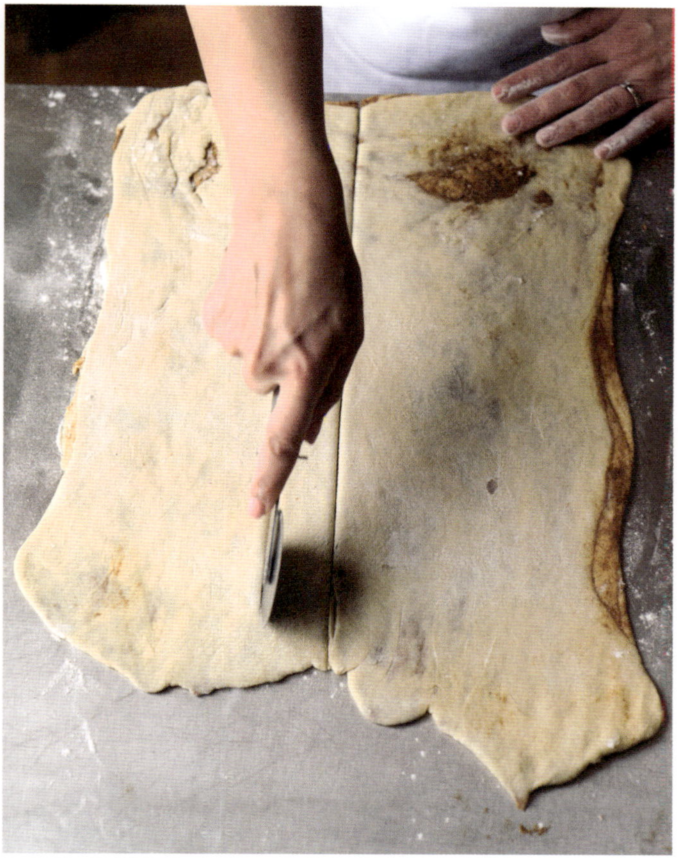
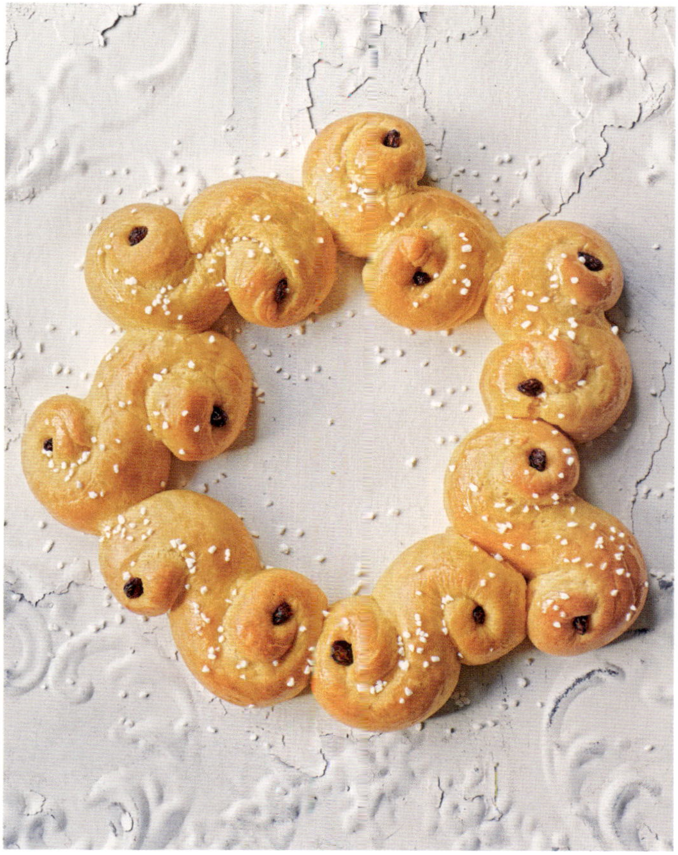
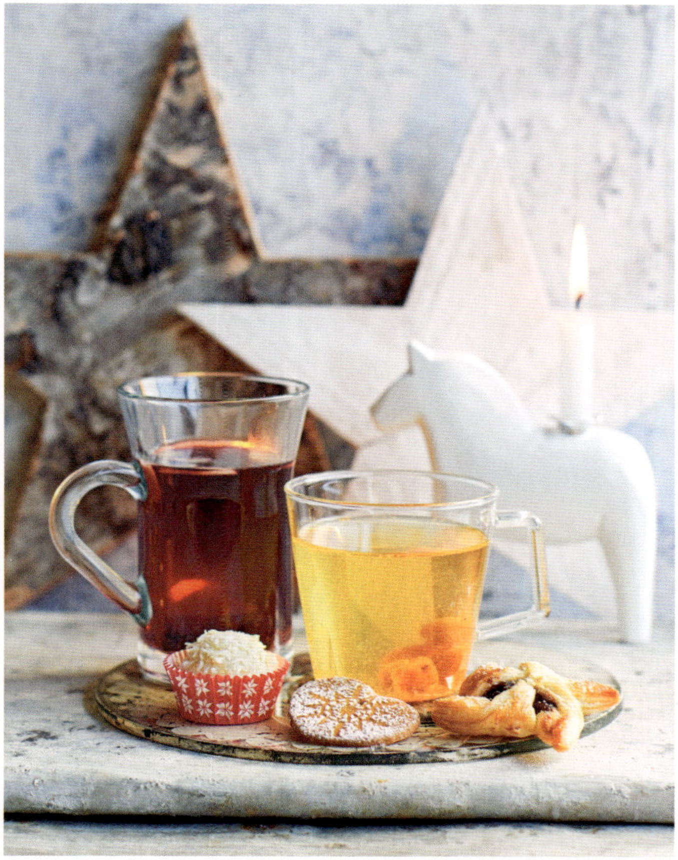
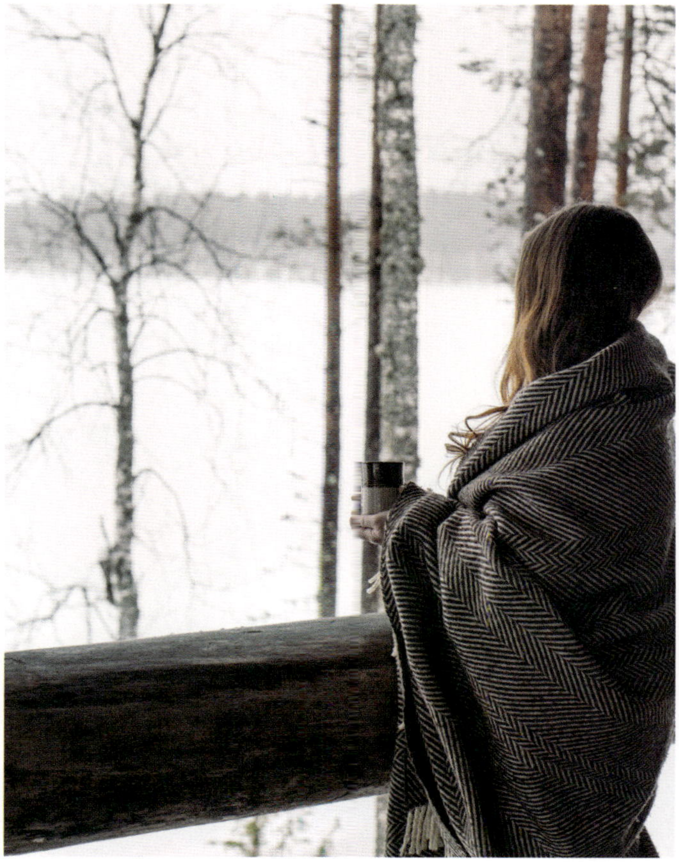

Chicken soup with meatballs & dumplings

Hønsekødssuppe med kød og melboller

This is my favourite comfort dish in the whole world. To me, this is childhood and home. It is not fancy, but it is hearty. In Denmark, most people (me included) buy this soup ready-made as it takes time to make from scratch. However, it is rewarding to make it yourself. If you don't have time to make both meatballs and dumplings, choose the one you like the most. You can also make all components ahead and freeze (freeze soup and balls separately and do not let the dumplings boil as they will split).

1 carcass from a roast chicken, or offcuts (a 1-kg/2 lb. 4-oz. carcass from the butcher is super cheap)

2 carrots, 1 onion, 1 leek, 1 parsnip and 2 celery sticks, all cut into large pieces

a handful of fresh parsley

a few sprigs of fresh thyme

3 bay leaves

salt and 10 peppercorns

TO CLARIFY
2 egg whites
1 onion and 1 leek, finely chopped

TO SERVE
2 carrots and 2 parsnips, cut into 5-mm/¼-inch pieces
1 large leek, sliced

MEATBALLS (MAKES 20–40)
400 g/14 oz. minced/ground beef and pork (half/half, or just beef)
1 egg
3 tablespoons plain/all-purpose flour
1 small onion, chopped
50 ml/3½ tablespoons milk

DUMPLINGS (MAKES 30–40)
75 g/5⅓ tablespoons butter
100 g/¾ cup plain/all-purpose flour
2 eggs

piping/pastry bag, with a 1-cm/ ½-inch opening

SERVES 4

Place the carcass in a large pan, cover with water (around 2 litres/quarts, depending on the size of the chicken) and add the vegetables, herbs, salt and peppercorns. Bring to the boil and skim off any foam that collects on top. Simmer for 2–2½ hours. Pour through a sieve/strainer and discard the vegetables and bones. Taste to check the seasoning, then place the stock in the fridge to cool down.

To clarify the broth, whisk the egg whites until thick and foamy (not stiff), add the chopped onion and leek, a dash of water and a pinch of salt to the whites and combine. Add the cold stock to a saucepan and turn on the heat. Add the foamy egg white to the top and bring to a boil for 4–5 minutes, then turn off heat and leave for 20–30 minutes to cool down again. This process will clean the stock and all the gunk will stick to the egg white. Carefully pour the broth through a sieve/strainer lined with muslin cloth or paper towels.

To make the meatballs, add all the ingredients to a food processor and mix well. Leave to set for 30 minutes before using. Heat a pan of water to a simmer. Put the meat mixture into the piping/pastry bag and squeeze out the meatballs, cutting them off with scissors, directly into the simmering water to cook for 3–4 minutes. If making larger meatballs, roll by hand. Remove the cooked meatballs with a slotted spoon and set aside.

To make the dumplings, add the butter to a saucepan with 200 ml/¾ cup water and bring to the boil. Whisk in the flour, then take off the heat and wait a few minutes, then whisk in the eggs, one by one, and mix until the dough is smooth and glossy. Season with salt.

Heat a saucepan of water and keep just below simmering. Transfer the dumpling mixture to the piping/pastry bag and pipe out individual dumplings, using scissors to cut each dumpling from the bag directly into the saucepan (or roll by hand). Leave to cook for a few minutes until the dumplings rise to the surface (do not let the water boil). Remove with a slotted spoon and set aside.

To serve the broth, add the carrots, parsnips and leek to the broth and heat until hot and the vegetables are just cooked through. Add the meatballs and dumplings, heat through and serve.

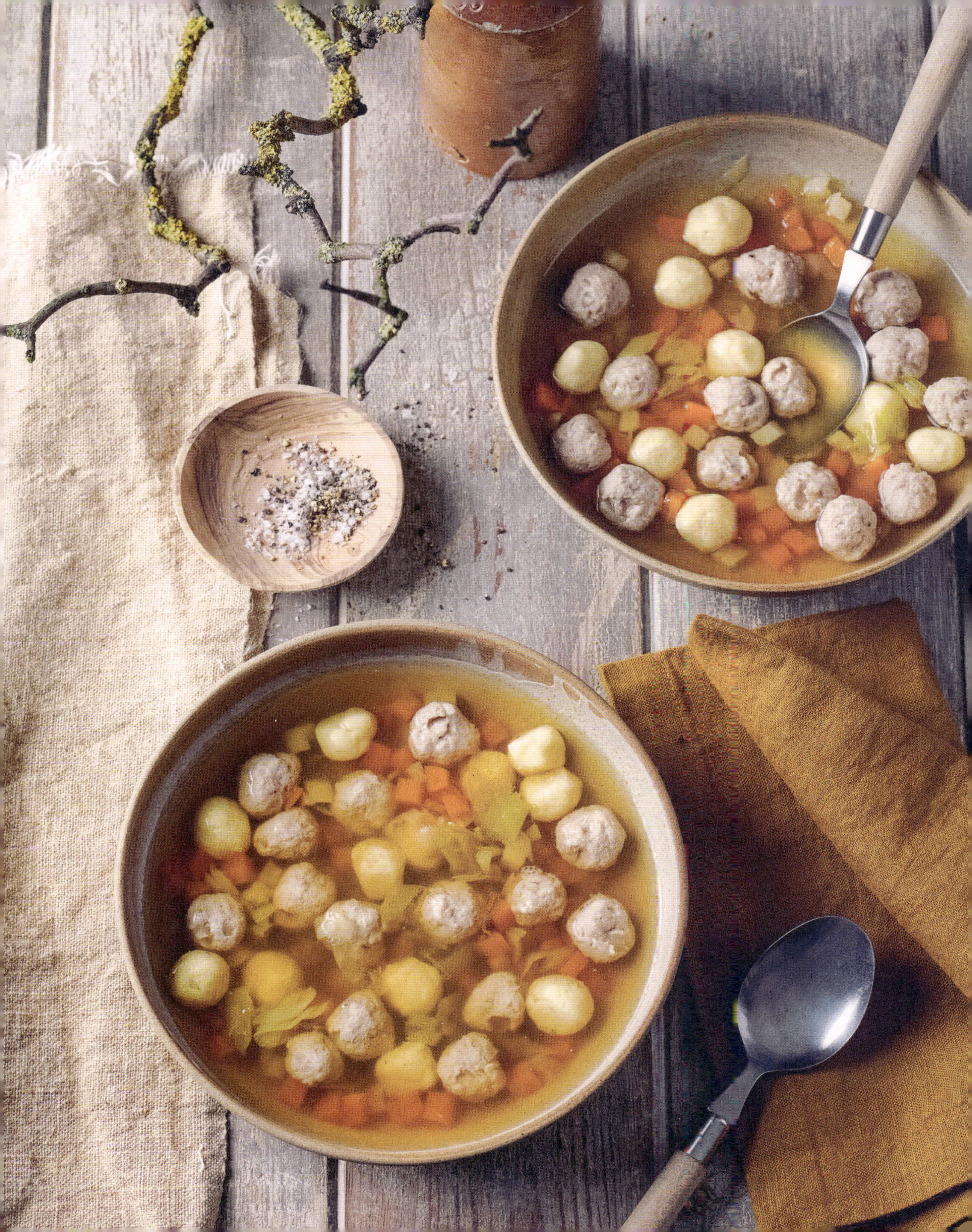

Västerbotten cheese scones

Västerbottensost scones

Not all *fika* needs to be sweet – and in my house, we are big fans of English scones, especially savoury ones. They are so quick to whip up and bake. Use a strong Cheddar if you can't get hold of Västerbotten cheese. I like to serve these with some cold smoked salmon and butter (or a dollop of sour cream).

250 g/2 cups plain/all-purpose flour
1 teaspoon baking powder
½ teaspoon bicarbonate of soda/ baking soda
½ teaspoon paprika
½ teaspoon salt
freshly ground black pepper
75 g/¾ stick cold butter, cut into cubes
100 g/3½ oz. Västerbotten cheese (or other hard cheese, such as pecorino), finely grated
125 ml/½ cup whole milk, with 2–3 drops of lemon juice added
2 tablespoons finely chopped chives
50 g/½ cup chopped walnuts (optional)
beaten egg or milk, for brushing

TO SERVE
150 g/5½ oz. smoked salmon
extra chives or dill sprigs
lemon wedges

6-cm/2½-inch cookie cutter

MAKES 8

Preheat the oven to 210°C/190°C fan/410°F/Gas 6½.

Put the flour, baking powder and bicarbonate of soda/baking soda, paprika, salt and pepper into a bowl and add the cold, cubed butter. Rub until the mixture resembles a crumble. Add the cheese and mix, then gradually add the milk and the chives. Mix in the chopped walnuts, if using. Try not to overwork the dough – less is more; it simply needs combining. The more you work the dough, the denser your scones will be.

Gently roll out the dough to a thickness of around 2 cm/¾ inch. Using the cookie cutter, punch out your scones (don't twist them out). You can gently re-roll the remaining dough to use it all up. You should get eight scones from this batch.

Place on a baking sheet, brush with egg or milk and bake in the preheated oven for around 12 minutes until browned, risen and baked through.

Serve with butter and smoked salmon and sprigs of dill or chopped chives, and big wedges of lemon for squeezing.

Venison stew

Viltgryt

Across the northern Nordic regions, lots of game meat is used for stews, from reindeer (very common) to venison and elk. It is not that easy to get hold of reindeer in the UK (although possible in speciality shops). Personally, I use venison when making game stew because Scotland especially has some great venison farms and the meat is excellent.

The meat can vary in terms of flavour, so taste your stew and spice up the result as necessary. I often find that stirring in a teaspoon of Marmite at the end can elevate a stew to new heights.

butter and oil, for frying
500 g/1 lb. 2 oz. venison pieces (make sure it's for slow cooking or the result will be tough)
80 g/3 oz. pancetta, cut into cubes
1 onion chopped
350 g/12 oz. root veg (carrot, celeriac/celery root, parsnip – whatever you love), cut into 2-cm/¾-inch pieces
200 ml/¾ cup red wine
600 ml/2½ cups beef or venison stock
1 bay leaf
3–4 sprigs of fresh thyme
8 allspice berries, crushed
1 heaped tablespoon brown sugar
200 g/7 oz. mushrooms
1 tablespoon lingonberry jam
200 ml/¾ cup sour cream or crème fraîche
white wine vinegar, to season
salt and freshly ground black pepper

SERVES 4

In a saucepan, melt a knob/pat of butter and a glug of oil and brown the meats all over, then remove with a slotted spoon and set aside.

Add the chopped onion to the saucepan and fry, covered, for at least 10–12 minutes until the onions are soft and starting to caramelise. Add the root veg and cook for a further 3–4 minutes uncovered. Add the wine and cook for a few minutes until the alcohol has evaporated, then return the meat to the pan along with the stock. Add the bay leaf, thyme, crushed allspice berries and sugar, bring to a simmer, then cover and leave to cook gently for 2 hours.

Check on the meat to see if it has started to soften – the final cooking time can easily be over 3½ hours depending on the cut. Add the mushrooms. Cook for a further hour and check again – once the meat starts to fall apart, it's nearly ready.

Season with a dollop of lingonberry jam and the sour cream. Taste and season again – it might need a little vinegar to balance the sauce out a bit.

NOTE I usually use beef stock because it is hard to get game stock, but if you can find game, do use this.

Oven pancake with apples & vanilla mascarpone

Ungspannkaka med äpple

In Sweden, an *ungspannkaka* – which means 'oven pancake' – is usually made in a rectangular tray and served in a large dish. You can use both sweet and savoury fillings – some serve it with lingonberry jam and whipped cream, some even serve it with fried bacon. I have a thing for what Americans call a 'Dutch Baby' (quite like an oven pancake, although made in smaller skillets and served as dessert), so this is how I make it at home (think a sweet Yorkshire pudding). You can make this in one large dish or several small ones. If you want to be traditional, serve with lingonberries. I love apple and cinnamon (to me, there is no scent that sends me back to my mother's kitchen more) with some toasted nuts and dollops of mascarpone. Crème fraiche also works if you prefer a more tart flavour.

20 g/1½ tablespoons butter and neutral oil, for the baking pan
250 g/9 oz. mascarpone cheese
seeds from 1 vanilla pod/bean
60 g/2½ oz. hazelnuts or pecan nuts, toasted, cooled and roughly chopped

BATTER
150 g/1 cup plus 2 tablespoons plain/all-purpose flour
1½ tablespoons caster/granulated sugar
½ teaspoon salt
1 teaspoon ground cardamom
1 teaspoon vanilla sugar or vanilla extract
4 eggs
240 ml/1 cup whole milk

TOPPING
20 g/1½ tablespoons butter
2 tablespoons brown sugar
3 tart apples, peeled and sliced into thin wedges
2 teaspoons ground cinnamon
a pinch of salt
1 tablespoon maple syrup (optional)

3 small or 2 larger ovenproof skillets or a large rectangular baking tray (approx. 20 x 30 cm/8 x 12 inches)

SERVES 3–6

In a bowl, combine the dry ingredients for the batter, then whisk in the eggs. Add the liquid bit by bit, ensuring all the ingredients are incorporated. Don't overmix – stop when it's a smooth batter. Chill in the fridge for 30 minutes before proceeding.

Preheat the oven to 240°C/220°C fan/475°F/Gas 9.

Place the butter and a glug of neutral oil in the skillets or baking pan. Place in the oven and heat until all the butter and oil have melted and the fats are super-hot.

Carefully pour in the batter and return to the oven. After about 10 minutes, reduce the heat to 210°C/190°C fan/400°F/Gas 6, but do not open the door for the first 20 minutes whilst baking. The sides will puff up slightly, like a massive Yorkshire pudding, and will start to brown.

Meanwhile, in a pan, melt the butter and brown sugar for the topping. Once melted, add the apples, cinnamon and salt and continue to cook for a few minutes until the apples start to soften. If you prefer soft apples, cook a bit longer – I like apples with a bit of bite, so I cook for less time. When done to your preference, stir in the maple syrup, if using, and take off the heat.

Whisk the mascarpone with the vanilla seeds (I like it tart, but if you prefer, you can add a bit of honey to sweeten). If the mascarpone is a little stiff, add a dash of milk to loosen.

Check the oven pancake(s) after around 25 minutes – they might need a further 5–8 minutes, but this depends on your oven. The base will stay quite soft, like a thick pancake, and the edges will be lighter.

Serve the pancakes in the skillets or baking pan, with the apples arranged in the middle and dollops of the mascarpone cream, topped with the toasted nuts. Enjoy immediately.

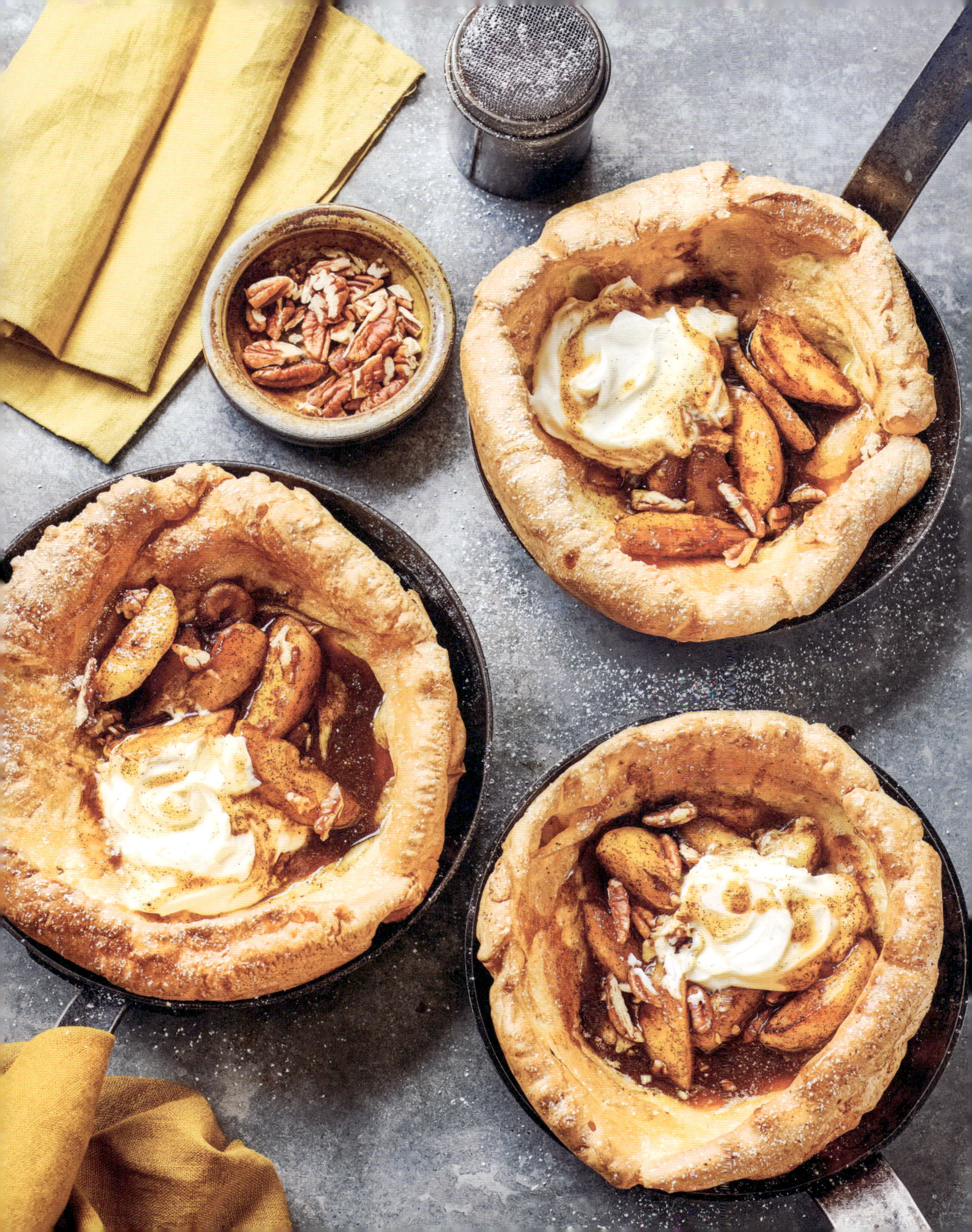

Six types of Christmas biscuits

Baking all the Christmas biscuits and cookies just ahead of the festive season is something I love. The whole family gets involved and we plan, prep and bake over several days. By the end of it, the whole house smells of Christmas and I've filled every tin to the brim (most keep for many weeks in airtight containers). There are so many more bakes than there is space in this book, so I've chosen some of the favourite ones I bake every year at my house.

Saffron biscotti
Saffransbiscotti

0.2 g saffron powder (equivalent to ½ sachet Swedish saffron)
2 tablespoons warm milk
75 g/5⅓ tablespoons butter, at room temperature
200 g/1 cup caster/granulated sugar
2 eggs
freshly grated zest of 1 lemon
1 teaspoon vanilla extract or vanilla sugar
350 g/2⅔ cups plain/all-purpose flour
2 teaspoons baking powder
75 g/2¾ oz. each of skin-on almonds and pistachios, toasted and roughly chopped

2–3 baking sheets, lined with baking parchment

MAKES APPROX. 40

Preheat the oven to 190°C/170°C fan/375°F/Gas 5.

Add the saffron powder to the milk and leave to infuse (if using stands, gently crush first).

Cream the butter and sugar in a stand mixer, add eggs one by one, then add the zest, saffron milk and vanilla. Sift in the flour and baking powder and mix by hand, adding the nuts at the end. Shape into two even logs, 25 cm/10 inches long, and place on the baking sheets.

Bake in the preheated oven for 30 minutes, then remove from the oven and reduce the heat to 140°C/120°C fan/275°F/Gas 1. Allow the logs to cool for about 10 minutes, then slice into biscotti 1–1.5 cm/⅜–⅝ inch thick). Place back on the baking sheets and back in oven for about 10 minutes to crisp up completely.

NOTE Allow all cookies to cool completely before eating. Store in an airtight container for 2–3 weeks.

Danish butter cookies
Vaniljekranse

180 g/1 cup minus 1½ tablespoons caster/granulated sugar
1 whole vanilla pod/bean
200 g/1¾ sticks butter, at room temperature
275 g/2 cups plain/all-purpose flour
100 g/1 cup ground almonds
50 g/½ cup finely hand chopped almonds
1 teaspoon bicarbonate of soda/baking soda
1 egg
a pinch of salt
1–2 teaspoons vanilla extract

2 strong plastic piping/pastry bags (or one fabric) and a medium star nozzle/tip

2–3 baking sheets, lined with baking parchment

MAKES 35–40

Preheat the oven to 200°C/180°C fan/400°F/Gas 6.

In a food processor, grind the sugar and whole vanilla pod/bean together. Remove any tough pieces of bark.

Cream the vanilla sugar and butter until just combined, then add the remaining ingredients and mix to an even dough. Don't overmix. The dough needs to be soft enough to push through a piping/pastry bag nozzle, but not too soft or it will not hold its shape during baking. Pipe out rolls 8–10 cm/3–4 inches long, then connect into circles and place on the baking sheets. Make sure the rolls are no thicker than your little finger, because they will spread during baking.

Bake for 8–10 minutes, or until just turning golden brown at the edges.

VARIATIONS Add orange zest, or add 15 g/2 tablespoons cacao powder (but reduce flour by the same quantity).

Cinnamon cookies
Jødekager

175 g/1½ sticks cold butter, cubed
200 g/1½ cups plain/all-purpose flour
1 teaspoon bicarbonate of soda/baking soda
100 g/½ cup caster/granulated sugar
1 egg yolk

TOPPING
1 egg white
2 teaspoons ground cinnamon
2 tablespoons granulated sugar
a small handful of chopped almonds

5-cm/2-inch round cookie cutter (optional)
2–3 baking sheets, lined with baking parchment

MAKES APPROX. 40

Combine the cold cubed butter with the flour and bicarbonate of soda/baking soda in a stand mixer with the paddle attachment. Mix briefly until you have a grainy, sand-like texture. Add the sugar and egg yolk and mix until the ingredients are just incorporated.

Roll the dough into a log (about 5 cm/2 inches in diameter) and wrap in clingfilm/plastic wrap. Chill in the fridge for a few hours, but ideally longer (overnight is good).

Preheat the oven to 180°C/160°C fan/350°F/Gas 4.

You can slice the dough (takes less time) or roll out on a floured surface and use a round cookie cutter. If slicing, using a sharp knife, carefully slice the log into thin slices. Place the cookies on the prepared baking sheets. Try not to handle them too much.

Brush the cookies with a little egg white using a pastry brush. Mix together the cinnamon and sugar and scatter over the cookies, then add a small sprinkling of chopped almonds to the middle of each.

Bake in the preheated oven for around 8–10 minutes or until they start to brown at the edges. Be aware that these biscuits burn easily, so keep an eye on them.

Danish ginger biscuits
Brunkager

100 g/½ cup caster/granulated sugar
150 g/¾ cup dark brown sugar
150 g/scant ½ cup golden/corn syrup
250 g/2¼ sticks butter
500 g/3¾ cups plain/all-purpose flour
3 teaspoons ground cinnamon
1 teaspoon ground cloves
1½ teaspoons ground ginger
1 teaspoons ground cardamom
1½ teaspoons bicarbonate of soda/baking soda
a pinch of salt
150 g/5½ oz. whole blanched almonds
80 g/½ cup mixed candied peel

2–3 baking sheets, lined with baking parchment

MAKES 100+ THIN BISCUITS

Melt the sugars, syrup and butter in a pan, then leave for 10 minutes to cool a little.

Mix the flour with the spices, bicarbonate of soda/baking soda and salt into the sugars to make a uniform dough. Add the nuts and mixed peel. Combine until smooth, then roll into logs around 5 cm/2¼ inches in diameter (it is easier to make 2–3 logs rather than one long one). Wrap in baking parchment and place in the fridge for at least 12 hours, or freeze to use later (you can bake these straight from frozen too).

Preheat the oven to 195°C/175°C fan/375°F/Gas 5.

Cut thin slices of the dough around 2 mm/⅛ inch thick. The knife needs to be sharp as it needs to slice not only the almonds but also the dough if it is slightly frozen. These do need to be thin to have that vital crunch once baked.

Bake in the preheated oven for 5–8 minutes only, until slightly browned. Take care not to allow the biscuits to be too dark as they'll taste quite bitter.

VARIATIONS Some people add pistachios for a change in flavour. You can also leave the mixed peel out or, as I usually do, only add mixed peel to half the batch, to have two options from one quantity of dough.

NOVEMBER

Danish peppernuts
Pebernødder

200 g/1¾ sticks butter, at room temperature
100 g/½ cup caster/granulated sugar
100 g/½ cup light brown sugar
1 egg
400 g/3 cups plain/all-purpose flour
1 teaspoon bicarbonate of soda/baking soda
a pinch of salt
75 ml/⅓ cup double/heavy cream

SPICE MIX
1 teaspoon ground cloves
1 teaspoon ground ginger
1 teaspoon ground cardamom
1 tablespoon ground cinnamon
1 teaspoon mixed spice
½ teaspoon ground white pepper
½ teaspoon ground black pepper

2–3 baking sheets, lined with baking parchment

MAKES 100+ BITE-SIZED BISCUITS

Cream the butter and sugars together in a stand mixer, then add the egg, then flour, bicarbonate of soda/baking soda, salt and the spice mix. Mix only until incorporated, then add the cream. Mix until combined into a dough and chill for at least 30 minutes.

Preheat the oven to 200°C/180°C fan/400°F/Gas 6.

Roll the dough into long rolls, the thickness of your index finger. Cut into small pieces 1-cm/½-inch thick and place on the baking sheets, or roll each one, which will take a long time but it will give you more uniform pieces (and keep smaller children occupied for hours, which is also a bonus).

Bake in the preheated oven for around 8 minutes. Do keep an eye on the baking time, because ovens vary and these little biscuits need to be only just golden, not any darker. Leave to cool and crisp up before eating.

VARIATIONS Add a little lemon or orange zest for a flavour pop. If you prefer a stronger flavour, increase the spices (but don't increase the pepper, or it can be overpowering).

Swedish ginger biscuits
Pepparkakor

550 g/scant 4¼ cups plain/all-purpose flour, plus extra for dusting
1 teaspoon bicarbonate of soda/baking soda
1½ teaspoons ground ginger
1 teaspoon ground cloves
1 tablespoon ground cinnamon
1 teaspoon ground cardamom
½ teaspoon ground allspice
a pinch of salt
100 g/½ cup granulated sugar
100 g/½ cup soft dark brown sugar
150 g/1¼ sticks butter, at room temperature
200 g/⅔ cup golden/corn syrup
150 ml/⅔ cup double/heavy cream

2–3 baking sheets, lined with baking parchment

MAKES 50–70 BISCUITS

In a stand mixer fitted with the paddle attachment, mix the flour, bicarbonate of soda/baking soda, spices, salt and sugars together. Add the rest of the ingredients and mix until you have an even dough. Shape into a log and wrap in clingfilm/plastic wrap. Rest it in the fridge at least overnight before using.

Preheat the oven to 200°C/180°C fan/400°F/Gas 6.

On a floured surface, roll out the dough very thinly (around 2 mm/⅛ inch thick), and use cookie cutters to cut your desired shapes. Make sure they are thin biscuits. Place them on the lined baking sheets.

Bake in the preheated oven – each batch will take 5–6 minutes, depending on the thickness. The biscuits should be a darker shade of brown without being burnt.

NOTE If you wish, you can let the kids decorate the biscuits with colourful icing – icing/confectioner's sugar mixed with beaten egg white and a few drops of freshly squeezed lemon juice makes the best decorative icing as it goes hard when it dries.

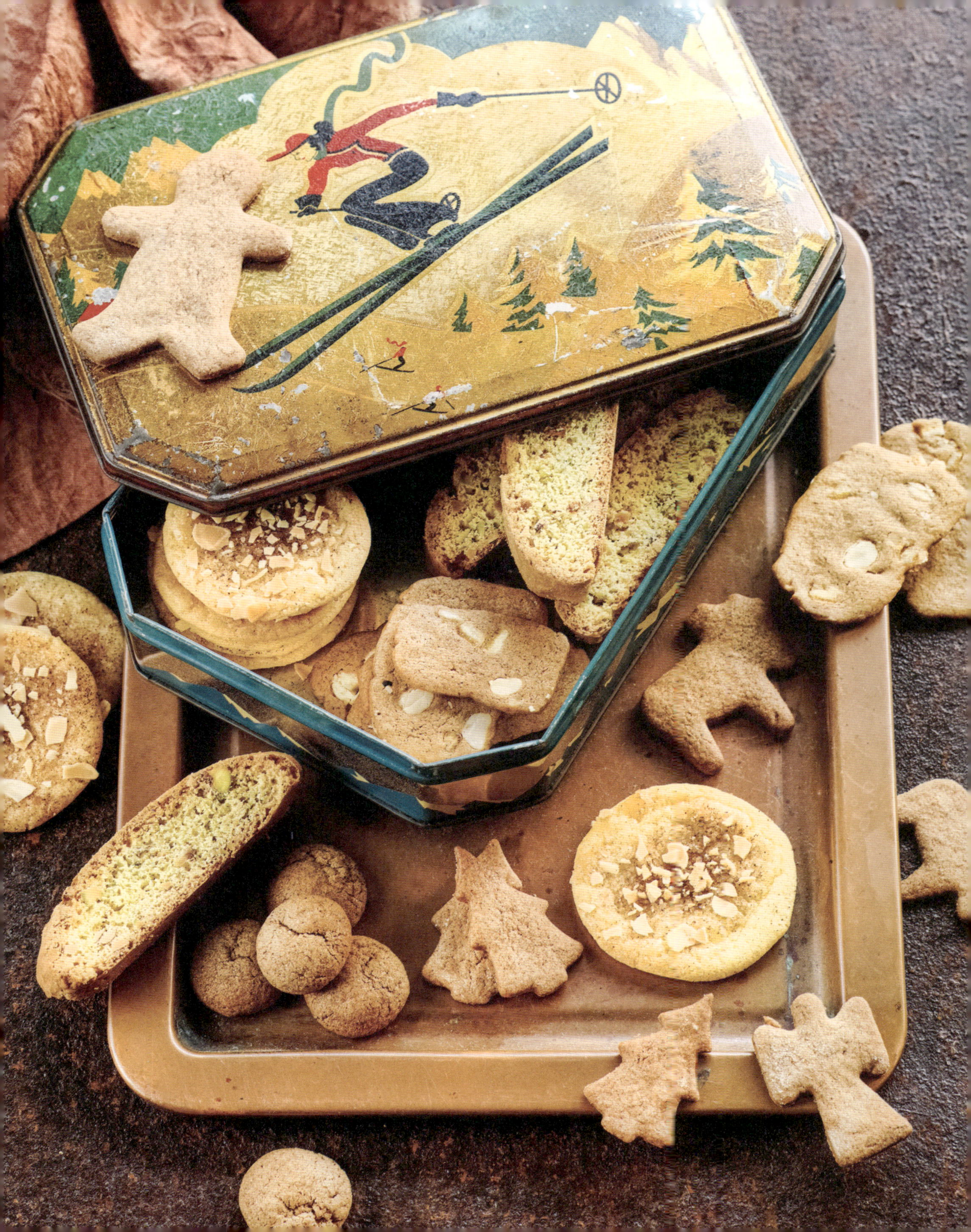

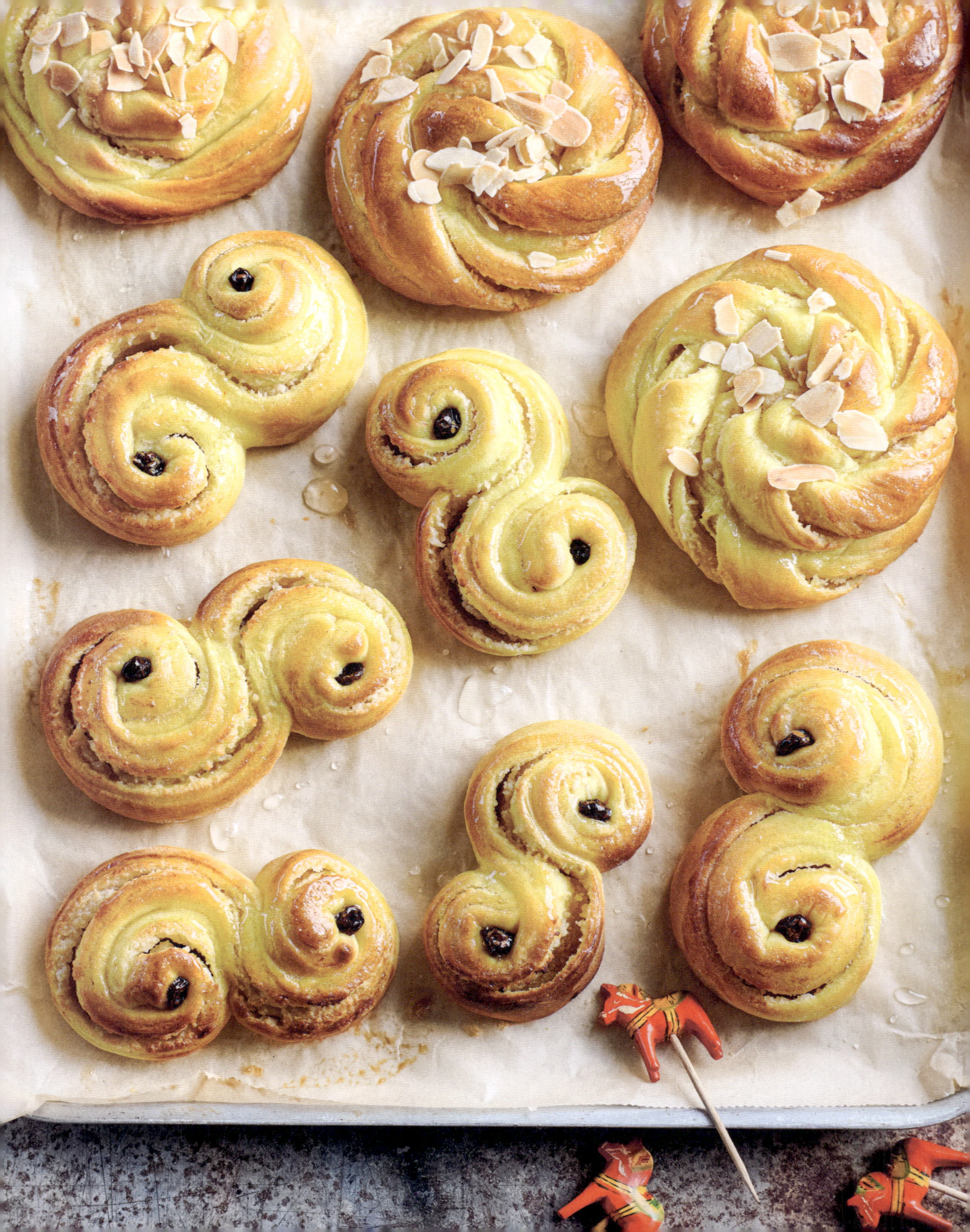

Saffron buns with marzipan
Lussebullar med marcipan

Saffron buns are served in Sweden and Norway during advent weekends and on the feast of Sankta Lucia (13th December). This is the base recipe for saffron buns. Getting the right sort of yellow requires the saffron to be ground, then added to a bit of liquid which really brings out the colour. In Scandinavia you buy saffron pre-ground, but using strands often results in slightly less yellow buns (but still with good flavour). The traditional shape of a *lussebulle* is an S-shape with a raisin in each fold. Here I layer it with a marzipan and butter filling, but you can make traditional S-shapes or knotted buns, as you prefer. For the traditional version, omit the marzipan filling.

200 ml/¾ cup whole milk

0.5 g saffron powder (equivalent to 1 sachet Swedish saffron)

25 g/⅞ oz. fresh yeast (or equivalent dry active granules)

75 g/6 tablespoons caster/superfine sugar

100 ml/⅓ cup plus 1 tablespoon Greek yogurt (or another type of soured yogurt product)

400–500 g/3–3⅔ cups strong bread flour, plus extra for dusting

½ teaspoon salt

100 g/7 tablespoons butter, very soft

1 egg, beaten (reserve half for brushing)

a handful of raisins (optional)

flaked/slivered almonds or pearl/nibbed sugar (optional)

FILLING

100–150 g/3½–5½ oz. Marzipan (see page 237), according to how much you want to add

50 g/3½ tablespoons butter, very soft

baking sheet, lined with baking parchment

MAKES 12–14 GENEROUS BUNS

Heat the milk in a saucepan until finger-warm (no more than 36°C/97°F), then add the ground saffron.

In a stand mixer, add the fresh yeast and the milk-saffron mixture. Mix for 1 minute, then add the sugar and stir until dissolved. Stir in the yogurt until incorporated, then mix in about half of the flour and combine, then add the salt. As you keep mixing, gradually add more flour, taking care not to add too much (saffron is very drying, so if you have a dry dough, the end result will also be dry). Add the butter and half of the egg and keep mixing, adding more flour as needed. This will take around 5 minutes.

When the dough is springy and well kneaded, leave to rest in a covered bowl in a warm place for about 40 minutes or until doubled in size.

For the filling, mix the marzipan with the softened butter and a dash of water to make it into an easily spreadable paste.

Turn out the dough onto a floured surface and knead. Using a rolling pin, roll the dough to a large rectangle approx. 30 x 40 cm/12 x 16 inches. Spread the filling all over, then fold the dough in half, to enclose the filling. Use your rolling pin to gently roll it out a little more, taking care not to squash the filling too much.

Using a pizza cutter of knife, cut the dough into 12–14 strips. Twist each strip and turn it in on itself into a swirl shape, taking care to ensure the end bits are tucked underneath (or these will unravel during baking). If making traditional S-shaped buns, add a raisin in each 'hole'.

Place the buns on the prepared baking sheet and allow to rise for a further 20 minutes.

Preheat the oven to 170°C/150°C fan/340°F/Gas 3½. Brush each bun lightly with the remaining egg wash and scatter over almonds or pearl sugar. Bake in the preheated oven for 10–12 minutes or until baked through.

Leave under a damp kitchen towel for at least 10 minutes as soon as they come out of the oven to ensure no crust forms. Saffron dough dries out quickly, so eat on the day of baking or freeze as soon as they are cool.

December is a month of icy outdoors and warm indoors. It's darkness and magical bright lights. It's tradition and new. December feels like a fairy tale to me – it's my favourite time of the year. Everything is about memories: reliving them, preserving them and creating new ones with the people I love. Those I let into my Christmas are in my heart.

As the snow starts to fall across our three countries (to be fair, probably more sleet than snow in the south, but giant snowfalls in the north), we prepare for the grand end of the year. Every weekend is spent visiting those close to us as we make, create, prepare and eat more biscuits than is good for our waistlines (but it's only Christmas once a year, so we just go on).

It's the month of peak *hygge*, peak *mys* (*mys* is the Swedish word for *hygge*), peak comfort. We have our winter wonderland and we have all the most magical food traditions. By the time of the celebration of Sankta Lucia bringing in her candlelit crown early in the morning of 13th December, *jul* – Yuletide – is firmly within our sights.

DECEMBER

CHRISTMAS IN SCANDINAVIA

When 13th December arrives, we celebrate *Sankta Lucia*. This tradition has both Christian and pagan roots. Aside from being the Feast of St Lucia of Syracuse, the day used to coincide with the winter solstice – the shortest day of the year (before calendar reforms). This is a good example of how Christianity merged with pagan rituals. The pagan *Lussinatt* was the darkest of nights when spirits, gnomes and trolls roamed the earth. Lussi, a feared enchantress, punished anyone who dared work, while legend has it that farm animals were able to talk to each other. Christianity brought with it Saint Lucia (both Lussi and Lucia are related to the Latin word for light, *lux*). Today, we drive the evil spirits away with someone wearing a crown of candles leading a procession of singers, emerging through the darkness early in the morning. It is a truly magical experience to see a Lucia celebration of any size and to me, the arrival of Lucia in December always signals that Christmas is here.

The big day around Christmas in Scandinavia is Christmas Eve, with the main festivities happening in the early evening. The Vikings believed a new day started at sundown, so some believe this forms part of the reason why we focus on the evening of 24th December rather than Christmas Day itself (that said, many other European countries also celebrate on Christmas Eve, so it is likely to be due to a multitude of cultural and traditional reasons).

Although Christmas Eve isn't a public holiday, many are either not working or will finish by lunchtime. Traditionally, this would be the day to bring in the Christmas tree from outside, although most people now get theirs several days earlier. You'll rarely find an artificial tree in a Scandinavian home (we do have plenty of real ones, after all). In Denmark, we have real candles on the tree that we light (think Victorian-style), and we do so for around 16 minutes on Christmas Eve when we dance around it and sing carols (as someone stands by with the bucket of water, just in case). It's a sight so beautiful and special that it justifies the annual risk.

Typically, families will be preparing Christmas food during the day. Each region has their own special dishes. Swedes typically have a full-on *smörgåsbord* of boiled ham, meatballs, sausages, beetroot, Jansson's Temptation and mustard herring; Danes prefer a dinner of roast duck and/or pork with caramelised potatoes and red cabbage. Depending on where you are in Norway, the dinner is either roast pork belly or *pinnekjøtt* (steamed smoked lamb ribs) or *lutefisk* (cod preserved in lye that is a very acquired taste, even for Norwegians).

In Norway, Christmas rings in at 3pm, while in Sweden it's when *Kalle Anka* (Donald Duck) starts on TV. The same Disney cartoon is broadcast every year and watched by the majority of Swedes, the end of the show signalling dinner time. In Denmark, everyone waits a little longer to start the celebrations in the evening.

After dinner, many households will receive a visit from either *Jultomte* or *Julenisse* (Father Christmas or the Christmas gnome), who will hand out gifts. We have both Father Christmas and the Christmas gnome in Scandinavia – though the two do seem to have merged into one these days. If you are not familiar with it, the story of the gnome is that there is a little creature (no taller than a metre or a few feet), living in every household and homestead, and present all year round though most prevalent at Christmas. He generally has a white beard and wears a red or grey woollen hat. They can be nice or naughty, depending on how you treat them. In many households, people put out a bowl of rice pudding for the house gnome on Christmas Eve – if not, for the rest of the year he will play tricks on you, such as stealing your socks and hiding your car keys.

Christmas Day is the start of the family *smörgåsbord* get-togethers and the following two or three days are spent visiting people, eating leftovers, drinking more *glögg* and eating the rest of the ginger biscuits.

As New Year's Eve comes around, people will get together with friends and have parties, like many others around the world. In Denmark, it's the night where everyone watches the King's speech (delivered live), and at midnight, eat a piece of *kransekage* and toast with Champagne while jumping off a chair into the new year, as is tradition.

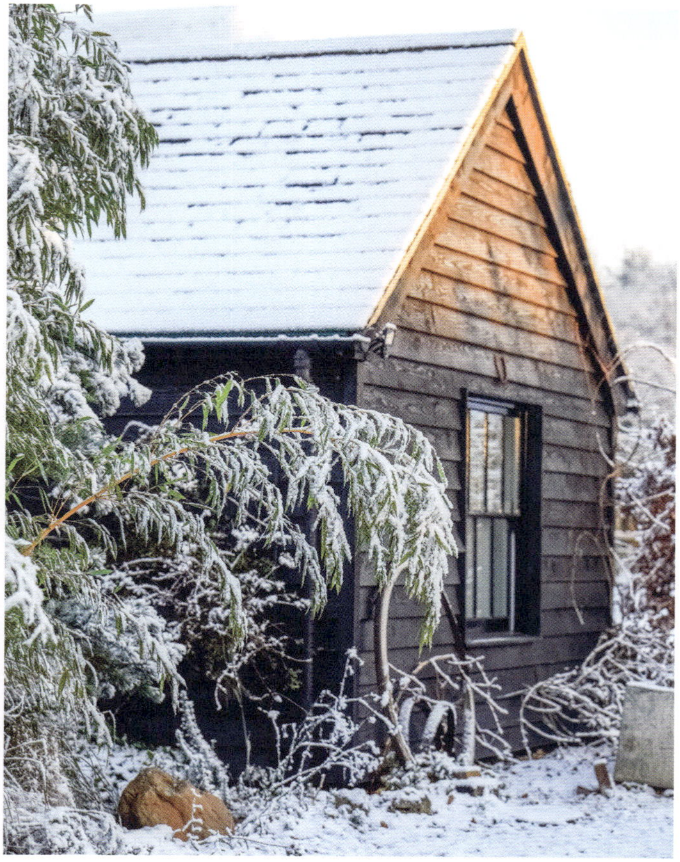
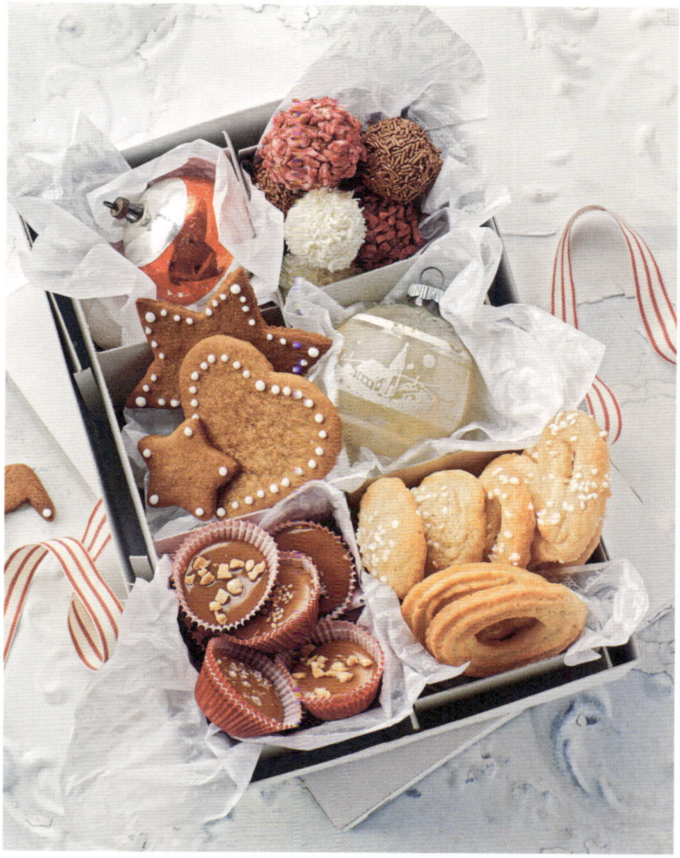
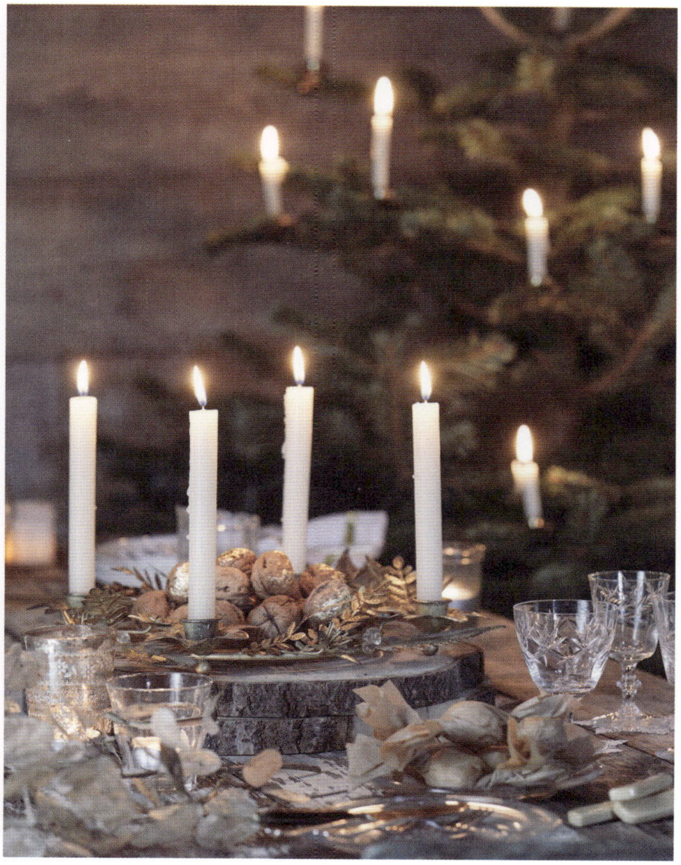
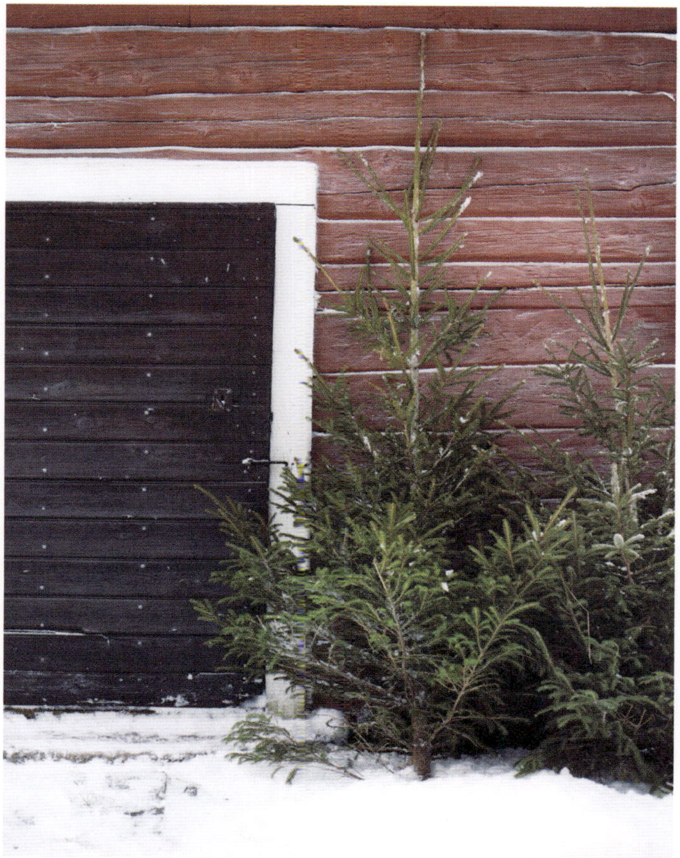

Beetroot tartare

Rødbedetartar

Being a huge beetroot fan (as is the Nordic way), this is a starter I often make when choosing meat-free options. Don't be put off by the initial prep: it is not as intensive as it seems, and the whole dish can be partly prepped ahead, simply adding the egg right before serving. You can even prep the poached eggs several hours ahead by pre-poaching until *just* set, keeping chilled, then simply re-heating for 30-40 seconds in simmering water just before serving (meaning zero poaching stress while your guests are waiting).

This dish works both as a starter or a lunch dish. You can even serve it on top of rye bread as an open sandwich (simply arrange on top of the bread).

40 g/⅓ cup hazelnuts
a glug of oil
½ small parsnip, cut into thin slices
4 eggs
2 avocados
approx. 2 tablespoons horseradish cream, or to taste
micro herbs, to taste (pea shoots work well)
freshly chopped dill, to garnish
4 slices of toasted rye or white bread, to serve

BEETROOT MIXTURE
200 g/7 oz. cooked beetroot/beets (pre-cooked is fine)
100 g/3½ oz. pickled beetroot/beets, finely chopped
2 tablespoons capers
2 small shallots, finely chopped
½ apple, finely chopped
3–5 cornichons, finely chopped
2 teaspoons freshly chopped dill
2 tablespoons freshly chopped flat-leaf parsley
2 teaspoons Dijon mustard
a few drops of Worcestershire sauce
a dash of extra virgin olive oil
salt and freshly ground black pepper

6–7-cm/2¾-inch round cookie cutter

SERVES 4

To make the beetroot/beet mixture, grate the cooked beetroot and place in a bowl. Add the other ingredients and stir to combine with a dash of olive oil (the mustard and oil help bring the mixture together a bit so it does not fall apart). Season to taste.

Toast the hazelnuts in a pan and leave to cool, then roughly chop.

In a small frying pan/skillet, heat a glug of oil, add the thinly shaved parsnip slices and fry until browned and crisp. Season and leave to cool.

If you need to make ahead, poach the eggs in hot water until just set, then drain on paper towels and keep cold until just before serving.

To serve, finely slice the avocados and arrange on four individual plates. Carefully place the cookie cutter on a plate and fill with one-quarter of the beetroot mixture, press gently to shape, then carefully pull the cutter away; repeat on the other plates. The beetroot should stay in shape. If you don't have a cutter, just arrange as best as you can, using a large spoon.

Heat a pan of water to a simmer and add the eggs to briefly re-heat but so they are still runny.

Top the beetroot with the poached egg and dollops of horseradish cream, to taste. Add the toasted hazelnuts, microgreens and crispy parsnips. Finish with a few sprigs of fresh dill and serve with the bread on the side.

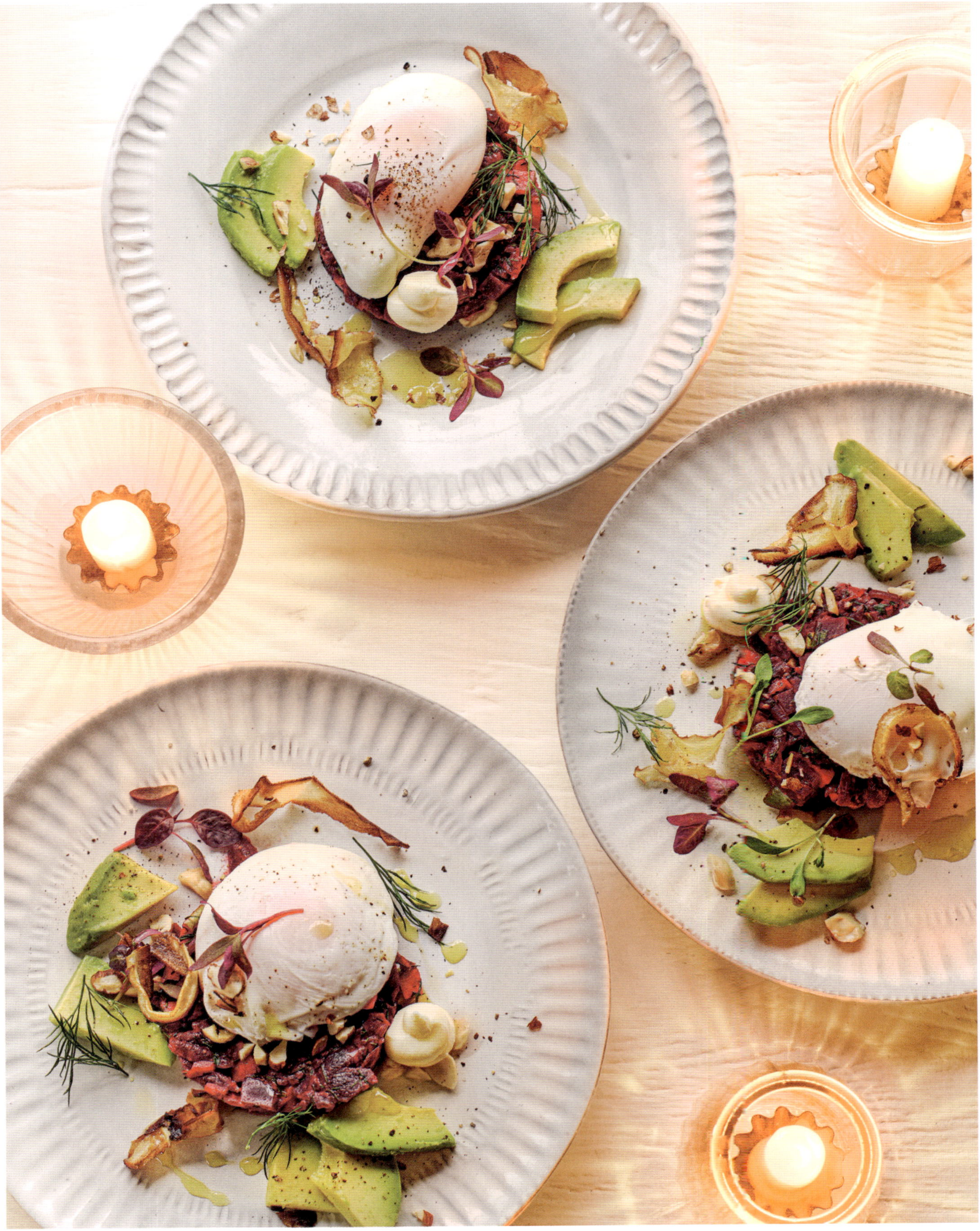

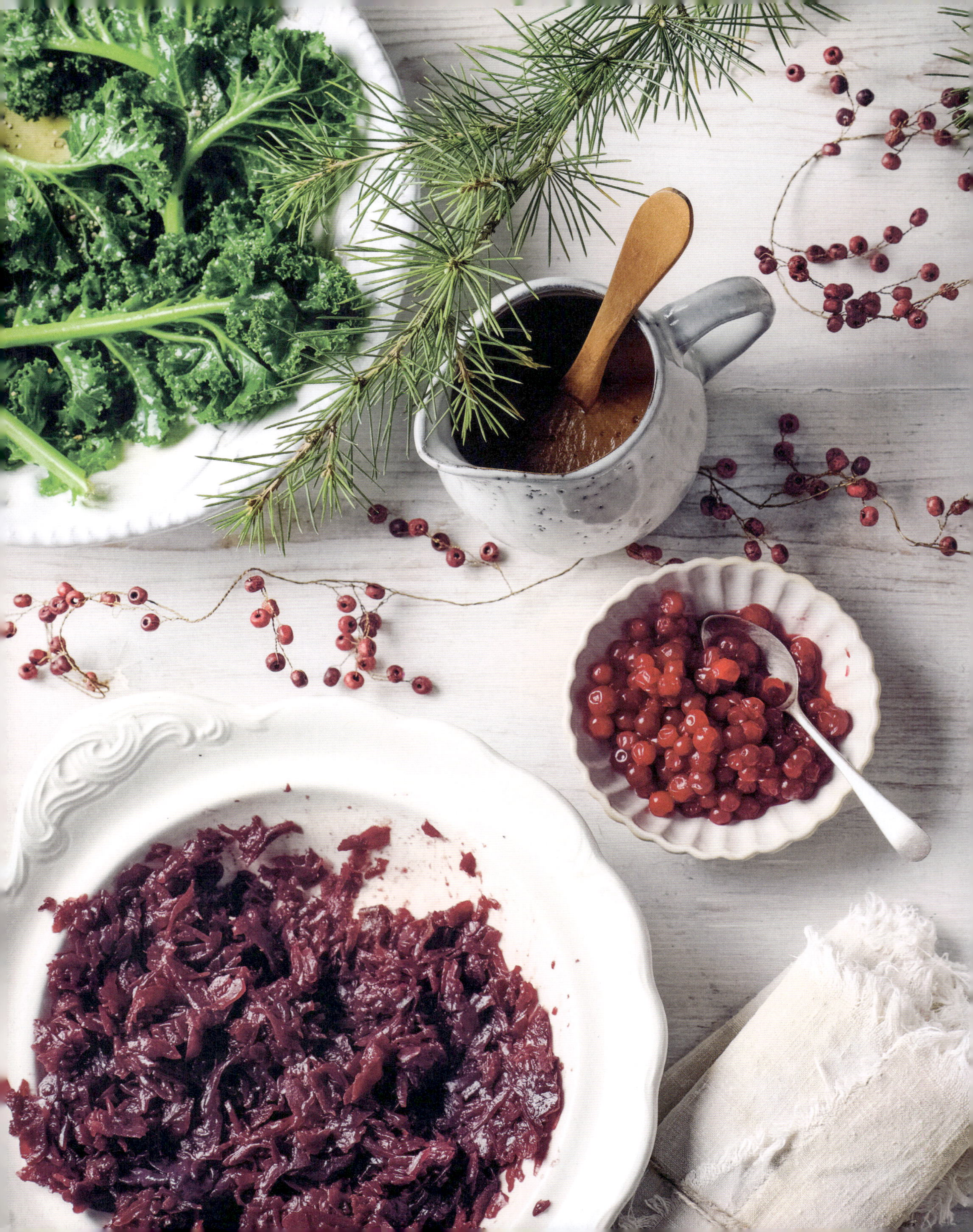

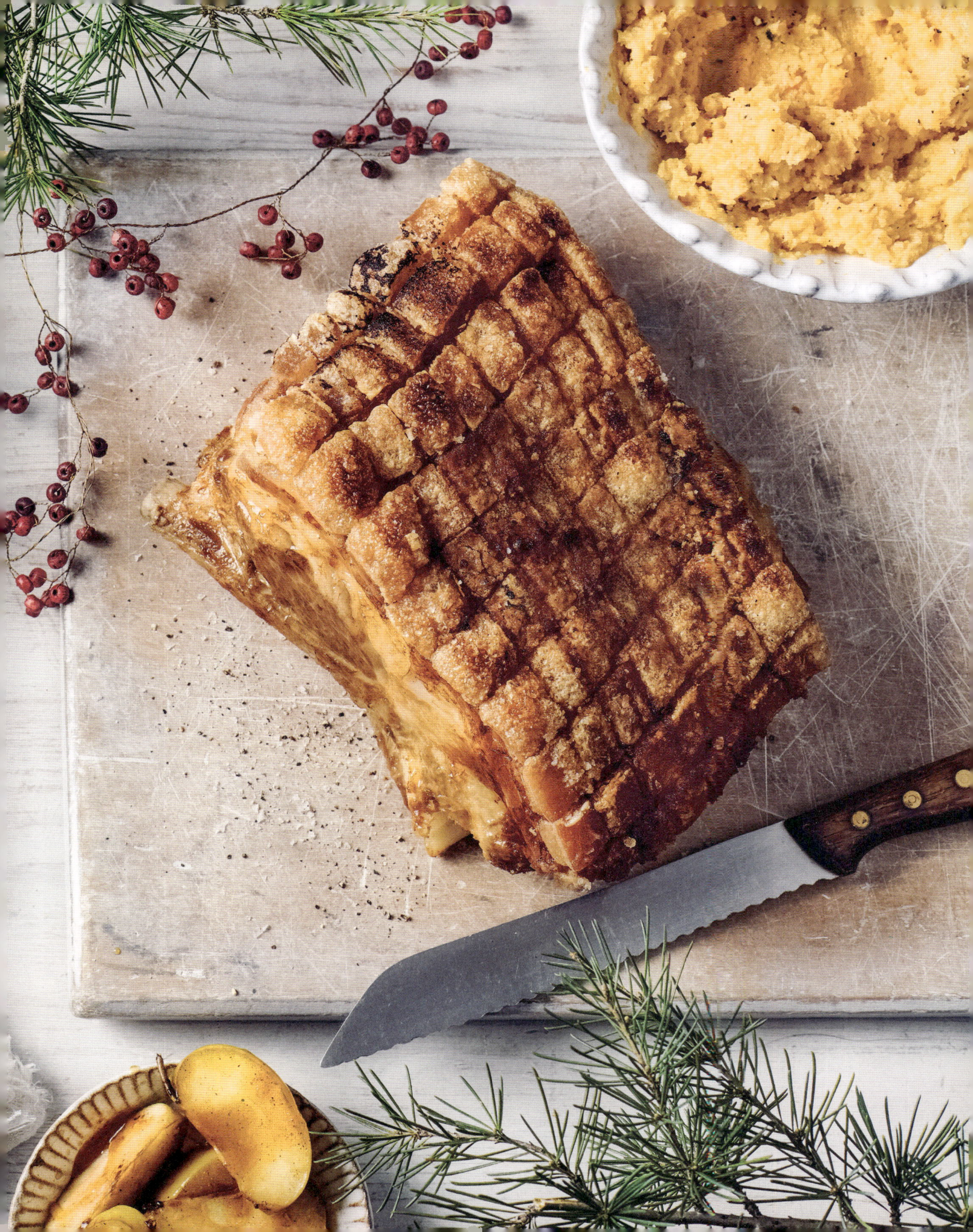

Norwegian pork belly roast

Ribbe

This is a dish served in many Norwegian homes on Christmas Eve, and in some places in Denmark, although there we slice it differently (and for Christmas Danes often favour the less fatty pork loin rather than belly, but I think this Norwegian pork belly is the way to go when it comes to pork roasting). In my childhood home we have some form of pork roast all year round and this cheaper belly cut is so full of flavour and the crackling is excellent when done properly. The stock from the roasting pan also makes the most deliciously thick gravy. Ask your butcher for a belly cut with the bones left in, but if you can't get hold of this, you can use 'normal' pork belly.

1.5-1.7 kg/3¼–3¾ lb. pork belly, bones left in if possible, skin scored deeply at 1-cm/½-inch intervals both ways (to make little squares all over)

200–300 g/7–10½ oz. mixed root vegetables (whatever you have – carrots, parsnips, onions), for stock

5 whole cloves

2 bay leaves

salt and freshly ground black pepper

SERVES 4–8

DAY MINUS 2 Liberally salt the pork on both sides and put in a dish, meat side down. Cover loosely with foil – not tight – and leave in the fridge for at least 24 hours, ideally 48 hours.

DAY 0 Turn the oven to 250ºC/230ºC fan/500ºF/Gas 9 (turn on the steam function if you have it).

Rinse the pork under cold running water, then dry and place in an ovenproof dish. Wrap foil around the dish to make a little dome (not touching the meat), then add water to reach the mid level of the dish. This will create steam and help start the cooking process.

Steam for 45 minutes, then discard the foil (save the water in the dish as this can be used for gravy). Turn the oven down to 160ºC/140ºC fan/325ºF/Gas 3. Check the scoring: the steaming should have helped separate the squares and it is now easier to cut where the butcher might have missed.

Add the cut veg to the base of the dish to flavour the stock. Add the herbs. Make sure the meat is level on top of the veg – this will help the fat run off the meat into the base of the dish as it roasts and your gravy will taste magnificent. Pop the meat back in the oven for 2–2½ hours until it is cooked through. Lower and slower gives the best flavour, but do keep checking as ovens vary.

Towards the end of the cooking time, turn the grill/broiler to high. Blast the top of the roast with heat and the little crispy pork rind squares will pop up. Keep a watchful eye as it burns easily.

Leave to rest for at least 20 minutes. Serve, cut into 5-cm/2-inch squares with thick brown gravy, potatoes and red cabbage.

GRAVY LIKE MAMMA MADE Save the cooking water from the potatoes or veg. In a saucepan, make a roux with some fatty stock from the pork and a few tablespoons of flour and keep whisking over heat. Add some water and keep whisking, add more stock and, as needed, more water. Leave to simmer and add more potato water as needed. Season and add a few drops of gravy browning. This gravy usually flavours itself, but if necessary, add a dash of Worcestershire sauce or a teaspoon of Marmite.

Christmas ham with mustard *Julskinka*

Boiled ham is essential on a Swedish *smörgåsbord*, known in this season as a *julbord* (Christmas table). Serve with grainy mustard and a mustard crust on spiced bread. You can make this in advance and add the mustard crust on the day. Serve it slightly warmed.

approx. 2.5 kg/5½ lb. lightly salted dry-cured unsmoked gammon, ideally with some fat on
1 onion, quartered
2–3 bay leaves
10 black peppercorns
salt

SWEDISH MUSTARD TOPPING
1 egg yolk
3 heaped tablespoons grainy Swedish mustard
3 heaped tablespoons breadcrumbs

SERVES 8–10 AS PART OF A CHRISTMAS SMÖRGÅSBORD

Place the ham in a saucepan, cover with water, add the onion, bay leaves, peppercorns and salt and bring to the boil. Skim off any fat that rises to the top. Reduce to a very slow simmer and cover. Cooking time depends on the size of the meat. A rule of thumb is 45–50 minutes per 1 kg/2 lb. 4 oz., but when the middle temperature reaches 72°C/162°F, it's done.

Remove the ham from the water and leave to cool. I usually cover it with clingfilm/plastic wrap to prevent the edge going dry.

To add the topping before serving, preheat the oven to 200°C/180°C fan/400°F/Gas 6. Trim any fat from the top of the cooked ham. Mix the topping ingredients and spread over the top of the ham (use your hands). Put the ham into the preheated oven for around 15 minutes to allow the topping to bake – you may need to pop it under a hot grill/broiler at the end so that the topping sets around the ham to give a mustard crust. Serve whole on the Christmas table and slice as needed.

Red cabbage *Rødkål*

Red cabbage is a staple across Scandinavia, especially during winter. You don't need to cook it for several hours, but that is what my mother did and so do I – it makes the best red cabbage and has deep flavour. Cook it less and you get more crunch.

50 g/3½ tablespoons butter
1 small red cabbage (approx. 500 g/1 lb. 2 oz.), first thinly sliced, then chopped slightly
1 apple, cut into small pieces
50 g/¼ cup light brown sugar
100 ml/7 tablespoons blackcurrant cordial (or redcurrant jelly)
50 ml/3½ tablespoons white wine vinegar
spices, to taste (star anise, bay leaf and allspice, or a cinnamon stick and a small bit of clove – discard hard spices after cooking)
salt and freshly ground black pepper

SERVES 4–6

Melt the butter in a saucepan and add the cabbage. Cook for a few minutes, then add the remaining ingredients and 100 ml/7 tablespoons water and bring to the boil. Turn down the heat and simmer over a low heat, covered, for about 2 hours. Check it from time to time to stir and see if it needs topping up with water.

Once the cooking time is up, check the seasoning, then leave to simmer, uncovered, for a further 30 minutes (check the water levels regularly). Check if the cabbage needs more salt, vinegar or sugar, to taste. You need a good balance of not too sour and not too sweet. My mother always said 'It should not irritate any areas of your tongue when you taste it'!

NOTE Norwegian white cabbage (*Surkål*) is also made at Christmas. Use white cabbage, cook for an hour and add caraway or cumin seed instead of red cabbage spices. Use stock from roast pork to add depth of flavour.

Jansson's temptation

Janssons frestelse

This is the iconic Swedish Christmas side dish. It's worth trying to get hold of the pickled sprats (known as *ansjovis*) to make this the 'right' way (do not use actual anchovies), but if you cannot get hold of Swedish sprats, use some pickled herring cut into small pieces instead.

There's some disagreement as to where the name of this dish comes from. Some say it is named after singer Pelle Janzon, others say it is from a silent movie from the 1920s called *Janssons Frestelse*. Either way, this is one of the more well-travelled Swedish recipes, and one that is worth adding to your recipe repertoire. This also works well as a side dish to roast lamb.

25 g/1¾ tablespoons butter, plus 20 g/1½ tablespoons to top
200 g/7 oz. white onions, sliced
700 g/1 lb. 9 oz. floury potatoes (I use Maris Piper)
300 ml/1¼ cups double/heavy cream
300 ml/1¼ cups whole milk
125-g/4½-oz. can Swedish pickled sprats (*ansjovis*) or finely chopped pickled herring
3–4 tablespoons dried breadcrumbs
salt and freshly ground black pepper

ovenproof dish approx. 30 x 15 cm/ 12 x 6 inches

SERVES 4, AS A SMÖRGÅSBORD SIDE

Preheat the oven to 180°C/160°C fan/350°F/Gas 4.

In a saucepan, melt the butter and fry the onions over a low heat for about 15 minutes.

Peel the potatoes and cut into matchsticks, a little thinner than French fries. Do this in one go and don't soak them in water as you want to keep the starch. Add the potatoes to the saucepan with the onion and mix. Add the cream and milk and allow to come to the boil briefly, then turn off the heat. Season with pepper and only a tiny bit of salt as you are adding salty fish too.

Add half the creamy potato to the oven dish, then add half the pickled sprats. Add the remaining potato mixture and then the rest of the sprats on top. Sprinkle breadcrumbs all over the top and add a few small knobs/pats of butter in five or six places.

Bake in the preheated oven for 30–35 minutes or until the potatoes are cooked through. Some potatoes soak up more liquid than others, so you may need to add more milk and cream during cooking. The final cooking time can vary quite a bit based on potato size – don't be tempted to turn up the heat as you don't want the cream to overcook. Lower and slower is better (although feel free to blast it for a few minutes at the end to brown the top if needed).

VEGGIE VARIATION Omit the *ansjovis* and this becomes a lovely veggie potato gratin. If you do this, I suggest adding a few drops of white wine vinegar to the milk and cream mixture and adjusting the seasoning. If you want a bit of a bite, add some capers.

MAKE IT DIFFERENT If you swap the pickled sprats with cooked ham (for example, leftover cubes of Christmas ham, see page 221) it becomes a dish called *Karlssons Frestelse* instead.

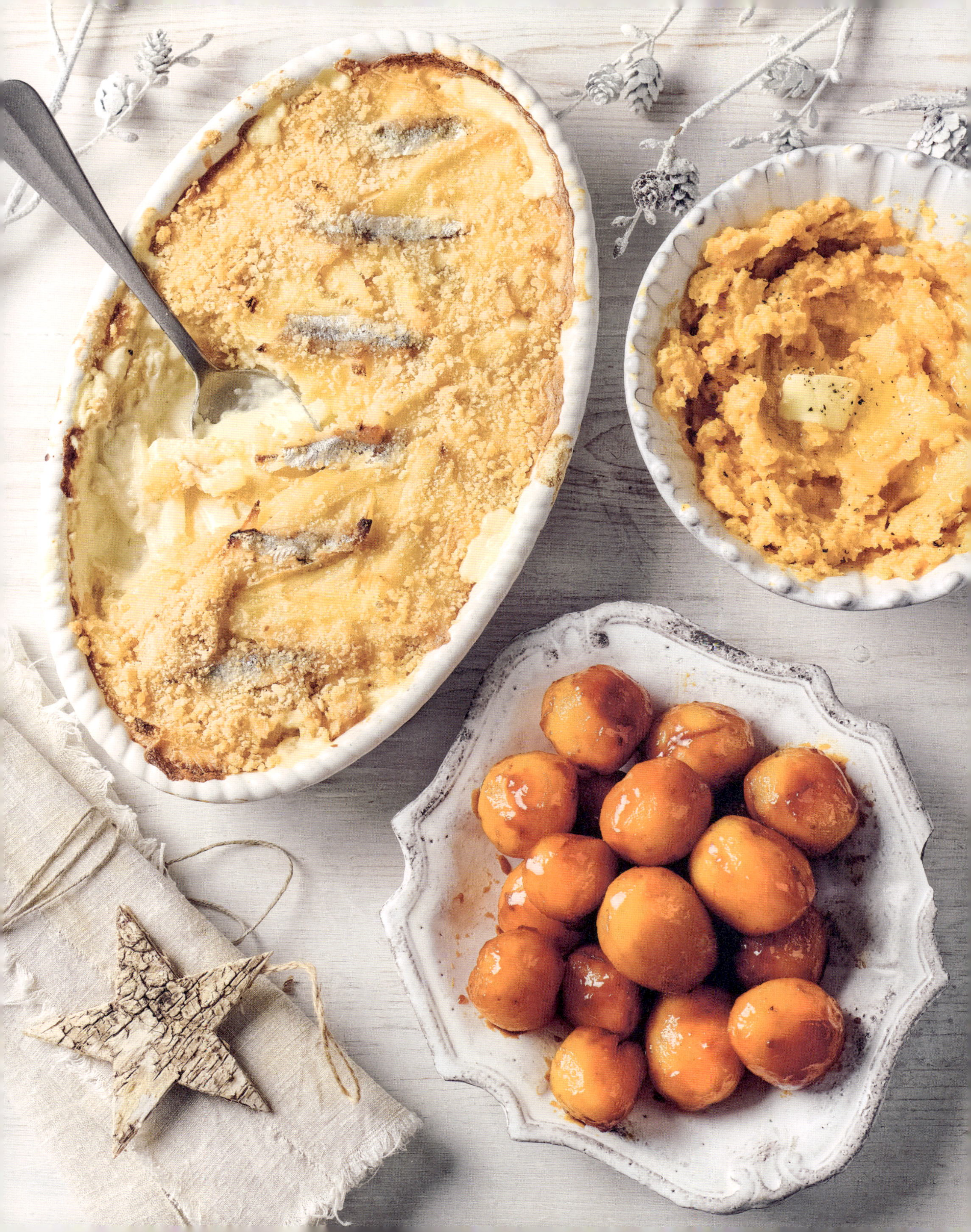

Caramelised potatoes

Brunede kartofler

These caramelised new potatoes are an obligatory side dish on Christmas Eve in Denmark. They are sweet and delicious with the thick gravy, meat and boiled potatoes. You only need to plan for a few of these potatoes per person as this is a rich and sweet addition – but it complements roast pork and duck so very well. This portion feeds at least six people if served alongside boiled potatoes.

1 kg/2 lb. 4 oz. small salad potatoes, cooked and peeled the day before
80 g/6 tablespoons caster/granulated sugar
25 g/1¾ tablespoons butter
salt

SERVES 6

The day before, boil the potatoes until only just done. Take great care not to overcook them, or the final dish will be mushy. I peel off the skin on the potatoes after cooking and cooling slightly. Store in the fridge overnight.

About 30 minutes before serving, add the caster sugar to a frying pan/skillet and shake the pan to spread it out. Turn the heat up high to allow the sugar to start melting, then lower the heat. Do NOT touch the sugar in the pan or stir. Once the sugar has melted, add the butter and stir carefully until everything is mixed. Add the cold potatoes to the pan and try not to move them too much for the first few minutes. Move the potatoes around the caramel from time to time over the next 15 minutes, keeping the heat at medium. Over that time the caramel will start to form a thin, sticky layer around the potatoes and any lumps will melt.

Season with salt at the end and serve immediately in a bowl next to Danish roast pork or duck for Christmas dinner.

Norwegian mashed swede

Kålrabistabbe

Swede/rutabaga is a hugely popular root vegetable in the Nordics. At Christmas, Norwegians serve it mashed with traditional dried and salted lamb ribs called *pinnekjøtt*. In Sweden, a variation of this dish is called *rotmos*, adding a few potatoes to the swede to bring a starchier result. For Swedish *rotmos*, simply add three medium potatoes to the ingredients below and reduce the swede by half.

1 kg/2 lb. 4 oz. swede/rutabaga
2 carrots
50 g/3½ tablespoons butter
100 ml/⅓ cup plus 1 tablespoon double/heavy cream
½ teaspoon freshly grated nutmeg
100 ml/⅓ cup plus 1 tablespoon meat stock (stock from the roast pork on page 220 is good for this)
salt and freshly ground black pepper
fresh thyme, to garnish

SERVES 4

Peel and cut the swede/rutabaga and carrots into equal-sized pieces, place in a pan and cover with water. Bring to the boil and cook until they are soft. Reserve the cooking water.

Add the butter, cream and nutmeg to the vegetables and mash until smooth. Taste, and add cooking water (and the stock, if using) to taste and according to the consistency you prefer. If you prefer a smoother mash, you can blitz it in a food processor or with a stick blender.

Season to taste, sprinkle with thyme leaves and serve.

Hasselback potatoes

Hasselback potatis

Invented in the 1950s by a trainee chef at Stockholm's *Hasselbacken* restaurant, these fancy potatoes are now famous around the world. They go well with any kind of roast dinner and you can vary the flavour by scattering breadcrumbs or hard cheese on top or adding fresh herbs. At my home in Denmark, these are always served with meatloaf (see page 52), and they are our go-to for most roast dinners.

1 kg/2 lb. 4 oz. roasting potatoes, such as King Edward or Maris Piper, peeled
a glug of neutral oil, such as sunflower
50 g/3½ tablespoons butter, melted
30–50 g/⅓–⅝ cup breadcrumbs (optional)
salt and freshly ground black pepper

SERVES 4

Preheat the oven to 220°C/200°C fan/425°F/Gas 7. Put a roasting pan with a generous glug of neutral oil in the oven to heat up.

Cut any large potatoes in half. Using a sharp knife, slice two-thirds of the way through the potatoes, 2 mm/⅛ inch apart (the thinner the slices, the crispier the result). Try placing the potato next to a chopping board and use the edge of the board to stop you cutting all the way through.

Add the potatoes, scored-side up, to the roasting pan with the very hot oil – take care as it might spatter a bit. Roast for 20 minutes.

Remove the potatoes from the oven, brush each potato with butter over the sliced area, then sprinkle breadcrumbs on top (if using). Season. Lower the heat to 200°C/180°C fan/400°F/Gas 6 and put the potatoes back in the oven for another 20 minutes or until they're done – the slices will be crispy, and the base of each potato cooked through.

TIP To prepare the potatoes hours ahead of roasting time, peel and slice and place in a bowl of cold water with a few drops of lemon juice – this will encourage the slices to open. Drain well before roasting.

Red cabbage salad

Rødkålssalat

A fresh alternative to the traditional cooked cabbages – we often serve this on the Christmas table as a lighter salad.

300 g/10½ oz. red cabbage, finely sliced
1 teaspoon Maldon sea salt
2 oranges, peeled
1 celery stick, finely chopped
2 tablespoons finely chopped parsley
40 g/1½ oz. pecan nuts, toasted and roughly chopped

DRESSING
2 tablespoons red wine vinegar
1 tablespoon maple syrup
1 tablespoon orange juice
5–6 tablespoons olive oil
salt and freshly ground black pepper

SERVES 4

In a bowl, lightly massage the red cabbage with the salt for a few minutes. Cut the oranges into 1–2-cm/½–¾-inch pieces (save the juice for the dressing). Add to the bowl, along with the celery and parsley. For the dressing, whisk the vinegar, syrup and juice, then slowly pour in the oil so it emulsifies. Season, then pour over the salad and mix well. Top with the pecans just before serving.

Rice pudding

Risengrød

Rice pudding has a huge place across Scandinavia at Christmas. We eat it hot during colder months with lots of cinnamon and butter (as pictured here) – perfect for any time of the day. From cold rice pudding, we make our Christmas Eve dessert – a creamy version with sauce. Each country has a different sauce (orange in Sweden, raspberry in Norway), but in my house we serve a warm cherry sauce. This dessert is very rich so I tend to serve in individual pots. It's traditional to hide an almond in the pudding – the person who finds it is given a little marzipan pig or chocolates.

200 g/heaped 1 cup pudding rice
1 litre/4 cups whole milk
½ vanilla pod/bean, sliced lengthways
salt, sugar or vanilla extract, to taste
butter, to serve
cinnamon sugar (mix 1 part ground cinnamon with 3 parts granulated sugar), to serve

SERVES 3–4

In a heavy-based pan, add the rice and 300 ml/1¼ cups water and bring to the boil for a few minutes. Add the milk and vanilla. Bring to the boil for 5 minutes, stirring constantly to avoid the rice sticking. Turn the heat to low and simmer, stirring occasionally, until the rice is al dente but not overcooked (20–25 minutes, but watch the pan as it can burn or boil over).

Once cooked, add a little salt to taste (I never add the salt until this stage). Add a little sugar if you prefer a sweeter pudding or a few extra drops of vanilla extract. The pudding may still feel a little too liquid when the rice is cooked, but the milk will soak into the rice as it cools slightly. If making the Creamed Rice Dessert (see below), cool and store in the fridge.

Serve the hot rice pudding topped with a knob/pat of cold butter in the middle and a generous amount of cinnamon sugar sprinkled over.

TIP Leftover rice makes delicious pancakes – *Klatkager* (dollop cakes). Mix 200 g/7 oz. cold rice pudding with 1 egg, 2–3 tablespoons plain/all-purpose flour, a bit of vanilla extract and 1 teaspoon baking powder, then fry in a pan in butter or oil, as you would for American-style pancakes. Serve with raspberry jam/preserves, dusted with icing/confectioner's sugar.

Christmas rice pudding
Risalamande

250 ml/1 cup whipping cream
2 tablespoons icing/confectioner's sugar
1 teaspoon vanilla sugar or extract
1 quantity Rice Pudding (see above), cold
50 g/⅜ cup blanched almonds, roughly chopped (one left whole)

SERVES 6–8

Whip the cream with the sugar and vanilla until thick, then gently fold into the chilled rice pudding. Add the almonds, including the whole one, and portion into individual serving pots. Chill in the fridge until ready to serve with cherry sauce on the side.

Danish cherry sauce
Kirsebærsovs

1 heaped tablespoon cornflour/cornstarch
2 x 300-g/10½-oz. cans black or morello cherries in syrup
1 teaspoon orange juice
2 tablespoons rum
sugar, to taste (optional)

Mix the cornflour/cornstarch with a small amount of syrup to make a paste. Bring the cherries and 250 ml/1 cup of the syrup to the boil in a pan, add the paste and stir. Boil for 1 minute to thicken, then take off the heat and add the orange and rum. Sweeten with sugar, if needed. Serve hot over *risalamande*.

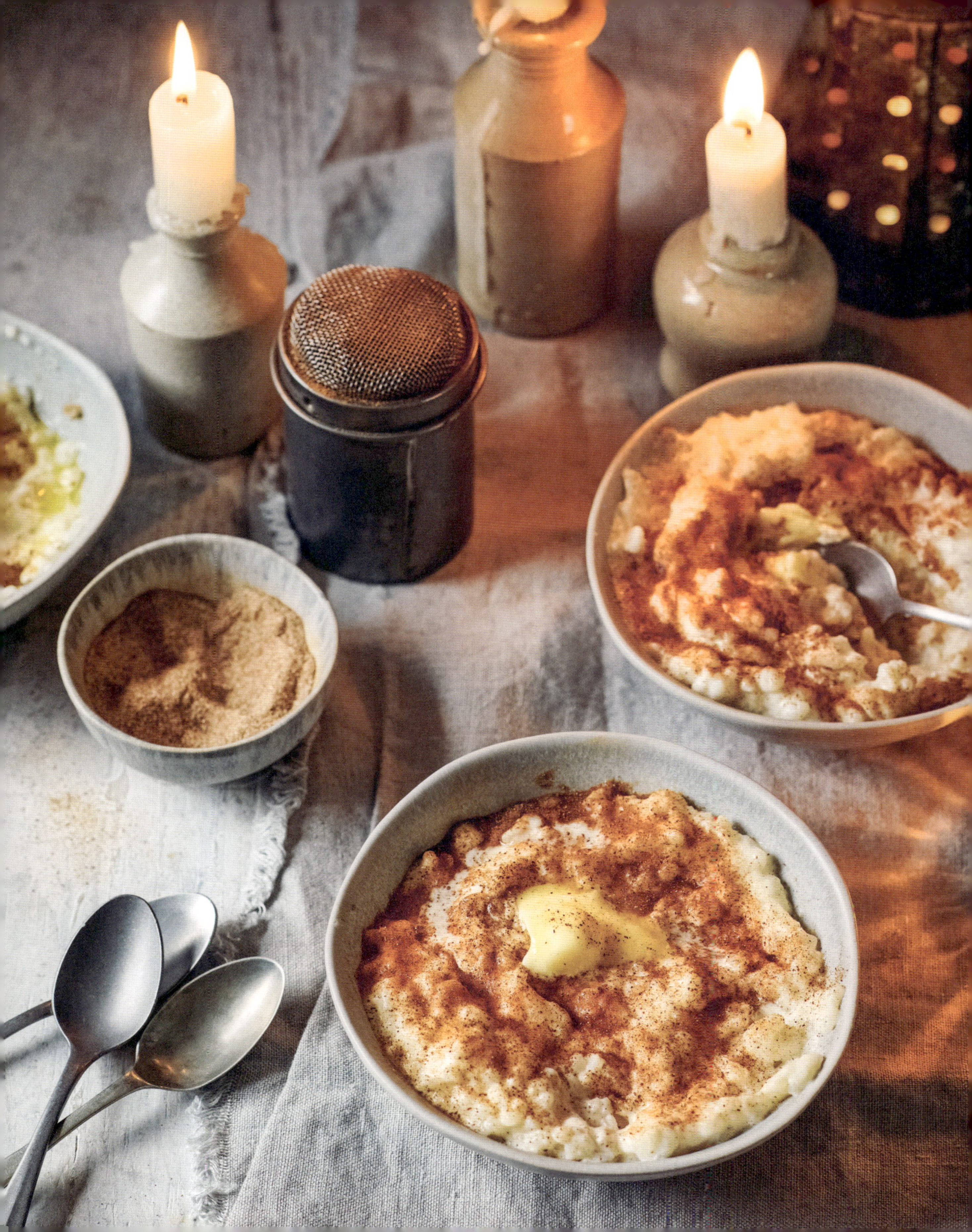

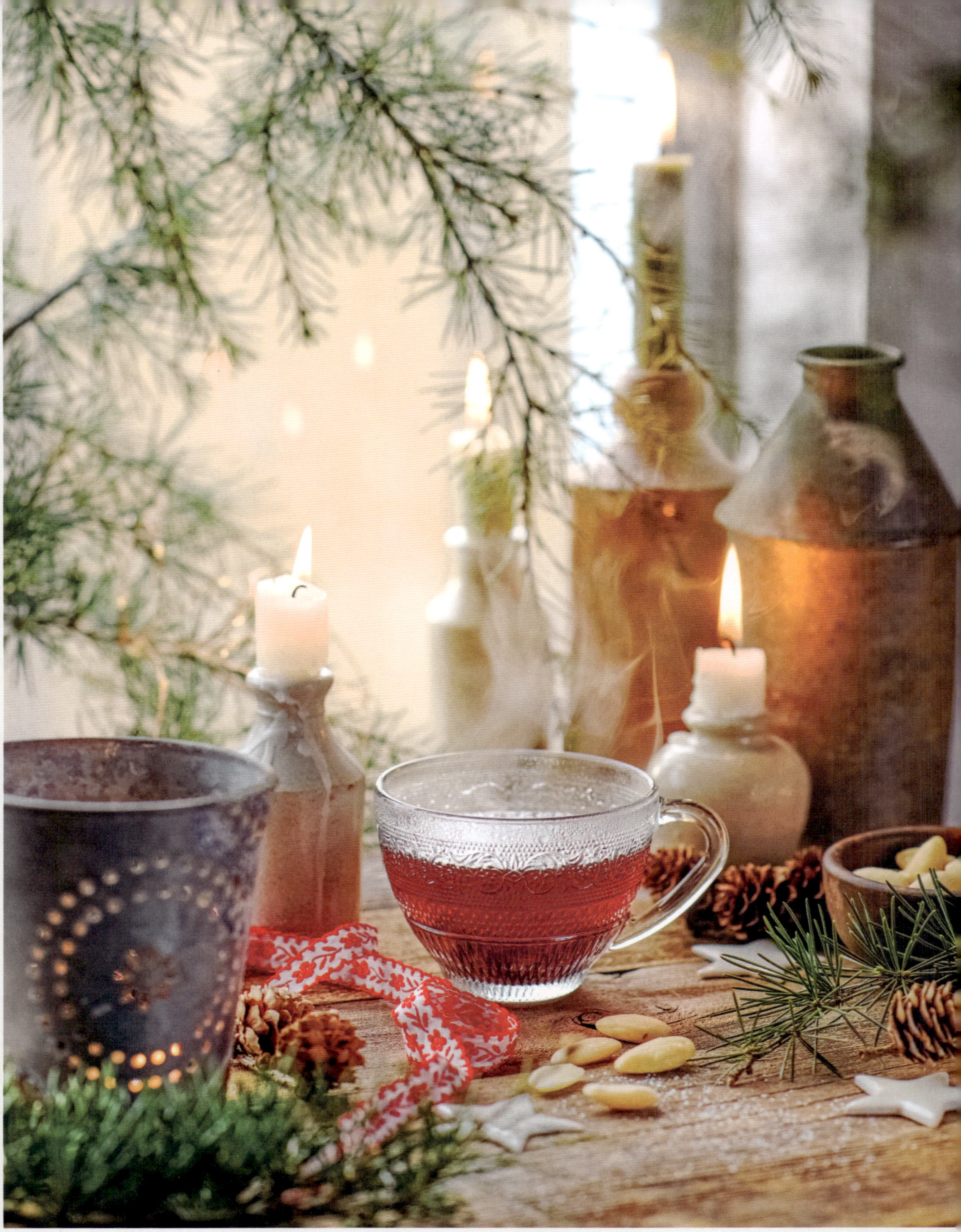

DECEMBER 229

Danish pancake bites

Æbleskiver

To make these, you need a special *æbleskiver* pan, which can be bought online (or use a Japanese Takoyaki pan). *Æbleskiver* are traditionally eaten in Denmark in December, when they are dusted with icing/confectioner's sugar and served with raspberry or strawberry jam/preserves on the side. In some places in America where second and third generation Danes live, *Æbleskiver* have evolved and are now served all year round for breakfast, which makes sense as these are a form of pancake.

3 eggs, separated
300 ml/1¼ cups buttermilk
100 ml/⅓ cup plus 1 tablespoon double/heavy cream
1 tablespoon caster/granulated sugar
½ teaspoon salt
1 teaspoon baking powder
½ teaspoon bicarbonate of soda/ baking soda
1 teaspoon ground cardamom
200 g/1½ cups plain/all-purpose flour
1 teaspoon vanilla extract
50 g/3½ tablespoons melted butter
icing/confectioner's sugar and strawberry or raspberry jam/ preserve, to serve

æbleskiver pan

MAKES APPROX. 30

Mix the egg yolks, buttermilk and cream in a bowl.

In another bowl, mix together the sugar, salt, baking powder, bicarbonate of soda/baking soda, cardamom and flour, as well as the vanilla extract.

In a third bowl, whisk the egg whites on high speed until stiff.

Mix together the wet and dry ingredients, then carefully fold in the whisked egg whites. Leave to rest for 30 minutes in the fridge.

Preheat the *æbleskiver* pan over a high heat, then reduce the heat to medium and add some melted butter to each hole. Carefully add enough batter to each hole to reach almost to the top. Leave to cook for a few minutes, then, using a fork, carefully turn the balls to cook the other side.

Once browned on all sides (this will take about 3–4 minutes per batch), keep the *æbleskiver* in a warm oven until you are done – this will also help to cook them through. Serve dusted with icing/confectioner's sugar and a little pot of jam/preserve for dipping.

Scandinavian mulled wine

Glögg

The basic Scandi *glögg* mulled wine most often contains a variation of these spices listed here and I think this is a good base from which to create your own twist on the recipe. If you can't get dried bitter orange, you can use fresh orange peel but the flavour is much fruitier so reduce the amount to taste. *Glögg* is made using a basic red wine – a cheap supermarket bottle will do.

1 bottle of inexpensive red wine
2 cinnamon sticks
1 thumb-sized piece of dried ginger
1 piece (approx. 6 g/¼ oz.) of dried bitter orange peel
8 whole green cardamom pods
15–16 whole cloves
80 g/6 tablespoons sugar

TO SERVE
100 g/¾ cup raisins
100 ml/7 tablespoons brandy or aquavit (or spirit of your choice)
60 g/¾ cup flaked/slivered almonds

SERVES 4

In a saucepan, heat the wine, spices and sugar to maximum 80°C/176°F (any higher and the alcohol starts to evaporate). Turn off the heat and leave to infuse for at least 1 hour, ideally longer.

Strain the *glögg*, pour back into the wine bottle and close.

To serve, soak the raisins in brandy or aquavit, ideally overnight. Heat the *glögg* to hot (not boiling). Add a few teaspoons of the alcohol-soaked raisins to a cup along with some flaked/slivered almonds and top with the hot *glögg*.

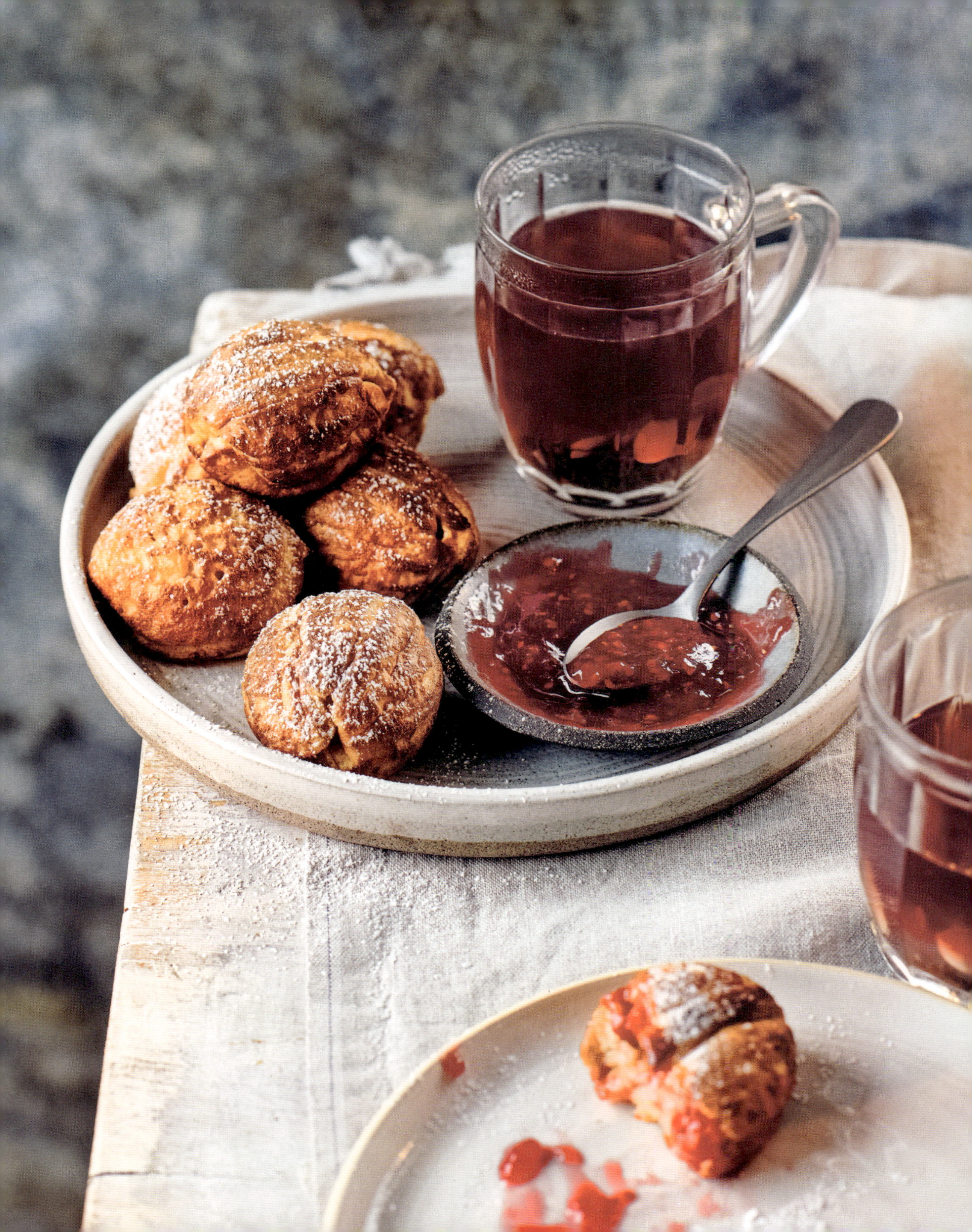

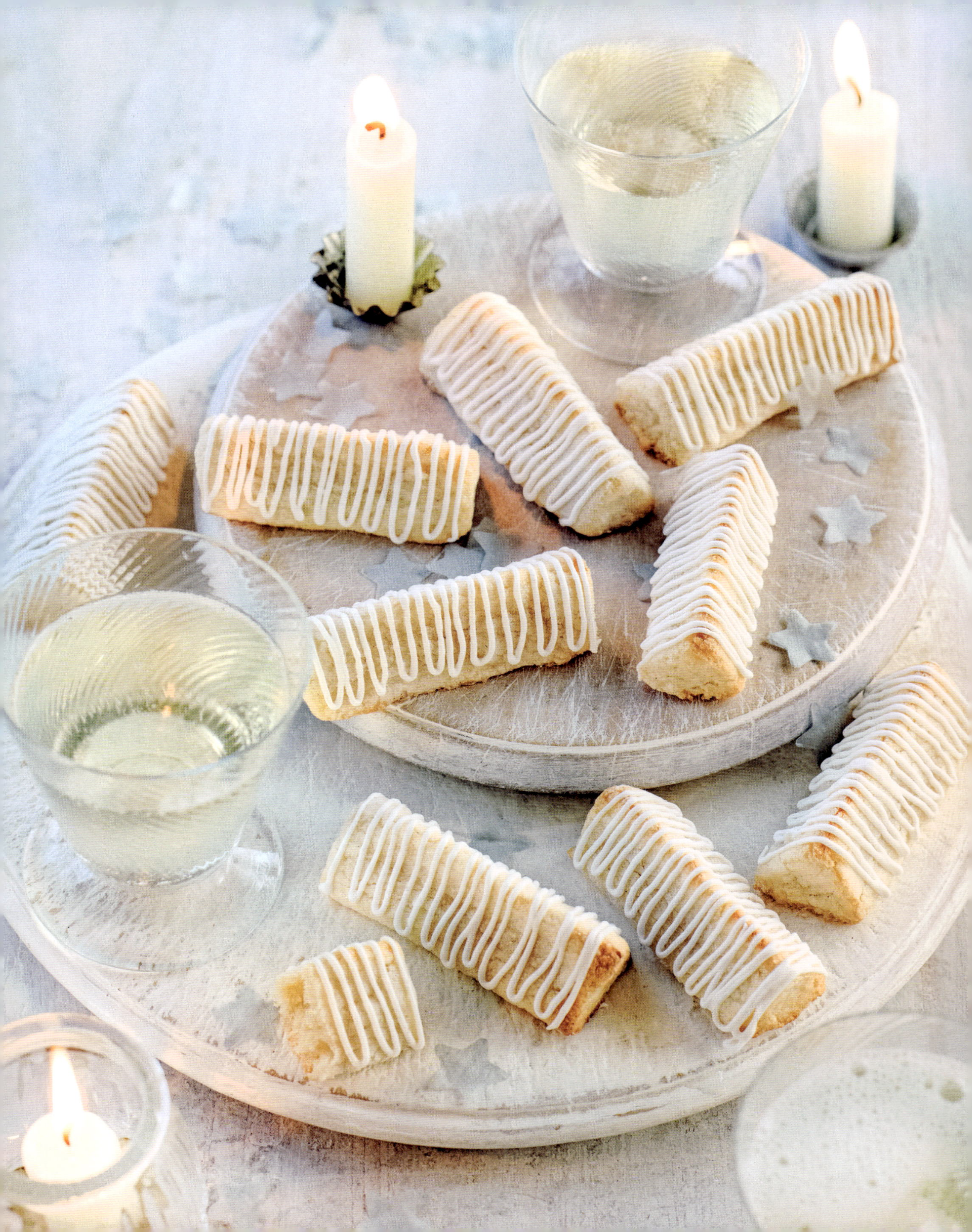

Almond cake bites
Kransekage

In Norway and Denmark, this is the ultimate celebration cake – for Norway's Constitution Day, weddings, big birthdays and on New Year (this is the cake Danes toast in the New Year with, usually after jumping down from a chair – as we do to jump into the New Year, see page 214). It's a very rich cake: a little goes a long way.

Most often you see a big *Kransekage* tower of rings (see tip, below) – it is the ultimate cake and not that easy to make, which understandably scares a lot of people. I agree, as getting the rings just right can be testing (along with the intricate amount of icing). Instead of the tower, I've included this recipe for bite-sized pieces – perfect during Christmas and New Year, with no stress of making the big tower.

50 g/1¾ oz. egg whites
75 g/¾ cup ground almonds
50 g/¼ cup caster/granulated sugar
50 g/heaping ⅓ cup icing/confectioner's sugar, plus extra for rolling
250 g/9 oz. Marzipan (see page 237)

ICING
100 g/¾ cup minus ½ tablespoon icing/confectioner's sugar
freshly squeezed lemon juice
½–1 egg white

baking sheet, lined with baking parchment

piping/pastry bag

MAKES 16 LARGE *KRANSEKAGE* LOGS OR 32 SMALLER PETIT-FOUR SIZED PIECES

In a bowl, whisk the egg whites until thick and foamy (not stiff). Add the almonds and sugars and whisk again until you have smooth paste. Grate the marzipan into the mixture and mix – the final mixture will be sticky. Place in the fridge for at least an hour.

Preheat the oven to 200°C/180°C fan/400°F/Gas 6.

Dust your worksurface with icing/confectioner's sugar. Roll your dough into logs around 1.5 cm/⅝ inch wide, cut into 16 or 32 pieces, depending on the size you prefer. The traditional shape is either round or with slightly pressed in sides, into a triangle.

Place on the baking sheet and bake in the preheated oven for around 10–12 minutes (depending on whether you're making the smaller or larger pieces). Keep an eye on them – they are done when they have a light brown colour, but take care not to over-bake. Leave to cool completely.

To make the icing, mix the sugar, a few drops of lemon juice and half of the egg white – you may not need all of it. Keep stirring until you have a very thick icing that can be piped – too liquid and it will run, too hard and you won't be able to squeeze it out. Add to a piping/pastry bag with a small hole cut at the end.

Decorate the logs, trailing the icing from side to side, like a radio wave pattern. These should be quite close together and it can take a steady hand to get it right. The icing will harden after some time.

These keep for a week or you can freeze, either before or after decoration.

TIP If you want to make a Norwegian/Danish *Kransekage* tower, double the recipe and it will give you enough for a ten-ring tower (serves 12–15). It is easiest if you buy the specialist baking pans, but you can roll and bake by hand. Adjust the baking time accordingly.

BASIC RECIPES

Basic bun dough
Dej til boller

This dough can be used for various Nordic buns. It is an enriched brioche-type dough. If you cannot get hold of compressed fresh yeast, use active dry yeast granules (not the fast-action yeast powder) – you need to activate the granules in warm liquid for 15 minutes until it froths up before continuing the recipe.

500 ml/2 cups whole milk, heated to 35–36°C/95–97°F
50 g/1¾ oz. fresh, compressed yeast (see tip) or 26 g/⅞ oz. dry active yeast granules
75 g/6 tablespoons caster/granulated sugar
150 g/1¼ sticks unsalted butter, super soft or just melted
2 teaspoons ground cardamom
900–950 g/6½–6¾ cups strong white bread flour
1 teaspoon salt
1 egg

MAKES 24–30 BUNS

Pour the warm milk into the bowl of a stand mixer fitted with a dough hook, then add the fresh yeast and start the machine on low. If using active dry yeast granules, add the yeast to the liquid with a spoonful of sugar and leave to develop for 15 minutes before proceeding to add mixture to the bowl of the mixer.

Add the sugar to the yeast mixture, then add the butter as you continue to mix. Add the cardamom. Start to add flour, bit by bit – you may not need it all so start with 800–850 g/5¾–6 cups. When the machine has been going for a minute or so, add the salt and the egg.

Continue kneading for around 5 minutes. You may need to add more flour – you want the mixture to end up a bit sticky, but not so much that it sticks to your finger if you poke it. It is better not to add too much flour as this will result in dry buns. You can add more later.

Once mixed, leave the dough in the bowl and cover with a kitchen towel or clingfilm/plastic wrap. Leave to rise for around 40 minutes or until it has doubled in size – always look for the size of the dough to double. If your kitchen is on the cooler side, this can take longer (or vice versa).

Choux pastry basic batter
Vandbakkelsedej

This dough is used for Danish Shrovetide buns, choux buns and Wales Cake.

100 g/7 tablespoons butter, cubed
1 teaspoon sugar
a pinch of salt
100 g/¾ cup plain/all-purpose flour
4 eggs, beaten

MAKES 20 SMALL CHOUX BUNS, 8 LARGER BUNS OR 1 CAKE

Preheat the oven to 200°C/180°C fan/400°F/Gas 6; you'll reduce the temperature to 180°C/160°C fan/350°F/Gas 4 halfway through the cooking time.

Pour 200 ml/¾ cup water into a saucepan and add the cubed butter. Bring to the boil and add the sugar and a pinch of salt. Sift the flour and add, in one swoop, to the pan. Mix vigorously until the dough starts coming away from the sides. Keep cooking and stirring over a low heat for 1 minute, then take off the heat and leave to cool down for 3–4 minutes.

Add the eggs to the batter in four parts, whisking with all your might after each addition.

Proceed as per your recipe, using these baking times:
Small choux buns: approx. 25–30 minutes
Larger choux buns: approx. 30–35 minutes
Full cakes: approx. 35–37 minutes

Do not open the oven for at least the first 20 minutes of the baking time, and remember to reduce the oven temperature halfway through cooking.

When you take them out of the oven, pierce the sides immediately to allow steam to escape and leave to cool on a baking rack. You can pop them back in the oven for a few minutes on residual heat to allow to crisp up a bit.

TIP When adding the egg to the dough, be careful not to add too much egg – you can test it to see if enough has been added by seeing if it drips in the 'V' shape. This recipe is for four medium eggs, but if you're unsure of your egg size, you can also mix the eggs and weigh out 180 g/6½ oz.

Shortcrust pastry
Tærtedej

A good base for savoury pies and quiches. Freeze any leftover for later use.

125 g/9 tablespoons cold butter, cubed
200 g/1½ cups plain/all-purpose flour
a pinch of salt
1 egg

MAKES ENOUGH FOR A 25-CM/10-INCH TART BASE

In a bowl, rub the butter into the flour with the salt until it resembles a sandy mixture, then add the egg and mix until you have a uniform dough. If it's a little dry, you can add a small dash of chilled water to help the dough hold together. Chill before using.

Sweet shortcrust pastry
Sød tærtedej

This is a versatile sweet pastry dough that can be used for most kinds of sweet pies and tarts, from *Mazarin* and raspberry slices to apple pie, and most things in between.

150 g/1¼ sticks cold butter, cubed
250 g/1¾ cups plus 2 tablespoons plain/all-purpose flour
80 g/scant ⅔ cup icing/confectioner's sugar
1 egg yolk
1 teaspoon vanilla extract (optional)

MAKES ENOUGH FOR A 23-CM/9-INCH TART BASE (BUT ENOUGH FOR A PIE LID, TOO, IF THINLY ROLLED)

Rub the butter and flour together to form a sandy mixture. Add the sugar, then add the egg yolk and vanilla (if using) and mix again. Add 3–4 tablespoons cold water to help the dough combine. Once you have a uniform, smooth dough, rest in the fridge for at least 30 minutes before using. If you're only using a base, freeze the remaining leftover dough for later use.

BASIC RECIPES 235

Basic Danish pastry dough *Wienerbrødsdej*

Making Danish pastry dough can be a bit of a faff, but once you get the hang of it, it's really satisfying. Do use cold ingredients and don't be tempted to use softened butter (however, make sure your butter hits the temperature sweet spot so you can roll it out together with the dough or you'll end up with butter lumps and it will bake unevenly).

30 g/1 oz. fresh yeast
200 ml/¾ cup cold milk
100 ml/⅓ cup plus 1 tablespoon chilled water
50 g/¼ cup caster/granulated sugar
600–650 g/4¼–4⅔ cups bread flour, plus more for rolling out (approx. 100–150 g/¾–1 cup)
3 medium/US large eggs (cold, if possible)
1½ teaspoons salt
500 g/4½ sticks cold butter

MAKES 1.6 KG/3½ LB. DOUGH

Add the yeast to a stand mixer with the cold milk and water, then add the sugar, 600 g/4¼ cups of the flour and the eggs. Knead for a minute or so until uniform, but don't over-knead. Add the salt to incorporate. Add more flour if the dough is still very sticky, making sure it has a consistency that can be rolled out. Turn the dough out onto a work surface.

Take the slab of cold butter and dust it liberally with flour. Beat it (a rolling pin is good) into a square 20 x 20 cm/8 x 8 inches. Chill the butter for 10–15 minutes if it starts to feel sticky.

Roll out the dough to a rectangle 45 x 25 cm/18 x 10 inches. Put the butter on top and then close the dough around the butter like an envelope – it will just fit, snugly. Make sure there are no gaps or openings.

Carefully roll out the dough again to measure 45 x 20 cm/18 x 8 inches, ensuring no butter escapes. This is the base layer. When you reach the right size, fold the dough in three (one-third of the dough to the middle and the other third dough on top). The dough should now be in nine layers. Chill for 20 minutes.

Repeat this twice more, so you end up with 27 layers, each time chilling for 20 minutes before proceeding. Chill the dough once more, then proceed to make individual pastries.

All Danish pastries (see pages 76–77) are baked at 210°C/190°C fan/410°F/Gas 6. Use baking trays with a lip as the butter melts whilst baking.

Almond filling *Remonce*

This is often used in Danish pastries, especially for traditional *kringle*. You can also use it in buns (add a dark brown sugar instead) or add cinnamon, if making *overskåren* (see page 77). If you prefer, use vanilla sugar.

125 g/4½ oz. marzipan (see opposite; if using store-bought, choose minimum 50% almond content)
125 g/9 tablespoons butter, softened
75 g/6 tablespoons caster/granulated sugar
1 teaspoon vanilla extract or vanilla sugar

MAKES 325 G/11½ OZ.

Grate the marzipan into a bowl and mix with the other ingredients.

CINNAMON REMONCE Mix 2 teaspoons ground cinnamon into the above recipe.

Pastry cream
Kagecreme

Kagecreme (or crème pâtissière, as the French version is called) is used in many Nordic desserts, from *Prinsesstårta* to Danish pastries. You can use it for layering trifles, filling layer cakes or serving with crumbles (you can thin it out with a drop or two of milk if necessary).

500 ml/2 cups whole milk
1 vanilla pod/bean, seeds scraped
3 egg yolks
50 g/¼ cup sugar
30 g/⅓ cup cornflour/cornstarch
a pinch of salt
20 g/1½ tablespoons butter (optional)

MAKES APPROX. 600 G/1 LB. 5 OZ. – YOU CAN HALVE THIS RECIPE IF YOU WISH (USE 2 EGG YOLKS)

In a saucepan, bring the milk to the boil with the scraped-out seeds from the vanilla pod/bean.

In a separate bowl, whisk together the egg yolks and sugar and add the cornflour/cornstarch.

When the milk has reached boiling point, take off the heat and pour one third into the egg mixture while whisking continuously.

Once whisked, pour the egg mixture back into the remaining hot milk. Return to the heat and bring to the boil, carefully. Whisk continuously as the mixture thickens, bubbling slightly for around 1 minute (take great care not to burn the mixture), then remove from the heat and stir in the salt and butter.

Pour into a cold bowl and place a sheet of baking parchment on top to prevent the cream from forming a skin as it cools. The mixture will keep in the fridge for a few days.

Marzipan
Marcipan

Marzipan is a big deal in the Nordics. In Sweden and Norway, mostly 50% marzipan is used (as in 50% sugar, 50% almond). In Denmark, however, you need around 63% almond content for it to taste right when making *Kransekage* (see page 233).

This version is made with sugar and liquid glucose and lasts for ages. The purpose of the liquid glucose is to stabilise the sugar as it boils. The reason I add almond extract to my marzipan is that in Scandinavia, you would traditionally use one single bitter almond for a stronger flavour, but those are not commonly sold in the UK (probably a good thing as they can be harmful when eaten raw, even in small quantities, as they contain traces of hydrocyanic acid).

1 generous tablespoon liquid glucose
60 g/5 tablespoons caster/granulated sugar
300 g/3 cups ground almonds
2 teaspoons almond extract

MAKES 400 G/14 OZ.

Put the liquid glucose and sugar in a pan with 4 tablespoons water, bring to the boil and leave to simmer for 4–5 minutes. Turn off the heat and allow to cool for a bit (lukewarm is fine).

In a food processor, grind the store-bought ground almonds for a few minutes to make sure they are as fine as can be.

Add the almond extract to enhance the almond flavour, then add most of the sugar syrup and blend. You might not need all the syrup, so check if it is sticking together (add the rest of needed). If it's a little too dry, you can add a tablespoon or two of water. Allow to cool down and set for a few hours and it's ready to use. Store in the fridge.

BASIC RECIPES 237

Index

A

almonds: almond cake bites 233
 almond filling 236
 marzipan 237
apples: Elsa's apple crumble 38
 Faeroese apple cake 173
 oven pancake with apples & vanilla mascarpone 204
 upside-down apple cake 170
aquavit: Jon-Anders' Nordic Bloody Mary 135
 Midsummer aquavit cocktail 114
asparagus: asparagus, pea & dill tart 108
 chicken vol-au-vents with asparagus 71
Astrid's sticky cake 42
avocados: dill-marinated carrot & avocado open sandwiches 90

B

bacon: chicken & bacon on rye 92
 Danish meatloaf 52
 Danish omelette with bacon 148
 potato pancakes with bacon 95
Barbro's salmon pâté 48
beef: chicken soup with meatballs & dumplings 200
 Danish beef in onion gravy 37
 Danish meatloaf 52
 Norwegian lobscouse stew 166
 Norwegian meatballs 36
 roast beef open sandwich 92
 Swedish beef stew 188
 Swedish meatballs 96
beer loaf, Danish 174
beetroot/beets: beetroot tartare 216
 haddock with beetroot and parsnips 16
 pickled herring with beetroot open sandwich 89
 roasted beets with dill 182
 Scandinavian beetroot salad 35
biscuits: cardamom biscuits 141
 Christmas biscuits 206–8
 one dough, seven biscuits 56–8
Bloody Mary, Jon-Anders' Nordic 135
bread: eight open sandwiches 88–93
 Danish beer loaf 174
 Danish carrot rolls 177
 Freja's buttermilk crescent rolls 154
 rye bread 23
 Swedish sandwich cake 118
 toasted wheat buns 99
 white loaf 189
brioche: toast skagen salad 151
brownie, my fudgy 42
brunch dishes 134–5
buns: basic bun dough 234
 big cinnamon buns 194
 Danish Shrovetide buns 59
 Lent buns 60
 Norwegian custard buns 100
 Riina's butter eye buns 61
 saffron buns with marzipan 211
 semlor buns 41
 sweet Funen 'focaccia' 80
 toasted wheat buns 99
buttermilk crescent rolls, Freja's 154

C

cabbage: red cabbage 221
 red cabbage salad 225
 roasted cabbage with Västerbotten cheese 35
cakes: almond cake bites 233
 Astrid's sticky cake 42
 Danish dream cake 193
 Danish lemon cake 121
 Faeroese cake 173
 Grandad's beard 157
 my fudgy brownie 42
 pistachio cake 83
 princess cake log 142
 Swedish strawberry cake 122
 sweet Funen 'focaccia' 80
 syrup cake 103
 that 80s chocolate cake 24
 upside-down apple cake with custard 170
caramel, salted: choux buns with salted caramel 27
 Faeroese cake 173
 salted caramel sauce 38
cardamom biscuits 141
carrots: creamed peas & carrots 70
 Danish carrot rolls 177
 dill-marinated carrot & avocado open sandwich 90
cauliflower open sandwich 91
caviar: Swedish rösti with caviar & salmon 68
celeriac/celery root: roast beef open sandwich 92
 simple celeriac salad 182
cheese: roasted beets with dill 182
 roasted cabbage with Västerbotten cheese 35
 spinach & cheese waffles 51
 Västerbotten cheese scones 202
 Västerbotten tart 152
 see also mascarpone
chequerboard cookies 58
cherry sauce, Danish 226
chicken: chicken & bacon on rye 92
 chicken soup with meatballs & dumplings 200
 chicken vol-au-vents with asparagus 71
chocolate: Astrid's sticky cake 42
 chequerboard cookies 558
 chocolate biscuits 56
 my fudgy brownie 42
 pistachio cake 83
 that 80s chocolate cake 24
 vanilla & chocolate biscuits with nuts 56
choux pastry: choux buns with salted caramel 27
 choux pastry basic batter 235
 Danish Shrovetide buns 59
 Wales cake 62
chowder, Riina's salmon 162
Christmas biscuits 206–8
Christmas ham with mustard 221
Christmas rice pudding 226
cinnamon: cinnamon cookies 207
 cinnamon Danish pastries 77
 cinnamon buns 194
 cinnamon bun French toast 135
cottage cheese: Swedish curd cake with raspberries 22
crayfish tails: Swedish sandwich cake 118
cream: choux buns with salted caramel 27
 Christmas rice pudding 226
 Danish Shrovetide buns 59
 Faeroese cake 173
 Lent buns 60
 princess cake log 142
 semlor buns 41
 Swedish strawberry cake 122
 Wales cake 62
crumble, Elsa's apple 38
curd cake, Swedish 22
custard see pastry cream

D

Danish beef in onion gravy 37
Danish beer loaf 174
Danish breaded meatballs 70
Danish brunch rolls 138
Danish butter cookies 206
Danish carrot rolls 177
Danish cherry sauce 226
Danish dream cake 193
Danish ginger biscuits 207
Danish jam slices 174
Danish lemon cake 121
Danish meatballs 20
Danish meatloaf 52
Danish Midsummer soup 141
Danish omelette with bacon 148
Danish pancake bites 230
Danish pastries 76–7, 236
Danish peppernuts 208
Danish remoulade 72
Danish Shrovetide buns 59
dough: basic bun dough 234
 basic Danish pastry dough 236
dumplings, chicken soup with meatballs & 200

E

eggs: Danish omelette with bacon 148
 egg & prawn open sandwich 90
 smoked salmon & egg open sandwich 89
Elsa's apple crumble 38

238 INDEX

F
Faeroese cake 173
fennel salad, simple 48
fish: Barbro's salmon pâté 48
  breaded plaice & new potatoes 117
  cured salmon with dill 116
  haddock with beetroot and parsnips 16
  hot-smoked trout salad & dill potato salad 128
  Jansson's temptation 222
  Jerusalem artichoke soup 12
  Jonas' midweek fish 151
  Midsummer plate 114
  pickled herring with beetroot open sandwich 89
  Riina's salmon chowder 162
  Scandinavian fishcakes 72
  smoked salmon & egg open sandwich 89
  Swedish rösti with caviar & salmon 68
  Swedish sandwich cake 118
  three herring dressings 133
  'focaccia', sweet Funen 80
Freja's buttermilk crescent rolls 154
French toast, cinnamon bun 135

G
ginger: Danish ginger biscuits 207
  Swedish ginger biscuits 208
grandad's beard 157
granola, seed 135
green salad with grandma dressing 128

H
ham, Christmas 221
hash, leftover 167
hasselback potatoes 225
hazelnuts, pan-roasted leeks with 131
hunka hunka burning love 165

J
Jansson's temptation 222
Jerusalem artichoke soup 12
Jon-Anders's Nordic Bloody Mary 135
Jonas' midweek fish 151

L
lardons: hunka hunka burning love 165
leeks, pan-roasted 131
leftover hash 167
lemon cake, Danish 121
Lent buns 60
lingonberry, potato pancakes with bacon 95
lobscouse stew, Norwegian 166

M
marzipan 237
  almond cake bites 233
  almond filling 236
  choux buns with salted caramel 27
  Danish lemon cake 121
  Lent buns 60
  princess cake log 142
  saffron buns with marzipan 211
  semlor buns 41
  Tosca tart 190
mascarpone, oven pancake with apples & vanilla 204
meat: leftover hash 167
meatballs: chicken soup with meatballs 200
  Danish breaded meatballs 70
  meatball sandwich 91
  my mother's Danish meatballs 20
  Norwegian meatballs 36
  Swedish meatballs 96
meatloaf, Danish 52
Midsummer aquavit cocktail 114
Midsummer plate 114
Midsummer soup, Danish 141
mulled wine, Scandinavian 230

N
Norwegian custard buns 100
Norwegian lobscouse stew 166
Norwegian mashed swede 224
Norwegian meatballs 36
Norwegian pork belly roast 220
Norwegian-style waffles 51
nuts, vanilla & chocolate biscuits with 56

O
oats: overnight oats 134
  seed granola 135
omelette with bacon, Danish 148
orange biscuits 56
overnight oats 134

P
pancakes 32
  Danish pancake bites 230
  oven pancake with apples & vanilla mascarpone 204
  potato pancakes with bacon and lingonberry 95
pancetta: Danish meatloaf 52
parsnips: haddock with beetroot and parsnips 16
  hunka hunka burning love 165
pastry: choux pastry basic batter 235
  poppyseed pastry 76
  shortcrust pastry 235
  sweet shortcrust pastry 235
pastry cream 237
  choux buns with salted caramel 27
  custard crowns 76
  Danish Shrovetide buns 59
  Norwegian custard buns 100
  princess cake log 142
  rhubarb & custard Danish pastries 77
  Swedish strawberry cake 122
  upside-down apple cake with custard 170
  Wales cake 62
pâté, Barbro's salmon 48
peas: asparagus, pea & dill tart 108
  creamed peas & carrots 70
  mashed peas 36
pesto: dill pesto potato salad 132
pink 'Brussels' biscuits 58
pistachio cake 83
poppy seeds: poppyseed pastry 76
  white loaf with white poppy seeds 189
pork: chicken soup with meatballs & dumplings 200
  Christmas ham with mustard 221
  Danish breaded meatballs 70
  fried pork belly with parsley sauce 153
  my mother's Danish meatballs 20
  Norwegian pork belly roast 220
  quick pork tenderloin pot 186
  Swedish meatballs 96
potatoes: breaded plaice & new potatoes 117
  caramelised potatoes 224
  dill potato salad 128
  hasselback potatoes 225
  hunka hunka burning love 165
  Jansson's temptation 222
  leftover hash 167
  Norwegian lobscouse stew 166
  potato pancakes 95
  Riina's salmon chowder 162
  Swedish rösti 68
  three potato salads 132
prawns/shrimp: egg & prawn open sandwich 90
  Swedish sandwich cake 118
  toast skagen salad 151
princess cake log 142
puff pastry: chicken vol-au-vents with asparagus 71

R
raspberries: princess cake log 142
  Swedish curd cake with raspberries 22
raspberry jam/preserve: cinnamon Danish pastries 77
  Danish jam slices 174
  Danish Shrovetide buns 59
  raspberry jam biscuits 58
remoulade, Danish 72
rhubarb & custard Danish pastries 77
rice pudding 226
Riina's butter eye buns 61
Riina's salmon chowder 162
roe herring dressing 133
rösti, Swedish 68
rye bread 23
  eight open sandwiches 83–93

S
saffron: saffron biscotti 206
  saffron buns with marzipan 211

INDEX 239

saffron pickled herring dressing 133
salads: green salad with grandma dressing 128
hot-smoked trout salad & dill potato salad 128
toast skagen salad 151
red cabbage salad 225
Scandinavian beetroot salad 35
simple celeriac salad 182
simple fennel salad 48
three potato salads 132
Waldorf salad 15
sandwich cake, Swedish 118
sandwiches, eight open 88–93
Scandinavian beetroot salad 35
Scandinavian fishcakes 72
Scandinavian mulled wine 230
scones, Västerbotten cheese 202
seed granola 135
semlor buns 41
shortcrust pastry 235
Shrovetide buns, Danish 59
soup: chicken soup with meatballs & dumplings 200
Danish Midsummer soup 141
Jerusalem artichoke soup 12
Riina's salmon chowder 162
Swedish pea soup 32
spelt grain, Waldorf salad with 15
spinach & cheese waffles 51
stews: Norwegian lobscouse stew 166
quick pork tenderloin pot 186
Swedish beef stew 188
venison stew 203
strawberry cake, Swedish 122
swede, Norwegian mashed 224
Swedish beef stew 188
Swedish crispy waffles 51
Swedish curd cake with raspberries 22
Swedish ginger biscuits 208
Swedish meatballs 96
meatball sandwich 91
Swedish pea soup 32
Swedish rösti with caviar & salmon 68
Swedish sandwich cake 118
Swedish strawberry cake 122
sweet Funen 'focaccia' 80
sweet shortcrust pastry 235
syrup cake 103

T
tartare, beetroot 216
tarts: asparagus, pea & dill tart 108
Tosca tart 190
Västerbotten tart 152
that 80s chocolate cake 24
toffee biscuits 58
tomato juice: Jon-Anders' Nordic Bloody Mary 135
Tosca tart 190

V
veal: my mother's Danish meatballs 20
vegetables: leftover hash 167
Norwegian lobscouse stew 166
Norwegian pork belly roast 220
venison stew 203
venison stew 203
vol-au-vents, chicken 71

W
waffles 51
Waldorf salad 15
Wales cake 62
wheat buns, toasted 99
wine, Scandinavian mulled 230

Y
yellow peas: Swedish pea soup 32

Acknowledgements

Jonas, Astrid and Elsa: Without whom nothing else matters.

My father Niels: The kindest, most wonderful *farmand* anyone could wish for.

My sisters Isabelle, Lone, Ulla, Ginny and Ditte and my flock of little Danish kitchen helpers Alfred, Kaia, Rosa, Magne and Ivan.

To my uncle Jens Blomhøj, for all his support, recipes and great food chats.

David Jørgensen for his red pen and wisdom: eternally grateful for your help on all my books.

Special thank you to Riina Salmela, Freja Haulrik, Stina Envall, Barbro McAusland, Jon-Anders Fjelsrud and Millicent Scott for contributing recipes and suggestions for this book.

Everyone at RPS for supporting me over this last decade of books about Scandinavian food: Julia Charles, Leslie Harrington, Megan Smith, Gillian Haslam, Patricia Harrington, Yvonne Doolan, Jack Duce – and the rest of the amazing team that worked on this book: Pete Cassidy, Kathy Kordalis, Tony Hutchinson, Ayushi Channawar, Lydia Mecklenburgh, Sadie Albuquerque and Maïté Franchi. It's a privilege and honour to work with you all.

To my agent Jane Maw for motivation, belief and the occasional much-needed push.

Thank you to our wonderful team at ScandiKitchen who turn up and make everything happen every single day: Riina, Maria, Freja, Emma, Amina B, Amina S, Ricky, Ida, Sini, Caterina, Emeliina, Marcus, Majka, Saara, Sheena, Mia, Chun, Vivek, Amanda, Aina, Sujith, Reka, Jolanta, George, Gabor, Ansku, Annie, Filippa, Frankie, Ro, Arthur, Ilona, Imie, John, Krupali, Myo, Nathan, Olga, Samira, Sofia – as well as Peter, David H, Chris and David C for keeping us on the straight and narrow.